THE BIRDS OF SICILY

An annotated check-list

by

Carmelo Iapichino

&

Bruno Massa

B.O.U. Check-list No. 11

British Ornithologists' Union, 1989
c/o Zoological Museum, Tring, Herts HP23 6AP, UK

ISBN 0 907446 10 8

Printed in Great Britain by Henry Ling Ltd., at the Dorset Press, Dorchester, Dorset

CONTENTS

Editor's Foreword   5

Preface   7

List of Figures and Plates   8

INTRODUCTION   9
   History   9
   History of Sicilian ornithology   9
   Geography   12
   Climate   15
   Vegetation   15
   Migration   16
   Breeding   21
   Conservation   24
   Isolation and other aspects of the Sicilian avifauna   28

ACKNOWLEDGEMENTS   32

SYSTEMATIC LIST   33

Gazetteer   118
Appendix 1 – Species rejected from the Sicilian list   124
Appendix 2 – Ringing and recoveries   126

BIBLIOGRAPHY. Includes all Sicilian ornithological references up to 1987   143

Index of scientific names of birds   160
Index of English names of birds   167

EDITOR'S FOREWORD

Sicily, with its outlying islands, situated at the toe of the long peninsula which is Italy, could be assumed to have a strategic role for migrant birds travelling between Europe and Africa. Most migration, however, is on a broad front and there is no evidence of defined inland routes, even though the number of transient species is high; many million individuals must cross Sicily at the migration periods, but without in any way being a conspicuous feature of the ornithological year. Sicily's mountainous areas and north coast create ideal habitats for many resident and migrant raptors. The importance of education in conservation of wildlife, the sharing of it with other countries, however, has yet to be recognised widely enough to remove the threats of traditional and pointless shooting habits, whereby thousands of birds of many species are slaughtered, mainly illegally, every year. Coincidental with this destruction are the draining of wetlands, deforestation and ever expanding urban sprawl over the last few decades, all incriminated in the near extinction of many species of breeding and wintering birds in Sicily, and the actual extinction of others.

Dr Massa and Dr Iapichino have devoted many years to obtaining detailed information, scientifically based, on the status of the Sicilian avifauna, including organising the *Atlas Faunae Siciliae – Aves* during the years 1979–1983 (see *Bull. Brit. Orn. Cl.* 107: 192). The present check-list, the eleventh in the British Ornithologists' Union's series, therefore comes at an appropriate time for a basic assessment to be made of the state of the avifauna of Sicily, both in regard to the species involved and the means whereby they may be protected in the future. For this task the authors are especially well qualified as a result of their wide personal knowledge and from their appreciation of the problems involved at first hand. It must sincerely be hoped that with increasing education in the field of natural history and conservation in Sicily, the next treatise on the Sicilian avifauna may be able to report a halt to the threats to its endangered species and a noticeable improvement in the present status of its many declining species, so comprehensively treated by the present authors.

James F. Monk

PREFACE

The importance of the Mediterranean islands for ornithology is shown in the extensive literature which has resulted from the work of North European ornithologists (particularly the British), but also of an increasing number of resident researchers.

Recently, annotated check-lists have been published for many Mediterranean islands: Balearic Islands (Bannerman & Bannerman 1983), Corsica (Thibault 1983), Cyprus (Flint & Stewart 1983), Malta (Sultana *et al*. 1975; Sultana & Gauci 1982). In Sicily, where ornithological literature is quite rich (but meagre in amount), the last annotated list of Sicilian birds dates back to Doderlein's work (1869–74). In 1976 one of us (BM) published a concise annotated list of 353 species known at that time. The present work has to fill the gap since then, utilising all the data gathered in Sicily in the last eleven years.

Our own observations and the data included in many journals, especially in the *Rivista Italiana di Ornitologia*, particularly in the last 30 years, are the basis of the list; unpublished data of other Sicilian ornithologists and bird-watchers have also been included. Information on the distribution of breeding species is largely taken from the *Atlas Faunae Siciliae – Aves* (Massa 1985). The older historical records have been included only after careful re-consideration and revision. However a work of synthesis such as this cannot but also point out the gaps in ornithological knowledge in Sicily. Unlike Malta there is as yet no systematic and regular study of migration, above all as regards Passerines, whereas data on the reproduction of most breeding species are still greatly lacking.

Another important aim of our work in Sicily is to help to rouse people's interest in the great problem of the preservation of its avifauna and its environment, no less severely threatened in Sicily than anywhere else in Europe.

For the future, we would be glad at any time to receive new data to update the list.

Carmelo Iapichino
Viale Teracati 81
96100 Siracusa
(Italy)

Bruno Massa
Istituto di Zoologia
Via Archirafi 18
90123 Palermo
(Italy)

June 1988

LIST OF FIGURES

Figure 1. Physical map of Sicily, showing names of some localities and rivers mentioned in the text. See also Figure 4 and Gazetteer.

Figure 2. Sicily in relation to the central Mediterranean.

Figure 3. Map of Sicily showing divisions used in the text.

Figure 4. Place names and Provinces in Sicily mentioned in the text. See also Figures 1, 6 and Gazetteer.

Figure 5. Map of woodland in Sicily according to Direzione Regionale delle Foreste della Regione Siciliana (updated 1983).

Figure 6. Map of Sicily showing the landscape. Black: montane habitat above 1000 m. White: natural vegetation (e.g. garigue, maquis, woods). Stippled grey: cultivated land. White with parallel lines: open grassland and grazing. Inland reservoirs (L.). Coastal wetlands (Trapani, Marsala, C. Feto, Gela, Pachino, Vendicari, Siracusa and Simeto).

Figure 7. Number of breeding species detected in each 10×10 km quadrant square of Sicily between 1979 and 1987 (Mercator's Universal Transverse projection).

Figure 8. Species/planar area correlation for terrestrial breeding birds of 37 Mediterranean islands from 0.5 km^2 to $25,709$ km^2 on a log–log scale. Data from Massa (1987c).

LIST OF PLATES

1) Typical cultivated landscape in the isle of Linosa, Sicilian Channel. (G. Massa)
2) Some extensive inland areas of Sicily are cultivated and lacking in natural vegetation. (A. Bisanti)
3) Eroded hills in the central strip of Sicily. (B. Massa)
4) Large inland areas of Sicily are seasonally covered by wheat. (A. Bisanti)
5) A typical valley of the Iblei Mts (locally called 'cava'), consisting of rich vegetation at the foot of calcareous massifs. (A. Ciaccio)
6) The dwarf broom-palm is comparatively rare in Sicily, but is well dispersed in the Nature Reserve of Zingaro, western Sicily. (B. Massa)
7) Sand dunes of the southern coast. (A. Dimarca)
8) The lake Biviere di Cesarò (1200 m) on the Caronie Mts. (A. Bisanti)
9) One of the several calcareous massifs scattered throughout Sicily. (B. Massa)
10) High cliffs of the western coast of the isle of Marettimo (Egadi). (B. Massa)
11) High Mediterranean maquis on the Madonie Mts. (B. Massa)
12) Rock massifs form the background to a Mediterranean evergreen wood on the Madonie Mts. (G. Massa)
13) A beech-wood on the Caronie Mts. (A. Ciaccio)
14) On the northern side of Aetna the pines are mixed with beech and birch trees. (B. Massa)
15) The volcano of Aetna, the highest peak of Sicily (3350 m). (A. Ciaccio)
16) The high montane vegetation of the Madonie Mts consists mainly of thorny xerophitic species and low beech-thickets. (A. Dimarca).

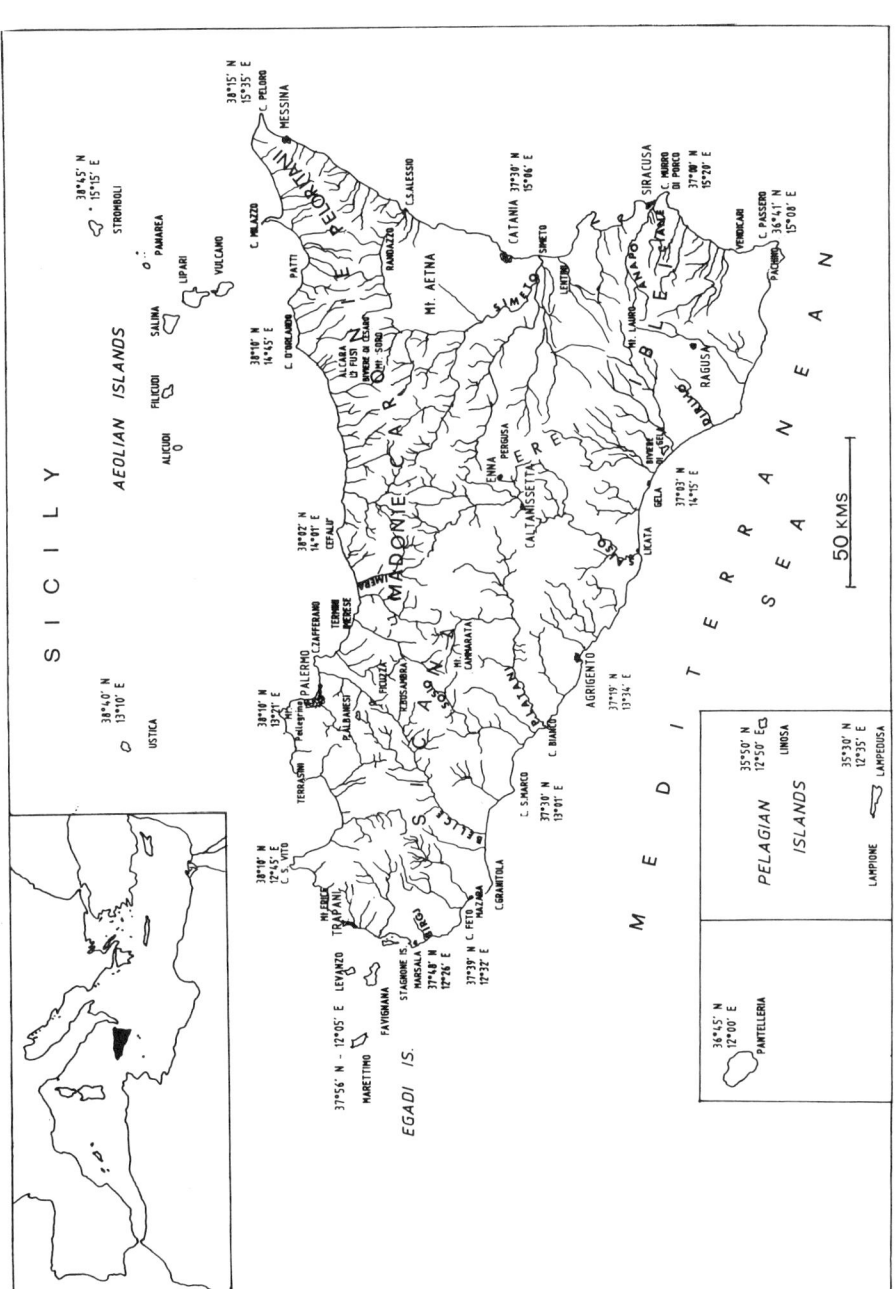

Figure 1. Physical map of Sicily, showing names of some localities and rivers mentioned in the text.

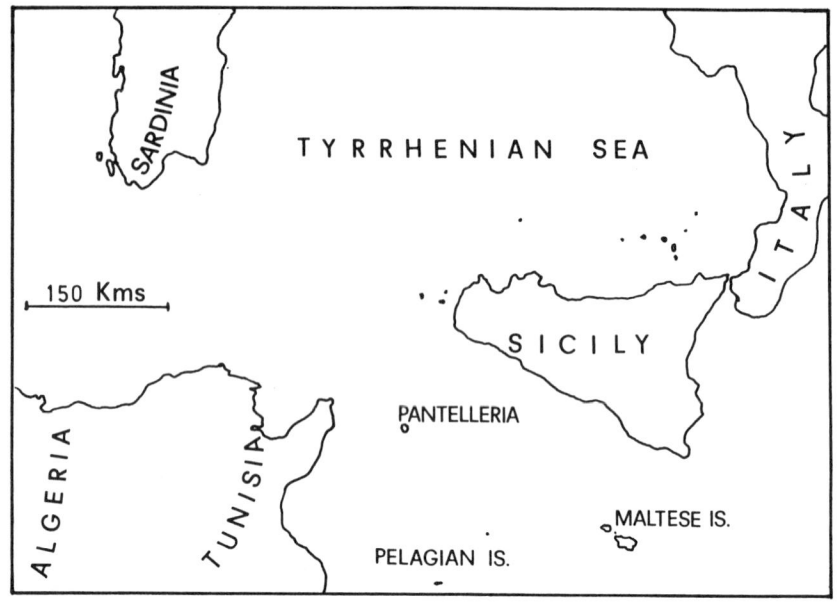

Figure 2. Sicily in relation to the central Mediterranean.

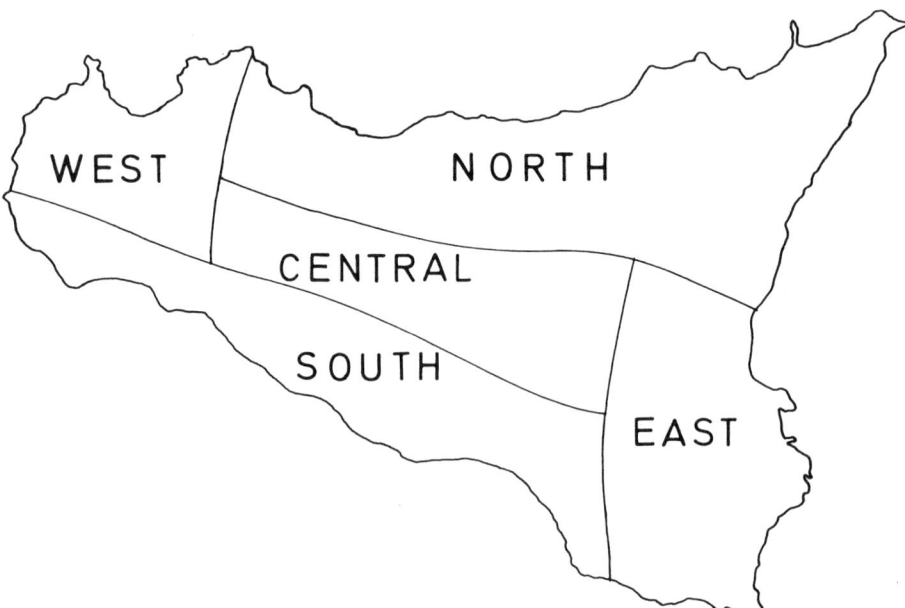

Figure 3. Map of Sicily showing divisions used in the text.

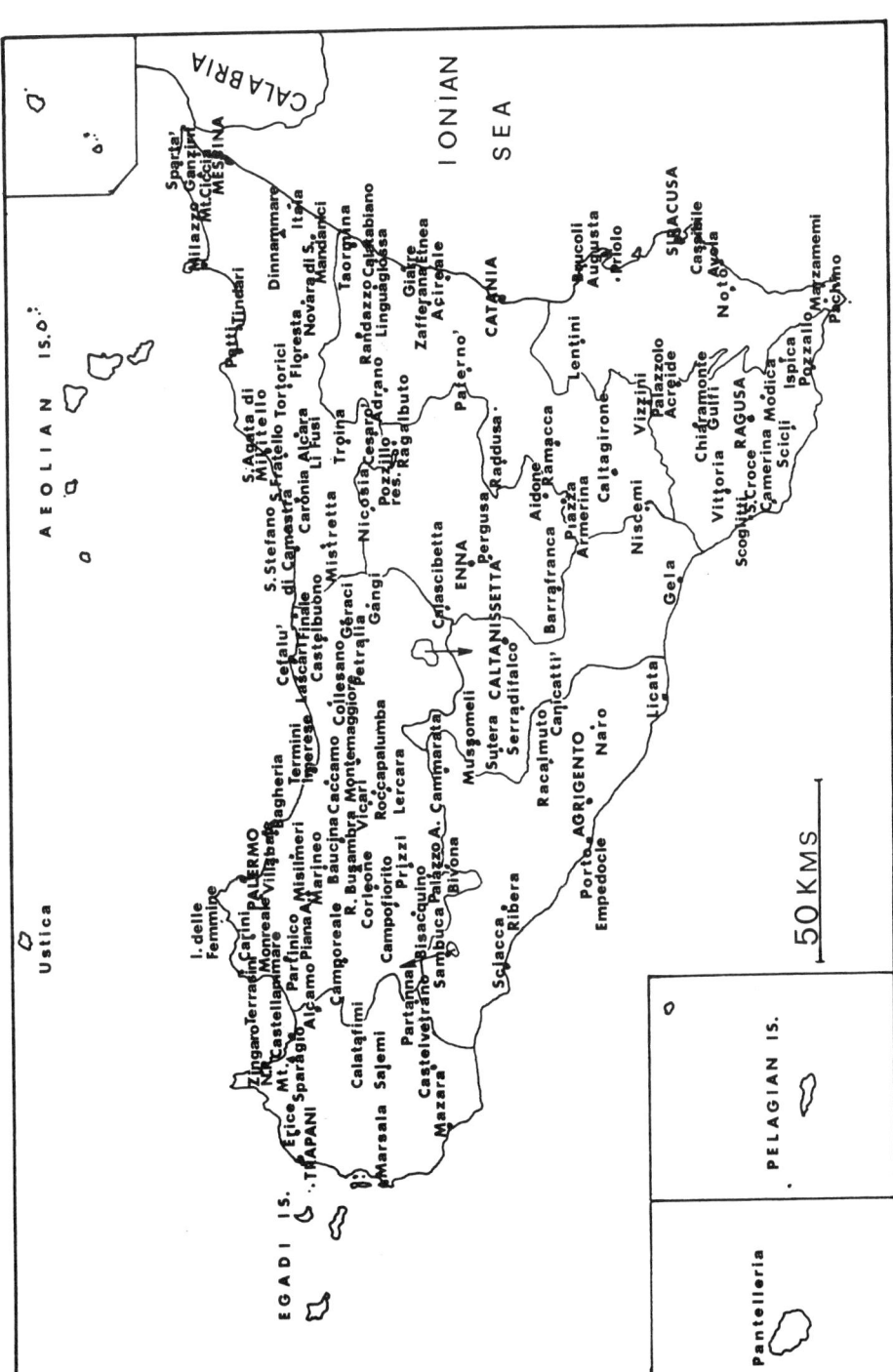

Figure 4. Place names and Provinces in Sicily mentioned in the text. See also Figure 1 and Gazetteer.

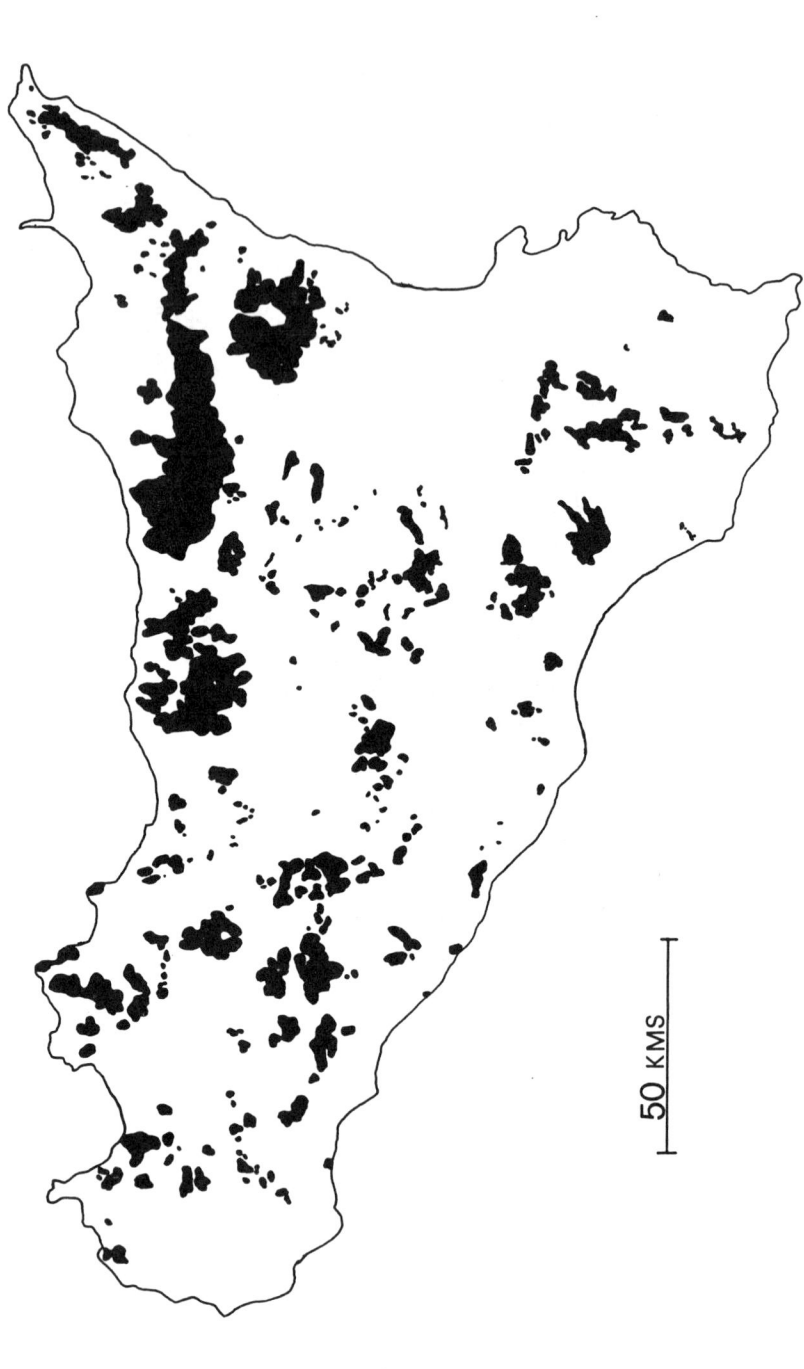

Figure 5. Map of woodland in Sicily according to Direzione Regionale delle Foreste della Regione Siciliana (updated 1983).

50 KMS

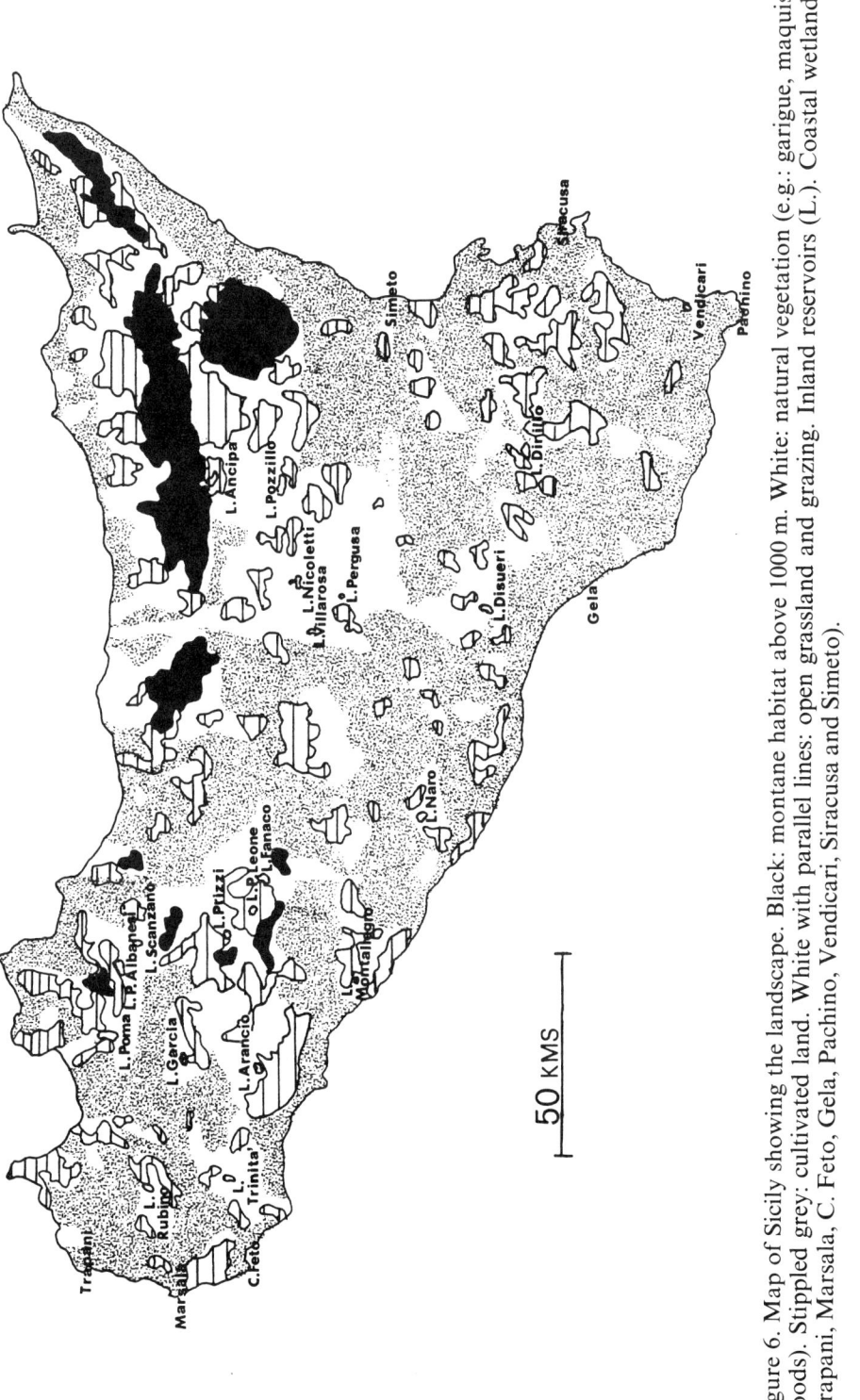

Figure 6. Map of Sicily showing the landscape. Black: montane habitat above 1000 m. White: natural vegetation (e.g.: garigue, maquis, woods). Stippled grey: cultivated land. White with parallel lines: open grassland and grazing. Inland reservoirs (L.). Coastal wetlands (Trapani, Marsala, C. Feto, Gela, Pachino, Vendicari, Siracusa and Simeto).

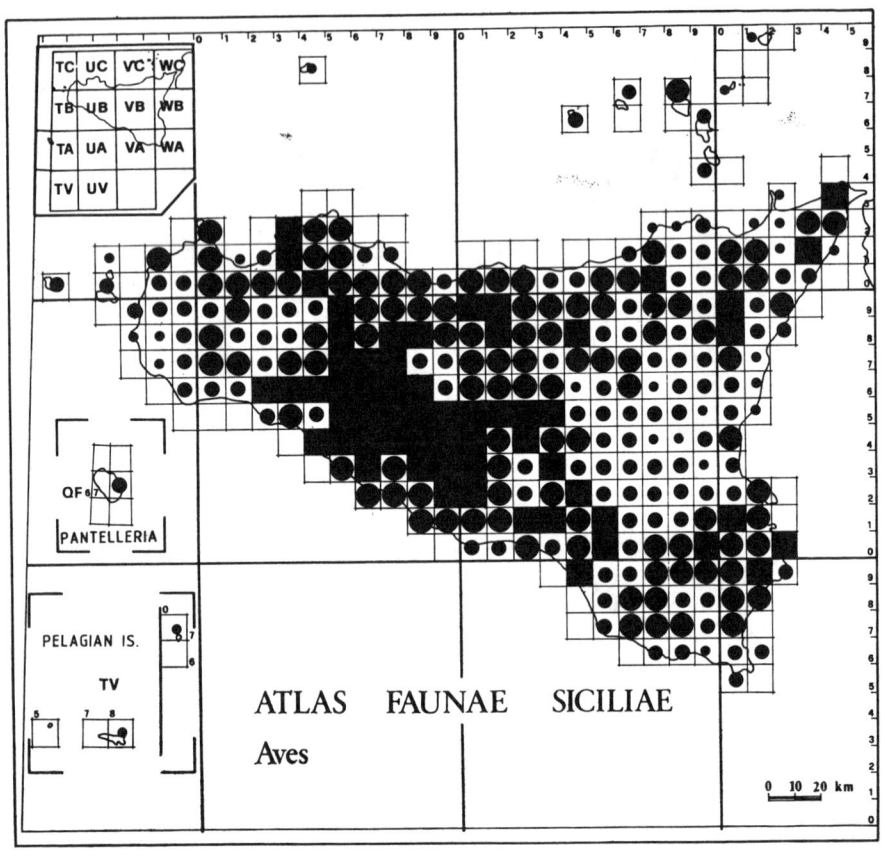

Figure 7. Number of breeding species detected in each 10 × 10 km quadrant square of Sicily between 1979 and 1987 (Mercator's Universal Transverse projection).
● < 21 species ● 21–35 species ● 36–50 species ■ > 50 species.

INTRODUCTION

HISTORY

Sicily's history spans a long period, from the Greek colonisation of the Sicilian coasts to the Roman conquest, and thereafter through several different foreign dominations (Arabs, Swabions, Normans, Spanish). In 1860 Sicily was annexed to the Italian kingdom, and since 1946 it has been a self-governing 'Region' of the Italian Republic. The Regional government, which is in Palermo, has full powers as regards many matters, among which are the management of the land, the conservation of the fauna and the hunting regulations.

HISTORY OF SICILIAN ORNITHOLOGY

A short history of Sicilian ornithology starts with a curiosity: it was in Sicily during the 13th century that one of the oldest and most famous books on birds was written, namely the well known treatise on falconry, 'De arte venandi cum avibus' by Emperor Federico II of Swabia, which included some observations on the life of birds.

At the beginning of the 18th century, Sicilian ornithological literature was very poor; references to birds were often included in works of general character, frequently having no scientific content. This was the result of a distinctly humanistic culture that used to consider natural sciences of only secondary importance. It is also important, nevertheless, to consider the problems involved in travelling through Sicily, still of great difficulty even at the beginning of this century, in some places even until recently. The shortage of roads, that often were usable only during parts of the year, and the widespread menace of brigands, together with the prevalence of malaria, made any travel dangerous and risky, especially inland. Only a few travellers, like Goethe, were brave enough to venture as far as the inland areas, far from the main cities. Palermo appeared always so distant from Europe that at the end of the 18th century an article in the *Encyclopédie Française* reported Palermo as having been totally destroyed by an earthquake in the previous century (Mack Smith 1968), which was very far from the truth. This aspect of Sicily's remoteness must be taken into account when considering the work of the ornithologists of the past.

A detailed reconstruction of all references to birds in the Sicilian literature from 1200 onwards was made by **Doderlein** (1869–74); all the authors he mentioned were of Sicilian origin — historians, botanists and lovers of natural sciences, who often made references to some species of birds. Among the most interesting of these were: **Francesco Russo**, who wrote *Breve descrizione di tutta sorta di uccelli conosciuti nella Sicilia* in 1680; **Francesco Cupani**, who wrote *Trattato di Storia Naturale* in 1696, and the famous *Pamphyton Siculum* in 1713, which included more than 200 etchings representing Sicilian birds; **Antonio Mongitore**, who wrote *Della Sicilia ricercata nelle cose più memorabili* in 1742; **Baldassare Palazzotto**, who wrote in 1820 the first complete work on Sicilian birds, but which remained unpublished; and **Giuseppe Galvagni**, author of some notes regarding the fauna of Aetna (1839–43).

In 1840 **Luigi Benoit** from Messina, published his book *Ornitologia Siciliana*, which was the first complete and methodical list of birds published. He described 270 species from the existing bibliography and from his own observations. Benoit's book can be considered to be the start of scientific ornithology in Sicily.

In 1842–43 a book by **Alfred Malherbe**, entitled *Faune ornithologique de la Sicile* was published in France. It is enough to read the second part of the introduction to realize how the author drew on Benoit's work for almost the whole book. Malherbe added 48 species (totalling 318) to Benoit's book, but it is difficult to ascertain what is original and reliable in a work which Trischitta (1919c) dubbed as 'plagiarism' (cf. De Murs 1844).

Twenty or so years later **Pietro Doderlein** came from Modena to hold the chair of Zoology and Comparative Anatomy at the University of Palermo. He was already a well-known zoologist and he set up a very rich zoological museum (cf. De Stefani 1918; Di Palma 1978). Thanks to a grant from Palermo University, he was able to explore the island, gathering original data and specimens. Between 1869 and 1874 he published *Avifauna del Modenese e della Sicilia*, which is very rich with valuable information. In the scientific reality of that time, Doderlein's work is the second important stage in, and the basis of, Sicilian ornithology. Some errors seem to be due to the author's good faith in reporting second-hand information, and only rarely are they due to inaccurate identification. Of great importance is the need to give critical attention to breeding statements about some species, these often being vague and lacking in details. In some cases, for example among wetland birds, the great changes the environment has suffered since Doderlein's time, make some cases of unproved breeding at that time probable or possible (e.g. breeding of Purple Heron *Ardea purpurea*, White-headed Duck *Oxyura leucocephala*, Marsh Harrier *Circus aeruginosus*). In other cases, mistakes become evident when species which have never bred or might possibly have bred in Italy, are listed as Sicilian breeders without any proof, purely on ecological grounds.

Minor works on local avifauna had been published prior to Doderlein's time and were quoted by him, e.g. notes on birds of Madonie Mts. by **Minà Palumbo** (1853–57) and of eastern Sicily by **Zuccarello Patti** (1844–46); others were issued later without adding anything new to Doderlein's work, e.g. like *Ornitologia Siciliana* by **Pistone** (1888) and *Gli Uccelli di Sicilia* by **C. Massa** (1891). The latter was criticised by Doderlein with regard to some species (e.g. the claimed breeding of Black-headed Bunting *Emberiza melanocephala*), criticisms that were handwritten on the reprint that C. Massa had sent to Doderlein (now in the library of the Istituto di Zoologia of Palermo).

Meanwhile Doderlein (1881) published a work on Sicilian vertebrates, with many references to birds. In 1893 he started a new paper, *Avifauna Sicula*, but was able to finish only the section on birds of prey before his death.

The end of the 19th century is characterised by the *Inchieste Regionali* (Regional Surveys) carried out by **Giglioli** (1889–1890) in many parts of Italy. Unfortunately his local correspondents were not always reliable and much of his data cannot therefore be considered authentic. Giglioli (1907) published the results of a second survey in a new book of much greater reliability than his first.

The present century is characterised in general by many contributions to Sicilian ornithology, but not by any work covering the entire avifauna like Benoit's and Doderlein's. We find some data in the papers of **Zodda** (1901–1905), continued by **Sturniolo** (1905–1907), and in those of **Joseph Whitaker**, who lived for many years in Sicily, though devoting himself much more to Tunisian avifauna. Nevertheless, in his 2 volumes *The Birds of Tunisia* (1905) there are often references to Sicily. It is also interesting to recall the note Whitaker (1899a,c) published on the Purple Gallinule *Porphyrio porphyrio* in *Il Naturalista Siciliano* and its English version in *Ibis*, dealing in particular with breeding in captivity, pointing out the great asynchrony of the breeding season of this bird. Although 50–60 years were still to elapse before this species became extinct in Sicily, Whitaker already had forebodings of its disappearance. A pad of rough notes, found in his library and dated 1920, seems to indicate

Plate 5. A typical valley of the Iblei Mts (locally called 'cava'), consisting of rich vegetation at the foot of calcareous massifs. (A. Ciaccio)

Plate 6. The dwarf broom-palm is comparatively rare in Sicily, but is well dispersed in the Nature Reserve of Zingaro, western Sicily. (B. Massa)

Plate 7. Sand dunes of the southern coast. (A. Dimarca)

Plate 8. The lake Biviere di Cesarò (1200 m) on the Caronie Mts. (A. Bisanti)

Plate 1. Typical cultivated landscape in the isle of Linosa, Sicilian Channel. (G. Massa)

Plate 2. Some extensive inland areas of Sicily are cultivated and lacking in natural vegetation. (A. Bisanti)

Plate 3. Eroded hills in the central strip of Sicily. (B. Massa)

Plate 4. Large inland areas of Sicily are seasonally covered by wheat. (A. Bisanti)

Plate 10. High cliffs of the western coast of the isle of Marettimo (Egadi). (B. Massa)

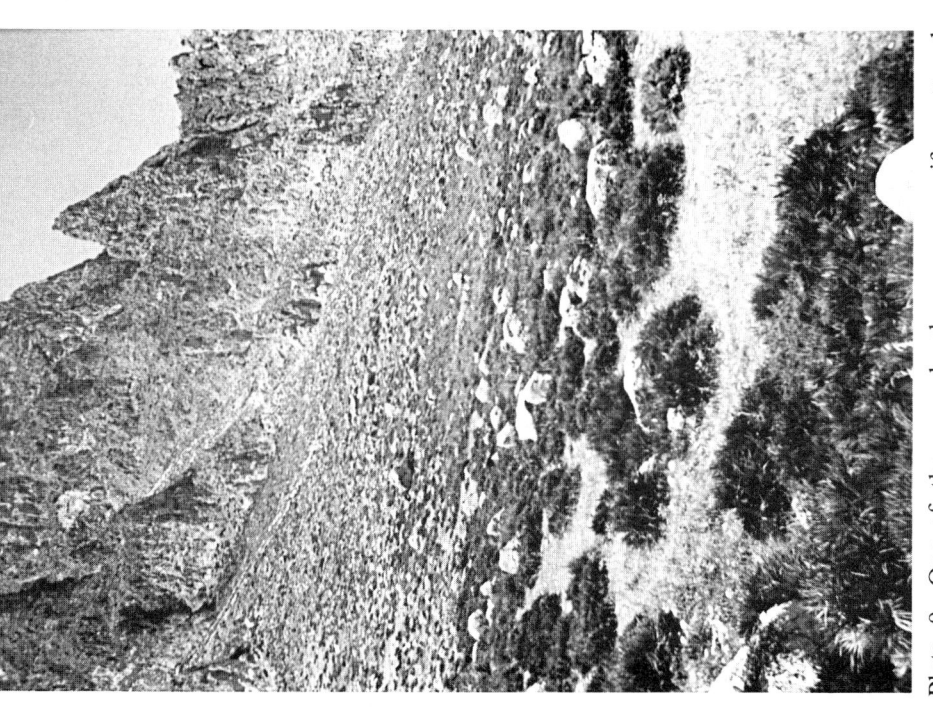

Plate 9. One of the several calcareous massifs scattered throughout Sicily. (B. Massa)

Plate 11. High Mediterranean maquis on the Madonie Mts. (B. Massa)

Plate 12. Rock massifs form the background to a Mediterranean evergreen wood on the Madonie Mts. (G. Massa)

Plate 13. A beech-wood on the Caronie Mts. (A. Ciaccio)

Plate 14. On the northern side of Aetna the pines are mixed with beech and birch trees. (B. Massa)

Plate 15. The volcano of Aetna, the highest peak of Sicily (3350 m). (A. Ciaccio)

Plate 16. The high montane vegetation of the Madonie Mts consists mainly of thorny xerophitic species and low beech-thickets. (A. Dimarca).

that Whitaker had in mind to write 'The Birds of Sicily' (Massa 1987d); however, the handwritten list did not add anything new, especially on breeding species, to the data already published in his Tunisian work of 15 years earlier.

In 1929 **Ettore Arrigoni degli Oddi** published his *Ornitologia Italiana*. In many respects it is still today a basic and unsurpassed text of Italian ornithology. There are many references to Sicily, mostly taken from existing literature; but the author himself visited Sicily and was in touch with Sicilian ornithologists, and was thus able to correct some former errors.

Among Sicilian ornithologists of this century **Antonio Trischitta** was probably the most original personality. After having published some notes on ornithology early in the century, he devoted himself to a study of a new method of zoological nomenclature, one which has never been adopted. He was really a connoisseur of ornithological literature and an experienced researcher, but unfortunately he did not produce very much about Sicilian ornithology.

Carlo Orlando's contribution was much more considerable; he wrote over 80 notes between 1935 and 1970. His most interesting works deal with species which became or were becoming extinct in Sicily in that period (e.g. Bearded Tit *Panurus biarmicus*, Lammergeyer *Gypaetus barbatus* and woodpeckers). His papers include many historical facts taken at first hand or facts which he obtained from people whom he considered to be reliable. He was also interested in taxonomy and described many different subspecies (mostly from Sardinia), which Vaurie (1959) considered to be synonymous with existing races, although in fact he did not examine Orlando's type series. Unfortunately Orlando did not pay much attention to distribution of breeding species and references to breeding are very scanty in his notes. He left a huge ornithological collection of skins (now at Museo Civico of Terrasini), which is a considerable source of information.

Angelo Priolo's contribution was remarkable, and his first paper dates back to 1946. Among his works, a cyclostyled contribution, issued in the first series of *Avocetta*, is very useful, since it sums up all his observations in Sicily from 1940 to 1953. Priolo also carried out much interesting research in taxonomy (e.g. in 1969 on the Marsh Tit *Parus palustris*, in 1970 and 1984 on the Rock Partridge *Alectoris graeca* and in 1979 on the Long-tailed Tit *Aegithalos caudatus*).

In the 1950s, many foreign ornithologists (especially Germans) visited Sicily. Their papers are a rich source of information. **E. Stresemann** published a work on Biviere di Lentini in 1943; it is a historical note, the last data on a wetland fauna that became extinct 6 years later with the complete reclamation of the lake. The results of his visit to Sicily were used again later (1955) to revise the first edition of the *Field Guide to the Birds of Britain and Europe* by Peterson, Mountfort and Hollom. Unfortunately some of Stresemann's revisions were not justified; he in fact visited the Biviere in April when many birds were still on migration, so that some species which he considered (without proof) to be breeders, could not have been included even in the 'possible' category of the present Atlas's criteria (see e.g. Savi's Warbler *Locustella luscinioides*).

Krampitz (1956b, 1958) published 2 works on Sicilian breeding birds, a complete and critical updating, with many interesting observations. In 1954–56 **Steinbacher**, and in 1957 **Mebs** published the results of their visits to Sicily. **Kumerloeve** (1968) published some data on the bird migration in the plain of Catania, and **Krapp** (1970) on the birds observed in the Egadi Is. Other original records from Pantelleria had been published by **Steinfatt** in 1934, and from Marettimo by **Suchantke** in 1960. Interesting data about Sicilian birds, especially moult of some *Sylvia* species, were collected in 1962 by the Oxford University Sicilian Expedition (Williamson 1976).

Compared with other Mediterranean islands, the number of non resident ornithologists who have visited Sicily is low and their papers usually refer to short visits. The political events in islands like Malta and Cyprus had engendered visits from foreign ornithologists, both short and longer stays, that have helped the development of local ornithology. Corsica has also been favoured by its proximity to France, a country of great ornithological tradition. Fortunately Sicilian islets were **Edgardo Moltoni**'s favourite destination in the 1960s and early 70s. Moltoni, the doyen of Italian ornithologists who died in 1980, published detailed and documented reports on birds of the Aeolian and Pelagian Is. and of Pantelleria. Exploration of islands surrounding Sicily has been completed thanks to the work of **Ajola** (1959, I. Ustica) and **Sorci** et al. (1973, Egadi and Stagnone Is.).

In the 1970s the contribution of Sicilian authors became more systematic in character; the first local lists resulting from regular observations were issued. They dealt with the salt-pans of Siracusa (Baglieri 1973a), the mouth of Simeto river (Priolo 1974a) and other areas.

In 1976 one of us (BM) published a complete list of 353 Sicilian species including some short notes on the status of each.

Since the early 1970s regular observations were being carried out in different areas of Sicily by an increasing number of observers. The developing interest in breeding birds and their distribution is the most evident result. From 1979 till 1983 a survey for an Atlas on the breeding birds in Sicily was carried out, with the collaboration of 27 amateurs (see Breeding). An annual Sicilian Ornithological Report was published in 1982, 1983 and 1984, while in most recent years many contributions on the breeding and feeding habits of some species, especially raptors and owls, on ecology and quantitative censuses have been issued. They are a welcome sign of a qualitative improvement in Sicilian ornithology.

In the Bibliography section of this book we provide a complete list of Sicilian ornithological literature.

GEOGRAPHY

Sicily, a land of harsh landscapes and contrasts, painted with strong colours, is the largest island of the Mediterranean, 25,780 km^2 (including islets); it is only 3 km away from the Italian peninsula and 145 km from Tunisia. It lies in the southern part of the central Mediterranean, at 38°18′–36°38′ N, 15°39′–12°25′ E. (Figs 1–3 and 6).

Coasts

Sicily has 1039 km of coastland (1350 km including islets). Overhanging cliffs, alternated or edged by small beaches form the eastern and central part of the north coast. Along the northwestern coast there are some rocky stretches, characterised by isolated mesozoic calcareous massifs, alternating with pebbly beaches. The western coast, from Trapani to Mazara, is a calcarenitic plain of Quaternary, formerly subjected to subsidence which caused the formation of the islets of Stagnone and other small rocky reefs (e.g. Formica, Maraone and others). There are extensive salt-pans along the coast between Trapani and Marsala and in the Isola Lunga islet. Unfortunately, many are now disused and reclaimed for built-up areas.

The southern coast is very different: it has a flat and uniform morphology, represented by an almost continuous succession of sandy beaches along the whole 350 km. Behind this coast are clay hills subjected to continuous erosion because of meteoric and eolic agents. Sand-dunal reefs are locally present along the southern coast, from Mazara to Portopalo near Capo Passero. They reach considerable size at the mouth of the Belice river and between Gela and Scoglitti (where they are called 'Macconi'). Unfortunately they are now in constant regression because of the heavy impact of agriculture (especially intensive cultivation in greenhouses). Rivers coming from inland form some coastal, highly cultivated, alluvial plains, such as the plains of the Ribera, Naro and Salso rivers, and at Gela which bounds the second largest plain of Sicily. Formerly, marshes were frequent in the coastal depressions, sometimes closed by sand-dunal reefs; now almost all have been drained. The most important remaining coastal wetlands are at Capo Feto, near Mazara, the fresh-water lake of Biviere near Gela, and the seasonal salt marshes of Longarini-Cuba near Pachino.

The 287 km of the eastern coast are more uneven. This coast is low and partly sandy as far as Catania. In its southeast part there are more salt marshes: Vendicari, between Noto and Pachino, probably shows the best preserved wetland habitat in Sicily (and is now a Nature Reserve), and there are the small salt-pans at Siracusa and Priolo. Behind Catania lies the largest plain of Sicily, 428 km^2 in extent, ploughed through by rivers like the Simeto, the longest in Sicily, where an intensive agriculture has developed. Here was to be found the famous lake Biviere di Lentini, the drainage of which was completed in 1949. North of Catania, the eastern coast below Aetna and the Peloritani Mts. is high and rocky; here are the lava reefs of Ciclopi, fronting a largely built-up coast. Coasts are steep between Taormina and Capo S. Alessio, but there are some beaches and low coasts again towards Messina.

Orography

Mountains represent 24% of the surface of Sicily, hills 56% and plains only 20%. The average altitude is c. 450 m above sea level; c. 70% of Sicily is higher than 300 m, but only 3% is higher than 1200 m. The maximum altitudes achieved are by Mt. Aetna (3350 m) and the Madonie Mts. (1979 m). Only the northern part of the island shows a regular range of mountains, constituted by the Peloritani, Caronie (also called Nebrodi, a term which formerly included the Madonie), and Madonie Mts. The Peloritani are schistose-crystalline and reach their peak of 1374 m at Mt. Grande. They are characterised by deep canyons dug by erosion, from which originated the largest rivers of Sicily, carrying towards the coast, during the winter floods, large amounts of stony materials.

The saddle of Filippazzo separates the Peloritani from the Caronie Mts. The latter are formed by sandstone rocks, often alternated by clays and interrupted by isolated calcareous massifs (Rocca di Novara, 1340 m). They culminate at Mt. Soro, 1847 m, and have a fresh, damp climate, which permits the growth of large beech forests. The saddle of Gangi and the Pollina river separate the Caronie from the Madonie Mts. The Madonie are high mountains irregularly distributed inside a large circular perimeter that penetrates inland from the coast. Their geological nature is calcareous-dolomitic, their physiognomy is steep and harsh, very different from that of the Caronie. Forests are developed mostly along the northern side and in the most sheltered valleys. The highest points are Pizzo Carbonara (1979 m), Mt. San Salvatore (1912 m) and Mt. Ferro (1906 m).

The Madonie and the Caronie are very important watersheds. Some of the longest rivers originate from their southern sides and flow to the south and east coasts of Sicily; such are the Alcantara, Simeto and Southern Imera rivers. The northern ridge also constitutes a natural barrier against the northern and southern winds, thus contributing to the separation of the fresher Tyrrhenian climate from the dry inland one.

Further west than the Madonie there are discontinuous calcareous reliefs of different height, generally aloof but also in groups along the coast, in the area between Mt. Erice (north of Trapani) and the Sicani Mts in the provinces of Palermo and Agrigento. The Sicani Mts. lie between the Belice and Platani rivers and provide the greatest part of their head waters. The highest mountain is Mt. Cammarata, 1584 m. The greatest number of calcareous massifs, characterised by rocky cliffs and karst formations, is found in this area. Nowadays these mountains, except for sparse xerophytic vegetation and some artificial plantations (generally pines), are barren. The plains below are fertile and intensely cultivated, a landscape marked and modified by the human presence. Here lies a great contrast between the sharp calcareous spires and the low clay hills: this contrast is most impressive at Rocca Busambra (1613 m), a mountain with rocky faces to the north, dominating the Mediterranean wood of Ficuzza, and with gentle slopes towards the cultivated lands of the south.

The central-eastern region of Sicily is characterised by the slight reliefs of the Erei Mts, whose highest points, c. 1000 m, are the urban areas of Enna and Calascibetta. This region, intensively cultivated for grain, is subjected to severe erosion and lack of natural vegetation, which during the dry season gives it a barren steppe-like appearance.

The southeastern part of Sicily is occupied by the Iblei Mts, whose highest point is Mt. Lauro (986 m). They are a calcareous plateau where erosion by rivers has dug many canyons, locally called *cave*, sometimes very deep. These narrow valleys are rich in water and vegetation, while higher parts of the plateau are extremely arid.

The volcano Aetna completes the orographic mosaic of Sicily. It is 3350 m high and is composed of many separate little volcanoes which have been destroyed by later explosive eruptions and erosion, and have then been partly or fully covered with lava cast out by the most recent eruptions. Aetna originated in the late Pleistocene, and covers 1500 km^2. It shows more than 200 secondary craters and a large depression on the east side (5 × 7 km), called Valle del Bove, makes its conical shape asymmetrical. This large volcano comprises a peculiar area of the island, differing from the others in its climate, soils and vegetation.

The islets

Fourteen islets lie off the north, west and south coasts of Sicily. Seven of them form the Aeolian archipelago, from east to west namely: Stromboli, 12·6 km^2 in area, Panarea 3·4 km^2, Vulcano 21 km^2, Lipari 37·6 km^2, Salina 26·8 km^2, Filicudi 9·5 km^2, Alicudi 5·2 km^2, with many small reefs around them. The Aeolian Islands have a volcanic origin (Stromboli and Vulcano are still active) and their heights range from 421 to 962 m. Their vegetation is Mediterranean maquis-type.

The Egadi Islands lie 13–33 km off the west coast. There are 3 main islets: Levanzo 6 km^2, Favignana 19 km^2 and Marettimo 12 km^2, and some small reefs. The highest point is 686 m, on Marettimo, which has on its western side wonderful cliffs falling sheer into the sea. The vegetation of the Egadi is a maquis, more (Levanzo) or less (Marettimo) degraded, while at Favignana only a low garigue remains. Marettimo holds several botanical endemics, mainly rock plants. Further south than the Egadi, there are the islets of Stagnone, low and very close to the coast.

Off the southern coast lies the largest of the Sicilian islets, Pantelleria, 83 km^2 in area, 100 km off Cape Granitola (Sicily) and 80 km off Cape Mustafà (Tunisia). Its origin is volcanic and its vegetation characterised by the beautiful features of Mediterranean maquis, still well preserved. It reaches its peak at 836 m and also holds a small natural lake with warm sulphurous water.

Further southeast from Pantelleria lie the islets of Linosa and Lampedusa (Pelagian Is.). Linosa, 5 km^2, is 161 km away from Sicily and 120 km from Malta. It is volcanic, with sparse low maquis. Lampedusa, 20 km^2 and 133 m high, is the southern most point of Italy. It is 205 km away from Sicily and 113 km from Tunisia, with a calcareous origin and appears like a totally barren plateau. About 17 km NW off Lampedusa lies the calcareous reef of Lampione, just 3 ha in area.

CLIMATE

The climate of Sicily is Mediterranean, and because of its strong characteristics of high temperatures and summer drought (due to the low latitude and to the proximity of the Saharan region), it is close to the sub-tropical type. According to the average temperatures recorded, 3 main climatic zones occur:

1) *the coastal zone*, up to 200 m above sea level, with average winter temperatures over 10°C and 5 months a year with more than 20°C on average. This zone is considered to cover 10,480 km² (41·2% of the total area);

2) *the warm temperature zone*, up to 1200 m, with average winter temperatures from 4°C to 9·9°C, and 3 months a year with more than 20°C. This zone covers 14,200 km² (55·7% of the total area);

3) *the cold temperature zone*, restricted to the areas over 1200 m. The average winter temperatures are below 4°C and the average yearly temperature is below 20°C. On Aetna, at over 2800 m the temperature is below zero in winter, while in summer it is below 10°C.

The average annual rainfall is 600–700 mm. Areas with the highest rainfalls (1200–1400 mm a year) are the Madonie and the Caronie Mts, the mountains around Palermo and Aetna. In most of the inland areas, along the southern coast and islets, rainfall is lower: max. 500–600 mm, and only 300–400 mm in the plains of Gela and Catania, on the southeast coast and near Trapani. 80% of the annual rainfall is concentrated in autumn and winter, with a peak from November to February.

Snow is occasional below 400 m, regular for a few days between 400 and 1000 m; it persists for months only over 1700–1800 m, mainly on Aetna, whose highest part, over 2200 m, is covered with snow for about 6 months in the year.

VEGETATION

Sicily was once covered by abundant woods and Mediterranean maquis. These were reduced to only small areas during different foreign dominations, and probably were largely destroyed by the Romans, when the island became the 'granary of the Empire'. After the downfall of the Roman Empire and the Moslem conquest, the nomadic pastoralists increased further the agricultural decay and the erosion and desertification of the land, which probably affected the flood/drought cycle of the rivers. Today the degree of aridity in areas of Sicily is related to different soils and substrates, being very high on the calcareous soils of the western, southern and southeastern parts. The aridity and its effects are reduced on the northern and eastern sides of the island, which show a cooler climate.

Cultivated olives are still the most widespread non-forest trees below c.700 m. The cultivation of Carobs *Ceratonia siliqua* today covers only a few areas, mostly in the southeast (e.g. the Iblei Mts). Almonds are widely scattered, especially on the poor soils of central Sicily. Along the coasts citrus plantations are increasingly cultivated. Re-afforestation has taken place using exotic species like *Eucalyptus*, in some cases by *Acacia*, and frequently by some species of pines, especially *Pinus halepensis*. Fig. 5 shows the present extent of woodland in Sicily; see also Fig. 6.

The landscape of Sicily is often dominated by Prickly Pears *Opuntia ficus-indica* and Agaves *Agave mexicana*, both imported.

The hills of the central and western zones are dominated by a very degraded vegetation, with scattered garigue, and are often characterised by *Ampelodesma mauritanica* or overgrazed open lands dominated by *Asphodelus*. Only in a few coastal calcareous localities a garigue occurs with the dwarf broom-palm *Chamaerops humilis*, which was once widespread along all the coasts.

The southeastern zone (Iblei Mts) shows a particular landscape. It is extremely dry on the calcareous plateau, and cool, with abundant water, along the narrow and deep valleys (the *cave*) where an abundant vegetation, characterised by thickets of Oak *Quercus ilex*, grows.

On the western side, the Sicani Mts are mostly denuded with scattered thickets of *Q. ilex* and *Q. pubescens* and widespread degraded shrubby vegetation. Only at Ficuzza and near Palazzo Adriano are there large woods, generally oak spp. (*Q. ilex, Q. pubescens* and *Q. suber*).

The most important arboreal cover is concentrated on the Madonie, Caronie, Peloritani Mts and Mt Aetna. The hill and mountain vegetation may be placed in the ilex oak association (*Quercion ilicis*–see Naveh & Lieberman 1984), which extends from the coast up to c.1200 m, which is its altitudinal limit. It is characterised by *Q. ilex, Q. pubescens*, Thorny Broom *Calicotome villosa, Pistacia terebinthus, Rhamnus alaternus, Euphorbia dendroides*, etc. Here and there grow scattered thickets of Evergreen Oaks *Quercus suber*, with an understorey of different species of Rockrose *Cistus*.

Mediterranean maquis, placed in the zonal vegetation of *Oleo-ceratonion* (op. cit.), is characterised by Lentisk *Pistacia lentiscus, Arbutus unedo, Cistus spp., Erica arborea, E.multiflora, Myrtus communis, Calicotome spinosa*, etc. It is thinly widespread, especially in some areas of the northern chain from the Madonie to Peloritani Mts, and also on the Aeolian Islands, at I. Marettimo (Egadi) and I. Pantelleria. Elsewhere it is degraded and shows little structural and floristic diversity.

Above 1200 m we find the upper Mediterranean vegetation level, characterised by the Quercetalia-Fagetea (Peterken 1981), with Oaks *Q. pubescens* and *Q. cerris*, beeches *Fagus sylvatica* (widespread on Madonie, and especially on Caronie Mts, more local on Aetna), Chestnut-trees *Castanea sativa*, different species of *Acer*, etc. On Aetna there are large pine-woods of *Pinus laricio* and small thickets of birch *Betula aetnensis* which, as *Genista aetnensis*, is particularly adapted for colonising the lava beds up to 2000 m. On Madonie Mts, the fir *Abies nebrodensis* once flourished, but today it is reduced to c.20 individual trees.

The highest mountain level, dominated by thorny and shrubby species, occurs only on the highest peaks of the Madonie Mts (characterised by *Astragalus nebrodensis*) and between 1800 and 2950 m on Aetna. There, up to 2450 m, *Astragalus siculus, A. aetnensis, Berberis aetnensis, Juniperus haemisphaerica*, etc. live; only some pioneer species, such as *Rumex aetnensis, Anthemis aetnensis* and *Viola aetnensis* grow up to 2950 m.

MIGRATION

Sicily, with is geographical position situated only 150 km northeast of the North African coast of Tunisia, can be expected to be of great significance in the migration routes between mainland Europe and Africa, and on the return journey. However, migration through the Mediterranean Sea occurs on a wide front, as observed by Moreau (1953, 1972) and Casement (1966), with no high concentrations over the straits, particularly as regards passerine night migrants. Their sight and radar records from ships crossing the Sicilian Channel, Tyrrhenian and Ionian seas, give an interesting picture of migration in this part of the Mediterranean and definitively confirm that no important concentration of passerines occurs on the Sicily–Tunisia route. Moreoever, Sicily has a regular coastline with few promontories and no

isolated capes of any size; nor does the complex inland orography favour the exis-
tence of well defined inland migratory routes. Therefore in most parts of Sicily
migrants are widely dispersed, and, although the number of migratory species is
high, migration in Sicily does not dominate the ornithological year as much as it
does in other Mediterranean islands.

Quite a different picture emerges on the surrounding islets, particularly the islets
to the south in the Sicilian Channel (the Pelagians and Pantelleria). These are the
most rewarding areas of Sicilian territory for the observation of migrant species,
especially of nocturnal migrants, which have passed largely undetected over the
main island. Unfortunately the absence of resident ornithologists on these islets
limits the gathering of data, so that the observations made in the 1960s and early
1970s by Moltoni remain fundamental. The low density of migratory passerines in
most areas of Sicily is confirmed by the lack of traditional trapping, which would
surely have taken place, as in other islands like Malta and Cyprus, if it had been
feasible. Until recently, only the migration of waterbirds and some game birds was
fairly well known.

Besides the surrounding islands, a few areas with some concentration of migrating
passerines can be found along the south and east coasts. The east coast is probably
the most exploited by migrants, which use the coast apparently to avoid the long sea
crossing of the Ionian Sea, as pointed out by Moreau (1953) and Casement (1966).

Geographical origins and destinations of migrants

Recoveries of ringed birds show that most migrants towards Sicily come mainly
from northern Jugoslavia, central Europe, Scandinavia and European Russia. This
confirms the assumption, also supported by comparative data on migration from
Apulia and along the Adriatic coast, that the main movement affecting Sicily is on a
NE/SW axis, from the direction of the Balkans further north and east, passing over
the Adriatic Sea to descend along the Italian coast. The number of birds moving
down Italy from north to south seems to be smaller.

The situation for E Sicily may be different from that for W Sicily. The western area
and coast shows evidence of a smaller movement of migrants from the northeast,
and, in contrast, is certainly more affected by migration from central Italy across the
Tyrrhenian Sea than is the east side of the island.

Some gulls and terns (Mediterranean Gull *Larus melanocephalus*, Slender-billed
Gull *Larus genei* and Sandwich Tern *Sterna sandvicensis*), largely coming from the
Black Sea and moving towards west Mediterranean or Atlantic wintering areas,
follow mainly an E/W route. The east and south Sicilian coasts serve as a guideline
for these species, as evidenced by the considerable coastal movements there, and
their absence near the islands of the Sicilian Channel.

A few species among passerines must take an E/W direction from their northern-
most breeding areas (e.g. Rufous Bush Chat *Cercotrichas galactotes* and Isabelline
Wheatear *Oenanthe isabellina*), regularly or occasionally reaching Sicily and Malta,
but only rarely other Italian regions. Sicilian and Maltese reports about eastern
forms of Lesser Short-toed Lark *Calandrella rufescens* and Trumpeter Finch
Bucanetes githagineus may also, though less likely, reflect regular movements of
eastern species.

Di Carlo (1973) considered the possibility of a route from Sicily to the Iberian
peninsula across the west Mediterranean, in particular for the Great Spotted
Cuckoo *Clamator glandarius*, though most years unrecorded in Sicily. Some support
comes from the recovery in west Sicily of a Night Heron *Nycticorax nycticorax*,
ringed as a nestling in Doñana in Spain in the previous spring, but such movements
cannot be regular or apply to more than very few species.

The lack of regular ringing in Sicily has greatly limited our knowledge of migration. Data on the African wintering areas of the birds migrating through Sicily are scarce, with the exception of some waterbirds which winter in the wetlands of Tunisia and whose trans-Saharan movements are unknown or rarely seen. Probably almost all individuals of the following species migrating through Sicily in fact winter in Tunisia: Black-necked Grebe *Podiceps nigricollis*, Cormorant *Phalacrocorax carbo*, Wigeon *Anas penelope*, Pochard *Aythya ferina*, Coot *Fulica atra*, Common Crane *Grus grus*, Oystercatcher *Haematopus ostralegus*, Turnstone *Arenaria interpres* and Slender-billed Gull. Confirmation is found in the good agreement between the estimated numbers of individuals of some of these species migrating through Sicily and the numbers obtained by winter censuses in Tunisia.

Weather and migration

A study of the relationships between migration and meteorology in Sicily has never been carried out. Few data only of local interest are generally reported by Ajola (1959), Moltoni & Frugis (1967) and Moltoni (1970, 1973a). It is likely that weather systems affect the local visibility, but the extent and rate of migration is generally regular from year to year.

Autumn migration

The waders of the genus *Tringa* are the first autumn migrants to arrive. They are already fairly numerous by the end of June. In July and August their passage is as evident as for some gulls or terns (e.g. Slender-billed Gull, Caspian Tern *Sterna caspia* and Black Tern *Chlidonias niger*).

The peak of migration for herons and other large waterbirds occurs in September; daily passage of hundreds of Grey Heron *Ardea cinerea* is sometimes reported. Ducks are scarce until late October and November, when large passages are observed along the east coast, with daily totals of 1000, rarely more (mainly Wigeon, Pintail *Anus acuta* and Pochard).

We still know very little about the autumn migration of raptors, which follow quite different routes in spring. No significant passage occurs in the area of Messina Straits, while a good number of Black Kites *Milvus migrans* and Honey Buzzard *Pernis apivorus* fly across west and central Sicily to converge over the islands of the Sicilian Channel (the Pelagian Islands, Pantelleria and Malta). We can assume that most of them come across the Tyrrhenian Sea, Corsica and Sardinia. Recently, hundreds of Honey Buzzards have been noticed during autumn migration in the Straits of Bonifacio between Corsica and Sardinia (Thibault 1983). A good passage also of Common Cranes is observed in autumn in west Sicily, with a peak between the end of October and November.

Movements of gulls are conspicuous along the east and south coasts from the end of October to mid-late November. With regard to Mediterranean Gulls and Sandwich Terns, this movement mainly consists of individuals wintering further west; it is not clear whether the same is true of Black-headed Gulls *Larus ridibundus*, the passage of which in Sicily might be limited to the local wintering birds.

The migration of some trans-Saharan migrant passerines starts between late July and early August (e.g. Garden Warbler *Sylvia borin* and Willow Warbler *Phylloscopus trochilus*) and continues up to mid-October, with a peak usually in the first half of September. Redstart *Phoenicurus phoenicurus*, Common Wheatear *Oenanthe oenanthe*, Whitethroat *Sylvia communis* and Spotted Flycatcher *Muscicapa striata* occur in good numbers. Among the diurnal migrants Sand Martin *Riparia riparia* and Swallow *Hirundo rustica* are usually the most numerous passerines. The autumn migration of trans-Saharan migrant passerines seems to be scarcer than in spring, possibly because Sicily, like the north African coast (Moreau 1972), is not important as a refuelling area.

In October and November movements of short-distance migrating passerines take place. Some of these winter further south than Sicily, along the Tunisian and Libyan littoral: e.g. Skylark *Alauda arvensis*, Meadow Pipit *Anthus pratensis*, Song Thrush *Turdus philomelos*, Starling *Sturnus vulgaris*, and finches like the Chaffinch *Fringilla coelebs* and other finches. Heavy passage of Skylarks and Meadow Pipits at sea around Sicily has been reported by many authors (Elliot & Monk 1952, Moreau 1953, Casement 1966), but the spectacular migration of Skylarks through the Gulf of Palermo, already described by Doderlein (1869–74) and Whitaker (1905) has largely decreased in recent years.

Winter visitors

Because of its mild climate, Sicily is a good wintering area for many species, most of them arriving between mid November (passerines) and mid December (wildfowl) and usually staying up to late February or mid-March. However, winter irruptions (January) are frequent , especially if bad weather lasts long in north Mediterranean countries, when populations of ducks, Coot, Lapwing *Vanellus vanellus*, Fieldfare *Turdus pilaris* and Chaffinch are usually affected. White Wagtail *Motacilla alba*, Robin *Erithacus rubecula*, Chiffchaff *Phylloscopus collybita*, Starling and Chaffinch are the most common wintering visitors, and are distributed uniformly all over the island. Only slightly less numerous are Skylark, Blackcap *Sylvia atricapilla* and other finches like Goldfinch *Carduelis carduelis* and Linnet *Carduelis cannabina*. Wintering site fidelity has been confirmed for the Robin in the outskirts of Palermo and for Woodcock *Scolopax rusticola* in Madonie Mts and in Ficuzza wood.

In the last few years between 3500 and 13,000 wintering ducks have been censused. They are mainly Pochard, Wigeon and Teal *Anas crecca*, which mostly concentrate on the lake of Pergusa. The number of wintering Coots shows less annual variation, with a maximum peak of c. 9000. We do not take in consideration the data reported by Caterini (1978) and the reports by local shooters, as listed acritically by Focardi & Spina (1986), do not seem to be reliable (e.g. the claimed wintering of Garganey *Anas querquedula* is certainly erroneous). It is likely that wintering ducks and Coots are increasing thanks to the creation of new protected areas; if all or at least the most important reservoirs were protected the duck numbers could increase considerably.

With the exception of Snipe *Gallinago gallinago*, the winter occurrence of waders is negligible.

Some recent censuses have shown how important Sicilian coasts are for wintering gulls: c. 21,000 Black-headed Gulls and c. 2000 Mediterranean Gulls were counted in January 1984. The latter were concentrated in a few areas of the south coast. Sicily seems to be the most important Italian wintering area for the Mediterranean Gull and Lesser Black-backed Gull *Larus fuscus*, and this is likely to be so also for the Gannet *Sula bassana*, which seems to be more numerous along the Sicilian shores in winter than on the upper and mid Tyrrhenian coasts.

In Europe, the Hoopoe *Upupa epops* overwinters only in Sicily, in Sardinia and in the southern Iberian peninsula: it is regularly present, but in small numbers, particularly along the south Sicilian coast.

Apart from the Hoopoe and waterfowl, the species wintering in Sicily and related to a peculiar habitat are quite rare; among them is the Alpine Accentor *Prunella collaris*, which overwinters only at the highest altitudes of the Caronie Mts, Rocca Busambra and probably the Madonie Mts.

Spring migration

For many species, mainly passerines, migration in spring seems to be more considerable than in autumn, though there are no data to stress a real difference in their numbers except for a few species that are known to follow different routes in spring and autumn. The apparent difference is possibly only the consequence of the birds' passage being more concentrated into a shorter period of time; but it is also necessary to consider that Sicily in spring is much more green than in autumn and therefore more attractive to migrants.

The spring passage starts during the middle of February with the arrival of some waterbirds, (e.g. Garganey, Black-tailed Godwit *Limosa limosa*, Ruff *Philomachus pugnax*) and the House Martin *Delichon urbica*. Occasionally Garganey and Black-tailed Godwit have been observed even in late January. In most years there is a heavy migration of Garganey between late February and late March, their passage often concentrated into a few days. Though there are no detailed counts, it is likely that thousands and sometimes tens of thousands of individuals pass in a single day. Among Garganeys there is often also a great number of Pintail *Anas acuta* and some Ferruginous Duck *Aythya nyroca*. This passage is evident only on the south coast and the east coast as far north as Siracusa. Some passerines also arrive mid February.

The spring migration of raptors in this part of the Mediterranean is not yet well known, but there are more data than about the autumn passage. Thiollay (1977) estimated that the minimum number of raptors migrating in spring from Cap Bon, Tunisia, to Sicilian coasts is more than 40,000. More recent data collected at Cap Bon (Dejonghe 1980, T. Gaultier) suggest lower estimates, though whether or not this reflects a decrease in the number of migrants is not known. Not all raptors migrating towards Sicily take off from Cap Bon; in fact, many harriers *Circus* spp. and falcons (mainly Kestrel *Falco tinnunculus* and Red-footed Falcon *Falco vespertinus*) cross the Sicilian Channel on a broad front, as evidenced by their frequent occurrence along the south and southeast coasts and in Malta. The actual arrival points, in fact, are not yet known, though their route towards the Straits of Messina is well recognised and seems to be restricted to the mountains along the north coast of Sicily. Good numbers are recorded over Palermo, particularly on Mt Pellegrino, at other isolated mountains, like Mt San Calogero, and at the Madonie and Caronie Mts. Some raptors leave west Sicily, crossing the Tyrrhenian Sea, of which some converge over I. Ustica, while others fly on as far as the Tuscan Islands or to the coasts of Latium; yet others may converge again on the area of the Straits of Messina by flying over the Aeolian Islands. Until 1984 raptors over the Straits of Messina were counted only occasionally, though sometimes passage of more than 3000 birds, nearly all Honey Buzzards *Pernis apivorus*, was recorded in only 2 days in mid May. Since 1984, the anti-poaching camps (see chapter on hunting) have coincided with some annual counts lasting one month from late April to late May. The total number of raptors counted has varied between 3200 and 8000, with over 60% of them Honey Buzzards, followed by Kestrel/Lesser Kestrel, Black Kite and Red-footed Falcon. It must be realised that where the counts took place represent only a fraction of the migratory front and that there were not always raptor specialists present, as these camps have mainly a conservationist character. The main difficulty in studying the migration in the Straits is due to the wide (40 km) front used by raptors between Sicily and Calabria; the maximum crossing distance is c. 25 km (between Roccalumera and Capo dell'Armi) decreasing northwards to 3 km, where the proper Straits lie. Even if the wind direction can cause local concentrations (see the Systematic List on Honey Buzzard), some passage seems to occur usually along the whole front. If we also consider the Aeolian Islands, where a remarkable passage towards the Calabrian coast north of Bagnara occurs, the migratory front is over 80 km.

A limiting factor in making observations is the flying height of the birds, which reach the Straits after having flown over, at a short distance from the coast, a high mountainous area (the average height of the ridge of the Peloritani Mts, of which

Dinnammare, the highest peak, is over 1000 m), the orography of which is complex and rich in thermals. Rather more detailed data on the migration of raptors over the Straits are reported by Massa (1975a, 1978e) and Dimarca & Iapichino (1984), with further analysis for this part of the Mediterranean being reported by Galea & Massa (1985).

The spring passage of the Common Crane in west Sicily is much more irregular in numbers than in autumn, though up to 500 have been counted in a single day over Palermo in early March.

The spring passage of waterbirds is mainly restricted to the wetlands and numbers greatly depend on the water level. Most species, e.g. herons, Spoonbills *Platalea leucorodia*, and large and medium sized waders, peak late Mar to late Apr, while the peak of some small-sized waders (e.g. Little Stint *Calidris minuta* and Curlew Sandpiper *Calidris ferruginea*) is in May, though they may still be present in early June. Herons, particularly Grey Heron and Little Egret *Egretta garzetta*, are usually in tens, mainly in coastal wetlands, while waders about the same time form the most numerous flocks with peaks of hundreds in wetlands around Capo Passero and Trapani.

Generally the spring migration of gulls and terns is smaller than the autumnal one; in spring the only species more numerous than in autumn are Little Gull *Larus minutus*, Gull-billed Tern *Gelochelidon nilotica*, Whiskered Tern *Chlidonias hybridus* and White-winged Black Tern *Chlidonias leucopterus*.

A few waterbirds regularly stop to oversummer in Sicily: e.g. some herons, increasingly so the Grey Heron, a few waders, and some Mediterranean Gulls, Black-headed Gulls and Audouin's Gulls *Larus audouinii*, the last only on southeast coasts.

A great migration of Turtle Doves *Streptopelia turtur* occurs from mid April to mid May, mainly on the south coast, the Messina Straits and the islets. Birds arrive usually in tens particularly in the early morning, but in the last few years they seem to be less numerous. The decrease in the numbers of the Quail *Coturnix coturnix* is much more evident; its spring passage occurs in the same areas as the Turtle Dove.

A few passerine species that winter in north Africa as well as Sicily show an obvious, though sparse, spring passage between February and March, e.g. Song Thrush and Starling. Passerines that have overwintered south of the Sahara are scarce until the last days of March, most species peaking mid April to mid May. Yellow Wagtail *Motacilla flava*, Redstart, Common Wheatear and Spotted Flycatcher, are probably the most numerous species, together with Swallows and House Martins *Delichon urbica*, which are also among the later migrants and can be still migrating in small flocks until mid June.

BREEDING

The number of species breeding in Sicily recorded 1979–1987 is 135, of which 70 can be considered as resident. Between 1979–1983 the surveys for the first Atlas of breeding birds was carried out (Massa 1985). The Atlas adopted a UTM grid and illustrates the confirmed, possible or probable breeding of each species inside the 297 10 km^2 quadrants. Fig. 7 (updated to 1987) shows the number of species found in each quadrant, represented by 4 symbols that represent the following categories of abundance: (1) less than 21 species; (2) between 21 and 35 species; (3) between 36 and 50 species; (4) more than 50 species. The average number of species for each 10 km^2 square is c. 40. Reference to distribution and breeding in the Systematic List is mostly taken from data for the Atlas, except that data collected after 1983, and therefore not included in the Atlas, are also used.

By this means the most interesting areas of the island, as regards the breeding birds, are pointed out: Sicani, the Madonie and Caronie Mts and Aetna. The distribution of species-richness coincides to a great extent with woodland in Sicily (Fig. 5). The highest number of species occurs in those areas in which there are also rock cliffs that create more habitat diversity and in which local species can also be found. The lowest number of species occurs in the plains, where agriculture is highly developed (Plain of Catania, some areas of Trapani district) and vegetation varies very little.

Among the islets, Pantelleria is the poorest in species in relation to its size; this may be because of its isolation. The Aeolian Islands are the richest, but all islets are generally poorer in species in comparison with similar habitats on the main island.

Unfortunately breeding biology data for many species, even the most common and widespread, are still insufficient. Even though some data can reflect the major or minor degree of coverage of some areas of the island or the easiness of recording some species rather than others, the Atlas gives a clear picture of the distribution and the relative frequency of breeding birds in Sicily. It has turned out that only one species, the Spanish Sparrow *Passer hispaniolensis*, was present in all 297 quadrants. Another 11 resident species are in more than 80% of the quadrants: Kestrel *Falco tinnunculus*, Crested Lark *Galerida cristata*, Stonechat *Saxicola torquata*, Blackbird *Turdus merula*, Sardinian Warbler *Sylvia melanocephala*, Great Tit *Parus major*, Magpie *Pica pica*, Hooded Crow *Corvus corone*, Serin *Serinus serinus*, Goldfinch *Carduelis carduelis*, Linnet *Carduelis cannabina* and Cirl Bunting *Emberiza cirlus*. These are the most widespread species in Sicily and show the most habitat-breadth. Another 19 species have been found to be present in more than 50% of the quadrants. These are also quite widespread and numerous, but show a stronger tie with particular habitats and are not uniformly present all over Sicily. Among them are: Swift *Apus apus*, House Martin *Delichon urbica*, Nightingale *Luscinia megarynchos* and Subalpine Warbler *Sylvia cantillans* (the 4 species which seem to be the most numerous migrant breeders); and Buzzard *Buteo buteo*, Turtle Dove *Streptopelia turtur*, Wren *Troglodytes troglodytes*, Fan-tailed Warbler *Cisticola juncidis*, Blackcap *Sylvia atricapilla* and Chaffinch *Fringilla coelebs*. Some other migrant breeders quite numerous in Sicily are: Hoopoe *Upupa epops*, Short-toed Lark *Calandrella brachydactyla*, Swallow *Hirundo rustica*, Spectacled Warbler *Sylvia conspicillata* and Woodchat Shrike *Lanius senator*.

There are about 15 species in Sicily that, regarding their breeding distribution, are related to the main mountains and to the woods at a medium or high altitude. These are confined to the Caronie and Madonie Mts and Aetna, or occasionally to the Peloritani, Iblei and Sicani Mts. Six of them do not seem to breed below 1000 m: Skylark *Alauda arvensis*, Redstart *Phoenicurus phoenicurus*, Rock Thrush *Monticola saxatilis*, Marsh Tit *Parus palustris*, Siskin *Carduelis spinus* and Crossbill *Loxia curvirostra*. Others live at a lower altitude, such as the Nuthach *Sitta europaea*. 400–500 m is usually the lowest altitude for the European Nightjar *Caprimulgus europaeus*, Whitethroat *Sylvia communis*, Chiffchaff *Phylloscopus collybita*, Long-tailed Tit *Aegithalos caudatus* and Coal Tit *Parus ater*.

It is interesting that in Sicily at least one species reaches one of its highest altitudes: the Spectacled Warbler *Sylvia conspicillata*, breeding on Aetna as high as 2200 m (only on Teide, in Tenerife, has it been found even higher, at 2400 m above sea level – Catalisano & Massa 1987b).

The most common wetland breeding species are Little Grebe *Tachybaptus ruficollis*, Moorhen *Gallinula chloropus* and Reed Warbler *Acrocephalus scirpaceus*. Water Rail *Rallus aquaticus*, Coot *Fulica atra*, Little Ringed Plover *Charadrius dubius* and Kentish Plover *Charadrius alexandrinus* are also quite well widespread. It is only recently, or after a long absence, that some wetland species have begun again to breed and some seem now to be regular (see below Changes in breeding status).

The 14 islets surrounding Sicily have interesting populations of sea birds, whereas Sicily holds merely 2 small colonies of Yellow-legged Gull *Larus cachinnans*. In the islets c. 5000 pairs of Yellow-legged Gull breed; the largest colonies, which are probably increasing, are on Lampedusa, Levanzo and Marettimo. About 15,000 pairs of Cory's Shearwater *Calonectris diomedea* breed in the islets too, of which c. 10,000 pairs have been estimated to nest on Linosa, one of the biggest Mediterranean colonies. Numbers of Manx Shearwater *Puffinus puffinus* and Storm Petrel *Hydrobates pelagicus*, though numerous, are probably underestimated; in Marettimo there are more than 1000 pairs of Storm Petrel, which is perhaps the second largest Mediterranean colony after Filfla in Malta. Only at Lampedusa does a small colony of Shags *Phalacrocorax aristotelis* exist, but it seems that a typical Mediterranean species, Audouin's Gull *Larus audouinii*, has never bred in Sicily or on Sicilian islets.

Among raptors, the large population of Peregrines *Falco peregrinus*, c. 150 pairs, is of interest; there are also c. 60 pairs of Lanner *Falco biarmicus* and c. 150 pairs of Eleonora's Falcon *Falco eleonorae*. While the number of Peregrines in Sicily is quite similar to that in Sardinia, the population of Lanners is surely the largest in Italy and probably one of the most numerous in Europe.

Changes in breeding status

It is difficult to define changes in status of the Sicilian avifauna because of data shortage about both distribution and abundance in the past. Moreover, it should be kept in mind that the authors of the past, from Benoit to Arrigoni, considered many species (that certainly today do not breed anymore) as breeders, often without entering into detail to prove it. They were not always very conscientious in reporting unconfirmed and second-hand information, as opposed to sure and confirmed records. Besides which, in the last 100 years the Sicilian environment has changed so much that great changes in the breeding avifauna are justifiably deduced, though without proof.

The great destruction of wetlands in the first half of the century (see section on Conservation — Destruction of nature) has surely been the cause of the extinction in Sicily of Red-crested Pochard *Netta rufina*, Purple Gallinule *Porphyrio porphyrio*, Bearded Tit *Panurus biarmicus* and perhaps other species whose breeding has never been confirmed, such as Cormorant *Phalacrocorax carbo*, Purple Heron *Ardea purpurea*, White-headed Duck *Oxyura leucocephala* and Marsh Harrier *Circus aeruginosus*. Some species like Black-necked Grebe *Podiceps nigricollis*, Mallard *Anas platyrhynchos*, Garganey *Anas querquedula*, Ferruginous Duck *Aythya nyroca* and Moustached Warbler *Acrocephalus melanopogon*, that are today rare or occasional breeders, perhaps used to be more common. On the other hand, the shortening of the spring hunting season in the last few years, has seen the return of some species that had probably become extinct in the past: Great Crested Grebe *Podiceps cristatus*, Black-winged Stilt *Himantopus himantopus* and Little Tern *Sterna albifrons*. For the same reason the Garganey and Ferruginous Duck might become (again?) regular breeders.

The Lammergeyer *Gypaetus barbatus*, Griffon Vulture *Gyps fulvus* Osprey *Pandion haliaetus*, Black Francolin *Francolinus francolinus*, Andalusian Hemipode *Turnix sylvatica*, Little Bustard *Tetrax tetrax* and Eagle Owl *Bubo bubo* became extinct in Sicily in the hundred or so years prior to the 1950–60s. Hunting, the change of the environment and, more recently, the use of pesticides, have caused many extinctions, but natural factors also could have had an effect, as some of the species probably had small populations, sometimes at the periphery of their range.

The destruction of woods has probably been a determining factor for the extinction of woodpeckers, namely *Picus viridis* and *Dendrocopus minor*, but the breeding of these species has never been confirmed.

Nowadays the most menaced species seem to be Red Kite *Milvus milvus*, Stone Curlew *Burhinus oedicnemus* and Dipper *Cinclus cinclus*, and their extinction in the next few years seems possible. Other species which are surely decreasing as breeders are Little Bittern *Ixobrychus minutus*, Lesser Kestrel *Falco naumanni*, Bee-eater *Merops apiaster*, Roller *Coracias garrulus*, Great Reed Warbler *Acrocephalus arundinaceus* and Chough *Pyrrhocorax pyrrhocorax*. Rock Partridge *Alectoris graeca*, Quail *Coturnix coturnix*, Calandra Lark *Melanocorypha calandra* and Woodchat Shrike *Lanius senator* are also decreasing, but are still quite widespread; Bonelli's Eagle *Hieraaetus fasciatus* is decreasing too and has probably already become extinct on Iblei Mts, where it was numerous in the past. Hunting, modifications of the environment and pesticides are involved in the decrease of all these species, though each in a different way.

The small populations of Golden Eagle *Aquila chrysaetos* and Egyptian Vulture *Neophron percnopterus* seem to be stable, but as some sites were recently deserted by the latter and some birds are killed every year by poachers, a decrease in numbers of Egyptian Vultures is possible. It seems that populations of the Peregrine *Falco peregrinus* and Lanner *Falco biarmicus* were not affected by the use of pesticides, but data on trends in their populations are lacking. It is of common knowledge that the last Sicilian colony of Griffon Vultures was destroyed with poisoned bait for foxes in 1965 (Priolo 1967).

Data about the increase of some species are still more approximate because there is no certain comparison with the past. The reduction of woods and high maquis and the creation of steppe-like habitats in some extensive inland districts probably favour some species like Crested Lark *Galerida cristata* and Corn Bunting *Miliaria calandra*. Reports of some local increase and the colonisation of some Sicilian islets in recent years seem to confirm an increase of the following species: Blackbird *Turdus merula*, Cetti's Warbler *Cettia cetti*, Serin *Serinus serinus* and Cirl Bunting *Emberiza cirlus*. Magpie *Pica pica*, Jackdaw *Corvus monedula* and Hooded Crow *Corvus corone* are also increasing, above all because of the increase of rubbish tips.

Recent colonisation of Sicily has been confirmed for 3 species: Pochard *Aythya ferina*, Black Kite *Milvus migrans* and Starling *Sturnus vulgaris*. In other cases the recent discovery of new breeding species is probably only apparent and reflects the increasing number of observers: Night Heron *Nycticorax nycticorax* (though this species possibly has really increased in recent years), Hobby *Falco subbuteo*, Long-eared Owl *Asio otus*, Kingfisher *Alcedo atthis*, Rock Thrush *Monticola saxatilis*, Siskin *Carduelis spinus* and Crossbill *Loxia curvirostra*. The recent issue of the Sicilian Atlas will surely allow assessment in the coming years of changes in status with more precision.

CONSERVATION

Hunting

Shooting is very common throughout Sicily and its destructive effect on wild birds is on a par with the extensive damage caused by destruction of the environment. In January 1983 hunting licenses in Sicily totalled 136,244 out of a population of 5 million (2·7%), and numbers have been slowly increasing since. The density of hunters in Sicily per km^2 is 5·2; this is less than in the Italian peninsula (7·3), but whereas in many parts of Italy shooting is mostly confined to resident species (Pheasants, Hares, etc.), in Sicily it is mostly addressed to migratory birds and only to a lesser extent to resident fauna (Rock Partridge *Alectoris graeca*, Rabbit *Oryctolagus cuniculus* and Hare *Lepus europaeus*).

The slack enforcement of hunting laws in other parts of Italy bears very little comparison to the dire situation in Sicily. The present Sicilian hunting law, approved by the Sicilian government on 30 March 1981, is similar to that in force all over Italy: the shooting season starts the last Sunday of August and ends the 28 February, during which season hunters must respect 3 closed days every week (Tuesday, Thursday and Friday). Only 32 species of birds may be legally shot, all amongst the most common ones (ducks, Coot, waders like Woodcock and Ruff, Turtle Dove, Quail and passerines such as Skylark and some species of thrushes). There is in addition a bag limit. Any kind of trapping and netting is forbidden, but, unlike other Mediterranean Islands, e.g. Malta or Cyprus, this is fortunately a little practised custom in Sicily. Only Robins *Erith-acus rubecula* and Goldfinches *Carduelis carduelis* are regularly trapped illegally in large numbers every year.

In the past, up to 1971, the law allowed Turtle Dove, Quail and raptors to be shot in spring (April and March) and, up to 1980, the hunting season lasted to 31 March. Conservation societies are asking for a further reduction of the shooting season, particularly a later start, but there is strong opposing political pressure from hunting societies to extend the season.

The above describes the situation on paper. Reality is different. Most hunters do not respect the law and there is no real effort by the authorities to enforce it. The list of species that can be shot is largely ignored, and very often hunters shoot protected and endangered species, either because they are not able to recognise protected birds, or, above all, because they ignore the law.

Taxidermy and collecting of stuffed birds are common in Sicily, resulting especially in the frequent quest for rare species, for which there is also a growing market. Birds of prey, protected by law since 1979, are still heavily shot; for example 448 birds of prey were stuffed by 9 taxidermists in the hunting season 1974/75, while 358 were stuffed by only 2 taxidermists in 1981 and 570 by 6 taxidermists in 1983 (Massa 1982 b, S. Falcone (see Table 1). If one takes into consideration that taxidermists in Sicily are probably numbered in hundreds, this data demonstrates that a law to control taxidermy is urgently required.

The limits of the shooting season are seldom respected, particularly in those areas in which the 'tradition' of spring hunting is strong. In April and May on islets (particularly Lampedusa, Linosa and Pantelleria) and along the southern coast, shooting of Turtle Dove and Quail (but in reality any kind of migratory bird) is as frequent now as when it used to be allowed by law. A particularly blatant breaking of the law is practised along the Straits of Messina, where it is a 'tradition' to shoot migrating raptors, especially Honey Buzzards *Pernis apivorus* in May. 'Adorni' (the local name for the Honey Buzzard) shooting is common in the terminal northern hills of the Peloritani Mts which line the Straits. Here are situated, in a few well-known strategic points, c. 100 brickwork shooters' hides, sometimes in reality small houses; hunters use them to conceal themselves and to shoot raptors which are gliding and soaring along the ridges of the mountains in search of thermals. On the Calabrian side of the Straits, Honey Buzzard shooting is even more popular than in Sicily, because there the raptors pass lower and over a wider area. According to data gathered by Lega Italiana Protezione Uccelli (LIPU) there are at least 5000 hunters who shoot raptors every year in Calabria, and around hundreds in Sicily; every year at least 1000 Honey Buzzards are shot, that is about one tenth of the total passing over the Straits. In addition an unknown number, probably thousands, of other species of raptors, such as Black Kite *Milvus migrans*, Kestrel *Falco tinnunculus*, Red-footed Falcon *Falco vespertinus*, are slaughtered. A small number of Black

Table 1. Birds of prey shot by hunters in Sicily between August 1974 and March 1975, and in 1981 and 1983 (January–December) and given respectively to 9, 2 and 8 taxidermists

Species	1974/75	1981	1983
Pandion haliaetus	5	1	3
Pernis apivorus	34	24	15
Milvus milvus	8	1	8
Milvus migrans	—	—	5
Neophron percnopterus	3	—	3
Gyps fulvus	—	—	1
Circaetus gallicus	—	2	2
Circus cyaneus	—	1	6
Circus pygargus	15	2	7
Circus macrourus	—	1	4
Circus aeruginosus	4	6	18
Accipiter nisus	12	14	8
Buteo buteo	91	70	141
Aquila pomarina	2	—	—
Aquila chrysaetus	2	1	3
Hieraaetus fasciatus	—	—	1
Falco naumanni	2	4	12
Falco tinnunculus	140	99	168
Falco columbarius	—	5	—
Falco vespertinus	3	1	4
Falco eleonorae	—	1	3
Falco subbuteo	4	10	9
Falco biarmicus	1	3	6
Falco peregrinus	4	2	9
Tyto alba	54	68	66
Asio otus	10	18	11
Asio flammeus	7	2	16
Otus scops	10	8	14
Athene noctua	24	9	9
Strix aluco	13	5	18
TOTAL	448	358	570

Storks *Ciconia nigra*, Egyptian Vultures *Neophron percnopterus* and Short-toed Eagles *Circaetus gallicus* are killed.

The authorities have tolerated this illegal hunting for many years. It must be noted that hunters do not shoot from areas particularly difficult to reach, but from sites near villages and even close to the main streets; in Calabria hundreds of shooters' hides are just a few metres from the motorway and some of them are even on the roofs of houses in the suburbs of Reggio Calabria. During the anti-shooting camp arranged by LIPU in 1984, more than 1200 shots against 3200 raptors were counted from 20 April to 19 May in the area of Mt Ciccia and Castanea in the Peloritani Mts, with a maximum on 30 April when 228 shots were fired in 2 hours and this despite the presence of policemen. In a situation like this any conservation action is difficult. Worse, in 1984 a bomb exploded in the LIPU office at Reggio Calabria the day before a demonstration against illegal shooting; threats and intimidations against bird-watchers in the field are frequent.

The authorities recently have arranged some anti-poaching measures to repress and prevent shooting mainly when conservationists are present, but all measures so far are quite insufficient to cope with the real problem. It will take many years and a lot of very hard work, particularly in education, to abolish this illegal extermination of raptors, which is one of the biggest threats to their survival still existing anywhere in Europe.

The illegal taking of eggs and chicks involves only a few species, but all of them require protection for their survival. Sicily is one of the areas greatly exploited by falconers, especially from Germany, because of the high density of Peregrines *Falco peregrinus* and Lanner Falcons *Falco biarmicus*. We estimate that falconers pillage more than 100 falcon chicks yearly in Sicily alone.

A particular kind of illegal collecting of eggs takes place at I. Linosa, where every year the inhabitants take at least 3000 eggs of Cory's Shearwater *Calonectris diomedea*. It is an old custom which, in the past, was justified by food requirements, but today it is only an anachronistic pastime.

There is little respect for the hunting laws because of the insufficient enforcement measures, which are entrusted to a body of gamekeepers, and to a voluntary body of hunting societies, whose response is limited, above all towards those types of hunting usually considered 'traditional'. Recently (1985) measures have also been entrusted to Foresters and this could mean an improvement of the present situation. Areas where shooting is forbidden are not extensive: in 1987 there were about 25,000 ha of Oasi di Protezione and Zone di Ripopolamento, and about 20,000 ha of Nature Reserves set up in 1984. Hunting is also forbidden in Regional woods, about 106,000 ha, many of which however are pine-plantations, rather poor in fauna. Actually, illicit hunting is fairly common even in most of these areas, particularly for some rare species by or for collectors, e.g. in the Nature Reserves at Vendicari and Foce Simeto, reports of Flamingos *Phoenicopterus ruber* and Spoonbills *Platalea leucorodia* being shot are supported by documentary evidence.

Sicily is surely today, for bird protection, one of the 'black spots' within EEC countries. Some improvement could be expected in the next few years, especially through the establishment of a good network of Nature Reserves and Parks, which are as yet mainly on paper. The interest for conservation amongst the population is still low, but it has greatly increased in the last 10 years; conservation societies like LIPU, WWF, Lega per l'Ambiente, in fact have nowadays some influence over local administrations, but paradoxically it is sometimes easier to stop destructive projects in areas of natural history interest than to act against direct bird killing. A definite improvement in the situation will probably follow if a widespread and long educational process, especially concerning teaching in schools, is set up.

Destruction of nature

Sicily has paid much more heavily than other Mediterranean isles for a thousand years of human pressures which have considerably changed the original landscape. In 1900 about 800 people (out of a total population of 3,500,000) owned one third of the whole island (the so-called *latifundia*). Particularly during the last decades, man has caused a great environmental and hydrogeological decay. The most remarkable consequence of his actions is shown in the broad expanse of arable land that reaches as far as 1200 m above sea level, and through the intensive cultivation along the coasts. This increase of cultivation has caused the decrease of the natural vegetation, which in many areas has been reduced to open grasslands or garigue, and only in a few places is it still possible to describe it as Mediterranean maquis.

Today woodlands are found only on the northern mountain ridges and on Aetna or in a few isolated areas, but in the past they spread over a great part of the island. The destruction of woods started with the Greek colonisation and increased with the Roman conquest, when Sicily used to be considered as the 'granary of the Empire'.

The increase of population and the colonisation of the coasts after the middle of the 16th century, was the period of the greatest destruction of the coastal forests. Around the middle of the 18th century much of the forest on Aetna, inhabited by animals like deer, disappeared (Mongitore 1742). According to Mack Smith (1968), in the 30 years before 1847 half the woodlands of Sicily were cut down, in particular to provide fuel for the sulphur mines. In 1911 there were only 98,000 hectares of woods.

The hydrogeologic imbalance is a consequence of the destruction of woods and of the intensive exploitation of the deforested lands: the flow of most sources and inland rivers has decreased enormously, and erosion is now very widespread inland – 40% of the Sicily's surface is officially considered to be subject to landslides. Today there are about 250,000 hectares of woodland; but re-forestation has been carried out by planting exotic species (mainly *Eucalyptus* spp.) of no natural history interest, or by planting conifers (*Pinus* spp.) that easily burn in the hot dry summer months (c. 7000 hectares were destroyed in 1983/84).

The destruction of wetlands in the last century has reduced this habitat from about 100,000 hectares in 1865 to 5000 hectares at this date. A century ago practically all the coastal plains were marshy throughout the year or during a part of it. Most reclamation was carried out between 1920 and 1950. It concerned particularly: the Plain of Catania and the marshes of the mouth of the Simeto river and the Biviere di Lentini (the largest natural lake in Sicily, c. 2000 hectares, completely reclaimed in 1949); the marshy areas of the southern and southeastern coasts, around Ispica, Pozzallo, Scicli and Gela; many sites near Licata, Agrigento, Selinunte and Mazara; and the salt-pans of Augusta (c. 600 hectares). Some of the salt-pans of Trapani have been reclaimed in the last 20 years for the expansion of the town and the development of agriculture, while the growth of many towns and the plans for tourist or industrial development are still menacing the few wetlands left. On the other hand, in the last 40 years, about 30 reservoirs of between 50 and 1000 hectares have been created and others are planned. They are usually in very bare habitats, having shores subject to landslides and lacking riparian vegetation; nevertheless some of them are frequented by good numbers of wildfowl.

In the last 30 years, however the most damage to nature in Sicily has been brought on by the huge expansion of built-up areas, partly because of the growth in the population, but mainly as a result of the increasing popularity of holiday houses along the coasts or in the mountains. Hundreds of new villages have been built up along the coasts, which are now almost completely covered with a strip of houses and touristic villages, usually inhabited for only a few months in the year. The same has happened on many islets and in some sites on Mt Aetna and the Madonie Mts of particular environmental interest. Almost all coastal sites of natural history interest have been completely destroyed in the last 20 years. The network of roads has increased considerably, with adverse effects on the fauna of inland and mountainous districts, where today the areas which are not disturbed are getting less and less.

By neither regional nor local authorities has there been any serious town-planning or territorial planning, if one considers that about one third of all buildings that exist today in Sicily have been built against the law or without any authorisation.

Only in 1984 were the first Nature Reserves established in Sicily; there are now 19, covering about 20,000 hectares in total. Others are planned for future years. A Regional Nature Park has been established on Mt Aetna and 2 others are in process of creation on the Madonie and Caronie Mts. Unfortunately the protection afforded to these areas is today (1988) still merely on paper, sometimes because of the local inhabitants' resistance, and no management plans have yet been established.

ISOLATION AND OTHER ASPECTS OF THE SICILIAN AVIFAUNA

Area influences the number of species on any island. Many authors have pointed out that the real meaning of any species/area slope should lie in the habitat diversity (cf.

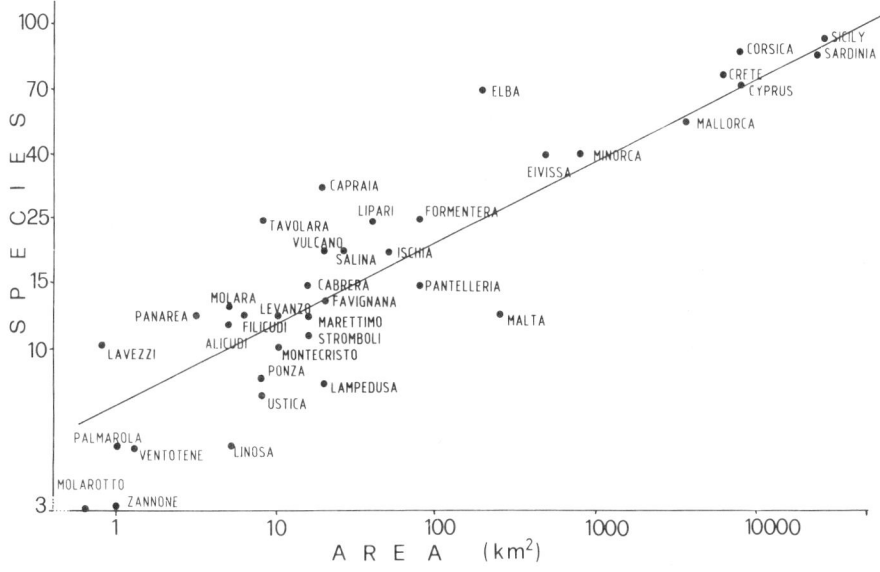

Figure 8. Species/planar area correlation for terrestrial breeding birds of 37 Mediterranean islands from 0·5 km² to 25,709 km² on a log–log scale. Data from Massa (1987c).

Williamson 1981). It seems that the number of species in the Mediterranean isles depend also on other parameters, such as area, altitude, latitude, longitude and distance from the continent; some of these are also responsible for habitat diversity (Lo Valvo & Massa, in press a). Fig. 8 shows the correlation species/planar area (on a log-log scale) for the terrestrial birds of 37 Mediterranean isles (cf. Massa 1987c; Catalisano & Massa 1987b). If we consider only the largest Mediterranean isles, the species richness of terrestrial birds seems to follow a gradient not directly dependent on the planar area; namely Sicily, Corsica, Sardinia, Crete, Cyprus. Planar as opposed to surface area, in some cases affects the data calculations significantly, e.g. for Corsica, which is very mountainous and has a surface effectively bigger than the planar area. Nevertheless planar area is useful for some comparison and consideration.

The slope of linear regression ($\log S = 0.271 \log A + 0.796$) corresponds to z and the intercept represents C in the Arrhenius' equation $S = CA^z$, where S is the number of species and A the area in km² (Preston 1962). The resulting values of z and C fall within those of isolated areas and mean that a 40-fold increase in area would be necessary to double the number of species.

Increasing insularity, measured as species impoverishment, is a phenomenon that can be observed working from north to south down Mediterranean peninsulas. A clinal decrease of breeding bird species has been observed throughout the Balkan peninsula to Crete and down the Italian peninsula to Sicily (Massa 1982 a, 1987 c). As already pointed out by Lebreton & Ledant (1981) and Flint & Stewart (1983), Cyprus and Crete are poorer in species than similar sized western Mediterranean isles, a finding which seems, however, to depend additionally at least upon the location, which is influenced by the Asiatic steppe climate.

As regards the families of birds, Sicily, the largest Mediterranean isle, contains the highest number in comparison with other islands. Within families, Sicily also has the highest number of species and consequently the highest number of predators, such as Accipitridae, Falconidae, Strigidae and Laniidae. Within Passerines, the families represented by the greatest number of species are Sylviidae and Fringillidae. Probably due to the close proximity of Sicily to the Italian peninsula, there are 11 continental species which have colonised Sicily but no other Mediterranean isle. These species, which have little tendency to disperse, are: Stock Dove *Columba oenas*, Eagle Owl *Bubo bubo* (now extinct), Tawny Owl *Strix aluco*, Redstart *Phoenicurus phoenicurus*, Chiffchaff *Phylloscopus collybita*, Marsh Tit *Parus palustris*, Nuthatch *Sitta europaea*, Lesser Grey Shrike *Lanius minor*, Starling *Sturnus vulgaris*, Siskin *Carduelis spinus* and Rock Bunting *Emberiza cia*.

Some species breeding in Sicily show broader ecological niches than in other isles or in continental areas, e.g. Rock Partridge *Alectoris graeca*, Spectacled Warbler *Sylvia conspicillata*, Subalpine Warbler *S. cantillans* and Wren *T. troglodytes* (Massa 1981b; Lo Valvo & Massa in press, b). Other species have populations of unusual density. Several censuses, using the point-count method with unlimited distances, allowed us to show the high frequency (i.e. their presence in the 100% category) of species such as Blackbird *Turdus merula*, Chaffinch *Fringilla coelebs*, Blackcap *Sylvia atricapilla* and Wren in broadleaved woods, and also Coal Tit *Parus ater* in conifer woods. Lo Valvo *et al.* (1983) found very high densities (100 pairs/10 ha) of Linnet *Carduelis cannabina* inside citrus plantations. The small total number of species in Sicily, and the consequent less frequent interspecific interactions, seem to account for these species' high abundance.

Some species show unusual and particular adaptations to habitat limitations. The Red Kite *Milvus milvus* and Black Kite *M. migrans* breed almost entirely on cliffs, and Buzzards *B. buteo* probably build over 50% of their nests on cliffs, while in Europe they are known to nest mainly on trees. Breeding Spectacled Warblers on Aetna reach 2200 m, an altitude surpassed only on Teide (Tenerife, Canary Is.) (Catalisano & Massa 1987 b).

Different authors have described several subspecies from Sicily, but Vaurie (1959, 1965) accepted only *Alectoris graeca whitakeri* and *Aegithalos caudatus siculus*. However only deeper research can establish whether populations of some species of Sicilian birds are forms within a wide range of variation (e.g. clinal) or are effectively genetically isolated. Up till now few studies only have been carried out. Orlando (1956a), and especially Priolo (1970, 1984), confirmed that Sicilian Rock Partridges are well differentiated from those living in the Italian and Balkan peninsulas, shown in their smaller size and a peculiar moult, and with more intense colouration. Priolo (1969a) examined some specimens of Sicilian Marsh Tit and concluded that the colour pattern was sufficiently different from that of individuals inhabiting southern Italy, recognizing the Sicilian subspecies described by De Borg as *Parus palustris siculus*. In 1979 Priolo also pointed out that the Sicilian Long-tailed Tit (which Vaurie had accepted as a subspecies – see back) is smaller than other European forms and that its pattern of colour distribution (especially on the head) is more similar to oriental forms; he hypothesized it could be a good species, just as Whitaker (1901) described it. Lo Valvo *et al.* (1986 and 1988), examining the wing length, wing formula and wing shape of Sicilian Blackcaps *Sylvia atricapilla*, have shown that their characteristics are similar to those of populations living in other Mediterranean islands and different from those of central Europe; a particular adaptation to shrubby habitats and sedentariness probably accounts for their shorter and more rounded wings. Finally, Massa (1987b) reported that Sicilian Crossbills *Loxia curvirostra*, like all Mediterranean populations, are adapted to live only on pines, as opposed to other conifers, and consequently have a stronger bill than central European ones. Their colouring forms part of a clinal variation south-wards between Europe and North Africa.

Finally, as regards the relationships between the species richness and the habitats, during research on the bird communities along an ecological succession of evergreen oaks, carried out in Corsica, Sicily, Crete and Cyprus (Massa in press), the highest number of species was found in the Mediterranean maquis, while a decrease of species richness was observed in thickets and mature wood. These findings, agreeing with those observed along the laurel forest succession on the Canary Is, are different from those on the continent, where the trend of species richness follows a regular increase to mature wood. The contrast is probably due to the greater isolation of most mature habitats in Sicily compared to shrubby ones (cf. Blondel 1982, 1986); colonisation by birds of mature habitats is probably a more difficult process than that of shrublands.

ACKNOWLEDGEMENTS

First we would like to thank Dr J. F. Monk, the Editor, whose patience, sympathy and irreplaceable help and encouragement have allowed us to start and complete this work.

We also thank the Sicilian ornithologists and birdwatchers who provided unpublished data for the list, particularly: Salvatore Baglieri, Adelaide Catalisano, Andrea Ciaccio, Angelo Dimarca, Salvatore Falcone, Gaspare Giambona, Anna Giordano, Emilio Giudice, Tommaso La Mantia, Gabriella Lo Verde, Fabio Lo Valvo, Mario Lo Valvo, Andrea Longo, Rosario Mascara, Angelo Priolo, Giovanni Salvo, Maurizio Sarà, Maurizio Siracusa, Gabriele Sorci and Salvatore Surdo. We are also grateful to Sabino Alvino, Aurelio Burgio, Andrea Cairone, Giuseppe Campo, Attilio Catapezza, Amedeo Falci, Fabrizio Germi, Giovanni Guadagna, Luigi Lino, Giovanni Malara, Mauro Mannino, Giuseppe Rannisi, Laura Russo, Fabrizio Scelsi and Salvatore Seminara. Our thanks too to all the collaborators of the *Atlas Faunae Siciliae – Aves*.

We would also like to thank Mario Lo Valvo for his help in the gathering of the data on the ringed birds; Carlo Violani for his helpful assistance in the ornithological literature and useful suggestions; John Borg, Patrizia La Vecchia and Maria Grazia Tornabene for improving our English and the translation of some introductory chapters.

We are particularly grateful to A. Priolo for assistance during our visit to his collection (now at Museo Civico of Randazzo); and V. E. Orlando for facilities afforded in the examination of specimens preserved at Museo Civico of Terrasini (mostly in coll. C. Orlando).

Particular thanks to Adelaide Massa, the wife of BM, for her patience and help during this long work.

Finally our apologies to anyone whom we may have negligently omitted to thank for their collaboration.

SYSTEMATIC LIST

In the systematic list the *scientific sequence and nomenclature* follow Voous (1973, 1977), while the subspecies follow Vaurie (1959, 1965). Only in 4 cases have we preferred to break away from this arrangement; we have followed Glutz & Bauer (1982) in according specific status to *Larus cachinnans*; we have also recognised the validity of *Hydrobates pelagicus melitensis*, in accordance with Hemery & D'Elbée (1985) and of *Parus palustris siculus* in accordance with Priolo (1969a). They are forms that Vaurie does not accept. We also include Sicily as probably in the range of *Sylvia atricapilla pauluccii* following some considerations of Lo Valvo *et al.* (1986, 1988). In a few other cases, though we have reported the forms Vaurie has accepted, we have thought it right to point out the lack of local studies and the necessity for deeper research.

The *English names* are the ones most in use and as given by Voous (1973, 1977).

The works reported in *the bibliography* have been examined closely before making the list. The references to Ornithological Reports of Sicily (1982–1986) have been omitted so as not to clutter the text. Personal communications are reported with the person's name preceded by initials. Records in the list, and the bibliography, are complete up to December 1987. The *abbreviations* used are as follows:

RB resident breeder   **PM** passage migrant
MB migrant breeder   **WV** winter visitor
OB occasional breeder   **AV** accidental visitor (up to 10 records)
FB former breeder

If more than one symbol is used for one species, they are given in order of importance.

The abbreviations N, S, E, W, Cen Sicily refer to the areas given in Fig. 3. 'Islets' means all the islands surrounding Sicily (except Malta). The abbreviations of Provinces are: AG Agrigento, CL Caltanissetta, CT Catania, EN Enna, ME Messina, PA Palermo, RG Ragusa, SR Siracusa, TP Trapani.

The *abundance scale* used is: accidental (up to 10 records); rare (more than 10 records but no proof of regular passage; and for breeding species, less than 20 pairs); scarce (up to c. 20 records per year or in most years, or 20–200 breeding pairs); uncommon; fairly common; common; abundant.

Whenever past authors are quoted, we give their own words, such as rare, scarce or common, literally translated from Italian. The meaning they gave to these words was sometimes, of course, probably different from the one we give in our abundance scale.

The word 'recent' refers to the period from c. 1970 onwards, that is, since observations have been more regular in Sicily.

The *abbreviations of the museums* used in the text are as follows: Museo di Zoologia of the University of Palermo (MZUP); Collezione Orlando in Museo Civico of Terrasini (MCT); Istituto Tecnico of Modica (ITM); Museo Civico di Storia Naturale of Milan (MM); Museo La Specola of Florence (MF); Coll. Whitaker in the Ulster Museum of Belfast (WMB); Coll. Priolo in Museo Civico of Randazzo (MCR); Coll. Trischitta in Federazione Siciliana della Caccia, Messina (TFC).

NON-PASSERINES

GAVIIDAE

1. GAVIA STELLATA   AV
    Red-throated Diver

Accidental visitor (*G. s. stellata*). 5 records: one at Madonie Mts. in coll. Whitaker (Orlando 1937d); one at Lascari, 14 Apr 1918, and one undated in coll.

Orlando (Orlando 1936b); one at I. Favignana, 'winter' 1962 (Sorci *et al*. 1973); one off Palermo, 6 Nov 1967 (Massa 1969).

2.   GAVIA ARCTICA   AV

Black-throated Diver

Accidental visitor (*G. a. arctica*). 7 confirmed records: one at Faro, 'winter' 1898, in coll. Orlando; one at Messina, 'winter' 1930, in coll. Trischitta; one at Siracusa, 29 Mar 1964; one at I. Pantelleria, 1 Nov 1969 (Moltoni 1973a); one long dead corpse at Portopalo, winter 1972; one at Augusta, 15 Nov 1974 (Fagotto & Baglieri 1976); one undated specimen from Mazara (Sorci *et al*. 1973).

PODICIPEDIDAE

3.   TACHYBAPTUS RUFICOLLIS   PM WV MB RB?

Little Grebe

Common passage migrant and migrant breeder (*T. r. ruficollis*) mainly at reservoirs; some birds probably resident. Recorded in breeding areas late Feb to Aug, peak numbers usually Sep–Nov with up to 400 together; overwinter in variable numbers, Dec–Jan, c. 500 counted late Dec 1983. Slight evidence of spring passage, Mar–Apr.

Breeding. T. r. ruficollis. At reservoirs and freshwater lakes or rivers up to 1250 m; at least 45 breeding areas counted 1979–1983 (Massa 1985), but with few details: recently fledged young found from mid May; second broods recorded at Pergusa. Whether any breeding pairs are resident is uncertain.

4.   PODICEPS CRISTATUS   PM WV RB?

Great Crested Grebe

Uncommon to fairly common autumn passage migrant and scarce winter visitor (*P. c. cristatus*) to harbours and reservoirs, early Sep (occasional late Aug) to mid Mar (occasional Apr–May), peaking late Nov to Dec; usually singly or up to 10 together. Up to 150 have overwintered in recent years, Dec to mid Feb. Also breeds.

Breeding. P. c. cristatus. Benoit (1840) and Doderlein (1869–74) listed it as a regular breeder in wetlands near Catania. Krampitz (1958) recorded one adult and one "young" at Pergusa, 25 Jun 1957. Breeding recently proved at Pozzillo reservoir: at least 4 adults and 20 downy young, 11 Aug 1984; 5 pairs with at least 15 downy young, 23 Jun 1985; 122 adults (20–30 pairs) and downy young, 12 Jul 1986 (Ciaccio & Siracusa 1985c, 1987); 30–37 pairs, Jul 1987. Summer records of 2–13 adults at Ogliastro and Rubino reservoirs suggest breeding 1984–1986 (A. Ciaccio & M. Siracusa); 3–4 pairs bred at Ogliastro, 1987. Whether any breeding pairs are resident is uncertain.

5.   PODICEPS GRISEGENA   AV

Red-necked Grebe

Accidental visitor: one collected at Gela, 1891 (Orlando 1978). Doderlein (1869–74) listed it, but gave no record.

6.   PODICEPS AURITUS   AV

Slavonian Grebe

Accidental visitor. 4 records: singles at Marsala, Dec 1900, (now at WMB), at

Poma reservoir, 10 Nov 1974 (Massa *et al.* 1979) (now at MZUP), at Simeto, 3 Nov 1981 (Ciaccio & Siracusa 1983) and at I. Lampedusa, 15 Dec 1984 (F. Petretti).

7.   PODICEPS NIGRICOLLIS   PM WV OB

Black-necked Grebe

Fairly common autumn passage migrant and winter visitor (*P. n. nigricollis*) along coasts and at reservoirs, late Jul to late Mar, singly or in 10s, sometimes up to 230 together, peak numbers usually Oct–Nov. Up to 300 have overwintered in recent years, but most reservoirs are usually not censused. Singles recorded in most years, Apr to Jun. 1–5 occasionally oversummered, 1979–1987.

Breeding. P. n. nigricollis. Claimed to be resident and regular breeder by Benoit (1840) and Doderlein (1869–74). Krampitz (1958) found adults and downy young at Pergusa (20–25 pairs), 25 Jun 1957. One pair had 2 downy young at Scanzano reservoir, 15 Jun 1966. One pair probably bred at Simeto, Jul 1972 (Priolo 1974a).

2 recoveries, of birds ringed in Czechoslovakia.

DIOMEDEIDAE

8.   DIOMEDEA EXULANS   AV

Wandering Albatross

Accidental visitor: one adult killed on the beach near Termini Imerese, 4 Oct 1957, showing no signs of captivity (Orlando 1958b). Specimen now at MCT.

PROCELLARIIDAE

9.   DAPTION CAPENSE   AV

Cape Pigeon

Accidental visitor: immature shot off Sciacca, early Sep 1964 (Massa 1974b).

10.   CALONECTRIS DIOMEDEA   MB PM WV

Cory's Shearwater

Fairly common migrant breeder (*C. d. diomedea*) at islets off Sicily. Frequently recorded along all Sicilian coasts, late Feb to early Nov, regular movements noted at Capo Murro di Porco where 1000s migrate south late Oct. Scarce mid Nov to mid Feb, overwintering probably regular only around Pelagian Islands. Sicilian populations have larger measurements than those of the Aegean Sea and are smaller than *C. d. borealis* of Selvages Islands (Iapichino *et al.* 1983, Massa & Lo Valvo 1986).

Breeding. C. d. diomedea. Breeding proved at Linosa (Moltoni 1970, Vaughan 1980), Lampedusa, Pantelleria, Ustica and Marettimo, but possible or probable at Levanzo, Favignana and Aeolian Islands. Breeding on mainland at S. Vito Lo Capo (Orlando *in* Krampitz 1958) never confirmed. Well known colony at Linosa contains c. 10,000 pairs despite intensive eggs collecting by locals. No counts at other colonies, but 5000 further pairs could broadly be supposed. Breeding colonies usually complete after mid Apr. Nests in crevices on cliffs or low-lying lava, sometimes several hundred metres from the sea; at Linosa 10s of pairs may lay in the same cave. Fidelity to nesting holes confirmed at Linosa. The single egg, laid late May to early Jun, is never replaced if lost; eggs hatch mid to late Jul and most young leave the burrows in Oct. Giglioli (1907) found many birds incubating eggs on 10

Aug, but in coll. Giglioli (MF) there are only 4 chicks c. 2 weeks old, collected on Lampione, 10 Aug 1882 (C. Violani).

4 recoveries, of birds ringed in France (Corsica) (1), Malta (1), Tunisia (1) and Portugal (1). 4 ringed in Sicily (I. Linosa) recovered in Algeria (3) and Tunisia (1).

11.   PUFFINUS GRISEUS   AV

Sooty Shearwater

Accidental visitor: one off Capo Passero, 25 Oct 1977 (Massa *et al.* 1979) and one off Capo Murro di Porco, Mar 1982 (Iapichino & Baglieri 1982b).

12.   PUFFINUS PUFFINUS   MB RB? PM WV

Manx Shearwater

Uncommon migrant breeder and fairly common winter visitor *P. p. yelkouan* at islets along all Sicilian coasts. Recorded all months, but movements still poorly known; some birds could be resident close around breeding colonies. Peak numbers, outside breeding areas, usually Nov–Feb in 10s or 100s, e.g. c. 3000 off Simeto, 22 Jan 1984 (A. Ciaccio). At Capo Murro di Porco autumn and winter movements usually southward. Large movements previously have been noted at Messina Straits, Jun–Aug (Giglioli 1890, Jany 1959), but there are no recent data.

Breeding. P. p. yelkouan. Proved at I. Marettimo, I. Levanzo, I. Favignana, I. Pantelleria, I. Lampedusa, the Aeolians Islands, and probably at I. Linosa. Breeding colonies never counted, but *P. puffinus* seems everywhere much less common than *Calonectris diomedea*. Few details known: nests in holes or old rabbit burrows; a single egg, usually mid to late Mar; recently hatched chicks from early May. At Egadi Islands some young are still collected by locals as food.

One recovery, of a bird ringed in Malta.

HYDROBATIDAE

13.   HYDROBATES PELAGICUS   MB PM

Storm Petrel

Scarce migrant breeder *H. p. melitensis*, locally common at I. Marettimo. No observations have been made of movements off Sicilian coasts. Singles or small parties occasionally recorded all months except Dec–Jan. Records from Ionian sea and E coast, Apr to late Sep, probably involve birds from Filfla colony in Malta. Recorded off I. Ustica, Oct–Nov (Ajola 1959), and between Trapani and I. Pantelleria, Apr–Oct (Doderlein 1869–74, Steinbacher 1956c, Foschi 1968, Moltoni 1970) — probably birds from the Marettimo or an unknown colony. In the past probably more common and widespread; Martorelli (1931) recorded 100s at Messina Straits. Breeding on mainland at S. Vito Lo Capo supposed by Orlando (*in* Krampitz 1958) never confirmed.

Breeding. H. p. melitensis has been confirmed as a good Mediterranean form (Hemery & D'Elbée 1985). This subspecies has also been recognised at I. Marettimo, where c. 1000 pairs are estimated to breed (Massa & Catalisano 1986a, b). Giglioli (1907) confirmed breeding at I. Vulcano, and Orlando (*in* Krampitz 1958) presumed it was still breeding there; no recent data from Aeolian islands. Breeding at I. Marettimo was confirmed by Krampitz (1957), Krapp (1970) and Massa (1973b). A probable breeding site at I. Levanzo (Massa 1973b) now seems deserted. Breeding at I. Lampione (near Lampedusa) confirmed by Moltoni (1970). Nests colonially in caves and holes in the ground; eggs, C/1, laid asynchronously, late Apr to early Jul, mostly mid May to mid Jun, hatching early Jun to mid Aug, fledging late Jul to mid Oct. Site tenacity confirmed at I. Marettimo.

7 recoveries, of birds ringed in Malta.

14.   OCEANODROMA LEUCORHOA   AV

   Leach's Petrel

   Accidental visitor. 3 records: one specimen from Siracusa, Jul 1854, at Florence Museum (Giglioli 1886), one taken near Palermo, 8 Dec 1968 (Cangialosi 1969a) and one found dead at Messina Straits, 3 Jan 1979 (Novelletto & Petretti 1980).

SULIDAE

15.   SULA BASSANA   PM WV

   Gannet

   Uncommon winter visitor (*S. b. bassana*), late Sep to mid May, mostly Dec–Feb, singly or in parties up to 40 in fishing areas. Twice, Jun. Recorded along all coasts and islets, apparently more common along E coast, where southward movements occur Oct–Nov; more than 3 per observation hour at Capo Murro di Porco each Jan 1975–1983 (Iapichino 1984a). Immatures outnumber adults in autumn, but not during winter months.

   5 recoveries, of birds ringed in Scotland (3), Channel Islands (1) and Ireland (1).

PHALACROCORACIDAE

16.   PHALACROCORAX CARBO   PM WV

   (Great) Cormorant

   Uncommon passage migrant and winter visitor (*P. c. sinensis*), increasing in recent years, (late Aug) mid Sep to early Apr, peak numbers usually mid Nov to Dec; on passage singly or in parties up to 15. Spring passage mid Feb or later, usually not obvious. Has overwintered regularly since late 1970s, mostly late Dec to mid Feb at harbours (e.g. Augusta and Sciacca) and at reservoirs: 30–50 in Jan censuses up to 1984, 350–425 from 1985 to 1987; Eerden & Munsterman (1986) estimated 700, Jan 1986. A few immatures occasionally stay into May, once into Aug. Breeding claimed by Benoit (1840), Doderlein (1869–74) and Giglioli (1886) at Biviere di Lentini and near Marsala, but never confirmed.

   15 recoveries, of birds ringed in Germany (6), Denmark (4), Holland (3), Poland (1) and Sweden (1).

17.   PHALACROCORAX ARISTOTELIS   RB

   Shag

   Resident (*P. a. desmarestii*) at I. Lampedusa; 30–40 pairs and 50–60 juveniles and immatures estimated summer 1980. Occasional away from Pelagian Islands: singles at Capo Murro di Porco, 5–8 Aug 1980, I. Marettimo, 27 Apr 1984 and I. Favignana, 31 May 1986, are the only confirmed records. Listed as scarce resident along Sicilian coasts by Giglioli (1907) and Arrigoni (1929), but this seems unlikely.

   Breeding. P. a. desmarestii. Nests on cliffs in W and NW Lampedusa. Few details: eggs found Jan–Mar, unfledged and recently fledged young Apr–Jun.

18.   PHALACROCORAX PYGMAEUS   AV

Pygmy Cormorant

Accidental visitor. 4 confirmed records: singles at Faro, 15 Sep 1907 and 18 Nov 1918 (Trischitta 1919a) and one at Ispica, 15 Nov 1968 (not late Oct 1970 as erroneously reported by Sorci *et al.* 1972); one undated specimen collected at Cefalú (Giglioli 1890).

PELECANIDAE

19.   PELECANUS ONOCROTALUS   PM

(Great) White Pelican

Rare and irregular passage migrant, probably commoner in past: "large flocks" reported at Messina, May 1834 (Benoit 1840) and at Capo Passero, Jan 1877 (Giglioli 1886, Orlando 1956b). A large influx occurred Oct to early Dec 1957, with c. 50 shot along all coasts (Orlando 1958d, Favero 1959). 10 records of 1–3, mostly from SE coast, 1967–1982: Oct (6), Apr, Jun, Nov, Dec one each.

20.   PELECANUS CRISPUS   AV

Dalmatian Pelican

Accidental visitor, one confirmed record: a single bird killed at Camporeale, May 1890, and preserved in MZUP (Riggio & De Stefani 1894). 3 killed near Pozzallo, Jan 1877, and listed by Balducci (1901) and Giglioli (1907) as *P. crispus* were in fact *P. onocrotalus* (Orlando 1956b).

ARDEIDAE

21.   BOTAURUS STELLARIS   PM

Bittern

Scarce but regular passage migrant (*B. s. stellaris*) to coastal wetlands, usually singly; 2–3 records in nearly all years, early Mar to mid May and Sep to mid Dec, mostly Apr and Sep. Twice Jan, once Feb in recent years. Breeding supposed by Doderlein (1869–74) and reported by others never confirmed.

22.   IXOBRYCHUS MINUTUS   PM MB

Little Bittern

Uncommon to fairly common spring passage migrant (*I. m. minutus*) to wetlands and rivers, mid Mar to early Jun (occasionally early Mar), peaking late Apr to mid May, usually singly; scarce on return passage, late Aug to early Oct, some years unrecorded. Twice Nov.

Breeding. I. m. minutus. Much more common in past when breeding habitat was plentiful. Doderlein (1869–74) reported that "thousands" bred in wetlands near Catania and Lentini; now less than 50 pairs, with breeding confirmed in 6 areas, 1979–1983 (Massa 1985).

2 recoveries, of birds ringed in Germany (1) and Belgium (1).

23.   NYCTICORAX NYCTICORAX   PM OB

(Black-crowned) Night Heron

Uncommon to fairly common passage migrant (*N. n. nycticorax*) at wetlands, mostly Cen and W Sicily, usually singly or up to 15, sometimes up to 50 together. Spring passage early Mar to mid May, mostly mid Apr. Up to 40, mostly immatures, regularly oversummer. Return passage mid Aug to early-mid Nov, peaking Sep. Once Feb. Probably largely overlooked because of its nocturnal migration. Recorded in much larger numbers in Malta, where it seems to be the most common heron (Sultana & Gauci 1982); it is likely that during a long sea-crossing, such as across the Sicilian Channel, migration is not strictly (or mainly) nocturnal and also birds are more easily observed at small islands (cf. *Ardea purpurea*).

Breeding. N. n. nycticorax. Doderlein (1869–74) and Giglioli (1907) supposed breeding but gave no details. One pair probably bred at Scanzano reservoir, spring 1982 (M. Sarà). Breeding confirmed at Biviere di Gela 1984–85: 2 nests and 5 recently fledged young, early Aug 1984; 4 pairs 1985, with 3 unfledged young late Jul and 13 recently fledged early Aug (Dimarca *et al.* 1987); adults recorded there throughout each breeding season since 1978. 1–2 pairs bred at Rubino reservoir and near Paternò 1986. One unfledged young found near Calascibetta, 1 Oct 1987 (A. Dimarca).

18 recoveries, of birds ringed in Hungary (11), Yugoslavia (2), Czechoslovakia (2), France (1), Spain (1) and N Italy (1).

24.   ARDEOLA RALLOIDES   PM OB?

Squacco Heron

Fairly common spring passage migrant to wetlands, usually 20 or less together, sometimes up to 60, late Mar to early-mid Jun, peaking late Apr. Up to 10 oversummering in recent years, late Jun to Jul. Scarce on return passage early Aug to Sep, usually singly. Once mid Mar and Nov. Doderlein (1869–74) supposed breeding at wetlands near Mondello (drained 30 years later), but gave no definite evidence. In Jun–Jul 1986 and 1987 supposed breeding near Paternò (adults showing alarm) (M. Siracusa, A. Ciaccio).

4 recoveries, of birds ringed in Yugoslavia (3) and Hungary (1).

25.   BUBULCUS IBIS   PM

Cattle Egret

Rare and irregular passage migrant (*B. i. ibis*). 9 confirmed records of 1–3, 1969–1987: May (3), Oct (2), Jun, Nov, Dec and "autumn"; but c. 10 undated specimens were collected near Catania in 1960s (Sorci *et al.* 1972). Malherbe (1843) stated that many were shot in Sicily, though Benoit (1840) surprisingly did not list it. Doderlein (1869–74) reported 2 specimens, from Trapani and from Messina. One labelled 16 May 1878 and shot locally is preserved at ITM.

26.   EGRETTA GULARIS   AV

Western Reef Heron

Accidental visitor, one confirmed record: a single bird (dark morph) flocking with *E. garzetta* at Simeto, 26 May 1976 (Priolo 1976).

27.   EGRETTA GARZETTA   PM WV OB

Little Egret

Common passage migrant (*E. g. garzetta*) to wetlands and along coasts, usually in 10s, sometimes up to 60, even 150 together. Spring passage early Mar to early Jun (occasionally late Feb), peaking Apr. Up to 70 regularly oversummering. Fewer records, but sometimes largest flocks, on return passage, late Jul to early Nov, mostly late Aug to Sep. Up to 15 have overwintered in most years since 1979 at Simeto and Vendicari, mid Nov to Feb.

Breeding. E. g. garzetta. Doderlein (1869–74) supposed breeding near Catania and Lentini but gave no details; c. 10 pairs had nestlings in reedbeds at Biviere di Lentini, Jun 1943 (Jany *in* Stresemann 1943).

11 recoveries, of birds ringed in Yugoslavia (7), France (3) and Tunisia (1).

28.   EGRETTA ALBA   PM

Great White Egret

Scarce passage migrant (*E. a. alba*), singly or up to 9 together. 1–10 records in most recent years, Mar to late Apr and Sep–Oct, less frequently May and Nov–Dec; once Jan, Jun and Aug.

2 recoveries, of birds ringed in Yugoslavia (1) and USSR (1).

29.   ARDEA CINEREA   PM WV OB

Grey Heron

Common passage migrant (*A. c. cinerea*) along coasts and to inland reservoirs, in 10s, occasionally up to 200 together, largest flocks on autumn passage. Spring passage mid Feb to mid May (sometimes early Feb), mostly mid Mar to mid Apr. Up to 100 regularly oversummer at wetlands and reservoirs. Return passage late Jul to late Nov, peaking mid to late Sep; c. 700 counted at Capo Passero, 19–22 Sep 1981. Up to 80 have overwintered in recent years at protected wetlands, mostly at Simeto, Dec–Feb.

Breeding. A. c. cinerea. Doderlein (1869–74) supposed breeding in wetlands near Catania but gave no details. First proof Jun 1987 at Pozzillo Reservoir: one nest and up to 22 adults (M. Siracusa, A. Ciaccio).

16 recoveries, of birds ringed in USSR (8), Hungary (3), Poland (2), France (1), Sweden (1) and Switzerland (1).

30.   ARDEA PURPUREA   PM

Purple Heron

Fairly common passage migrant (*A. p. purpurea*) at wetlands and reservoirs mid Mar to late May (sometimes early Mar), peaking early to mid Apr, singly or up to 40 together. 1–3 regularly oversummer, Jun–Jul. Sometimes scarcer on return passage, early Aug to late Oct, mostly Sep; often recorded in mixed flocks with *Ardea cinerea*. Once Nov. Like *N. nycticorax*, more common in Malta. Doderlein (1869–74) listed it as a common breeder and winter visitor at wetlands near Catania and Lentini. Stresemann (1943) believed it bred at Lentini, but its breeding has never been confirmed.

25 recoveries, of birds ringed in Hungary (12), Yugoslavia (5), Holland (3), N Italy (2), Czechoslovakia (2), Switzerland (1).

CICONIIDAE

31. CICONIA NIGRA   PM

Black Stork

Scarce spring passage migrant, singly or in parties up to 15 late Mar to late May, mostly early May and majority at Messina Straits. Return passage late Aug to late Oct, up to 5 records of singles in a year, mostly in SE wetlands. Twice Nov, once Feb (Benoit 1840) and Dec.

32. CICONIA CICONIA   PM

White Stork

Uncommon spring passage migrant (*C. c. ciconia*), late Feb to mid May, peaking Mar; usually 1–8 together, but flocks of 20–50 recorded in most years at Messina Straits and probably regular. Scarce on return passage, mid Aug to Oct, singly or up to 12 together. Once Jul, Nov and Dec. 3 oversummered near Paternò, early Jun to mid Aug 1986, and 2 there Jun–Jul 1987.

5 recoveries, of birds ringed in Germany (2), Holland (1), Switzerland (1) and Algeria (1).

THRESKIORNITHIDAE

33. PLEGADIS FALCINELLUS   PM

Glossy Ibis

Uncommon to locally fairly common spring passage migrant, mostly at SE wetlands, in variable numbers mid Mar to mid-late May, peaking late Mar to mid Apr, singly or in 10s. Also up to 150 together; on occasion heavy passage occurs, with up to 4–6 reports of such large flocks over a few days. Occasional Jun–Jul. Scarce on return passage mid Aug to Oct, usually 1–4, occasionally up to 15 together. Once Nov. Breeding supposed by Doderlein (1869–74), and reported by others on his authority, never confirmed.

2 recoveries, of birds ringed in Hungary.

34. PLATALEA LEUCORODIA   PM

Spoonbill

Uncommon passage migrant (*P. l. leucorodia*) at coastal wetlands, particularly at Vendicari, usually 15 or fewer together, sometimes up to 40–60; largest flocks usually on return passage, exceptionally 106 at Vendicari, 20–22 Mar 1986. Spring passage mid Feb to early Jun, peaking Mar to mid Apr; return passage mid Jul to late Oct, peaking Aug–Sep. Occasionally Nov–Jan. One overwintered at L. Gorgo, Dec 1986 to Jan 1987, and 9 at Biviere di Gela, Nov 1987 to Feb 1988. Up to 15 have oversummered in recent years, Jun to early Aug.

6 recoveries, of birds ringed in Hungary (4), Yugoslavia (1) and Austria (1).

PHOENICOPTERIDAE

35. PHOENICOPTERUS RUBER   PM

Greater Flamingo

Scarce but regular passage migrant (*P. r. roseus*) at coastal wetlands, recorded all months, usually 1–4, sometimes up to 30 together; small influxes of 10s occasionally occur, e.g. Dec 1984 to Jan 1985. Most records late Feb to mid Apr and late Aug to Nov. 2–3 overwintered at Vendicari, Nov to Feb 1979–80 and 1986–87; another was present there Nov 1982 until shot in Aug 1983. One oversummered at I. Salina, May–Aug 1987 (S. Giani).

5 recoveries, of birds ringed in France.

ANATIDAE

36. CYGNUS OLOR   WV

Mute Swan

Rare and irregular winter visitor. 6 records of 1–2, 1966–1983: Nov (3), once each Feb, May and Dec. An exceptional influx occurred, mainly at E and S coasts, 9–12 Dec 1984: 3–9 shot near Siracusa, c. 10 shot near Gela, 2 shot inland at Mussomeli, one shot at I. Lampedusa. One adult and 5 immatures overwintered at Vendicari, 9 Dec 1984 to 18 Feb 1985. At least 11 on E coast, Dec 1986. In past Doderlein (1869–74) reported it as accidental, but Zuccarello Patti (1845) recorded up to 15 in autumn 1845.

37. CYGNUS COLUMBIANUS   AV

Bewick's Swan

Accidental visitor; one record of 3, autumn 1952 at Simeto (Sorci *et al.* 1973, A. Burgio).

38. CYGNUS CYGNUS   PM

Whooper Swan

Rare and irregular passage migrant. 11 records: one at Milazzo, winter 1838 (Benoit 1840) (1828 according to Doderlein 1869–74); some at Biviere di Lentini (Massa 1890); one at Castelvetrano in 1897 (Venezia 1897d); 2 at Cefalù, 6 Jan 1898 (Maggio 1898); one at Filaga, 2 Dec 1943; 3 at Lentini, Catania and Raddusa 1940–53 (Priolo 1954); one at Marzamemi, Dec 1958; 2 near Mazara, c. 1960 (Sorci *et al.* 1973); 4 at Nicosia, late Nov 1969 (Sorci *et al.* 1971b). Benoit (1840) reported that "other swans" were seen in previous years at Lentini. Doderlein (1869–74) listed it as irregular.

39. ANSER FABALIS   AV

Bean Goose

Accidental visitor in recent years (subspecies not determined). 8 documented records of 1–10 since 1968: Jan (3), Dec (2), once each Feb, Mar and Nov. Much more common in the past; Benoit (1840) and Doderlein (1869–74) listed it as "very common" in winter at wetlands near Catania and Lentini. Ajola (1959) listed it as regular at I. Ustica, but gave no records.

40. ANSER ALBIFRONS   PM

White-fronted Goose

Rare and irregular passage migrant (subspecies not determined). 11 documented records of 1–7 in 5 years since 1969: Oct (5), Dec (3), once each Feb and Sep and one undated. In past never recorded by Doderlein (1869–74), but some winter records by Trischitta (1923a) and Priolo (1954) and (doubtfully) 35 at I.

Lipari, 10 Jan 1967 (Moltoni & Frugis 1967). Ajola (1959) listed it as regular at I. Ustica, but gave no records.

41.   ANSER ERYTHROPUS   AV
Lesser White-fronted Goose

Accidental visitor: one at Trapani, Feb 1937 (Caterini 1938).

42.   ANSER ANSER   PM WV
Greylag Goose

Scarce passage migrant and winter visitor (*A. a. anser*) to wetlands and coastal plains, singly or up to 15 together, occasionally up to 60, mid Nov to mid Feb, mostly Dec. In recent years up to 7 have stayed at Simeto for up to 20 days in Jan, and overwintering there could be regular were it not for illegal shooting. One overwintered at Vendicari, 7 Jan to 18 Feb 1979. Occasional Sep, Oct and Mar, once Apr. One taken at Siracusa, 24 Nov 1965, resembled *A. a. rubrirostris* (S. Baglieri).

43.   BRANTA BERNICLA   AV
Brent Goose

Accidental visitor (*B. b. bernicla*): one overwintered at Simeto, late Dec 1986 to early Mar 1987 (Ciaccio 1987).

44.   TADORNA FERRUGINEA   WV
Ruddy Shelduck

Rare and irregular winter visitor. 14 records of singles, only 5 since 1950: Dec (4), Jan (3), Nov (2) and 5 undated specimens (Arrigoni 1929, Priolo 1954, Ajola 1948, Fagotto & Baglieri 1976, Duchi *in* Toso 1986).

45.   TADORNA TADORNA   PM WV
Shelduck

Uncommon passage migrant and winter visitor, late Sep to mid Apr, most Nov–Feb; 80–346 in Jan census 1975–87, almost all at Vendicari. Singles regular, May–Jul; early migrants, mostly juveniles, occasionally arrive late Jul.
One recovery, of a bird ringed in USSR.

46.   ANAS PENELOPE   PM WV
(European) Wigeon

Fairly common autumn passage migrant and winter visitor to wetlands and reservoirs. Autumn passage mid Aug to mid Dec, peaking Nov, in 10s or 100s. Up to 2600 in Jan census 1975–87, but usually c. 1000. Most leave mid-late Feb, a few not until late Apr. Usually no obvious spring passage. Occasional May and Jun.
One recovery, of a bird ringed in USSR.

47.   ANAS STREPERA   PM WV
Gadwall

Uncommon autumn passage migrant and winter visitor. Usually scarce till mid Dec, but has been recorded from mid Aug; 42 at Pergusa, 14 Sep 1982, was exceptional. Up to 189 overwintered 1975–87, most till mid Feb, last mid Apr.

48.   ANAS CRECCA   PM WV
Teal

Fairly common passage migrant and winter visitor (*A. c. crecca*) to wetlands and reservoirs, in 10s or 100s, mid Aug to late Mar; peak numbers usually late Oct to mid Dec; up to 2500 in Jan census 1975–1987. Most depart mid to late Feb. Scarce, Apr, occasional May to early Aug. Benoit (1840) supposed breeding near Siracusa and Doderlein (1869–74) in S Sicily, but their statements seem unlikely (Lo Verde & Massa 1985).

3 recoveries, of birds ringed in England (1), France (1) and USSR (1).

49.   ANAS PLATYRHYNCHOS   PM WV OB
Mallard

Uncommon autumn migrant and winter visitor (*A. p. platyrhynchos*) late Aug to early Apr, mostly Dec, usually 20 or less together. Up to 348 in Jan census 1975–87, but usually less. Much more common in the past (Doderlein 1869–74). In most recent years has irregularly oversummered, May–Jul.

Breeding. A. p. platyrhynchos. Old authors, from Benoit (1840), listed it as a regular breeder. Priolo (1954) reported no breeding records 1940–53. Has bred only 3 times in recent years: just fledged young at L. Preola, Jul 1973; female with 5 downy young at Pergusa, 24 Jun 1980; one pair with 6 downy young at Biviere di Gela, Jul 1987 (A. Falci).

50.   ANAS ACUTA   PM WV
Pintail

Fairly common passage migrant and uncommon winter visitor (*A. a. acuta*), mostly along coasts. Autumn passage from early Sep, peaking late Oct to Nov, in 10s or 100s. Up to 355 in Jan census 1975–87. Spring passage early Feb to mid Apr, in variable numbers, some years very few, but passage of 100s, even 1000s, occurs along S and E coasts, e.g. late Feb 1975, late Mar 1977, early Mar 1985. Occasional May.

2 recoveries, of birds ringed in USSR.

51.   ANAS QUERQUEDULA   PM OB
Garganey

Common spring passage migrant in variable numbers, some years very common. Spring passage mid Feb to late May, peaking early to mid Mar (sometimes late Feb or late Mar); usually in 10s or 100s, but passages of 1000s, sometimes even 10,000s, occur on a few dates in most years along S and SE coasts, especially at Mazara, Gela and Capo Passero. During strong passage, 1000s usually flock at sea all day and approach land at dusk. Some years passage is concentrated into a few days: e.g., 10,000s recorded at S coast, 27 Feb 1975, but no others all spring. Uncommon on return passage, early Aug to late Oct, 10 or less together, occasionally up to 60. Occasional late Jan to early Feb and Jun–Jul, once Nov. Sometimes reported Dec, but confusion with other *Anas* never ruled out. Overwintering since 1983 claimed in winter counts carried out by hunters' associations (cf. Focardi & Spina 1986), is unsupported.

Breeding. Occasional breeder, possibly regular in past (Benoit 1840, Doderlein 1869–74). Single pairs bred at L. Gurrida, 1954 (A. Priolo), at Siracusa salt-pan,

1973 and 1976 (Fagotto & Baglieri 1976); 2 pairs had 14 downy young at Biviere di Gela, 5 Jul 1984, and 7 pairs there, Jul 1985 (A. Dimarca). Total of 16 pairs and 122 downy young at Biviere di Gela and L. Soprano, mid Jul 1986, 2 pairs at Biviere di Gela, Jul 1987 (A. Falci).

3 recoveries, of birds ringed in USSR (2) and Mali (1).

52. ANAS CLYPEATA   PM WV
Shoveler

Fairly common passage migrant and uncommon winter visitor, mid Aug to late Apr, mostly mid Nov to Jan, occasionally in 100s on passage. Up to 466 in Jan census 1975–87. Evidence of spring passage in most years, mid Feb to early Apr, sometimes in 10s, sometimes up to 120 together. Once each Jun and Jul. Breeding reported in the past (Malherbe 1842–43) is unconfirmed (Doderlein 1890, *ms*).

53. MARMARONETTA ANGUSTIROSTRIS   AV
Marbled Teal

Accidental visitor in the past. Arrigoni (1929) reported 6 records: one, Aug 1866; one at Lentini, Nov 1881; 1–3 at Catania, 5 Aug 1892, 21 Nov 1892, 8 Dec 1892; one undated specimen. Bertiaio (*in* Giglioli 1907) reported flocks near Catania, Jun–Dec 1892. No records since.

54. NETTA RUFINA   FB PM WV
Red-crested Pochard

Scarce (and irregular?) passage migrant and winter visitor, formerly common (Doderlein 1869–74, Giglioli 1907). 1–4 recorded in most years since 1975, early Nov to Jan, once each Oct and Jul. Sorci *et al.* (1973) mentioned 2 undated specimens and that in previous years it was "not rare" near Trapani. First confirmed breeding by Benoit (1840) at Biviere di Lentini, confirmed by other authors including Arrigoni (1929). Last confirmed breeding 13 Jun 1943: 10 pairs at Biviere di Lentini (Jany *in* Stresemann 1943). (The Biviere di Lentini was drained in late 1940s.)

55. AYTHYA FERINA   PM WV MB
Pochard

Fairly common autumn passage migrant and winter visitor, mostly at L. Pergusa and at reservoirs, where it is the commonest duck. Autumn passage mid Aug to late Dec, peak numbers at Pergusa (3000–4000) late Oct to mid Dec, when most are still on passage. Up to 7100 in Jan census 1975–1987. Most leave late Feb to early Mar; regular Apr and occasional May–Jun outside breeding areas.

Breeding. Regular breeder since 1982: 10 pairs at Pergusa, 1982–1983 (Dimarca & Falci 1983); 10 pairs at Pergusa and 2–5 at L. Ogliastro, 1984; 5–6 pairs at L. Soprano and 26 at Pergusa, 1985 (A. Dimarca). Total of 52 pairs and 435 downy young at the above lakes and at Biviere di Gela, Jul 1986, but only 16 pairs in 1987 (A. Falci). Downy young recorded after early-mid Jun. Breeding success variable: at Pergusa 92 fledged young counted in 1982, only 19 in 1983 due to predation by dogs, 48 in 1984 (A. Dimarca). Most breeders leave early Sep. Breeding followed the first winter that shooting was banned at Pergusa.

56. AYTHYA NYROCA   MB PM WV

Ferruginous Duck or White-eyed Pochard

Uncommon passage migrant and winter visitor, numbers sharply reduced in last decades, but no figures available. Spring passage mid Feb to Apr, in recent years usually singly, sometimes in 10s and up to 60; passage of 100s reported at Gela, Mar 1985 (E. Giudice). Non breeders occasional May–Aug. Return passage less obvious, late Sep to Dec, singly or occasionally up to 100 together. 50 or less in Jan census 1975–87.

Breeding. Benoit (1840) supposed breeding at Lentini, later authors repeating this statement, or listed it as a breeder (Arrigoni 1929), but gave no proof. First confirmed breeding 1983: pair with 7 downy young at Simeto, 7 Jul 1983 (Ciaccio & Siracusa 1984). Pair with 3 downy young at Simeto 23 Jun 1984 (A. Ciaccio & M. Siracusa); 2–4 pairs yearly at Biviere di Gela, 1984–87, with up to 25 downy young recorded early–mid Jul, 3 pairs with 22 downy young at L. Soprano, Jul 1986, and one pair there, Jul 1987 (A. Dimarca, A. Falci).

57. AYTHYA FULIGULA   WV PM?

Tufted Duck

Scarce winter visitor (and passage migrant?), mid Nov to Mar, usually singly or up to 10, but 150 at Pergusa, late Jan 1982, once mid Oct (A. Dimarca). Occasionally reported Aug to early Oct, but confusion with *A. nyroca* possible.

58. AYTHYA MARILA   AV

(Greater) Scaup

Accidental visitor. 4 documented records: one 9 Dec 1953 near Catania (A. Priolo); one at Prizzi reservoir, 3 Jan 1971 (Sorci *et al.* 1972); one at Pantano Cuba, Dec 1974; one at Vendicari, 13 Dec 1986.

59. MELANITTA NIGRA   AV

Common Scoter

Accidental visitor, one confirmed record: flock of 18 at Simeto mouth, late Nov 1987 to late Jan 1988 (A. Ciaccio).

60. BUCEPHALA CLANGULA   AV

Goldeneye

Accidental visitor. 3 records: male at Trapani c. 1930 (Sorci *et al.* 1973); female at Lago Faro, winter 1927; female at Simeto, 8–17 Dec 1981 (Ciaccio & Siracusa 1983a). Formerly listed as common or scarce in winter (Benoit 1840, Doderlein 1869–74, Minà-Palumbo 1857, A. Burgio).

61. MERGUS ALBELLUS   AV

Smew

Accidental visitor, one record: juv female, Paternò, 4 Jan 1932 (C. Orlando). Listed as rare by previous authors, but no record reported (Arrigoni 1929, Sorci *et al.* 1973).

62.   MERGUS SERRATOR   PM WV

Red-breasted Merganser

Scarce and regular autumn migrant and winter visitor along coasts, singly or up to 12 together, late Oct to Feb, mostly Nov. Usually wanders, but 4 overwintered at Augusta harbour, 31 Dec 1984 to 7 Feb 1985. Once Apr.

63.   MERGUS MERGANSER   AV

Goosander

Accidental visitor (*M. m. merganser*). 6 records in the last 35 years: 2 at I. Ustica, 1950 and 1955 (Ajola 1959); one at Siracusa, 8 Nov 1955 (Fagotto & Baglieri 1976); one at Pantelleria, 7 Dec 1972 (Moltoni 1973a); undated specimen from Marsala (Sorci *et al.* 1973); 3 at Simeto, 16 Nov 1980 (Ciaccio & Siracusa 1983a).

64.   OXYURA LEUCOCEPHALA   AV FB?

White-headed Duck

Now an accidental visitor. 7 documented records since 1930: male at Mazara, c. 1930 (Sorci *et al.* 1973); one at F. Torto, 13 May 1935 (Orlando 1936c); female at Pantelleria, 12–14 Jul 1954 (Moltoni 1957); female at Siracusa, 9 Nov 1970, 2 shot at Pachino, Nov 1974, 2 at Simeto, 6 Dec 1981 to 3 Jan 1982 (Ciaccio & Siracusa 1983a); one at L. Soprano, 11–18 Dec 1983 (A. Dimarca). Listed as breeder and common or very common winter visitor at Biviere di Lentini (Benoit 1840, Doderlein 1869–74, Arrigoni 1929), but no definite evidence of breeding reported, though Zuccarello Patti (1845) recorded many individuals from E Sicily, including some in breeding plumage.

ACCIPITRIDAE

65.   PERNIS APIVORUS   PM

Honey Buzzard

Locally common passage migrant. In spring, early-mid Apr to mid Jun, peaking 5–20 May. Spring passage in Sicily moves from W coast (reached from Cap Bon, Tunisia) along mountains bordering N coast to Messina Straits. Here passage of 100s even 1000s in one day is regular. A second, but not well known route is in E Sicily and involves the few spring migrants crossing through Malta. Over Messina Straits birds pass on a wide front, including the Aeolian Islands, crossing the 3–20 km width of the Straits in most conditions of weather. The route from the Peloritani Mts, which faces east across the Straits, varies with the wind: with SE winds birds pass at low altitude, but heavier passages seem correlated with light N and NE winds. Birds arrive in flocks of up to 200, more usually in parties up to 15, from early morning to dusk, when they attempt to roost in pine trees. Some afternoons increase in numbers is often noted. No complete counts: 1876 were recorded 20 Apr to 19 May 1984 (Dimarca & Iapichino 1984); 3138 from 20 Apr to 20 May 1985; c. 7300 1–30 May 1986 with 1056 as late as 27 May; over 3000 in only 2 days, 11–12 May 1979; but in all years only a fraction of the wide front was covered. According to Thiollay (1977) at least 16,000 birds cross the Sicilian Channel at C. Bon. (See also the introductory chapter on hunting.)

In autumn smaller numbers pass mid Aug to late Oct, peaking mid or late Sep, but autumn migration is poorly known: no relevant passage seems to occur in Messina

Straits nor on the E and SE coasts, but flocks of up to 70 are recorded fairly regularly, mostly in W and Cen Sicily. Occasional Nov and Mar, 2 records late Dec. 6 recoveries, of birds ringed in Sweden (4) and Finland (2).

66.   MILVUS MIGRANS   PM MB
Black Kite

Fairly common to locally common passage migrant (*M. m. migrans*). Spring passage along N coast and Messina Straits, early Mar to late May, peaking late Mar to early Apr, usually in small flocks, but up to 80 together at Messina Straits. 244 counted at Messina, 20 Apr to 19 May 1984 (Dimarca & Iapichino 1984), but the main passage has never been counted. More numerous on return passage, mostly in W Sicily and I. Pantelleria, early Aug to late Oct, peaking late Aug to mid Sep, in 10s or 100s, e.g. 135 at Alcamo, Sep 1982, 400 at Pantelleria, 6 Sep 1978 (Galea & Massa 1985), c. 1200 at Rocca Busambra, 29 Aug 1976. Occasional Feb, Jul and Nov. One overwintered Dec 1987 to Jan 1988 near Corleone (T. La Mantia, M. Sarà).

Breeding. M. m. migrans. Rare and local migrant breeder in mountainous areas in Palermo and Agrigento districts. Breeding confirmed 1979 (Massa 1980), but had probably occurred since 1950s (Mebs 1957, C. Orlando). Breeding population now c. 15 pairs, probably increasing. Nests on inland cliffs or in big shrubs or trees on cliffs; pair restoring nests recorded Mar–Apr, pairing mid Apr to mid May. Eggs, C/2 to C/3, early to mid May, young fledge late Jun to early Aug.

3 recoveries, of birds ringed in Poland, (1), Germany (1) and Switzerland (1).

67.   MILVUS MILVUS   RB WV PM
Red Kite

Scarce resident breeder, numbers augmented Oct–May, by winter visitors (*M. m. milvus*). Both the breeding population and winter visitors have greatly decreased in the last 15 years. A few regularly recorded on spring passage, Mar–May, Messina Straits (Galea & Massa 1985). Winter roosts now contain up to 15–20 birds; e.g. one roost of 50 recorded by Massa (1976a) decreased in following years: 16 Sep 1970(50), 24 Oct 1976(30), 11 Dec 1977(22), 20 Dec 1981(21), 17 Jan 1988(7), in the same area where Orlando (1943) recorded largest flocks. Roosts at Iblei Mts now deserted: 50–60 in different roosts 1969–71, a few 1972–73, singles 1976–78, none since then (Baglieri & Fagotto 1980). Last flocks at roosts in spring, mostly immatures, seen late Mar to early Apr, e.g. 10 at Rocca Busambra, 1 Apr 1976.

Breeding. M. m. milvus. Galvagni (1839–43) reported breeding at Aetna and Doderlein (1869–74) at Madonie Mts, Ficuzza, Calatafimi and Mt Cuccio. Giglioli (1907) listed it as scarce. Probably still widespread in 1950s: Mebs (1957) found many pairs at Rocca Busambra 1 km apart. Decreased in 1970s: bred last at mountains around Palermo (Conca d'Oro) in 1971, at Iblei Mts c. 1975 (Baglieri & Fagotto 1980), at mountains near Trapani in 1977. Massa (1985) estimated c. 90 pairs at inland mountains (Sicani, Madonie and Caronie), now probably less than 40 pairs. Nests in holes or ledges on cliffs, sometimes in trees, up to 1400–1500 m, but recorded up to 1800 m in breeding season (Krampitz 1958). Flight displays Jan–Mar, occasionally Apr–May; mating late Feb to mid Mar. Eggs, C/2–3 late Mar to early Apr; young fledge early to mid Jul, rarely Jun. Post breeding flocks recorded after Jun, e.g. 30 at Mistretta, 24 Jun 1973, 10 at Vicari, 10 Aug 1978 (F. Tirrito).

2 recoveries of birds ringed in Germany.

68.   HALIAEETUS ALBICILLA   AV

White-tailed Eagle

Accidental visitor. 8 records of immatures: one near Carini, May 1869 (Doderlein 1869–74); 3 near Catania (Doderlein 1893); one at I. Ustica and one at Buonfornello, Sep 1946 (Orlando 1955c, Ajola 1959), one at I. Salina, 8 Dec 1960 (Moltoni & Frugis 1967) (now at MCR) and one at Palazzolo Acreide, 28 Nov 1973 (S. Baglieri). Erroneously quoted by De Stefani Perez (1905a).

69.   GYPAETUS BARBATUS   FB AV?

Lammergeier

Former breeder (*G. b. aureus*), but only one documented breeding record: one pair near Castelbuono, Madonie Mts, 1839–1840 (Minà Palumbo 1853–57). Benoit (1840) never recorded it. Doderlein (1869–74) reported 2 specimens: one immature, 1865, and one adult, between P. Albanesi and S. Giuseppe Iato, 1866; one specimen from Sicily, *ante* 1893 (Doderlein 1893), now at MM. One killed near Reggio Calabria, 1879, may have crossed from Sicily. 4 killed since 1906: one adult near Cefalù, 8 Jan 1906, one adult near Siracusa, 1910, one at Gangi (Madonie Mts), 1911, and one at Mt Ciccia (Messina Straits), 30 Mar 1916 (Costantino 1918, Arrigoni 1929, Orlando 1958h, who corrected Arrigoni's dates). A doubtful sight record at Madonie Mts, Feb 1935 (Orlando 1935a, 1936c).

70.   NEOPHRON PERCNOPTERUS   MB PM WV?

Egyptian Vulture

Scarce passage migrant and rare migrant breeder (*N. p. percnopterus*). No evidence of large movements through Sicily (Galea & Massa 1985) in spite of 100s recorded in Tunisia by Thiollay (1977) on spring migration. Spring passage mid Feb to late May, peaking mid Apr to early May; 14 counted at Messina Straits, 20 Apr–19 May 1984 (Dimarca & Iapichino 1984). Immatures occasionally on passage late May to Jun (Ajola 1939, Krampitz 1958, S. Falcone). Autumn passage late Aug to early Oct (Suchantke 1960, Galea & Massa 1985). Usually singly, occasionally up to 8–10 together. Giglioli (1907) listed it as resident, but overwintering seems only exceptional: last winter record, one adult, 27 Jan 1971 (Sorci *et al.* 1972). A few non-breeders probably oversummer. Usually recorded in pairs, sometimes in small flocks at carrion: 9 at Madonie Mts, Sep 1970; 7 at Rocca Busambra, Oct 1970 (Sorci *et al.* 1972); 5 at Piana Albanesi, 17 Jul 1973 (G. Giambona). Recorded in breeding areas till Oct, sometimes Nov–Dec: one at Piana Albanesi, 22 Nov (Orlando 1958g), one juvenile near Palermo, late Nov 1971, one immature at Tagliavia, early Dec 1975 (G. Cangialosi).

Breeding. N. p. percnopterus. Doderlein (1869–74) listed it as rare; regularly reported by later authors (e.g. Mebs 1957, Krampitz 1958). Breeding population now c. 20 pairs; decreased in some areas (e.g. near Palermo) in 1970s. At least 2 sites deserted in last 10 years. Some pairs breed at irregular intervals, one pair doing so 3 times in 5 years. First arrivals mid Feb, mostly early Mar. Nests, in cavities on cliffs, lined with wool. Noted for site fidelity lasting many years. Flight displays recorded Mar to May, pairing Mar to early Apr. Eggs, C/1–2, early Apr, young fledge early–mid Aug. Breeding success: 0·7–1 (2 chicks in one nest are not rare).

71.   GYPS FULVUS   FB AV

Griffon Vulture

Formerly a common resident, extinct now as breeder since 1965. Accidental visitor (*G. f. fulvus*) in recent years; 10 records of singles, 1970–1985: juvenile killed at Mazara, 20 Sep 1970 (Sorci *et al.* 1973), adult recorded at Mt Pellegrino, 24 Dec 1978, 2 immatures killed at Agrigento and Iblei Mts, 1978–79 (E. Giudice), immature recorded at Madonie Mts, May 1983 (M. Terrasse), immature observed near Trapani, 25 Sep 1983 (S. Surdo), immature killed at Piana Albanesi, 8 Oct 1983 (A. Guarraci), immatures recorded at Mt Gallo and Raffo Rosso, Sep 1984, P. Albanesi Dec 1984 (F. Lo Valvo) and at Sutera, 28 Aug 1985 (M. Inglisa). These birds probably came from N Africa — a few are irregularly recorded at Cape Bon (Tunisia) in spring (Thiollay 1977, T. Gaultier).

Benoit (1840) and Doderlein (1869–74) listed it as a common resident. Widespread in Sicily till 1930s (G. Ajola, C. Orlando, A. Priolo), with small colonies still present at Caronie Mts (Priolo 1954), Madonie Mts, Rocca Busambra and mountains near Palermo (Orlando 1958g); previously, at Iblei Mts, where no colony was known, and listed as "not rare" by Riera (1923). Breeding on Aetna reported by Galvagni (1843). A colony of 30–40 birds in the surroundings of Palermo (Doderlein 1869–74), mostly at Mt Gallo, was deserted after 1926 due to a quarry installation, but 3 birds were recorded there again, 7 May 1944, and one pair nested in nearby Mt Pellegrino till 1939 (Orlando 1958g). A colony at Rocca Busambra survived till early 1960s: 10 birds, 1932 (Orlando 1958g), at least 2 pairs, 1957 (Mebs 1957, Krampitz 1958), one pair 1959–1964; in the same area a long dead corpse was found in 1967, and a single adult observed at least 25 times, 1973–1984. The colony at S. Vito, first recorded by Doderlein, existed till 1930s, perhaps 1940s. Colony at Madonie Mts, first recorded by Minà Palumbo (1853–57), survived till early 1960s: at least 2 pairs, 1957–58 (Orlando 1958g, Krampitz 1958), 2 birds, 19 Aug 1962 (C. Orlando 1962); a single adult recorded at least 6 times in the same area, Jul 1974 to Aug 1977 (Priolo 1974, Fazio 1976, A. Carapezza). The colony at S. Giuseppe Iato disappeared in 1950s, that at Piana Albanesi was deserted in early 1960s, one nest being recorded there 1957 (Krampitz 1958) and one immature killed there Feb 1968 (Sorci *et al.* 1972). Breeding was confirmed at one colony near Alcara Li Fusi (Caronie Mts) till 1965, when 18 birds, the whole colony, were killed by poisoned bait (Priolo 1967).

72.   CIRCAETUS GALLICUS   PM WV

Short-toed Eagle

Scarce passage migrant (*C. g. gallicus*), unrecorded some years. Spring passage early Mar to early Jun, autumn passage early Sep to Nov. Twice Jul (Moltoni 1973a, A. Ciaccio). Usually singly, occasionally in twos. Evidence for any large movement through Sicily is lacking (Dimarca & Iapichino 1984, Galea & Massa 1985) in spite of 100s observed in Tunisia on spring passage by Thiollay (1977). Recently a regular winter visitor: 1–4 in S Sicily, Dec–Feb 1980–1986 (Mascara 1984b, A. Ciaccio & A. Falci) and one shot near Caltagirone, 1 Jan 1960 (A. Priolo). Breeding claimed by Arrigoni (1929) never confirmed.

73.   CIRCUS AERUGINOSUS   PM WV FB?

Marsh Harrier

Fairly common passage migrant (*C. a. aeruginosus*) in variable numbers. Spring passage late Feb to late May, peaking late Mar to late Apr, singly or up to 10 together. 149 counted at Messina Straits, 20 Apr to 19 May 1984 (Iapichino &

Dimarca 1984). Usually less common on autumn passage, mid Aug to early Nov, peaking mid to late Sep. Scarce late Nov to mid Feb; 1–4 regularly overwintered at Simeto. Occasional Jul to early Aug. Breeding recorded by Benoit (1840) and Doderlein (1869–74) at Lentini and near Siracusa, but not confirmed this century.

2 recoveries, of birds ringed in Germany (1) and Poland(1).

CIRCUS spp.

All 4 harriers migrate across Sicily on a broad front, but there is evidence of some concentration at Messina Straits and along E coast. Females and immatures of *C. pygargus/C. macrourus* are more numerous than males, particularly mid Apr onwards. Out of 143 harriers counted at Messina Straits, 20 Apr to 19 May 1984, 32 were *C. pygargus*, 2 *C. macrourus*, 110 *pygargus* or *macrourus* (Dimarca & Iapichino 1984); out of 52 in spring 1980–1984 at Capo Murro di Porco, 15 were *C. pygargus*, 11 *C. macrourus*, 26 were 'ringtails'.

74.   CIRCUS CYANEUS   PM WV
Hen Harrier

Scarce passage migrant (*C. c. cyaneus*) mostly in spring, early Mar to mid May and Sep to late Nov. 1–2 regularly overwinter at inland areas, Nov to early Feb. Doderlein (1869–74) listed it as common and claimed breeding, but this seems a mistake (Lo Verde & Massa 1985).

75.   CIRCUS MACROURUS   PM
Pallid Harrier

Scarce spring passage migrant, mid Mar to early May, mainly early Apr, usually singly. Irregular on return passage, Sep. Twice Feb and once Oct and Nov. More numerous in past; Doderlein (1890, ms.) listed it as the commonest harrier in Sicily.

3 recoveries, of birds ringed in Tunisia.

76.   CIRCUS PYGARGUS   PM
Montagu's Harrier

Uncommon to locally fairly common spring passage migrant, late Feb to late May, mostly mid to late Apr; singly or in parties up to 8. Occasional Jun. Scarce on return passage, late Aug to mid Oct, sometimes Nov. Doderlein (1869–74) listed it as rare. (See *Circus* spp.)

2 recoveries, of birds ringed in France (1) and Sweden (1).

77.   ACCIPITER GENTILIS   AV
Goshawk

Accidental visitor. 6 records of singles since 1900: Castelbuono, 1900 (specimen at MCT); Erice, Mar 1953, Marsala, Mar 1953 and Ustica, Apr 1953 (Steinbacher 1955); Rocca Busambra, 26 Apr 1957 (Mebs 1957); Palermo, 16 Jan 1962 (G. Ajola). Mongitore (1742) recorded it at Aetna, Sabatini (1915) recorded it at Aeolian Islands. Benoit (1840) and Doderlein (1869–74, 1893) listed it as breeder, but gave no proof.

52   Accipitridae

78. ACCIPITER NISUS   PM WV RB

Sparrowhawk

Uncommon passage migrant and winter visitor (*A. n. nisus*). Slight evidence of passage at islets (Aeolian, Egadi and Ustica) and at Messina Straits, Mar to mid May, and Aug–Oct. Usually singly. A very few overwinter, Nov–Feb, in natural woods and pine plantations.

Breeding. A. n. nisus. Benoit (1840) listed it as a migrant, Doderlein (1869–74) as a common resident. Breeding population unknown, apparently scarce and local, probably decreasing and some localities now deserted, e.g. P. Albanesi, where Orlando (1943b) recorded one pair. Breeding confirmed at Madonie, Caronie and Peloritani Mts, Aetna and some areas of Sicani Mts, 1979–1983 (Massa 1985), and possibly at Iblei Mts. Nests in trees in hilly or mountainous woods. Very few details: one nest, C/3, found early Jun, 2 nests with 2 and 3 chicks recorded mid Jul.

2 recoveries, of birds ringed in Sweden (1) and Germany (1).

79. BUTEO BUTEO   RB PM WV

Buzzard

Common resident breeder, passage migrant and winter visitor (*B. b. buteo*). Spring passage, early Mar to late May, peaking late Mar to early Apr; very few from mid Apr: 40 counted at Messina Straits, 20 Apr to 19 May 1984 (Dimarca & Iapichino 1984). Apparently scarcer on return passage, Sep–Oct, sometimes early Nov (Galea & Massa 1985). Uncommon winter visitor, wintering birds usually appearing darker than residents. *B. b. vulpinus* is possibly overlooked, but at least 7 records: May (3), Jan, Feb, Apr and Nov; but "many" at I. Marettimo, Sep 1960 (Suchantke 1960). Most of spring migrants at C. Bon (Tunisia) resemble *vulpinus*.

Breeding. B. b. buteo. Benoit (1840) listed it only as a migrant, Doderlein (1869–74) as a common breeder. Common to locally very common, resident breeder; breeding population 1000–1500 pairs. Occurs in hilly and mountainous areas, open, rocky and woody habitats; also breeds at Egadi and Aeolian Islands. Massa (1980) recorded one pair/15 km^2, Cairone (1982) one pair/12 km^2, and Mascara (1984c) 2 pairs one km apart. Nests on ledges on cliffs or in trees, more frequently on cliffs in mountainous areas (Krampitz 1958). Flight displays recorded Jan–Apr, mainly Mar, pairs restoring nests, Feb–Mar and pairing Mar to early Apr. Eggs, C/2–4, usually C/3, late Mar to early May, young fledge mid June to late Jul, mostly early Jul. Breeding success: 2·4–2·7 juveniles per pair (Massa 1980, Mascara 1984c), only 0·02 at Roccapalumba, where chicks are usually taken by young boys (Cairone 1982).

4 recoveries, of birds ringed in Tunisia (3) and USSR (1).

80. BUTEO RUFINUS   AV

Long-legged Buzzard

Accidental visitor. 4 records: 2 at Agrigento, Feb 1874 (Arrigoni 1929); one shot between Corleone and Prizzi, 22 Dec 1951 (Orlando 1954); one near Floresta, 28 May 1954 (Orlando 1955f); one shot at Pachino, 4 Jan 1973 (T. Mingozzi). One was recorded on Calabrian side of Messina Straits coming from Sicily, 18 May 1978. Good numbers recorded at C. Bon (Tunisia) by Thiollay (1975, 1977) were possibly local residents, not crossing the Sicilian Channel (Galea & Massa 1985).

81.   BUTEO LAGOPUS   AV

Rough-legged Buzzard

Accidental visitor: one near Priolo, Oct or Nov 1968 (S. Baglieri). Doderlein (1869–74) listed a specimen from Siracusa on Benoit's authority, but Benoit (1840) did not mention it.

82.   AQUILA POMARINA   PM

Lesser Spotted Eagle

Rare passage migrant (*A. p. pomarina*), could be regular at Messina Straits in spring. 14 confirmed records since 1959: Oct (4), Mar, Apr and Sep (2), "autumn" (2), once May and "spring" (Giambona 1971, Priolo 1972b, Dimarca & Iapichino 1984). On Calabrian side of Messina Straits 2 on 14 May 1986, and 2 doubtful records, May 1987, all coming from Sicily (G. Malara). 2 unidentified eagles near Palermo, 9 May 1936 (Orlando 1936c) and 14 Mar 1978 (A. Carapezza) were probably this species. Benoit (1840) listed it as resident, but this seems a mistake. Doderlein (1893) reported only one specimen, from Bivona.

83.   AQUILA CLANGA   PM

Spotted Eagle

Rare and irregular passage migrant. At least 16 records of immatures: 2 near Gibilrossa c. 1890, one near Palermo 1877 (Doderlein 1893); one between S. Giuseppe Iato and Monreale 15 Sep 1897 (De Stefani Perez 1898); one, undated, near Castelvetrano, one at Villabate, 16 Oct 1932 (Orlando 1935b); one at St. Flavia, 16 Oct 1954 (G. Ajola); one at I. Ustica, 1 Nov 1958 (Ajola 1959, who reported that in autumn "black eagles" occasionally occurred at the islet); one near Palermo, 1952 (I. Venchierutti); one at Pachino, 1963; one at Simeto, 1–25 Feb 1981 (Ciaccio & Siracusa 1983); 4 undated (Doderlein 1893, Orlando 1935b). One undated specimen at TFC.

84.   AQUILA HELIACA   AV

Imperial Eagle

Accidental visitor (*A. h. heliaca*). 3 records of immatures: Montemaggiore, 30 Nov 1947 (Ajola 1948b); Monte Lauro, May 1959, Pachino, Oct 1973 (Massa *et al.* 1979). One immature was recorded on the Calabrian side of Messina Straits coming from Sicily, 19 May 1986 (G. Malara). A specimen from Madonie Mts, Sep 1968, claimed to be Imperial Eagle by Randazzo (1972b) was in fact a Golden Eagle *Aquila chrysaetos* (Massa *et al.* 1979).

85.   AQUILA CHRYSAETOS   RB

Golden Eagle

Rare resident breeder. (*A. c. chrysaetos*). Immatures wander far from breeding areas and occasionally leave Sicily: 4 records at Messina Straits, late Apr 1974, 2 May 1975, 15 Apr 1981, 3 May 1984 (Dimarca & Iapichino 1984).

Breeding. A. c. chrysaetos. 15 pairs known in mountainous areas, inland or, occasionally, near the coast. Doderlein (1869–74) listed it as a rare resident. Distance between 2 breeding sites, 10–42 km (Falcone *et al.* in Fasce & Fasce 1984). Nests on cliff ledges. Flight displays recorded Nov–Apr, mainly Feb–Mar, pairs restoring nests and mating Feb–Mar (occasionally early Apr). Eggs, C/1–2, early

Apr, young fledge Jul, usually mid to late Jul. 4 recent records of 2 fledged young from one nest, 1984–1987 (A. Ciaccio, S. Falcone, P. Valguarnera). Breeding success, 0·84 (±0·49) juveniles per pair. During breeding season apparently preys on frogs (Priolo 1973) and snakes (Massa 1981a). Orlando (1955e) listed 31 killed in previous 25 years; at least another 30 killed since then.

86.   HIERAAETUS PENNATUS   PM

Booted Eagle

Scarce passage migrant, late Sep to late Dec and Apr–May, once Feb and late Mar. Influxes occurred Nov–Dec 1985, with at least 14, mostly in SE, and at Messina Straits with 35, Apr–May 1986, and 15, Apr–May 1987 (A. Giordano, G. Malara). Only 6 records before 1975, but possibly overlooked in view of recent records and of regular spring passage at Cape Bon.

87.   HIERAAETUS FASCIATUS   RB

Bonelli's Eagle

Rare resident breeder. Massa (1976c) estimated c. 10 pairs in 1974; in 17 areas, breeding confirmed in 5, probable in 6, possible in 6 others, 1979–1983 (Massa 1985). Numbers probably greatly reduced in last decades, but details on trend lacking. At Iblei Mts, where now almost extinct, said to be fairly common in past (A. Priolo). Many specimens are found in public or private collections. Juveniles and immatures wander, but no evidence of birds moving to or from Sicily.

Breeding. Occurs in main mountains, but also on isolated cliffs and on one islet. Nests in holes or ledges of cliffs. Flight displays Jan–Apr, less frequently May–Jun. Eggs, C/1–2, mid Feb to early Mar. Prey caught by male and young fed by female. Young fledge late May to early Jun. Breeding success less than 1·5 juveniles per pair. The commonest mammal prey is Rabbit *Oryctolagus cuniculus* (c. 30%), but small to medium sized birds, such as Jackdaw *Corvus monedula* and Rock Dove (*Columba livia*) compose c. 50% of prey (Massa 1976c, 1981a, Salvo in press).

PANDIONIDAE

88.   PANDION HALIAETUS   PM FB

Osprey

Uncommon passage migrant (*P. h. haliaetus*) at wetlands, reservoirs and along coasts, mid Mar to mid May, mostly mid to late Apr, and late Aug to late Oct, mostly late Sep to early Oct, usually singly. Occasional Jan, Feb, Jun and Nov. Generally more records in spring, except in SE Sicily. Riera (1923) reported overwintering at Biviere di Lentini.

Breeding. P. h. haliaetus. Doderlein (1869–74) listed it as a breeder, but gave no evidence; Orlando (1936a) supposed breeding at Capo Zafferano. One pair bred at I. Marettimo till 1960s and an old nest was found there 1971 (Massa 1973b).

13 recoveries, of birds ringed in Finland (9) and Sweden (4).

FALCONIDAE

89.   FALCO NAUMANNI   PM MB WV

Lesser Kestrel

Uncommon passage migrant, singly or in parties up to 20. Spring passage early Mar to early Jun, from late Apr mostly females and immatures (Dimarca &

Iapichino 1984) (see also *F. tinnunculus*). Return passage late Aug to late Oct. Doderlein (1869–74, 1893) recorded it as a winter visitor, but no records since until 1980s: 1–5 in 2 localities, Dec–Feb 1981–1983 (Ciaccio *et al.* 1983), 7–15 at L. Rubino, 13 Jan 1984 and 28 Jan 1986 (A. Dimarca).

Breeding. Benoit (1840) listed it as a migrant, Doderlein (1869–74) first recorded it as breeding. Now an uncommon and local breeder, mainly in Cen and S Sicily, but some colonies also in W and NE. Breeding population c. 200 pairs, probably decreasing in last 30 years: Mebs (1957) listed it as commoner than *F. tinnunculus*, Krampitz (1958) found colonies of up to 40–50 pairs. Now colonies are usually of 3–4 pairs, a few up to 20–25; single pairs sometimes recorded. Densities recorded: $10.9 \ km^2$ per pair in S Sicily (Mascara 1984c), 16.8 and $22.5 \ km^2$ in W Sicily (Massa 1980, Cairone 1982). Occurs in open and dry areas, from c. 250 up to 700–1000 m. Nests in holes and ledges on cliffs, sometimes in old buildings; one colour-ringed young was recorded for 2 years at the same colony. First arrive mid Mar, colonies completed by mid Apr. Mating recorded Mar to early May; eggs, C/2–6, usually C/3–5, May–Jun, young fledge Jul–Aug. Breeding success, 3.2–4.5 juveniles per pair (Massa 1980, Cairone 1982). At colonies c. 10% of birds are immatures.

2 recoveries, of birds ringed Austria (1) and Tunisia (1).

90.   FALCO TINNUNCULUS   RB PM WV

Kestrel

Common resident breeder, passage migrant and winter visitor (*F. t. tinnunculus*). The commonest migrant falcon, late Feb to early Jun, peaking Apr, and late Aug to Nov (Dimarca & Iapichino 1984, Galea & Massa 1985). No specific counts at Messina Straits, but 314 *F. tinnunculus/naumanni* counted there 20 Apr to 19 May 1984 (Dimarca & Iapichino 1984).

Breeding. *F. t. tinnunculus*. The most widespread breeding raptor, population c. 2000–2500 pairs including islets, in a wide variety of habitats: open, cultivated, rocky, wooded and urban areas. Densities recorded: 5.6–7.5 pairs/km^2 (Massa 1980, Cairone 1982). Nests in holes and ledges on cliffs or buildings, rarely in old nests of *Corvus corone* and, probably, of *Garrulus glandarius* and *Pica pica*, from sea level up to c. 1800 m. Mating Apr–May (occasionally early Jun); eggs, C/3–5, once C/6, late Apr to early Jun, fledging mid Jun to late Jul. Breeding success: 2.0–4.2 juveniles per pair. At Roccapalumba success is reduced to 1.08 due to taking of chicks by locals (Cairone 1982). High mortality due to shooting, e.g. 140 specimens stuffed by taxidermists of 8 towns, 1974–1975 (Massa 1976a) and 159 by only 2 taxidermists at Catania, 1981–1982 (A. Ciaccio).

41 recoveries, of birds ringed in Tunisia (36), Finland (2), France (1), Sweden (1) and USSR (1).

91.   FALCO VESPERTINUS   PM

Red-footed Falcon

Fairly common spring passage migrant (*F. v. vespertinus*) in variable numbers, late Mar to early Jun, usually peaking late Apr to mid May. Usually 20 or less together (Dimarca & Iapichino 1984), but passage of more than 100 in a day sometimes reported: 100s at I. Ustica, late Apr 1958 (Ajola 1959), 120 at Capo Zafferano, 20 Apr 1970; c. 500 at Capo Murro di Porco, 21 Apr 1977 (S. Baglieri). 120 at Messina Straits, 1 Jun 1987 (G. Malara). Rare and irregular on return passage, Sep.

2 recoveries, of birds ringed in USSR (1) and Tunisia (1).

92.   FALCO COLUMBARIUS   PM
Merlin

Scarce passage migrant (*F. c. aesalon*), singly Mar to mid May and Sep to mid Dec, mostly in autumn. Some years unrecorded. 2 records, Jan one doubtful Jul (Priolo 1972b).

One recovery, of a bird ringed in Norway.

93.   FALCO SUBBUTEO   PM MB
Hobby

Fairly common spring passage migrant (*F. s. subbuteo*), late Mar to early Jun, peaking late Apr to early May; 82 counted at Messina Straits, 20 Apr to 19 May 1984 (Dimarca & Iapichino 1984). Apparently scarce on return passage, late Aug to Oct, mostly late Sep, in spite of high numbers recorded at Malta (Galea & Massa 1985). Usually singly. Overwintering claimed by Doderlein (1869–74) seems an error.

Breeding. F. s. subbuteo. Breeding supposed by Giglioli (1907), Priolo (1954) and Krampitz (1958), but first proved in 1978 (Massa 1980). Breeding population is < 10 pairs, in hilly wooded habitats. Eggs late Jun, in old nests of *Corvidae*, recently fledged young late Aug–mid Sep.

94.   FALCO ELEONORAE   MB PM
Eleonora's Falcon

Scarce passage migrant and local breeder at some islets. Spring passage, mid Apr to mid Jul, peaking late May to early Jun. Occasional from late Mar, and up to late Jul. Only 9 counted at Messina Straits, 20 Apr to 15 May 1984 (Dimarca & Iapichino 1984). Apparently scarcer on autumn passage, early Sep to early Nov. Occasional Aug, mostly immatures (Massa 1978b). A few non-breeders are recorded irregularly at I. Pantelleria, where it probably oversummers (Moltoni 1973a, Massa 1978b).

Breeding. Doderlein (1893) reported the first specimen from Sicily, Mt Pellegrino, 10 May 1891. Giglioli (1890, 1907) first confirmed breeding at the small islet of Lampione (near Lampedusa), estimating c. 12 pairs in 1882. Colony at I. Lampedusa first recorded by Zavattari *et al.* (1960); Moltoni (1970) estimated c. 150 birds there 1968. Colonies at Aeolian Islands first recorded at I. Alicudi and I. Filicudi by Moltoni & Frugis (1967), and at I. Salina by Massa (1978b); breeding suspected at I. Panarea by Allavena (1965). Present Sicilian breeding population c. 150 pairs (Massa 1978b, Spina *et al.* 1985). First arrive at colonies late Apr, mostly May–Jun; probably only immatures arrive Jul. Nests in holes or ledges on sea cliffs. Giglioli (1907) found nests on the ground at Lampione, close to those of *Calonectris diomedea*, but now this does not occur. Eggs, C/2–3, late Jul to early Aug, recently hatched young late Aug to early Sep (Giglioli 1907, Spina *et al.* 1985). Young fledge early Oct, colonies being deserted by late Oct to early Nov.

95.   FALCO BIARMICUS   RB PM
Lanner Falcon

Scarce and local resident breeder and rare (and irregular?) passage migrant (*F. b. feldeggii*, but see below). A few, mostly immatures, occasionally recorded at Messina Straits, Feb–Mar (Galea & Massa 1985). One specimen at MZP, taken at Modica, c. 1890, was referred to *F. b. erlangeri* (of NW Africa) by Trischitta (1939a), but this is considered a mistake by Orlando (1957d). Threatened by shooting: at least 35 killed in 15 years, 35% of them immatures.

Breeding. F. b. feldeggii, or probably a clinal form between *feldeggii* and *erlangeri*, named *orlandoi* by Trischitta (1939b). Doderlein (1869–74) listed it as an occasional migrant, Giglioli (1907) as resident. Mebs (1957) first recorded nests. Breeding population now c. 60 pairs (Ciaccio *et al.* in press). Occurs in grasslands and rocky areas from sea level up to c. 1100 m, usually inland, only one pair recorded on sea cliffs (G. Salvo). Nests on ledges or in holes or old nests of *Corvidae* (once of *Hieraaetus fasciatus* – A. Ciaccio) on small cliffs geologically friable, rarely on high calcareous cliffs. Minimum distance from a *F. peregrinus* site is 200 m, usually much more (5–6 km). Pairing recorded late Jan to late Feb; eggs, C/2–4, usually C/3, mid Feb to mid Mar, fledging late Apr to early Jun, mainly early May, juveniles at breeding sites till Sep. Fidelity to sites not so strong as in *F. peregrinus*. Breeding success, c. 2·5 juveniles per pair (Mebs 1957, Mascara 1984c, 1986, A. Ciaccio, A. Dimarca, S. Falcone, G. Salvo). Average weight of prey in Sicily c. 110 g, while for Peregrines it is c. 90 g. (Siracusa *et al.* in press).

96. FALCO CHERRUG   AV

Saker

Accidental visitor (*F. c. cherrug*). 6 recorded since 1967: one near Palermo, Oct 1967; one at Chiaramonte, Feb 1970, erroneously reported as "autumn 1969" by Sorci *et al.* (1972) (S. Baglieri); 2 shot near Messina, spring 1971 (Sorci *et al.* 1972); one near Siracusa, Aug 1978 (S. Baglieri); one undated specimen from Egadi Islands (Sorci *et al.* 1973). One collected at Mt Pellegrino, Jun 1868, listed as Saker by Doderlein (1869–74) was in fact a Peregrine *F. peregrinus* (Salvadori 1872, Doderlein 1890 ms.).

97. FALCO PEREGRINUS   RB PM

Peregrine

Scarce resident breeder, also on islets, and scarce passage migrant. A few, mostly immatures, recorded at Messina Straits and islets, Feb–Mar (Galea & Massa 1985), some probably *F. p. peregrinus*. 10 confirmed records of *F. p. calidus*, Oct–Feb.

Breeding. F. p. brookei. Only in rocky areas, but frequently recorded in open habitats. Present breeding population c. 150 pairs, density one pair/86 km² (Schenk *et al.* 1983). Average distance between 2 nest sites, 5 km (Falcone & Seminara 1981). Nests in holes and on ledges on calcareous cliffs, along coasts and inland up to 1300 m. Flight displays recorded from Jan, mating Jan–Feb. Eggs, C/2–4, generally C/3, Feb, fledged young late Apr to early May, rarely mid May. High fidelity to nest site all year. Breeding success, 1·6–2·0 juveniles per pair (Falcone & Seminara 1981, Schenk *et al.* 1983). At least 150 shot in last 55 years (75% immatures), but falconry is the main threat (see introductory section on shooting). In past at I. Ustica chicks were collected sometimes as food by locals (Doderlein 1869–74).

98. FALCO PELEGRINOIDES   AV

Barbary Falcon

Accidental visitor: one immature near Siracusa, 30 Mar 1977 (Massa *et al.* 1979).

PHASIANIDAE

99. ALECTORIS GRAECA   RB
Rock Partridge

A. g. whitakeri, an endemic race, is smaller than Italian and Balkan races: wing of male 166 mm, of female 156 mm (Priolo 1984), weight of adults respectively c. 570 and c. 450 g; for further differences in plumage and moult see Orlando (1956a) and Priolo (1970, 1984). Fairly common resident breeder from sea level up to c. 2000 m (Spanó *et al.* 1986). In past very common in hilly, rocky, mountainous, wooded and also cultivated areas, now decreasing and local because of hunting, pesticides, and introduction of different forms (*A. g. saxatilis, A. chukar*), fortunately unsuccessful up to now (Massa 1976d, Priolo 1970, Priolo & Sarà 1986). Commoner in Madonie, Sicani, Caronie, and Iblei Mts and Aetna; rare along coasts but still present in a few areas (e.g. Zingaro Nature Reserve). Spallanzani (1793) recorded it at I. Lipari, where it became extinct c. 1880 (Sabatini 1913). Doderlein (1869–74) reported it as resident at I. Pantelleria, but it disappeared from there in the last century (Moltoni 1973a).

Doderlein (1869–74) recorded an albino population on the verge of extinction, known in Sicily since 1700. Many albino specimens are preserved in Sicilian collections and museums (Iannizzotto 1910a, Arrigoni 1929, Ajola 1939, Orlando 1956a, Priolo 1984).

Breeding. A. g. whitakeri. On the ground, usually near a herbaceous plant. Eggs, C/8–14, usually (probably) C/10–12, Apr–May, newly hatched chicks late May to mid Jul, young fledge early Jul to late Aug. Family parties are recorded all autumn not far from the breeding site.

100. FRANCOLINUS FRANCOLINUS   FB
Black Francolin

Former resident breeder (*F. f. francolinus*), widespread till 1840s, extinct c. 1869. Benoit (1840) recorded it in S Sicily, still widespread, mainly near Gela and Caltagirone, but sharply decreasing (due to hunting) and becoming rare, even though protected since 1550 by Viceroy De Vega. Extinction first claimed by Lilford (1862). Doderlein (1869–74) stated it was formerly abundant near Castelvetrano, Partanna, Sciacca, Licata, Gela, Caltagirone, Misilmeri, S. Giuseppe Iato, Madonie Mts and Parco della Favorita at Palermo, where it was introduced c. 1800. He also reported that the last 2 had been shot near Gela in 1865 and at Falconara in 1869. Giglioli (1890) listed it as formerly abundant at Finale plain and near Falconara, where he shot "many", 1844–45. Orlando (1958l) reported a doubtful capture of one later than 1872. About 20 Sicilian specimens are preserved in museums. All authors agree extinction was caused by hunting (Pratesi 1976) except Amari (1937), who blamed land reclamation.

Used to occur mainly in open areas, probably low maquis, but also in crops. Benoit (1840) stated it nested close to bushes of *Chamaerops humilis.* Eggs C/10–14. According to Arrigoni (1929) it was probably imported into Sicily by "crusaders".

101. COTURNIX COTURNIX   PM MB WV
Quail

Fairly common to locally common passage migrant (*C. c. coturnix*), numbers greatly reduced since 1950s at least and still decreasing. Spring passage mid Mar to late May, peaking late Apr to mid May; most numerous at islets (Pantelleria,

Ustica), at Messina Straits and along S coast. In recent years singles or 10s in a day at one locality, in past much more numerous, e.g. up to 100 in a day shot by a single hunter at I. Ustica in 1920s (Ajola 1959). Scarcer on return passage, mid-late Aug to Nov, mostly Sep to mid Oct; very scarce Dec; irregularly reported, Jan to mid Feb, but probably a few regularly over winter. Occasional on passage late Feb and early Aug.

Breeding. C. c. coturnix. Migrant breeder, locally still fairly common but rapidly decreasing. Many areas deserted in most recent years. Occurs in open cultivated or uncultivated areas, more widespread in W, Cen and S Sicily; occasionally bred at islets (Favignana, Pantelleria, Ustica). Eggs, C/8–14, May, newly hatched young usually late May to early Jun (G. Salvo).

119 recoveries, of birds ringed in Italy (74), Tunisia (41), Hungary (2), France (1) and Switzerland (1). 2 ringed in Sicily recovered in Malta.

RALLIDAE

102. RALLUS AQUATICUS   RB WV

Water Rail

Scarce or uncommon resident breeder (*R. a. aquaticus*) at wetlands, also inland; c. 30 breeding areas counted 1979–1983 (Massa 1985), but is probably overlooked. Some local increase, Oct–Feb, suggests influx of migrant birds.

Breeding. R. a. aquaticus. In reedbeds at freshwater wetlands. Few data available due to secretive habits: adults building nests early Apr, recently fledged young recorded usually early Jun, but downy young occasionally as late as early Sep, possibly second broods.

103. PORZANA PORZANA   PM

Spotted Crake

Scarce spring passage migrant to wetlands, early Mar to late Apr, easily overlooked. Usually scarcer on return passage, Sep to late Nov. One Dec. On 24 Jun 1979, one male and 2 females recorded in reedbed at Foce Birgj (Iapichino & Baglieri 1981). Benoit (1840) and Doderlein (1869–74) listed it as very common on passage and supposed breeding near Catania. Cramp & Simmons (1980) include E Sicily in the breeding range.

104. PORZANA PARVA   PM OB

Little Crake

Scarce spring passage migrant, Mar to mid May, usually singly, occasionally up to 10 together, easily overlooked. Once Sep and Oct, 2 records Nov.

Breeding. Giglioli (1907) supposed breeding but gave no proof. One confirmed breeding: 2 shells of recently hatched eggs found at Longarini marsh, Jun 1980 (Iapichino & Baglieri 1981).

105. PORZANA PUSILLA   PM

Baillon's Crake

Rare (and irregular?) spring passage migrant (*P. p. intermedia*), Mar–Apr. Once Nov.

106. CREX CREX   PM
Corncrake

Scarce and decreasing spring passage migrant; singles recorded late Feb to late May, mostly early May. Rare on return passage, Sep to early Nov. Once Jan. Doderlein (1869–74) listed it as a common spring migrant and regular winter visitor. Palazzotto (1801) claimed that it occasionally bred in wet meadows.

107. GALLINULA CHLOROPUS   RB PM WV
Moorhen

Common resident, passage migrant and winter visitor (*G. c. chloropus*) to wetlands, rivers, canals, reservoirs, little dams. Local increases and records outside breeding areas (e.g. at islets) suggest passage mainly late Sep to Oct and Mar–Apr.
Breeding. G. c. chloropus. Common resident breeder everywhere in suitable habitat up to 1200 m. Few details: eggs, C/6–10, mid Mar to Jul, mostly Apr, recently fledged young after mid May.
2 recoveries, of birds ringed in Poland (1) and Germany (1).

108. PORPHYRULA ALLENI   AV
Allen's Gallinule

Accidental visitor. 5 records (not 8 as erroneously stated by Massa *et al.* 1979): one at Pachino, 17 Dec 1881 (Giglioli 1886); one near Catania, 4 Dec 1902 (Whitaker 1903, now at WMB); one undated specimen from Lentini (Arrigoni 1929, Orlando 1958f); one at Siracusa salt-pan, 5 Dec 1975 (Massa *et al.* 1979); one at Dirillo mouth, 15 Feb 1988 (S. Baglieri).

109. PORPHYRIO PORPHYRIO   FB AV
Purple Gallinule

Former resident breeder (*P. p. porphyrio*) in wetlands near Catania, Lentini, Siracusa, Gela and Mazara; now an accidental visitor: 2 near Trapani, autumn 1969 (Sorci *et al.* 1973). Benoit (1840) and Doderlein (1869–74) listed it as a fairly common resident in the Catania plain, especially at Biviere di Lentini, and also along Anapo river near Siracusa, rare elsewhere and an irregular migrant (see also Cavendish Taylor 1886). Giglioli (1890) stated it was common at Lentini, scarcer at Biviere di Gela. Whitaker (1899a,c) recorded it also near Vittoria (probably S. Croce Camerina) and at Mazara marshes. At Lentini was abundant indeed; c. 1500 were shot yearly to be sold at markets (Martorelli 1906). Decrease probably started in the first decades of this century; by 1929 Arrigoni (1929) reported only 100 shot yearly at Lentini, though Orlando (1957f) considered it common there till 1930s, and it had certainly greatly decreased by 1943 (Stresemann 1943) and disappeared finally after the drainage of the lake ended in 1949. Many moved to wetlands near Simeto mouth, but were exterminated by shooters within a few years (Priolo 1974a). Became extinct at Siracusa salt-pan in 1956 (Fagotto 1976) and at Gela in 1950s; last confirmed records at Biviere di Gela, 8 Apr 1951 and Nov 1953 (Orlando 1957f), but Krampitz 1958) stated it was still present in the lake. At Mazara it disappeared in early 1950s (Sorci *et al.* 1973).
Arrigoni (1929) listed 8 records of *P. p. madagascarensis*: Siracusa, Oct 1851; Messina, autumn 1865; Agrigento, autumn 1869; Lentini, Mar 1908; 4 undated.
Breeding. P. p. porphyrio. Eggs, C/2–4, laid Feb–Mar (Benoit 1840). Whitaker (1899) recorded laying in captivity, Jan, Mar, Apr and Jul. Jany (*in* Stresemann

1943) found 3 old nests in reedbeds at Lentini, one with shells of a hatched egg, 13 Jun 1943.

110. FULICA ATRA   WV PM RB

Coot

Common autumn passage migrant and winter visitor (*F. a. atra*) at wetlands and reservoirs, late Aug to early Apr, peak numbers late Oct to mid Dec. Up to 9600 annually in Jan census 1975–1987, commonest at Pergusa (maximum 4800, Jan 1986). Most leave late Feb to mid Mar. Usually no conspicuous spring passage.

Breeding. F. a. atra. Uncommon resident breeder, found regularly at Pergusa, L. Soprano, Simeto, Biviere di Gela and in a few other areas. Breeding population c. 200 pairs, possibly increasing; probably much more numerous in past when breeding habitat was plentiful. Eggs recorded after mid Mar, recently fledged young late May to Jul.

2 recoveries of birds ringed in Hungary (1) and USSR (1).

111. FULICA CRISTATA   AV

Crested Coot

Accidental visitor: one shot at Biviere di Lentini, Oct 1864 (Giglioli 1886). Malherbe (1843) claimed that one had been shot near Siracusa, but gave no details.

TURNICIDAE

112. TURNIX SYLVATICA   FB

Andalusian Hemipode

Former resident breeder (*T. s. sylvatica*), extinct not later than 1920, probably due to both hunting and land reclamation. Occurred mainly in garigue with *Chamaerops humilis*, along S coast from Gela to Mazara, probably scarcer near Catania and Ragusa. Absent in N Sicily; one shot near Palermo reported as exceptional by Doderlein (1869–74). Giglioli (1906) recorded it near Messina. Fairly common in the last century (Benoit 1840), Doderlein (1869–74) could shoot 10–15 daily on S coast, 1862–70. Greatly decreased in the last decades of last century, Giglioli (1889) and Angelini (1892) listing it as nearly extinct. Whitaker (1896, 1905) reported that it was once plentiful in all parts of the southern and southwestern districts, where its favourite haunts were tracts of uncultivated moorland, among the clumps of dwarf broom-palm and other scrub vegetation. Last documented records: singles shot at Falconara, autumn 1910 (Orlando 1958m) and at Castelvetrano, 1913 (Sorci *et al.* 1973), doubtfully at Agrigento, Nov 1914 (Arrigoni 1929). Extinction as late as 1940–50s claimed by Orlando (1958m) seems a mistake.

Less than 20 Sicilian specimens in collections and museums. One previously unreported specimen recently found at ITM.

GRUIDAE

113. GRUS GRUS   PM

Common Crane

Fairly common passage migrant (*G. g. grus*), recorded in flocks up to 500, usually 30–80; sometimes commoner on autumn than on spring passage. Spring passage early Mar to early Apr, return passage late Aug to early Dec, mostly mid Oct to late Nov; occasional influxes till late Dec, e.g. 50 at Gela, late Dec 1985. Occasional Jan, but overwintering never proved. Once May. Most records are from W Sicily, where usually recorded overhead. Though few figures available, some passage is likely to involve 1000s, sometimes in a few days, e.g. over 500 over Palermo, 6 Mar 1983 (A. Guarraci), c. 1000 over Alcamo, Mar 1983 (G. Campo), over 600 in 15 flocks in W Sicily, 14–24 Nov 1984, and over the same dates "hundreds" reported over Sciacca. Listed as common by all previous authorities but no figure reported. Calcara (1846) stated that "large flocks visited Lampedusa annually in May and Jun destroying the whole harvest".

114. ANTHROPOIDES VIRGO   AV
Demoiselle Crane

Accidental visitor. 2 documented records: one shot near Agrigento, Mar 1879 (Giglioli 1907); one shot at Marsala, 6 Sep 1964, claimed to be one of 2 (Sorci *et al.* 1973). Doubtful records reported by Doderlein (1869–74) and Moltoni (1970); breeding at Lampedusa claimed by Schembri (1843) is clearly an error.

OTIDIDAE

115. TETRAX TETRAX   FB AV
Little Bustard

Former resident breeder, definitely extinct in early 1960s, now an accidental visitor. Benoit (1840) listed it as a common resident near Caltagirone, Gela, Vizzini and Palermo. Doderlein (1869–74) recorded it as a fairly common resident in S Sicily, but also near S. Vito and between Catania and Siracusa, rare near Messina and a passage migrant in Mar near Agrigento. Giglioli (1890) recorded large flocks near Gela, Mar–Apr, single pairs in other months. Whitaker (1905) has written it "used to be more plentiful a few years ago than it is now [1905], and was far from uncommon in some of the less cultivated districts on the south and south-west of the island". Specimens from Buonfornello plain, 21 Nov 1934, and Nicosia (Caronie Mts), Mar 1928, are preserved in coll. Orlando. Arrigoni (1929) did not report its breeding in Sicily. Greatly decreased in 1930–40s, because of spring shooting and land reclamation (Orlando 1935, Priolo 1969b). Last confirmed breeding in W Sicily c. 1940, and one shot near Marsala, Oct 1969 (Sorci *et al.* 1973). Last breeding in Cen Sicily, at Pietralonga, c. 1955, and in E Sicily, at Ramacca, in 1964 (A. Priolo). A female was shot at Capo Murro di Porco, 19 Nov 1970 (S. Baglieri).

Orlando (1958e) considered *T. t. tetrax* the resident form and *T. t. orientalis* as an irregular passage migrant, but Vaurie (1965) indicates that western and eastern populations' measurements overlap and does not separate them.

116. CHLAMYDOTIS UNDULATA   AV
Houbara Bustard

Accidental visitor. 4 records: one near Siracusa, winter 1844 and one at I. Pantelleria, 15 Nov 1911 (Arrigoni 1929), both of them *C. u. undulata*; one at Pachino, 7 Nov 1923 (Di Carlo 1972) and one at Capo Passero, Sep 1971 (Baglieri 1972b) were both *C. u. macqueenii*.

117. OTIS TARDA   AV

Great Bustard

Accidental visitor (*O. t. tarda*):– 5–6 near Catania, 1845–1846 (Doderlein 1869–74); one near Catania, Feb 1846 (Zuccarello Patti 1846); one at Alcamo, 1864 (Doderlein 1869–74); singles at Agrò river 1902, near Trapani 1926–29, near Terrasini Oct 1932 (Orlando 1958e); one killed at Giarre, Mar 1949 (Priolo 1972b). One doubtful record reported by Sorci *et al.* (1972).

HAEMATOPODIDAE

118. HAEMATOPUS OSTRALEGUS   PM

Oystercatcher

Uncommon passage migrant (*H. o. ostralegus*), mainly in autumn along E coast. Spring passage mid Mar to mid May, usually 1–5 birds on a few dates. Singles occasionally, Jun. Flocks up to 50–80 regular early Jul to late Aug at SE wetlands, with a few birds to mid Oct.

RECURVIROSTRIDAE

119. HIMANTOPUS HIMANTOPUS   PM MB

Black-winged Stilt

Uncommon to fairly common spring passage migrant (*H. h. himantopus*) and scarce migrant breeder to wetlands, also inland, early-mid Mar to mid May, mostly Apr, singly or in 10s, and up to 40 together. Usually fewer on return passage, mid Jul to mid Sep, peaking mid Aug; some years no obvious autumn passage but difficult to assess because of confusion with breeders. Some recorded Jun outside breeding areas are probably immatures. Occasional late Sep, once Dec.

Breeding. H. h. himantopus. In past, breeding supposed by Doderlein (1869–74). Arrigoni (1929) listed it as an occasional breeder in Sicily, but reported that breeding was common 70 years before. Regular breeder since 1976 or possibly 1973 (Massa 1978c) mainly in coastal wetlands, mostly at Trapani salt-pan and Longarini. 20–50 pairs nested annually 1976–1987, but only one pair in 1978 and c. 10 in 1980–1981. Number of pairs per breeding season depends on water levels. Eggs, usually C/4 (occasionally C/3 and C/5) late Apr to mid Jul, mostly mid May to early Jun. Unfledged young late May to late Aug. Breeding success variable, 0·12–2·2 juveniles per pair. First departures mid Jul, mostly mid-late Aug.

A pullus ringed in Sicily was recovered in N Italy c. 2 months later.

120. RECURVIROSTRA AVOSETTA   PM WV OB

Avocet

Uncommon to fairly common passage migrant to wetlands, occasional inland. Uncommon on spring passage, late Mar to mid May, sometimes early Mar and into early Jun, in flocks of 10 or less, occasionally up to 30. Recorded mid to late Jun most years. More numerous on return passage early-mid Jul to Nov, sometimes into Dec, peaking mid Aug to Sep, in 10s up to 100 together, mostly on E coast. Irregular in winter, when some movement still occurs. 3 definite records since 1977 of 2–6 overwintering, Dec to Feb, at Simeto and Vendicari.

Breeding. Breeding supposed by Doderlein (1869–74) near Siracusa seems doubtful. One pair with 3 unfledged young recorded at Trapani salt-pan, 19 Jun 1986 (Surdo 1987), 10 pairs in 1987 (S. Surdo, M. Sarà).

BURHINIDAE

121. BURHINUS OEDICNEMUS   PM WV RB or MB
Stone Curlew

Scarce and decreasing breeder (Priolo 1954, Orlando 1958p), probably mainly resident, but definite evidence is lacking. Uncommon passage migrant (*B. o. oedicnemus*), mid Mar to May and Sep–Nov, and winter visitor, Dec–Feb. Sometimes in small flocks; up to 20–40 together at some inland areas in winter (A. Ciaccio, A. Dimarca). In past much more common, including in winter (Orlando 1958m). Occurs in open areas, stone banks along rivers, semi-arid and cultivated areas with scattered trees, coastal plains, from sea level up to c. 1000 m.

Breeding. Many breeding areas deserted in recent years. Eggs, C/1–3, usually C/2, Apr–Jul (Aug), mainly May–Jun. Young fledge late May to mid Sep; newly hatched chicks found early Sep (E. Giudice) suggests second brood.

B. o. saharae collected at I. Pantelleria, 28 Apr 1977 (Cambi 1977). Vaurie (1965) stated that *B. o. saharae*'s range included islands of the Mediterranean, though "very rare" now in most of them, but he had examined no specimens from Sicily. There is no conclusive evidence about the race breeding in Sicily, and the overlap with migrant and wintering populations adds difficulty, but many Sicilian specimens are lighter and smaller than the nominate form.

GLAREOLIDAE

122. CURSORIUS CURSOR   PM
Cream-coloured Courser

Rare and irregular passage migrant (*C. c. cursor*) along coasts. 22 records of singles, 3 of 2 together: Mar (6), Apr (3), Feb, May and Oct (2), Jun, Sep, Nov, "spring", "autumn" and 5 undated.

123 GLAREOLA PRATINCOLA   PM MB
(Collared) Pratincole

Scarce spring passage migrant (*G. p. pratincola*) along coasts, singly or less than 10, sometimes higher numbers, once up to 26 together, Apr to late May; non breeders wander occasionally to SE wetlands, Jun–Jul. 2 records late Mar, 3 in Oct.

Breeding. G. p. pratincola. Rare and irregular breeder, formerly more common. Doderlein (1869–74) stated that large numbers bred near Catania, Siracusa and Agrigento. Giglioli (1890) supposed breeding inland near Caltanissetta, but this is dubious. Kramptiz (1958) stated that it bred in former years at Gela, Licata and Pachino. Massa (1978c) recorded 8–10 pairs displaying at Pachino and 4 at Simeto, Apr–Jun 1973, but breeding was not confirmed. First confirmed breeding 1974: 3 pairs at Simeto (Massa 1978c). One pair was with a recently fledged juvenile at Pachino, 14 Jun 1978; 1–3 pairs at Biviere di Gela, 1983–84 and in 1986, had unfledged young early Jul (Mascara 1987a, A. Dimarca); one pair with one unfledged young at Trapani salt-pan, late Jun 1986 (S. Surdo). There are undated eggs from S Sicily in a private collection (A. Pazzuconi).

124. GLAREOLA NORDMANNI   AV

Black-winged Pratincole

Accidental visitor: a specimen from Marsala, 27 Apr 1904 (Whitaker 1904), now at WMB.

CHARADRIIDAE

125. CHARADRIUS DUBIUS   PM MB WV?

Little Ringed Plover

Fairly common passage migrant (*C. d. curonicus*) to wetlands, reservoirs and rivers, in 10s and up to 120. Spring passage mid-late Feb to mid May, peaking Mar to early Apr; usually scarcer on return passage, early Jul to Nov. Irregular in winter, 2 recent records at Ogliastro reservoir: one, 21 Jan 1979, and 4 on 13 Jan 1980. 3 at Catania, 3 Jan 1985 (A. Ciaccio). Up to 8 reported overwintering at Termini (Gatto 1980).

Breeding. C. d. curonicus. Nests on freshwater wetlands, mostly at inland reservoirs and along rivers, occasionally at salt-marshes (Iapichino & Baglieri 1978). Massa (1978c) estimated 70 pairs at least; breeding confirmed in 44 areas, 1979–1983 (Massa 1985). Eggs C/3–4 May–Jun. Recorded as a breeding species by all previous authorities since Doderlein (1869–74), but data on population trends are lacking.

2 recoveries of birds ringed in Germany (1) and Czechoslovakia (1).

126. CHARADRIUS HIATICULA   PM WV

Ringed Plover

Uncommon to fairly common passage migrant (*C. h. hiaticula*) to coastal wetlands and inland reservoirs, singly or in 10s up to 80. Spring passage late Mar to mid Jun, peaking late Apr to mid May; return passage mid Jul to late Nov, mostly Aug-Sep. 1–4 have wintered regularly in recent years at SE wetlands. Breeding claimed by Arrigoni (1929) is doubtful — pullus from Castelvetrano that he stated to be *Charadrius hiaticula* was in fact *Charadrius alexandrinus* (Massa 1978c).

Both the nominate race and *C. h. tundrae* are likely to occur but the only reported occurrence of the latter (Orlando 1936c) is doubtful (Massa 1978c).

127. CHARADRIUS ALEXANDRINUS   PM MB WV

Kentish Plover

Common passage migrant and migrant breeder (*C. a. alexandrinus*); no evidence of resident birds. Spring passage early Mar to early May, usually in 10s, sometimes from mid Feb. Post-breeding flocks regular after mid Jun, when some migration probably occurs. Common on return passage early-mid Jul to Nov, peaking Aug, in 100s up to 500 together at SE wetlands and at Trapani salt-pan. Uncommon winter visitor, Dec to Feb, in variable numbers along coasts, c. 110 in 1984 winter census, probably more in dry winters. Rare inland, but 3 overwintered at L. Pergusa, Dec 1983 to Feb 1984 (A. Dimarca).

Breeding. C. a. alexandrinus. Along sandy coasts and salt wetlands. Massa (1977) estimated 400–450 pairs, with densities 0·09–0·19 pairs/ha. Eggs, usually C/3 (once C/5), mid Mar to mid Aug, mostly mid May to mid Jun; some evidence of second broods. Incubation c. 25 days, unfledged young usually Jun-Jul, sometimes till early

Sep; mortality of young c. 45% (Massa 1978c, 1985). Most breeders probably leave late Aug to Sep.

One recovery, of a bird ringed in Hungary.

128. CHARADRIUS ASIATICUS   AV

Caspian Plover

Accidental visitor: one shot near Catania, 30 Mar 1978 (Fantin 1982).

129. CHARADRIUS (= EUDROMIAS) MORINELLUS   PM

Dotterel

Uncommon and decreasing autumn passage migrant, late Aug to late Nov, mostly Oct, singly or up to 15 together. Rare on spring passage, mid Mar to early May, singly or up to 10. Listed as fairly common, sometimes in 100s, at Malta (Sultana & Gauci 1982), so probably overlooked. Doderlein (1869–74) listed it as common in spring at Agrigento and Gela.

130. PLUVIALIS DOMINICA   AV

Lesser Golden Plover

Accidental visitor. (*P. d. fulva*). 2 records: one shot at Punta Raisi, 25 Aug 1974 (G. Pellerito); one taken at Siracusa salt-pan, 6 Oct 1979 (Iapichino & Baglieri 1982b).

131. PLUVIALIS APRICARIA   PM WV

Golden Plover

Uncommon to fairly common passage migrant and winter visitor; both *P. a. apricaria* and *P. a. altifrons* occur, the latter perhaps more commonly. Mostly inland at meadows and arable fields, in 10s, sometimes in 100s. On passage in very variable numbers, mid Feb to mid Apr and Oct–Nov, occasional May, Jun and late Sep; some movement also in winter; up to 400 at Simeto in Jan.

132. PLUVIALIS SQUATAROLA   PM WV

Grey Plover

Uncommon passage migrant along sandy coasts and wetlands, singly or up to 20 together, mid Mar to mid-late Jun, mostly early May, and late Jul to Nov. Singles, or up to 10 together, regularly overwinter, Nov–Mar, mainly at Simeto and Vendicari.

133. CHETTUSIA GREGARIA   AV

Sociable Plover

Accidental visitor. 2 records: one at Capo Feto, c. 1940 (Sorci *et al.* 1973); one at Ispica, 1955. The latter was erroneously reported by Di Carlo (1972) as *Vanellus spinosus* (Massa 1978c).

134. CHETTUSIA (= VANELLUS) LEUCURA   AV

White-tailed Plover

Accidental visitor: one at Longarini, 19 Apr 1975 (Massa *et al.* 1976).

135. VANELLUS VANELLUS   WV PM

Lapwing

Fairly common winter visitor in 10s, sometimes in 100s, mostly inland at arable fields. Usually no obvious spring passage; recorded till late Apr. Once mid May, Jun and Jul. Singles regularly after mid-late Aug, main numbers arriving mid Nov to Dec, but passage possibly regular into Jan. Up to 300 overwintered at Simeto, Dec–Mar.

4 recoveries, of birds ringed in N Italy (1), Germany (1), Holland (1) and Sweden (1).

SCOLOPACIDAE

Calidridinae

136. CALIDRIS CANUTUS   PM

Knot

Scarce but probably regular passage migrant (*C. c. canutus*) to coastal wetlands, 1–3 birds in most years, late Apr to mid Jun and mid Jul to late Sep. Once Mar and late Nov. One at Finale, Feb 1860 (Doderlein 1869–74).

137 CALIDRIS ALBA   PM WV

Sanderling

Uncommon to fairly common spring passage migrant to wetlands and sandy coasts, mid Apr (possibly late Mar) to late May, peaking early–mid May, singly or in 10s, and up to 50, exceptionally up to 100 together. Once Jul. Scarcer on return passage, early Aug to Nov, usually 10 or less. Up to 17 have overwintered at least 4 times in recent years, mid Dec to Mar, mostly at Simeto.

One recovery, of a bird ringed in Norway.

138. CALIDRIS MINUTA   PM WV

Little Stint

Common passage migrant to wetlands and, in small numbers, to inland reservoirs, in 100s up to 2000 together, numbers strongly depending on water-levels. Spring passage mid Mar to early Jun, peaking early May. Scarce mid Jun to early Jul. Return passage mid Jul to Nov, mostly Aug-Sep. In recent years up to 100 have overwintered, Nov–Mar, but winter movements also occur; in some years there are no winter records.

3 recoveries, of birds ringed in Sweden (1), Malta (1) and Tunisia (1).

139. CALIDRIS TEMMINCKII   PM

Temminck's Stint

Scarce passage migrant but easily overlooked. Singles or parties up to 10 recorded annually mid Apr to late May (occasionally late Mar), and Aug–Oct. 1–3 overwintered at Vendicari mid Dec 1980 to mid Mar 1981. Arrigoni (1929) stated that it wintered in Sicily.

140. CALIDRIS MELANOTOS   AV

Pectoral Sandpiper

Accidental visitor: one taken at Siracusa salt-pan, 15 Sep 1968 (Baglieri 1973); one at Imera mouth, 20 Mar 1982 (G. Giambona).

141. CALIDRIS FERRUGINEA   PM

Curlew Sandpiper

Fairly common to common passage migrant to coastal wetlands, early Apr to early Jun, mostly early-mid May, usually flocks up to 100–300, but sometimes up to 1000 together, at SE wetlands. A few, regularly, mid-late Jun. Usually in smaller numbers in autumn, early-mid Jul to mid Oct. Twice Mar, once Nov and Dec. Doderlein (1869–74) claimed that it wintered, but this is unlikely.

2 recoveries, of birds ringed in Sweden (1) and Mauritania (1).

142. CALIDRIS ALPINA   PM WV

Dunlin

Common autumn passage migrant to wetlands and reservoirs. Both *C. a. alpina* and *C. a. schinzii* occur, the latter identified from skins on only a few occasions in Feb and Mar (Massa 1978c). Scarce on spring passage, mid Mar to May, in flocks of 10 or less, occasionally up to 50; occasional Jun. In 10s or 100s, up to 400 together, mid Jul to Nov, peaking late Aug to early Oct. Regular in winter, numbers depending on water-levels; up to 150 have overwintered, Nov to late Mar, a few into mid Apr.

2 recoveries, of birds ringed in Germany (1) and Czechoslovakia (1).

143. LIMICOLA FALCINELLUS   AV

Broad-billed Sandpiper

Accidental visitor (*L. f. falcinellus*), but could have been overlooked. 5 records of singles in recent years: Siracusa, 20 Sep 1972; Pachino, 27 Aug 1973; Priolo, 1 Sep 1976 (Massa 1978c); Simeto, 10 Oct 1982; Priolo, 16 Sep 1984. Doderlein (1869–74) recorded one near Agrigento.

144. TRYNGITES SUBRUFICOLLIS   AV

Buff-breasted Sandpiper

Accidental visitor. 3 records: one at Longarini, 21 Sep 1976 (Massa *et al.* 1979); one at Priolo salt-pan, 19 Aug 1985, one at Biviere di Gela, 13 Oct 1985 (Dimarca *et al.* 1986).

145. PHILOMACHUS PUGNAX   PM

Ruff

Common passage migrant in spring, mid Feb to early Jun; 100s, sometimes 1000s, Mar-Apr, at coastal wetlands but also at reservoirs and wet meadows inland. Singles regularly, Jun. Autumn passage, early Jul to early Nov, usually in 10s. Occasional in winter; 6 records of 2–10 wintering in recent years. Doderlein (1869–74) listed it as common in winter.

6 recoveries, of birds ringed in Finland (3), Sweden (1), Norway (1) and Tunisia (1).

Gallinagininae

146. LYMNOCRYPTES MINIMUS   PM WV
Jack Snipe

Uncommon passage migrant, easily overlooked, but has decreased in recent years. Singles on passage, Oct-Nov and early Mar to mid Apr, most records Nov. Scarce, but possibly regular winter visitor, Dec-Feb. Occasional Sep.

One recovery, of a bird ringed in Germany.

147. GALLINAGO GALLINAGO   PM WV
Snipe

Common passage migrant and winter visitor (*G. g. gallinago*) mid Aug to mid May. Autumn passage most marked mid Oct to early Dec. Overwinters in variable numbers. Spring passage less obvious, Mar-Apr. Occasional late May to early Aug. Usually singly, but 10s or even 100s in suitable areas.

148. GALLINAGO MEDIA   PM
Great Snipe

Scarce passage migrant and decreasing – some years unrecorded; singles or twos mid Mar to mid May, mostly Apr, sometimes from Feb. Irregular on return passage, late Sep to Nov. Doderlein (1869–74) listed it as common.

Scolopacinae

149. SCOLOPAX RUSTICOLA   PM WV
Woodcock

Common autumn passage migrant and winter visitor, mid Oct to mid Mar, peaking Nov to mid Dec; slight evidence of spring passage early Feb to mid Mar; very scarce Apr, occasional early May and late Aug (Orlando 1956d,f). During passage more numerous at islets. Overwinters in variable numbers in wooded areas and along some rivers throughout. At dusk leaves to feed at night in clearings on many Diplopoda, Coleoptera, Lumbricidae and Gasteropoda. Ringing evidence of winter site fidelity.

3 recoveries of winter ringed birds, one recovered 2 winters later and another one winter later, and one within the same winter.

Tringinae

150. LIMOSA LIMOSA   PM
Black-tailed Godwit

Fairly common spring passage migrant (*L. l. limosa*) in 10s or 100s up to 400, early Feb to mid May, peaking late Feb to late Mar, largest flocks usually recorded overhead. Scarce on autumn passage, early Jul to Oct, singly or up to 7 together. 1–5 regularly late May to Jun; occasional Nov-Dec, but no evidence of overwintering; also mid-late Jan, probably early return migrants.

One recovery, of a bird ringed in Hungary.

151. LIMOSA LAPPONICA   PM
Bar-tailed Godwit

Scarce passage migrant (*L. l. lapponica*) to coastal wetlands. Apparently irregular in spring, 5 records, Apr-May; 1–7 birds usually in autumn, early Sep to late Oct. Once Jul.

152. NUMENIUS PHAEOPUS   PM
Whimbrel

Scarce to fairly common spring passage migrant (*N. p. phaeopus*) along coasts, mid Mar to mid May, peaking late Mar, usually 10 or less, but sometimes 100s; c. 500 counted Capo Murro di Porco, 24–25 Mar 1985, and "large flocks" reported near Pachino, Mar 1977 (S. Baglieri). Uncommon on return passage early Jul to Sep, mostly Aug, singly or up to 7. Once Feb and Oct, twice Nov. Doderlein (1869–74) stated that it wintered.

153. NUMENIUS TENUIROSTRIS   AV
Slender-billed Curlew

Only an accidental visitor, singly, in recent times: at Siracusa, 13 Sep 1930; at I. Ustica, 13 Sep 1947 (Ajola 1959); near Palermo, May 1969, and at Priolo salt-pan, Feb 1971. One specimen from Agrigento, 1902 at TFC (Massa 1978c). Formerly a fairly common visitor (Doderlein 1869–74); Giglioli (1890) and Arrigoni (1929) stated that it was the commonest *Numenius* sp.

154. NUMENIUS ARQUATA   PM WV
Curlew

Uncommon to fairly common passage migrant (*N. a. arquata*) to wetlands and reservoirs. Spring passage, late Feb to mid May, peaking late Mar, in variable numbers, usually singly, sometimes in 10s. Occasional early-mid Jun. Usually more records on return passage, late Jun to Nov, 10 or less, occasionally up to 25 together. A few have overwintered regularly in recent years, up to 13 in Jan, mostly at Simeto, Vendicari and Mazara. Doderlein (1869–74) listed it as common in winter.

155. BARTRAMIA LONGICAUDA   AV
Upland Sandpiper

Accidental visitor: one taken at Buonfornello, 27 Sep 1969 (Massa & Cangialosi 1969b).

156. TRINGA ERYTHROPUS   PM WV
Spotted Redshank

Uncommon passage migrant, usually singly or up to 15 together, occasionally up to 50, mid Mar to late May and mid Jun to late Oct or early Nov, mostly Aug-Sep. Up to 30 have regularly overwintered since 1980 mainly at Simeto, L. Ogliastro and Pergusa, Nov to Mar; wintered occasionally in previous years (Doderlein 1869–74, Massa 1978c).
   2 recoveries, of birds ringed in Finland (1) and Czechoslovakia (1).

157. TRINGA TOTANUS   PM WV
Redshank

Fairly common to common passage migrant (*T. t. totanus*) to coastal wetlands and inland reservoirs. Singles or up to 30 together, occasionally up to 100, early Mar to early Jun, mostly Apr. A few probably oversummer, but numbers difficult to assess because of early migrants. Common on return passage, mid Jun to early Nov, peaking early Jul to mid Aug, in 10s or 100s, up to 400 together; some, probably still on passage, mid Nov to Dec. Wintering status given by all authorities since Doderlein (1869–74). Up to 60 regularly overwintered in recent years at protected wetlands and lakes, Nov to early-mid Mar.

2 recoveries, of birds ringed in Germany(1) and Denmark (1).

158. TRINGA STAGNATILIS   PM

Marsh Sandpiper

Uncommon spring passage migrant to wetlands, also inland, early Mar to late May, mostly Apr, singly or in flocks up to 25. Scarcer in autumn, mid late Jun to mid Oct, singly or up to 9. 3 records Dec.

159. TRINGA NEBULARIA   PM

Greenshank

Uncommon to fairly common passage migrant to wetlands and reservoirs. Tens or less, mid-late Mar to early Jun, but c. 150 at Trapani, 28 Apr 1984; sometimes common on autumn passage, 50–200 together mid-late Jun to Oct, mostly Aug. Almost regularly recorded Nov; 4 records Dec, once late Feb and early Mar; c. 30 at Pergusa, 12 Jan 1986 (A. Dimarca) but overwintering not proved.

160. TRINGA OCHROPUS   PM

Green Sandpiper

Uncommon to fairly common passage migrant to wetlands, rivers, also little dams, usually singly but also, mostly in spring, in 10s up to 50. On passage late Feb to May and mid Jun to Oct, peaking Jul to mid Aug. Occasional in winter; 4 records in recent years: late Dec (2) and Jan (2). Breeding supposed by Doderlein (1869–74) is unlikely.

161. TRINGA GLAREOLA   PM

Wood Sandpiper

Fairly common passage migrant, mostly at coastal wetlands. Spring passage mid Mar to early Jun, peaking late Apr when up to 200 together; autumn passage mid-late Jun to mid Oct, peaking Jul-Aug, usually in smaller numbers, but c. 500 recorded 11 Jul 1977 at Priolo and 5 Jul 1984 at Longarini.

3 recoveries, of birds ringed in Sweden (2) and Finland (1).

162. XENUS CINEREUS   PM

Terek Sandpiper

Rare and apparently irregular passage migrant to coastal wetlands; one record inland. 10 singletons and 2 once in 8 years since 1974, mid Aug to early Oct (8), May (2), once Jun (Massa et al. 1979, Iapichino & Baglieri 1982, Norante 1982, Ciaccio & Siracusa 1983a). One taken near Pachino ante 1974 (Fagotto & Baglieri 1976). Singles, 9 May 1912 and Nov 1900 (Arrigoni 1929).

163. ACTITIS HYPOLEUCOS   PM WV

Common Sandpiper

Fairly common passage migrant along coasts and rivers and at reservoirs. Spring passage early Mar to early Jun, mostly mid Apr to early May; return passage late Jun to Oct, peaking Jul-Aug. Recorded singly or in 10s, up to 60 together, largest flocks on return passage. Scarce winter visitor, Nov-Feb, usually singly; 30 at Pergusa, 17 Jan 1982, was exceptional. Recorded Jun in suitable breeding areas, but breeding, supposed by Doderlein (1869–74), Arrigoni (1929) and Sorci *et al.* (1973), has never been confirmed.

2 recoveries, of birds ringed in Sweden (1) and Germany (1).

Arenariinae

164. ARENARIA INTERPRES   PM

Turnstone

Uncommon passage migrant (*A. i. interpres*) singly or in flocks up to 20, along coasts and to wetlands, late Mar to early Jun, peaking mid May; in smaller numbers early Aug (Jul) to late Oct. Once Nov and Dec (Massa 1978c).

One recovery, of a bird ringed in Sweden.

Phalaropinae

165. PHALAROPUS LOBATUS   AV

Red-necked Phalarope

Accidental visitor, but possibly overlooked. 7 records: one near Palermo, 4 Oct 1952; one at Prizzi reservoir, Nov 1969; one taken near Scoglitti, Mar 1970 (Sorci *et al.* 1971b) and claimed to be in a flock of 10; one at Longarini, 26 Aug 1974. 2 off E coast 19 Sep 1974 and another 10 Sep 1975 (Massa 1978c, Massa *et al.* 1979); one at Siracusa salt-pan, 21–25 Aug 1985.

166. PHALAROPUS FULICARIUS   AV

Grey Phalarope

Accidental visitor. 2 records: one at I. Pantelleria, Aug 1966 (Foschi 1968); one taken off Capo Passero, 7 Dec 1976 and claimed to be in a flock of 12 (Massa *et al.* 1979).

STERCORARIIDAE

STERCORARIUS spp.

Sorci *et al.* (1971) considered that *S. parasiticus* and *S. pomarinus* were not rare and were regular winter visitors in the Mediterranean and along Sicilian coasts. The relative frequency of recording of each species is not easy to assess. Out of 73 birds recorded 1967–1977, mostly shot, 39 were *S. pomarinus* and 34 *S. parasiticus* (Sorci *et al.* 1971c, Baglieri 1973c, S. Baglieri); out of 79 birds observed at Capo Murro di Porco, 1975–1983, mostly Jan 1980 to Mar 1983, 38 were positively identified as *S. pomarinus* and 9 as *S. parasiticus* (Iapichino 1984d). At least one skua is recorded at Capo Murro di Porco on most days when sea-watching occurs mid Oct to Jan, nor are records much fewer Feb-Apr. Occasional May-Sep. Numbers seem to have increased in recent times (Sorci *et al.* 1971c); very few records in the past century (Trischitta 1919b).

167. STERCORARIUS POMARINUS   PM WV

Pomarine Skua

Uncommon passage migrant and winter visitor, recorded all months, singly or up to 5 together; at Capo Murro di Porco peak numbers mid Oct to Nov, when most move south. Spring passage, Mar-Apr, but not so obvious as in *S. parasiticus* (see also *Stercorarius* spp.)

168. STERCORARIUS PARASITICUS   PM WV

Arctic Skua

Scarce but regular passage migrant and winter visitor along all coasts, recorded all months except Aug, singly or up to 3 together. Most records late Feb to Apr (see *Stercorarius* spp.)

169. STERCORARIUS LONGICAUDUS   AV

Long-tailed Skua

Accidental visitor, possibly overlooked. 4 records: one undated specimen (Giglioli 1886); one at Palermo, 22 Jul 1897 (Trischitta 1919b); one off Brucoli, Mar 1969 and 2 off Palermo, 4 Oct 1970 (Sorci *et al.* 1971c).

170. STERCORARIUS SKUA   WV PM?

Great Skua

Rare but possibly regular winter visitor (*S. s. skua*) (and spring passage migrant?), mostly off E coast. 12 records of singles, 11 since 1974: Mar (5), Jan (3) and once each Feb, Apr, Sep and Oct (Sorci *et al.* 1971, Massa 1978c, Massa *et al.* 1979, Baccetti & Mongini 1981).
2 recoveries, of birds ringed in Scotland.

LARIDAE

171. LARUS MELANOCEPHALUS   PM WV

Mediterranean Gull

Fairly common winter visitor, late Nov to mid Feb, along S and SE coasts; c. 2000, mostly adults, counted in 1984 winter census at harbours and coastal wetlands, but probably more winter offshore. Spring passage, mid Feb to mid Apr, usually not very evident. Up to 100 regular May-Aug at Augusta and Siracusa harbours. First juveniles recorded mid Jul during weak migration. Main autumn passage mid Oct to late Nov, peaking 25 Oct-10 Nov, when hundreds are regularly counted migrating at Capo Murro di Porco (Iapichino 1984a).
76 recoveries, of birds ringed in USSR (Black Sea).

172. LARUS MINUTUS   PM WV

Little Gull

Uncommon to fairly common passage migrant and winter visitor in variable numbers along coast, occasionally inland. Spring passage mid Feb to early May, usually in 10s or less, but 100s, up to 500 together, mostly immatures, occurred mid Mar to Apr on E coast, 1982, 1984 and 1985. Return passage not conspicuous, mid

Aug to Nov, usually singly. Scarce or locally fairly common in winter: 100s at many coastal areas, Oct 1970 to Feb 1971 (Sorci *et al.* 1972); 169 in Jan census 1984; c. 100 at Siracusa, early Jan to late Feb 1985. Occasional Jun-Jul. Listed as irregular and rare in the past (Doderlein 1869–74, Ajola 1950).

One recovery, of a bird ringed in USSR.

173. LARUS RIDIBUNDUS   WV PM OB
Black-headed Gull

Common winter visitor along coasts, uncommon inland. Small migration from early Jul in 10s or 100s, but major arrivals late Oct to early Dec; southward passage recorded on E coast, Nov; c. 22,000 in 1984 winter census, with 1000s recorded at 8 locations. Most leave late Feb to late Mar. Up to 200 regularly oversummer. The number of oversummering birds and early migrants, Jul-Aug, has increased in recent years on E coast.

Breeding. One pair nested at Longarini marsh, Jun 1980, but nest (C/2) was robbed (Baglieri *et al.* 1980).

62 recoveries, of birds ringed in Hungary (25), Czechoslovakia (10), Finland (10), USSR (8), Yugoslavia (3), Poland (3), Denmark (1), Austria (1) and Sweden (1).

174. LARUS GENEI   PM WV
Slender-billed Gull

Recorded in all months. Uncommon spring migrant, early Mar to late May, usually less than 10, but flocks up to 40 recorded mid Apr. Up to 10 regularly, Jun. Return passage early Jul to mid Oct, with a few until late Nov; autumn flocks of 10s or 100s fairly common in wetlands along E coast, where sometimes they stay for weeks — 150–200 regularly recorded mid Aug to mid Sep at Vendicari and Priolo salt-pan. A few have overwintered in recent years: 4–15 recorded annually at Vendicari and Simeto, late Nov to mid Feb. In past recorded irregularly in winter.

42 recoveries, of birds ringed in USSR (40), Tunisia (1) and Sardinia (1).

175. LARUS AUDOUINII   PM WV?
Audouin's Gull

Scarce to locally uncommon summer visitor (non breeders) and passage migrant on E coast. Up to 50, mostly immature, have regularly oversummered, particularly at Priolo salt-pan, late May to mid-late Aug, sometimes into Sep, since 1974 at least (Priolo 1975). Autumn passage late Jul to early Nov, peaking Aug-Sep, with increasing numbers of adults and juveniles (up to 24 together) at wetlands; also up to 12 records per year of ones or twos moving southward at Capo Murro di Porco. 5 records late Nov to early Feb. Small but regular passage mid Feb to Apr, 1–4 records of singles in most years, but 8 at Pachino, 6 Mar 1972. Prior to 1974 thought to be rare and irregular, with only 11 documented records (Priolo 1975, Massa 1978c).

176. LARUS CANUS   WV
Common Gull

Rare and apparently irregular winter visitor (*L. c. canus*), probably overlooked. 13 records of 1–2, 9 since 1970: Jan (5), Mar and Nov (2) once Feb, May, Sep and Dec (Ajola 1950, Moltoni & Frugis 1967, Sorci *et al.* 1971, 1973, Moltoni 1973, Massa 1978c, G. Rallo). Doderlein (1869–74) and Arrigoni (1929) listed it as common, possibly due to misidentification.

177. LARUS FUSCUS   WV PM

Lesser Black-backed Gull

Fairly common winter visitor along S and E coasts in 10s, up to 230 together.
First arrivals late Aug, most Nov-Dec, usually no obvious passage. c. 400 in 1984
winter census, but difficult to count because of marine habits. Some increase
Feb-Mar suggests migration. Regular Apr; singles oversummer in most years. In
lower Sicilian Channel flocks of 10s were common 25 Sep to 10 Oct 1982 (M. Sarà).
Breeding supposed by Doderlein (1869–74) and Giglioli (1907) is unlikely.

L. f. fuscus, *L. f. graellsi* and *L. f. intermedius* occur; most resemble *intermedius* in
blackish mantle and head-streaking.

9 recoveries, of birds ringed in Denmark (4), Sweden (2), Finland (2) and England
(1).

178. LARUS CACHINNANS   RB

Yellow-legged (Herring) Gull

Common resident breeder, mainly at islets, locally increasing. Usually uncommon along Sicilian coasts in winter; large flocks of immatures and non-breeders
recorded May-Aug, mainly along S and E coasts. Autumn and spring movements,
occasionally noted, probably referring to breeding birds. For specific status of
cachinnans see Glutz & Bauer (1982).

Breeding. On all islets, largest colonies at Lampedusa, Levanzo and Marettimo.
Breeding population c. 5000 pairs in 20 colonies. Breeding on rocky coasts of main
island, claimed by Doderlein (1869–74), Mebs (1957) and Krampitz (1958), is not
common; small colonies exist at Tindari (Massa 1978b) and between S. Vito Lo
Capo and Zingaro Nature Reserve. Odd pairs bred at inland reservoirs of Scanzano
and Piana, 1983–1984 (M. Sarà), at Mazara harbour (Sorci *et al.* 1973) and near
Cefalù, 1985 (B. Zava). Nests on ledges of cliffs or among vegetation on flat topped
islets. Eggs, C/1–3, average C/2.8 (M. Lo Valvo), late Mar to late Apr, hatching mid
Apr to late May, occasionally early Jun, mainly early May (M. Lo Valvo). Young
fledge Jun and colonies are then partly deserted.

179. RISSA TRIDACTYLA   WV

Kittiwake

Scarce but regular winter visitor, mostly off N and E coasts; 43 records of 1–8
since 1975, mid Nov to mid Mar, mostly Jan–Feb; twice Oct, once Sep. Possibly
overlooked in past. Doderlein (1869–74) reported an influx in 1872–73 winter and
Orlando (1937f) in 1936–37 winter.

2 recoveries of birds ringed in England (1) and USSR (1).

STERNIDAE

180. GELOCHELIDON NILOTICA   PM

Gull-billed Tern

Uncommon to fairly common spring passage migrant (*G. n. nilotica*) along
coasts, sometimes inland. Usually 10 or less, but up to 30 together, (mid) late Mar to
early-mid Jun, peaking late Apr to early May. Up to 40 recorded late Jun to Jul;
oversummering is possibly regular. Scarce Aug to late Sep, singly but occasionally
up to 10 together. Twice Oct and Nov. One winter record: 2 at I. Pantelleria, 13 Jan
1971 (Moltoni 1973a).

181. STERNA CASPIA   PM

Caspian Tern

Scarce on spring passage, mid Mar to May, 1–4 records of 1–3 in most years. Occasional Jun, one at Simeto, 25 Feb 1981 (Ciaccio & Siracusa 1983a). Fairly common autumn passage migrant mostly along E coast, mid Jul to early Nov, peaking mid Aug to early Oct, usually in twos at sea, but up to 25 together at wetlands. One winter record: 4 off S coast, 4 Jan 1978 (Massa 1978c). Possibly overlooked in past; Priolo (1974a) and Baglieri & Fagotto (1977) called it regular, while previous authorities listed it as rare and irregular, except Mayaud (1956) and Kumerloeve (1968), who noted the importance of the E Sicilian coast for migrating terns.

35 recoveries, of birds ringed in Finland (17), Sweden (10) and USSR (8).

182. STERNA BENGALENSIS   AV

Lesser Crested Tern

Accidental visitor on E coast. 5 records: one near Messina, Mar 1833 and one near Siracusa, c. 1839 (Doderlein 1869–74, Arrigoni 1929); one at Priolo salt-pan, 3–4 Aug 1983 (Iapichino 1984b); one at Simeto, 30 Jun 1984 (A. Ciaccio); one at Priolo, 24–31 May 1985, probably the same as the bird found dead in Siracusa salt-pan, 6 Jun 1985.

183. STERNA SANDVICENSIS   PM WV

Sandwich Tern

Fairly common to common passage migrant and winter visitor (*S. s. sandvicensis*) along coasts, occasionally inland. Spring passage in variable numbers late Feb to Apr, usually 10 or less, but up to 50 together. Up to 60 oversummer May to early Aug, mostly at Priolo salt-pan. Return passage late Jul to late Nov, peaking late Oct; common on SE coasts, 1403 in flocks of up to 63 moving south at Capo Murro di Porco during 81 observation hours, 1 Sep to 28 Nov 1982 (Iapichino 1985c). Regular Dec to mid Feb, singly or up to 25 together; difficult to count because of erratic flock movements. Breeding claimed by Doderlein (1869–74) and Arrigoni (1929) was never confirmed and seems dubious.

7 recoveries, of birds ringed in USSR (Black Sea).

184. STERNA HIRUNDO   PM

Common Tern

Rare and irregular passage migrant (*S. h. hirundo*) singles or occasionally up to 10, Mar-Apr. 1–2 recorded Jun-Jul in most years; oversummering proved at Priolo 1977 and 1985. Twice, May, Aug and Nov. Some winter records at I. Pantelleria: up to 8 early-mid Jan 1971, one 8 Dec 1972, at least 2, 20–27 Feb 1973 (Moltoni 1973a). Doderlein (1869–74) listed it as very common and supposed breeding; Sorci *et al.* (1971b) also listed it as regular and common but such status is unlikely.

185. STERNA PARADISAEA   AV

Arctic Tern

Accidental visitor. 2 confirmed records: one at Simeto, 24 Jul 1973 (Priolo 1974a) and 3 off Capo Passero, 10 Jul 1976 (Massa *et al.* 1979). One undated specimen "from Sicily" reported by Arrigoni (1929); Steinbacher (1956a) observed "many" near Siracusa, Oct 1955, but gave no details.

186. STERNA ALBIFRONS   PM MB

Little Tern

Scarce passage migrant (*S. a. albifrons*) along coasts and at wetlands, mid-late Apr to early Jun, and late Jul to early Oct, singly or up to 10 together. Usually very few records outside breeding areas, though some wander along coasts, Jun-Jul. 2 records Mar and one at Simeto, 6 Nov to 21 Dec 1983 (Ciaccio & Siracusa 1985a).

Breeding. S. a. albifrons. Zuccarello Patti (1844) listed it as a common breeder at Simeto where he collected one downy young. Doderlein (1869–74) and Orlando (*in* Krampitz 1958) claimed breeding in S Sicily, but gave no proof. Breeding proved at Priolo salt-pan, Jun 1974 (Baglieri & Iapichino 1974); 10–30 pairs regularly bred at Trapani salt-pan and Stagnone di Marsala, 1977–1987; at Longarini 15 pairs bred in 1977, 1–3 in 1978–1983, none in 1981, c. 10 in 1984, c. 25 in 1985 , 2 in 1986, c. 10 in 1987. 1–2 pairs occasionally breed at Vendicari and Priolo. Eggs, C/3, sometimes C/1 or C/2, late May to early Jul, mostly early Jun, recently hatched young late Jun to early Aug. Very low breeding success due to disturbance and shooting, e.g. most birds at Longarini colony were shot the first day of the shooting season, 25 Aug 1985.

187. CHLIDONIAS HYBRIDUS   PM

Whiskered Tern

Scarce coastal passage migrant (*C. h. hybridus*), also inland, mid Apr to early Jun and Jul to Aug (twice Sep), singly or up to 7 together. Recorded Jun most years; oversummering, proved 1983 and 1985 — could be regular. 5 winter records; one at Simeto, 26 Dec 1981 (Ciaccio & Siracusa 1983a); a single bird overwintered 3 times at Siracusa salt-pans, Oct–Mar 1984–87, 4–8 at Biviere di Gela, 5–24 Jan 1985. (A. Dimarca). Doderlein (1869–74) reported only one record, in 1839 near Siracusa.

188. CHLIDONIAS NIGER   PM

Black Tern

Fairly common spring passage migrant (*C.n. niger*) to wetlands and reservoirs, late Mar to mid-late May, peaking late Apr to early May, in 10s, up to 150 together, but some years very few. Much more common on autumn passage in 10s or 100s, early Jul to Oct, mostly mid Aug; peak number at E wetlands usually c. 500 but sometimes up to 1300 together. 1–4 recorded Jun in most years, once mid Mar and Nov.

2 recoveries, of birds ringed N Italy (1) and Holland (1).

189. CHLIDONIAS LEUCOPTERUS   PM

White-winged Black Tern

Uncommon passage migrant mid Apr to early Jun, in 10s or less, maximum 70 together. Return passage early Jul to Sep, 2–5 records of ones or twos in most years. Most recorded at coastal wetlands.

ALCIDAE

190. ALCA TORDA   WV

Razorbill

Rare and irregular winter visitor. At least 11 records: one at Messina in winter 1835 (Benoit 1840); Castellammare *ante* 1869 (Doderlein 1869–74); Stretto di

Messina 1894 and 1896 (5 birds), Palermo, Dec 1905 and winter 1907, Cefalù 1909 (MCT); 2 at Trapani, 9 Dec 1905, one at Mazara, 8 Jan 1925, 2 at I. Favignana, Nov 1970, undated specimen from W coast (Sorci *et al.* 1971b). Some undated records from Catania and Siracusa (Doderlein 1869–74).

191. FRATERCULA ARCTICA   WV
Puffin

Rare but possibly regular winter visitor, mostly off N coast, more common in the past. 8–10 at Messina (Benoit 1840), large influxes in winter 1885–1886 (Venezia 1900a, Trischitta 1918b) and Mar 1898–1906 (Giglioli 1907, Trischitta 1918b). Also recorded in 1897 (Leonardi 1897), 1911, 1914, 1918 (Trischitta 1918b). 17 records of 1–10 since 1938, 13 between 1970 and 1987: Jan (3), Feb (6), Mar (5), once May, Aug (long dead corpse) and Dec (Moltoni & Frugis 1967, Baccetti & Mongini 1981, Sorci *et al.* 1971b, 1973, M. Sarà, G. Scafidi). Sabatini (1913) reported many in winter 1912 at Aeolian Islands, where he stated it was regular.
One recovery, of a bird ringed in Great Britain.

PTEROCLIDIDAE

192. PTEROCLES SENEGALLUS   AV
Spotted Sandgrouse

Accidental visitor: 2 (one shot) near S. Croce Camerina, 28 Apr 1909 (Whitaker 1910), now at WMB.

COLUMBIDAE

193. COLUMBA LIVIA   RB
Rock Dove

Uncommon to fairly common resident breeder (*C. l. livia*), scarcer in E Sicily, but true status sometimes difficult to assess because of gene flow with feral pigeons, which are common in every town or village. Also breeds at most islets, but at I. Ustica has become extinct (Ajola 1959).
Breeding. C. l. livia. Birds in the pure form usually found in colonies of 30–80, in rocky, woody or cultivated areas up to c. 1500 m. Nests usually on cliffs up to 50 m above ground; eggs, C/1–2, Apr–Aug, unfledged young regularly as late as Dec at villages on Madonie Mts.

194. COLUMBA OENAS   PM WV RB or MB
Stock Dove

Now rare and irregular passage migrant and winter visitor (*C. o. oenas*), Oct–Apr, mostly in autumn, but up to 20 years ago regular and sometimes fairly common (Massa 1985, S. Baglieri). Only one recent winter record: 31 near Avola, 29 Jan 1984 (S. Baglieri).
Breeding. C. o. oenas. Rare and local (resident?) breeder. One pair building a nest at Ficuzza wood, mid Jun 1980 (Massa 1985), is the only proof of breeding. A few summer records at Madonie, Sicani and Caronie Mts suggest breeding (Orlando 1937, Krampitz 1956, Massa 1985, M. Sarà).

195. **COLUMBA PALUMBUS**   RB WV PM

Woodpigeon

Fairly common resident, autumn passage migrant and winter visitor (*C. p. palumbus*). Numbers increase early Sep to Feb, peaking late Oct to Dec with flocks of 10s (sometimes 100s up to 300), probably most of them migrants. Some evidence of spring passage at I. Ustica, Feb–Mar (Ajola 1959).

Breeding. C. p. palumbus. Fairly common resident, scarcer in W Sicily. Occurs in woods, thickets or cultivated areas (e.g. almond tree plantations), from sea level up to 1800 m, scarcer in plains along coasts. Nests in trees, 2–8 m above ground; eggs, C/2, late Apr to May.

One recovery, of a bird ringed in France.

196. **STREPTOPELIA DECAOCTO**   AV

Collared Dove

Accidental visitor. 2 confirmed records: one at I. Linosa, Apr 1984 (M. Lo Valvo) and one at I. Pantelleria, Sep 1985 (F. Lo Valvo).

197. **STREPTOPELIA TURTUR**   PM MB

Turtle Dove

Common spring passage migrant (*S. t. turtur*), mainly at islets and along S coast, apparently decreasing in recent years. Spring passage late Mar to early-mid Jun, peaking late Apr to early May (sometimes mid May). Along S coast arrives in flocks usually up to 50, mostly in early mornings, sometimes 1000s in a day in some areas. Fewer and in smaller flocks on return passages, late Aug to mid-late Oct, peaking early Sep.

Breeding. S. t. turtur. Fairly common and widespread migrant breeder from sea level up to c. 1100 m, in woods, open areas with scattered trees or valley bottoms and thickets. Eggs, C/2, May-Jun, with some evidence of second broods. Most breeding areas deserted by mid Aug.

7 recoveries, of birds ringed in Czechoslovakia (3), Tunisia (2), Poland (1) and N Italy (1).

198. **STREPTOPELIA SENEGALENSIS**   AV

Palm Dove

Accidental visitor. 3 confirmed records: one at I. Pantelleria, 30 Aug 1974 (Brucher & Lehmann 1975), one at Simeto, 17 Nov 1985 (A. Ciaccio), one at I. Linosa, late Apr 1987 (M. Lo Valvo).

CUCULIDAE

199. **CLAMATOR GLANDARIUS**   PM

Great Spotted Cuckoo

Rare spring passage migrant, early Feb to May, mostly Mar. Most years unrecorded. Once Jun and Sep, 2 records each Jan and Oct.

200. **CUCULUS CANORUS**   PM MB

Cuckoo

Fairly common spring passage migrant (*C. c. canorus*), late Mar to mid May, peaking mid to late Apr, usually singly. Scarcer on return passage, early Aug to mid

Oct. Occasionally on passage early Jun and early Jul (cf. Whitaker 1899d). Once mid Mar.

Breeding. C. c. canorus. Probably a fairly common and widespread migrant breeder in wooded areas from sea level up to c. 1800 m. Highest densities are in pine forest on Aetna. Occurs in breeding areas from early May, but no details. One old record of egg in nest of *Saxicola torquata* (Whitaker 1920 ms).

201. COCCYZUS AMERICANUS   AV

Yellow-billed Cuckoo

Accidental visitor: one shot near Giarre, 2 Nov 1932, (Di Mauro *in* Moltoni 1933), specimen preserved at MM, lost in the Museum's fire 1943.

TYTONIDAE

202. TYTO ALBA   RB PM? WV?

Barn Owl

Common and widespread resident breeder (*T. a. alba*), from sea level up to c. 1500 m. Resident also at some islets (Aeolian, Egadi and Pantelleria). Possibly a scarce passage migrant and winter visitor (*T. a. alba*); unusual abundance noted in winter 1950 (Ajola 1951b) and in autumn-winter 1969–70 (Massa & Cangialosi 1970b). Occasional at I. Ustica and Pelagian Islands (Ajola 1959, Moltoni 1970); one flying off Gulf of Palermo, 10 Oct 1980 (T. Di Natale). Small mammals, particularly Savi's Pine Vole *Microtus savii* (23–74%), constitute the main diet in Sicily (Massa 1981a, Massa & Sarà 1982, Sarà & Massa 1985, Siracusa & Ciaccio 1985, Catalisano & Massa 1987a). Contoli *et al.* (1978) found, exceptionally, remains of bats in pellets from Vendicari.

Breeding. T. a. alba. In open and cultivated areas, towns, villages, sometimes wooded areas. Nests in buildings, old churches, ruins, bridges, viaducts, cliffs. Eggs, C/2–6, usually C/4, Apr–Jun; second broods not confirmed. Young fledge late May to late Jul, sometimes early Aug.

STRIGIDAE

203. OTUS SCOPS   RB MB? PM WV

Scops Owl

Common resident breeder (*O. s. scops*), widespread throughout, mainly up to 1200 m, but occurs up to 1700 m on Aetna (M. Sarà). Breeds at some islets (Aeolian and possibly Egadi). Unknown if all breeders are strictly resident or partly migrant. Fairly common passage migrant (*O. s. scops*) along coasts and at islets, early Mar to early May, and, much more numerous, Sep-Nov, usually peaking late Sep to mid Oct. Very abundant in the past century during autumn migration at I. Ustica (Doderlein 1893). Summer diet consists of arthropods (60%) and small mammals (40%).

Breeding. O. s. scops. In wooded or cultivated areas with scattered trees, gardens in suburban and urban areas. Nests in holes in trees, buildings, ruins, walls or viaducts. Calls Feb-Jul, less frequently in summer and Nov-Jan. Eggs, C/2–5, usually C/4, late Apr to late May, fledged young early Jul to early Aug.

2 recoveries, of birds ringed in Tunisia (1) and Morocco (1).

204. BUBO BUBO   FB

Eagle Owl

Former breeder; last confirmed breeding was at St. Nicola l'Arena, summer 1935 (Orlando 1957a). Doderlein (1869–74) listed it as rare on Madonie Mts and Ficuzza wood, and at Mt. Pellegrino he collected a chick, which is preserved with 2 adults at MZUP. Giglioli (1890) listed it as a rare breeder near Messina and Palermo, scarce at Modica, and reported breeding in Apr at Manche di Alfano near Geraci, Madonie Mts. 25 Sicilian specimens known, 12 collected 1932–1976: Geraci, autumn 1932 (labelled Oct 1920 in coll. Orlando) and St. Giuseppe Iato, autumn 1935 (Orlando 1957a); Bisacquino, Nov 1938 (Ajola 1939); Racalmuto, 1940 (G. Salvo); Scillato, autumn 1941, Prizzi, Mar 1945, Madonie Mts, c. 1948 (Orlando 1957a); near Enna, Nov 1954 (Priolo 1972); Cefalù, Jun 1955 (Orlando 1957a); Baucina, winter 1961 (M. Sarà); Cesarò, Jun 1964 (Priolo 1972b) and Capodarso, Jan 1976 (A. Dimarca). Extinction probably more recent than last breeding record suggests. Calls heard by Baglieri & Fagotto (1978) along Anapo river probably belonged to an escaped bird. Extinction has been confirmed by extensive surveys in all suitable areas aided by tape recorded calls, 1983–86 (Sarà *et al.* 1987).

Orlando (1957a) described *B. b. meridionalis* for Sicily and S Italy, but Vaurie (1965) considered *meridionalis* a synonym of *B. b. bubo*.

205. ATHENE NOCTUA   RB PM?

Little Owl

Common resident breeder (*A. n. noctua*), from sea level up to 800–900 m, scarcer up to 1700 m at Madonie Mts (Krampitz 1958, M. Sarà). Breeding at I. Lipari stated by Sabatini (1912) and Moltoni & Frugis (1967), not confirmed 1979–1983 (Massa 1985). Occasional records at islets (where it does not breed) and at unusual localities along coasts are the only evidence of small movements from and to Sicily.

Breeding. A. n. noctua. In open, cultivated and rocky areas, scarcer in urban areas, rare in woods. More widespread in Cen and W Sicily and at Iblei and Peloritani Mts. Nests in buildings, mainly ruins, bridges, viaducts, old trees, heaps of stones and sometimes in old burrows of rabbits. Calls Mar-Jun and Oct-Dec, less frequently Jan-Feb and in summer. Eggs, C/3–5 mid Apr to early May, recently fledged young early Jun to early Jul. In winter-spring, feeds mostly on arthropods (52.9%) and small mammals (42.4%), whereas in summer a high percentage of prey is arthropods (88.1%) (see also Lo Verde & Massa, in press).

206. STRIX ALUCO   RB

Tawny Owl

Fairly common but rather local resident breeder from sea level up to c. 1600 m. Occasionally wanders: 2 autumn records at Egadi Islands (Sorci *et al.* 1973).

Breeding. Cramp & Simmons (1985) suggest *S. a. sylvatica* for southern Italy, but taxonomical studies in Sicily and Italy are lacking. Occurs mainly in woods, but also in rocky habitats and open areas, sometimes near towns and villages. At Ficuzza wood 55 were counted on 4270 ha (M. Sarà). Nests in trees or old buildings. Eggs, C/4, Apr-Jun, occasionally Jul; recently fledged young late Jun to late Aug. In Sicily feeds mainly on small mammals, especially Wood Mouse *Apodemus sylvaticus* (see also Massa 1981a, Sarà & Massa 1985).

207. ASIO OTUS   PM RB

Long-eared Owl

Scarce, but easily overlooked, autumn passage migrant and winter visitor (*A. o. otus*), Oct to late Feb, mostly Dec. Occasional on passage Mar–Apr. Most records inland, so some probably refer to vagrant Sicilian birds.

Breeding. A. o. otus. Probably a rare and local resident breeder, but breeding range still unknown. Doderlein (1869–74) and Riera (1923) listed it as a scarce resident but gave no detail. Breeding proved twice: 3 unfledged young robbed from a nest near Scordia, early Apr 1978, and another brood robbed from a nest on Aetna, May 1984 — all being found later at a 'pet' shop at Catania (Ciaccio & Siracusa 1985). Recorded during breeding season in suitable breeding areas near Palazzo Adriano, at Caronie and Aetna Mts up to 1700 m, 1984–86 (M. Sarà).

208. ASIO FLAMMEUS   PM

Short-eared Owl

Uncommon passage migrant (*A. f. flammeus*), late Feb to late Apr, and mid Sep to early Dec, mostly late Sep to late Oct; 2 records, Jan. Doderlein (1869–74) and Giglioli (1907) listed it as sedentary but gave no proof of breeding.

CAPRIMULGIDAE

209. CAPRIMULGUS EUROPAEUS   PM MB

Nightjar

Uncommon to locally fairly common but decreasing passage migrant (*C. e. europaeus* and *meridionalis*), mainly in spring, late Mar to late May, peaking late Apr. Fewer on return passage, late Aug to late Oct. Occasional Dec.

Breeding. C. e. meridionalis. Scarce and local breeder (Madonie, Caronie Mts, and Aetna). Occurs in scrub and lightly wooded hills at 500–1700 m; eggs, C/2, usually mid May.

One recovery, of a bird ringed N Italy.

210. CAPRIMULGUS RUFICOLLIS   AV

Red-necked Nightjar

Accidental visitor: one San Vito Lo Capo, 3 Jun 1898 (De Stefani Perez 1898) (specimen now lost); one at Catania, 26 Apr 1948, referred to *C. r. desertorum* (Priolo 1946, 1968a).

211. CAPRIMULGUS AEGYPTIUS   AV

Egyptian Nightjar

Accidental visitor (*C. a. saharae*). 5 confirmed records: one at Agrigento (Doderlein 1869–74), one at Modica, Dec 1879, one at Palermo, 23 Apr 1899 (Whitaker 1899b) (now at WMB); one near Mazara, May c. 1955 (Sorci *et al.* 1972); one at Lentini, 30 Mar 1977 (Massa *et al.* 1979).

APODIDAE

212. APUS APUS   PM MB

Swift

Abundant passage migrant and migrant breeder (*A. a. apus*), mid Mar to mid Oct; passage obscured by large number of breeders, but peak numbers mid Apr to mid May. Less common on return passage, peaking late Jul to mid Aug. Confusion with *Apus pallidus* not always ruled out in Oct records. Once Jan.

Breeding. A. a. apus. Abundant and widespread breeder in towns and villages, but also on cliffs, from sea level up to c. 1500 m. Some local decreases noted in recent years. Also breeds at I. Pantelleria and at some of Egadi and Aeolian Islands. Very few details: some birds visit the nest as early as mid Mar, most breeders arriving early to mid Apr. Most young fledge early Jul and almost all birds have left the colonies by mid or late Jul.

213. APUS PALLIDUS   PM MB

Pallid Swift

Uncommon passage migrant, mid Mar to early Jun and Aug to late Oct, but probably overlooked; apparently more numerous on return passage.

Breeding. A. p. brehmorum (see below). Uncommon and local migrant breeder, but many colonies probably still unknown. Nests on buildings in towns (Palermo, Catania, Caltanissetta) and on sea cliffs, in colonies of up to 30 pairs. Breeding confirmed at I. Pantelleria and I. Marettimo, but may nest also at I. Salina and I. Filicudi. No details; most birds visit nests late Mar to late Aug, but a few regularly remain at colonies till early Nov.

Sicily is usually considered in the breeding range of *A. p. brehmorum* (Vaurie 1965 mentions "southern Italy"); no local study has been made and the race breeding in Sicily has not been properly ascertained.

214. APUS MELBA   PM MB

Alpine Swift

Fairly common passage migrant (*A. m. melba*), mid Mar to late May (sometimes Jun), and early Aug to early Nov; usually in 10s, sometimes in 100s mainly late Aug–Sep. Once early Dec.

Breeding. A. m. melba. Uncommon and local migrant breeder on cliffs from sea level up to c. 1000 m; largest colonies contain c. 100 birds. Also breeds at I. Lipari and probably at I. Pantelleria. Few details; fledged young mid Jul to late Aug, last recorded at colonies mid to late Oct.

ALCEDINIDAE

215. ALCEDO ATTHIS   PM WV RB or OB

Kingfisher

Fairly common autumn passage migrant and uncommon winter visitor (*A. a. atthis*) at wetlands, reservoirs and rivers, early Aug to Apr; peak numbers usually Aug–Sep. Scarce and local May–Jul.

Breeding. A. a. atthis. Most authors since Benoit (1840) have listed it as a fairly common resident, but without details. Breeding first proved 1985: one pair at nest, late Mar to Apr, at Simeto (Ciaccio 1986); deserted nests and recently fledged young recorded at Siracusa salt-pan, Jun 1985–1987. Breeding season records suggest breeding possibly in other areas.

3 recoveries, of birds ringed in Germany (1), Hungary (1) and Czechoslovakia (1).

MEROPIDAE

216. MEROPS SUPERCILIOSUS   AV

Blue-cheeked Bee-eater

Accidental visitor (*M. s. persicus*). 3 records: one at Messina, c. 1890 (Arrigoni 1929), one at Castelvetrano, May 1912 (Venezia 1912); one shot near Siracusa, May 1979 (Iapichino & Baglieri 1982). 2 doubtful records reported by Malherbe (1842–43) and Doderlein (1869–74). Regular migration erroneously reported on E coast by Zodda (1902).

217. MEROPS APIASTER   PM MB

Bee-eater

Uncommon spring passage migrant to islets and along coasts, mid Apr to early Jun, peaking late Apr to mid May. Usually 10–50 together, but passage of 100s in one day sometimes reported. Rare on return passage, late Aug to Sep. 3 records Mar, twice Oct, occasional on passage, Jul.

Breeding. First confirmed 1982, 15–18 pairs in 3 colonies near Catania (Ciaccio & Siracusa 1983), in the same area where Zuccarello-Patti (1844b) stated breeding. Deplorably and incomprehensibly these colonies were exterminated by poachers 1983–1984. One small colony recorded along a river in S Sicily (A. Ciaccio). At least 1–3 pairs bred near Niscemi, Jun 1984 (Mascara 1984a). Eggs laid late May to early Jun, recently fledged young found mid to late Jul (Ciaccio & Siracusa 1983b, Mascara 1984a).

CORACIIDAE

218. CORACIAS GARRULUS   PM MB

Roller

Scarce and decreasing spring passage migrant (*C. g. garrulus*), early Apr to late May, mostly late Apr; usually singly, most records from islets. Rare (and irregular?) on return passage, late Aug to Sep.

Breeding. *C. g. garrulus*. Uncommon and local migrant breeder; breeding population c. 200 pairs (Lo Verde & Massa 1985). More frequent in Cen and S Sicily, in open cultivated hills. Nests in old buildings, on bridges, cliffs or in river banks (Mascara 1987d). Recorded in breeding areas late Apr to mid Aug; eggs, C/2–3 mid to late May, recently fledged young Jun. Much more common in Doderlein's time.

UPUPIDAE

219. UPUPA EPOPS   PM MB WV

Hoopoe

Fairly common to common spring passage migrant (*U. e. epops*), late Feb to May, mostly late Mar to mid Apr. Occasionally mid Feb and early Jun. Fewer in autumn, early Aug to Oct. Scarce and local winter visitor, Nov–Feb (Massa 1978d); regularly overwinters at Vendicari, Biviere di Gela, near Vittoria and possibly elsewhere in S Sicily.

Breeding. *U. e. epops*. Fairly common migrant breeder, more widespread in S Sicily, in cultivated areas with scattered trees or woods, up to 1800 m, but scarcer below 500 m. Eggs, C/4–6, from mid May.

2 recoveries, of birds ringed in Poland (1) and Germany (1).

PICIDAE

220. JYNX TORQUILLA   PM WV MB

Wryneck

Uncommon to locally fairly common passage migrant, mid Mar to early May, and mid Aug to Nov, peaking Sep. Rare winter visitors, singles recorded in most years, mainly along coasts, Dec to early Feb. Once Jul at I. Panarea.

Breeding. J. t. tschusii. Rare and local migrant breeder (or resident?) in a few wooded areas on mountains (Madonie, Aetna, Peloritani and possibly Iblei). Nests in trees and walls; unfledged young early Jul. *J. t. torquilla* occurs on passage.

4 recoveries of birds ringed in Finland (2) and Hungary (2).

221. PICUS VIRIDIS   FB? AV

Green Woodpecker

Probably a former breeder (*P. v. viridis*) in the last century, but no definite breeding record. Benoit (1840) stated it was common in Sicily, but rare near Messina. Doderlein (1869–74) listed it as a rare breeder, but later (1881) as an irregular migrant from Italy. Orlando (1956c) said it occurred in the Palermo, Messina, Catania, Enna and Caltanissetta districts at the end of the last century, but that it became very rare in the first years of this century, when it was present only in Messina, Catania and Palermo districts; he also reported 2–3 shot near Castelbuono (Madonie Mts), c. 1904, one at Gibilmanna (Madonie Mts), 1916 or 1917 (preserved at MCT) and some doubtful records at Malabotte wood and Madonie Mts till 1930s. Singles recorded in pine woods on Aetna, near Bronte, 22 Nov 1981 (F. Tassi) and May 1982 (A. Priolo) were possibly vagrants from Italy.

222. DRYOCOPUS MARTIUS   AV

Black Woodpecker

Accidental visitor, only one confirmed record. Benoit (1840) listed it as very rare and probably resident near Messina. Doderlein (1869–74) listed it as very rare and reported one specimen collected at Zafferana (Mt Aetna), preserved in coll. Auteri at Catania, but in 1881 considered it an irregular migrant from Italy. Giglioli (1907) did not find Auteri's specimen in 1881, and doubted the species was present in Sicily. Trischitta (1919c) recorded one specimen from Messina, summer 1900 or 1901, in coll. Pistone and one undated specimen, probably coming from Sicily, was preserved by Sturniolo — previously in coll. Benoit (Messina), now at MCT. Judging from above references, breeding in Sicily in the past is unlikely.

223. DENDROCOPUS MAJOR   RB

Great Spotted Woodpecker

Uncommon and local resident breeder (*D. m. italiae*) in wooded areas of Peloritani, Aetna, Caronie, Madonie, Sicani and Erei Mts, from c. 100 up to c. 1800 m. High densities observed in some areas: one pair per 10 ha at bottom of wooded valley at Ficuzza (M. Sarà) and on coniferous woods on Aetna.

Breeding. D. m. italiae. In broadleaved and coniferous woods, sometimes in pine plantations, exceptionally in *Eucalyptus* plantations. Prefers mature woods but also occurs in copses with scattered old trees. Nests in holes in trees with trunks at least 25–30 cm wide, usually 40–50 cm. Eggs, C/3–5, late Apr to mid May, recently fledged young early Jun to early Jul.

The Sicilian race *Picus major siciliae* (Orlando 1956c), is considered a synonym of *D. m. italiae* by Vaurie (1965).

224. DENDROCOPUS MINOR   ·   FB?

Lesser Spotted Woodpecker

Probably former breeder. Benoit (1840) and Doderlein (1869–74) listed it as a resident breeder but much less numerous than *D. major*. Giglioli (1890) listed it as rare near Messina. Probably present till 1930s at Madonie and Caronie Mts but it died out in 1950s (Orlando 1956c). A specimen labelled Gibilmanna 1908 (Orlando 1956c) is now at MCT.

PASSERINES

ALAUDIDAE

225. AMMOMANES CINCTURUS   AV

Bar-tailed Desert Lark

Accidental visitor (*A. c. arenicolor*): one taken near Siracusa, 28 Mar 1975 (Massa *et al.* 1976).

226. MELANOCORYPHA CALANDRA   RB PM

Calandra Lark

Fairly common but decreasing resident breeder (*M. c. calandra*), more widespread in Cen and S Sicily and at Iblei Mts. A few records at islets and along coasts, Mar to early May and Oct–Nov, suggest scanty passage (Ajola 1959, Moltoni 1970, 1973a, Steinbacher 1955b). Post breeding flocks of 10s, occasionally up to 200, recorded Jul–Jan.

Breeding. M. c. calandra. In open arable land or garigue, from sea level up to c. 1000 m, highest densities in flat stoney areas near the sea. Eggs, C/4–5, late Mar to May.

227. MELANOCORYPHA BIMACULATA   AV

Bimaculated Lark

Accidental visitor: one shot near Vendicari, 4 Oct 1978 (Baglieri & Iapichino 1979).

228. CALANDRELLA BRACHYDACTYLA (=CINEREA)   PM MB

Short-toed Lark

Fairly common migrant breeder and spring passage migrant (*C. b. (=c.) brachydactyla*), early Mar to late Oct, spring passage peaking early to mid Apr. Occasional early Nov.

Breeding. C. b. (=c.) brachydactyla. Nests on the ground in open arable land, garigue or stony river beds, from sea level up to c. 900 m; more numerous in Cen Sicily, Iblei Mts and along W coast. Post breeding flocks of 10s or 100s common, Jul–Aug, in breeding areas; most leave early to mid Sep. Also breeds at all islets except Aeolian Islands and Marettimo. Eggs, C/4–5, late Apr to early Jun.

229. CALANDRELLA RUFESCENS   AV

Lesser Short-toed Lark

Accidental visitor. 4 records of singles: Siracusa salt-pan, 26 Nov 1966 (Massa *et al*. 1976), Capo Murro di Porco, 1 Nov 1975 (Massa *et al*. 1979), Capo Murro di Porco, Nov 1986 and near Siracusa 15 Feb 1987 (S. Baglieri).

The first 2 birds were referred to *C. r. heinei* (Massa *et al*. 1979).

230. GALERIDA CRISTATA   RB

Crested Lark

Common and widespread resident breeder. No evidence of any regular movements; occasionally recorded at I. Pantelleria (Moltoni 1973a).

Breeding. In open cultivated areas with scattered trees, arable land, garigue, salicornia beds, from sea level up to c. 1000 m. Also breeds at I. Favignana and I. Levanzo. Usually singly or in small family parties till Sep. Nests on the ground; eggs, C/4 (sometimes C/5), mid Apr to mid Jun. Recently fledged young recorded May–Jul.

Sicily is usually considered to be in the breeding range of *G. c. meridionalis* (Vaurie 1959), but no local study has been made and the race breeding in Sicily has not been properly ascertained.

231. LULLULA ARBOREA   RB PM

Woodlark

Uncommon but widespread resident breeder and scarce autumn passage migrant (*L. a. pallida*), Oct–Dec; some birds (migrant or resident?) overwinter along coasts, far from nearest breeding areas.

Breeding. Nests on the ground in lightly wooded hills, but also in rocky and open areas, from 200 m up to c. 1800 m. No details available.

232. ALAUDA ARVENSIS   PM RB or MB

Skylark

Common autumn passage migrant and common winter visitor (*A. a. cantarella* and *A. a. arvensis*), mid Sep to mid Apr, peaking mid Oct to mid Nov. Flocks of 10s or 100s up to 400 are common in autumn along coasts and, in winter, in open areas, particularly in Cen Sicily. Usually some evidence of spring passage, late Feb to Apr. Occasional early Sep and early May. Doderlein (1869–74) considered it was not an exaggeration when Rafinesque (1814) stated that on some days of peak autumn migration as many as one million Skylarks crossed the Gulf of Palermo daily, and over 10 million during the whole season. Such numbers were continued to be reported by many hunters up to 1950 (G. Ajola, E. Catalano), but are now very much reduced. Whitaker (1905) reported that Skylarks in the Gulf of Palermo were once regularly shot by hunters: "numbers of small boats, each with one or two gunners in them, lining the roadstead, their occupants keeping up a lively fusilade at the poor birds as they arrive in small flocks. This may be carried on for several hours, and any stranger arriving in Palermo by the daily postal steamer might imagine that a miniature naval battle was being waged, or that a revolution had broken out!".

Breeding. A. a. cantarella. Scarce and local breeder in open areas above 1000 m (Aetna and Madonie Mts). Nests on the ground, eggs, C/3–4 late Apr. No evidence whether breeding birds are resident.

233. EREMOPHILA ALPESTRIS   AV

Shore Lark

Accidental visitor. 2 collected near Messina (Pistone 1888), no date; one at
Capo Murro di Porco, May 1985 (S. Baglieri).

HIRUNDINIDAE

234. RIPARIA RIPARIA   PM

Sand Martin

Common spring passage migrant (*R. r. riparia*), early Mar to early Jun, usually
peaking late Apr to early May, when 100s or 1000s up to 3000 together, are recorded
along coasts and at wetlands. Very scarce mid Jun to Jul, perhaps in suitable
breeding habitat. Much less numerous on return passage, early Aug to late Oct,
mainly Sep. Occasionally Nov, twice Dec. Benoit (1840), Doderlein (1869–74) and
Riera (1923) claimed breeding, but gave no definite evidence. Breeding at I. Panarea
stated by Moltoni & Pirovano (1980) seems an error. Benoit (1840) and Doderlein
(1869–74) listed it as a winter visitor.
One recovery, of a bird ringed in Sweden.

235. PTYONOPROGNE RUPESTRIS   RB PM WV

Crag Martin

Uncommon and local breeder, some recorded all year in breeding areas, so
probably resident. Scarce autumn passage migrant and winter visitor, Oct–Feb
(Mar), usually in small parties, sometimes up to 50 together. Some (or most) winter
records probably refer to seasonal movements of residents, but records at islets
confirm that a small passage occurs. Has overwintered at Aeolian Islands (Moltoni
& Frugis 1967). No regular spring passage but c. 100 over Palermo, 16 Apr 1984
(T. La Mantia).
Breeding. In rocky areas from sea level up to c. 1000 m, mostly in mountains along
N coast and at Sicani Mts. Colonies of 4–5 pairs. No details, but a colony near
Cefalù was re-occupied 1–20 Mar 1985 (A. Dimarca).

236. HIRUNDO RUSTICA   PM MB

Swallow

Common passage migrant (*H. r. rustica*) early Mar to late Jun, mostly Apr to
mid May. In most autumns seems less numerous than in spring, early Aug to late
Nov, mostly Sep to mid Oct. Irregular Dec and Feb. 1–2 overwintered at Simeto, 9
Dec 1983 to 22 Jan 1984 (A. Ciaccio). Passage of 100s or 1000s in a day are frequent
at islets and in some coastal areas, e.g. Messina Straits, where 183 per hour on
average were counted 15–17 May 1979 (see also Steinbacher 1956e). Doderlein
(1869–74) referred some reddish birds to *H. r. savigny*, but the occurrence of this race
has still to be confirmed.
Breeding. H. r. rustica. Locally fairly common migrant breeder, more widespread
in Cen and S Sicily, absent at islets. Nests in farm-houses, wells, cowsheds, in open
areas or villages. Nest building from Mar; first broods early Mar to late Jun, second
broods 12–14 days after first young fledge, third brood in Jul. Of 25 pairs, 92% were
double brooded, 32% triple brooded, only 8% single brooded; eggs, C/2–7, usually
C/4–5, average C/5·7 in Mar, C/3·0 in Jul, with breeding success of 4·1 juveniles per
pair (Dimarca & Lo Valvo 1987).

8 recoveries of birds ringed in Tunisia (2), Denmark (2), Poland (1), Sweden (1), France (1) and Belgium (1).

237. HIRUNDO DAURICA   PM OB?

Red-rumped Swallow

Scarce passage migrant (*H. d. rufula*), late Mar to late May and mid Aug to Oct; usually in mixed flocks with other hirundines, singly or up to 6 together (Baglieri 1977), but c. 30 near Palermo, 10 Sep 1971 (Sorci *et al.* 1972). Most spring records are at Pelagian Islands. No definite evidence of breeding, but Priolo (1972b) recorded c. 15 birds at Calatabiano in suitable breeding habitat, Jun to late Aug 1970, and observed some birds collecting mud (to build nests?).

238. DELICHON URBICA   PM MB

House Martin

Common passage migrant and migrant breeder (*D. u. urbica*). Spring passage mid Feb to mid Jun, peaking mid Mar to early May. Migrant flocks usually of 10s or 100s up to 500, occasionally up to 1000. Scarcer on return passage, mid Aug to late Oct, with a few into Nov. Occasional early Feb and Dec. Doderlein (1869–74) recorded "many" in winter in S Sicily, but there are no recent records of birds overwintering.

Breeding. D. u. urbica. Common and widespread, probably more numerous in Cen and S Sicily, in nearly all towns or villages, and on cliffs, from sea level up to c. 1300 m. Most colonies number 20–50 pairs, but some 150 or more. First recorded at nests early Mar, most arriving late Mar to early Apr. Few details: recently fledged young late May to Sep, mostly mid Jun to Jul (first broods); most leave late Aug to mid Sep, last seen at colonies late Sep, occasionally Oct.

One recovery, of a bird ringed in England.

MOTACILLIDAE

239. ANTHUS NOVAESEELANDIAE   PM

Richard's Pipit

Rare but possibly regular passage migrant (*A. n. richardi*), at islets and along coasts, Mar–Apr and Sep–Oct, occasionally Feb and up to mid Dec, once early Jun. Usually singly, occasionally up to 6; 100–200 at I. Marettimo, 4–5 Oct 1955 (Steinbacher 1956a) seems an error. Orlando (1935) considered the species was probably overlooked.

240. ANTHUS CAMPESTRIS   PM MB

Tawny Pipit

Fairly common spring passage migrant (*A. c. campestris*), mid Mar to mid May, peaking Apr, singly or in parties up to 10. Uncommon on return passage, late Aug to late Oct. Once Jan and Dec, twice Nov.

Breeding. A. c. campestris. Uncommon migrant breeder, more widespread in western Cen and in S Sicily; also breeds at I. Marettimo. Occurs in open areas, meadows, highlands, from c. 100 up to 2300 m (Aetna), mainly above 500 m. Eggs, C/3, mid to late May, recently hatched young, mid Jun to mid Jul.

241. ANTHUS TRIVIALIS   PM OB

Tree Pipit

Common spring passage migrant (*A. t. trivialis*), early Mar to late May, peaking early Apr to early May. Numbers vary, 10s or 100s in one day, mainly at islets. Less numerous on return passage, late Aug to early Nov. Once Jan (Moltoni 1973a) and Dec.

Breeding. A. t. trivialis. Recorded breeding once only (Massa 1976b, Lo Verde & Massa 1985) – just fledged young with adult at Piano Cervi (Madonie Mts), Jun 1973.

242. ANTHUS PRATENSIS   PM WV

Meadow Pipit

Common autumn passage migrant and winter visitor (*A. p. pratensis*) in every kind of open habitat, mid Oct to late Mar; heavy passage sometimes recorded, late Oct to Nov. Scarce Apr, occasional May; 2 records late Sep. Breeding claimed by Steinbacher (1955b) seems an error.

243. ANTHUS CERVINUS   PM

Red-throated Pipit

Fairly common spring passage migrant, early Mar to early Jun, mostly early Apr to early May. Recorded in variable numbers, usually singly or up to 30 together, mainly at coastal wetlands. Scarcer on return passage, mid Oct to early Dec. Once early Jul (2 birds) and Jan.

One recovery, of a bird ringed in Sweden.

244. ANTHUS SPINOLETTA   PM WV

Water Pipit

Scarce autumn passage migrant and winter visitor (*A. s. spinoletta*), mid Oct to late Mar, mostly Oct-Dec. Some evidence of irregular spring passage, Mar. Once Apr and Aug (Moltoni 1970, Moltoni & Frugis 1967). Usually recorded at wetlands, singly or up to 8 together. Rock Pipit *A. s. littoralis* has been recorded 8 times at Malta (Sultana & Gauci 1982), but never in Sicily.

245. MOTACILLA FLAVA   PM OB

Yellow Wagtail

Common spring passage migrant, early Mar to early Jun, peaking mid Apr to early May when 100s, and up to 1000 together, recorded at wetlands, islets and along coasts. Uncommon mid Jun to Jul. Usually in rather smaller numbers on return passage, early Aug to late Oct, peaking Sep. Irregular Nov, once Dec.

M. f. flava is the most numerous race, followed by *M. f. cinereocapilla; M. f. feldegg* is usually the commonest in the first period of spring passage. *M. f. thunbergi* is rare, but possibly regular. 4 confirmed records of *M. f. iberiae*: Mar, Apr, Jun and Oct. 3 records of *M. f. flavissima*: Apr (2) and Sep. One confirmed record of *M. f. beema*: Palermo, 1931 (Orlando 1936b). Races are sometimes difficult to ascertain due to the occurrence of hybrids, e.g. birds resembling *feldegg* but with pale superciliary stripes are recorded in most years and were reported as *xanthophris* or as *superciliaris*. The few birds recorded mid Jun to Jul are usually *cinereocapilla*, but 1–2 *feldegg* oversummered at Longarini, Jun–Jul 1984, and at Trapani salt-pan, 1986 (S. Surdo).

Breeding. M. f. cinereocapilla. Occasional breeder; Doderlein (1869–74) and Krampitz (1958) listed it as breeder, but recent records are few: one pair at Biviere di Cesarò (1250 m), Jun 1974; at least one pair bred at Biviere di Gela in 1984, when 4 recently fledged young were recorded 1 Jul, 15 pairs in 1985 (Dimarca *et al.* 1987).

2 recoveries, of birds ringed in N Italy (1) and Nigeria (1).

246. MOTACILLA CITREOLA   AV

Citrine Wagtail

Accidental visitor (*M. c. citreola*): one male at Siracusa salt-pan, 12 May 1986

247. MOTACILLA CINEREA   WV RB PM

Grey Wagtail

Fairly common autumn passage migrant and winter visitor (*M. c. cinerea*), Sep to Apr, mostly mid Oct to Feb, singly or up to 3–5 together.

Breeding. M. c. cinerea. Uncommon resident breeder, more widespread in N Sicily and at Iblei and Sicani Mts. Occurs along rivers, streams, near lakes or little dams, but also on sea cliffs and in old towns (e.g. Palermo where it is increasing), from sea level up to c. 1800 m. Eggs, C/4–5 from mid Mar, fledged young from early May. Double brooded.

One recovery, of a bird ringed in Malta.

248. MOTACILLA ALBA   WV PM RB

White Wagtail

Common autumn passage migrant and winter visitor (*M. a. alba*), late Aug to late Mar, mostly from mid Oct. Winter roosts of 100s or 1000s up to 3000 recorded in many towns and villages, Nov to late Feb. Slight evidence of spring passage, Mar to Apr. One confirmed record of *M. a. yarrelli*, Nov 1973 (Massa 1976b).

Breeding. M. a. alba. Uncommon and local resident breeder from sea level up to c. 1800 m, usually in open areas near rivers or streams. Nests in walls, ruins or trees; one pair regularly bred on a ship-wreck in Siracusa harbour. Eggs, C/4–5, Apr–May.

One recovery, of a bird ringed in Hungary.

BOMBYCILLIDAE

249. BOMBYCILLA GARRULUS   AV

Waxwing

Accidental visitor (*B. g. garrulus*). 5 records of singles: Cefalù, 1963; Randazzo, 23 Jan 1966 and 6 Feb 1966 (specimens at MCR); Iblei Mts, Nov 1975 (S. Baglieri); Capo Gallo, 23 Mar 1984 (G. Guadagna).

CINCLIDAE

250. CINCLUS CINCLUS   RB

Dipper

Rare resident breeder above 400 and up to 1200 m, greatly decreasing because of transformation and canalisation of rivers. Probably vagrant in autumn: some shot at Prizzi reservoir, Oct 1970, far from known breeding areas.

Breeding. C. c. meridionalis. Doderlein (1869–74) listed it as fairly common along rivers near S. Giuseppe Iato and at Madonie Mts. Found near Nicosia (Orlando, *in* Krampitz 1958) and along Alcantara river (Priolo 1954), and along Sosio river, but breeding never confirmed (Krampitz 1958). Breeding confirmed at Madonie (between Gangi and S. Mauro Castelverde) and possible in 4 areas (Mt Soro, Novara di Sicilia, Mandanici, Anapo river), 1979–1983 (Massa 1985). No recent records at Alcantara river, where it still bred in 1970s (A. Priolo). Nests in holes between rocks or under wooded slopes along rivers; eggs, no figure, usually May, recently fledged young Jun–Jul.

TROGLODYTIDAE

251. TROGLODYTES TROGLODYTES   RB PM
Wren

Common and widespread resident breeder (*T. t. troglodytes*) from sea level up to c. 2300 m; also breeds at Aeolian Islands and has colonised I. Favignana in recent years. Some evidence of small passage at islets (Pantelleria, Egadi) where it is occasional, Sep–Oct (Moltoni 1973, Sorci *et al.* 1973).

Breeding. T. t. troglodytes. In a variety of habitats, mainly in woods with undergrowth and rocky areas with dense vegetation; also in citrus plantations and urban areas. Highest density recorded: 35 pairs per 10 ha in surburban areas of Palermo (Lo Valvo *et al.* 1985). Birds building nests recorded from mid Feb; nests placed in crevices and holes, c. 45–500 cm above ground, eggs, C/4–5, mainly Mar–Apr, unfledged young occasionally Jul (T. La Mantia).

PRUNELLIDAE

252. PRUNELLA MODULARIS   WV PM
Dunnock (Hedgesparrow)

Uncommon autumn passage migrant and winter visitor (*P. m. modularis*), late Oct to late Mar, mostly Dec-Feb; slight evidence of spring passage, late Feb to mid Apr, especially at I. Ustica. Occasionally from mid Sep, once late Apr and Aug (Orlando 1937c). Doderlein (1869–74) listed it as partly resident but this is unlikely. Krampitz (1958) recorded singing males at Piano Zucchi, 1100 m, Jun 1957, but no recent confirmation. Vaurie (1959) says it breeds in Sicily, probably referring to Doderlein.

253. PRUNELLA COLLARIS   WV PM
Alpine Accentor

Scarce passage migrant and winter visitor (*P. c. collaris*), Oct to late Mar, mainly Nov-Dec, usually on highest mountains (Rocca Busambra, Caronie, Madonie); singly or in parties up to 10 (Priolo 1965b, 1972b, Orlando 1967a), but at Rocca Busambra c. 100, late Dec 1970 (Sorci *et al.* 1972), c. 200 early Dec 1973, and 10s, 6 Mar 1977.

TURDIDAE

254. CERCOTRICHAS GALACTOTES   PM
Rufous Bush Chat

Rare spring passage migrant (*C. g. galactotes*), possibly regular at Pelagian Islands and at I. Pantelleria, as it is in nearby Malta (Sultana & Gauci 1982). 15

records of 1–3 since 1956, early Apr to mid May, only 2 in mainland Sicily (Orlando 1957b, Moltoni 1970, 1973a, Fantin 1975, Cambi & Cambi 1977, Iapichino & Baglieri 1982). One undated record reported by Doderlein (1869–74). The few specimens examined belong to *C. g. galactotes*.

255. ERITHACUS RUBECULA   WV PM RB

Robin

Abundant autumn passage migrant and winter visitor (*E. r. rubecula*), late Sep to early Apr, mostly early to mid Oct to mid Mar; usually only slight evidence of spring passage, Mar; scarce mid to late Apr but occasionally recorded till Jun in wintering areas. Fidelity to wintering site noted at Palermo.

Breeding. E. r. rubecula. Locally fairly common resident breeder in woods with thick undergrowth from 400 up to c. 1800 m; 14 pairs per 10 ha counted at Ficuzza wood (M. Sarà).

13 recoveries, of birds ringed in Poland (2), Germany (2), Czechoslovakia (2), USSR (2), Malta (1), Austria (1), Sweden (1), Finland (1) and Hungary (1).

256. LUSCINIA MEGARHYNCHOS   PM MB

Nightingale

Common passage migrant and migrant breeder (*L. m. megarhynchos*). Spring passage late Mar to mid May, peaking early to mid Apr. Occasional mid Mar. Scarcer on return passage, mid Aug to early Oct.

Breeding. L. m. megarhynchos. Widespread migrant breeder from sea level up to c. 1200 m, in woods or areas with thick vegetation. Few details: singing males late Mar to Jul, recently fledged young late Jun to Jul.

One ringed in Sicily recovered in Libya.

257. LUSCINIA SVECICA   PM WV

Bluethroat

Scarce passage migrant, late Feb to early May and late Sep to early Dec. Possibly a regular winter visitor at large reedbeds of Biviere di Gela and Siracusa salt-pan, with at least 25 records of 1–3, late Dec to Jan 1974–1987 (Massa *et al.* 1979, Iapichino & Baglieri 1982, A. Dimarca). Both *L. s. svecica* and *L. s. cyanecula* occur; only 2 confirmed records of *L. s. svecica*: Palermo, Oct 1930 (Orlando 1935a) and Gela, 23 Dec 1983 (Mascara 1985).

258. PHOENICURUS OCHRUROS   WV PM RB

Black Redstart

Fairly common autumn passage migrant and winter visitor (*P. o. gibraltariensis*), early Oct to mid Mar, peak numbers Nov–Jan; scarce late Mar, occasional Apr outside breeding areas. Overwinters also in urban areas.

Breeding. P. o. gibraltariensis. Uncommon and local resident, more widespread in N Sicily. Occurs in rocky open areas or bushy and wooded hills, from 300 up to c. 1800 m. Eggs, C/3–4, early Apr to mid Jun, recently fledged young late Apr to early Jul.

One recovery, of a bird ringed in Germany.

259. PHOENICURUS PHOENICURUS   PM MB or OB

Redstart

Fairly common to locally common passage migrant, (*P. p. phoenicurus*), occasional mid to late Mar, main passage early Apr to early May, peaking mid to late Apr, last seen early Jun. Once early Mar. Return passage mid to late Aug to early Nov, peaking Sep to early Oct. No satisfactory winter record. Up to 50 may be recorded in the same area at islets or along coasts.

Breeding. P. p. phoenicurus. Minà Palumbo (1853) and Doderlein (1869–74) stated that a few pairs bred in mountains. Evidence of breeding (pairs carrying food) twice recently: edge of pine forest at Aetna 1750 m above sea, Jun 1982, and edge of beech forest at Madonie Mts, c. 1800 m, Jun 1983.

260. PHOENICURUS MOUSSIERI   AV

Moussier's Redstart

Accidental visitor: one at I. Lampedusa, 27 Feb 1987 (Lo Verde 1987).

261. SAXICOLA RUBETRA   PM

Whinchat

Fairly common passage migrant, early Apr to late May, peaking late Apr to early May, irregularly from mid Mar; singly or up to 50 in the same area mainly at islets. Scarcer on return passage, mid Aug to late Oct, mostly Sep. Occasionally Nov to early Dec; at least 2 at I. Pantelleria, Jan 1971 (Moltoni 1973a); one (locality unknown), late Jan, at MCT; 2 at Mozia, 2 Feb 1983 (F. Germi); one at Siracusa, 19 Feb 1977, probably an early migrant. Breeding claimed by Doderlein (1869–74) and Krampitz (1958) was never confirmed.

262. SAXICOLA TORQUATA   RB WV PM

Stonechat

Common resident breeder, passage migrant and winter visitor (*S. t. rubicola*), with increased numbers early Oct to Mar. Peak numbers at islets and along coasts usually mid Oct to Nov.

Breeding. S. t. rubicola. Common and widespread resident in open cultivated or natural areas from sea level up to 1920 m (Aetna). Aeolian Islands colonised in 1980s. Nests on the ground or on small slopes, eggs, C/3–6 (usually C/5), mid Mar to early Jun, fledged young from early Apr; double brooded.

S. t. archimedes Clancey 1949 (from Sicily) is a synonym of *S. t. rubicola* (Vaurie 1959).

263. OENANTHE ISABELLINA   PM

Isabelline Wheatear

Scarce spring passage migrant, now regular, late Feb to mid Apr. First recorded in 1974 near Siracusa (Baglieri 1974a), since when 1–20 birds are recorded annually near there, with 6 records from I. Linosa, I. Marettimo and W Sicily (Massa *et al.* 1976, 1979, Iapichino *in* Toso 1981, Iapichino & Baglieri 1982). One autumn record: one at I. Alicudi, 4 Oct 1977 (Massa *et al.* 1979).

264. OENANTHE OENANTHE   PM MB

Common Wheatear

Common passage migrant (*O. o. oenanthe*), mid Mar to early Jun, usually peaking late Mar to mid Apr, and early Aug to early Nov, peaking Sep. Occasional early Mar and late Nov. 10s, and up to 100–200 together regularly counted at islets and along coasts. 5 confirmed records of *O. o. leucorhoa*, all singles: at I. Pantelleria, late Aug 1966 and 28 Aug 1971 (Moltoni 1973a); at I. Linosa, 4 May 1967 and 26 Apr 1982; at I. Marettimo, 20 Apr 1974.

Breeding. O. o. oenanthe. Widespread and locally fairly common migrant breeder, mainly in Cen Sicily, in open areas and on arable, from c. 100 m up to c. 2000 m (Aetna), more numerous above 700 m. Few details; eggs, C/2–3, late Apr to early May, recently fledged young mostly mid Jun to early Jul.

3 recoveries, of birds ringed in Tunisia (2) and Hungary (1).

265. OENANTHE HISPANICA   PM OB

Black-eared Wheatear

Uncommon to fairly common spring passage migrant, mid Mar to early Jun, mostly mid to late Apr, singly or up to 10 in the same locality. Scarcer on return passage, late Aug to late Sep. Once Oct. Both *O. h. hispanica* and *O. h. melanoleuca* occur, the latter in slightly larger numbers.

Breeding. O. h. melanoleuca. Males holding territories recorded on Aetna, Jun 1982, and near Caltanissetta, Jul 1982 and Jun 1983. Two nests with 5 and 3 unfledged young found in a rocky area near Caltanissetta, 12 Jun 1986; one pair with 4 unfledged young at Biviere di Gela, 18 Jun 1986 (A. Dimarca, A. Longo). Steinbacher (1955b) supposed breeding at I. Favignana.

266. OENANTHE DESERTI   AV

Desert Wheatear

Accidental visitor (*O. d. atrogularis* — Massa *et al.* 1979). 8 records of singles: Palermo, 20 Nov 1891 (Giglioli 1907); Siracusa, 20 Mar 1973 (Baglieri 1973b); Siracusa, 9 Mar 1975, 27 Apr 1975, 8 Mar 1976 and 24 Mar 1977 (Massa *et al.* 1976, 1979); I. Linosa, 7 Sep 1981 (not 1982 as reported by Iapichino & Baglieri 1982); Siracusa, 18 Mar 1982 (Iapichino & Baglieri 1982).

267. OENANTHE LEUCURA   PM OB?

Black Wheatear

True status uncertain, probably rare and irregular passage migrant (and occasional breeder?). Singles recorded at Messina, May 1902 (*O. l. syenitica*, Arrigoni 1929), near Palermo, "summer" 1902 and 11 Sep 1935 (Orlando 1936a); at Lo Zucco Montelepre, Apr 1967, 3 May 1968, 28 Apr 1969 and Sep 1969 (Massa 1973b). Egadi Islands: singles at Favignana and Marettimo, May 1968 (F. Krapp), one at Marettimo, 7 Jun 1971 (Massa 1973b). Aeolian Islands: 2 at Lipari, 9 Jun 1911 (Nagy 1912), one at Vulcano, 11 Jan 1967 (Moltoni & Frugis 1967). Doderlein (1869–74) listed it as an uncommon breeder, Riera (1923) as "common" in stone plains around Ragusa, but neither gave any breeding details.

268. MONTICOLA SAXATILIS   PM MB
Rock Thrush

Scarce spring passage migrant, mid Mar to late May, mostly Apr. Irregular on return passage, late Aug to mid Oct.

. *Breeding.* Rare and local breeder. Minà Palumbo (1857) supposed breeding at Madonie Mts. Breeding recently confirmed at Aetna and Madonie, between 1400 and 1800 m (Lo Valvo 1983). Birds visited nests late May, recently fledged young late Jun. Breeding thought possible at lower altitudes (Salvo 1984a), not confirmed later.

269. MONTICOLA SOLITARIUS   RB
Blue Rock Thrush

Fairly common and widespread resident breeder (*M. s. solitarius*) in Sicily and at all islets (especially Levanzo and Favignana); now absent at I. Linosa, where recorded by Moltoni (1970), Oct–Mar. No evidence of regular movements or migration, but locally commoner in winter along coasts and in towns.

Breeding. M. s. solitarius. In rocky areas with garigue, mountain or sea cliffs, also in suburban areas, from sea level up to c. 1700 m (Madonie Mts). Nests in holes in cliffs, caverns and old buildings; few details: eggs, C/4–5, late Apr to early Jun, recently fledged young early May to late Jun.

270. ZOOTHERA DAUMA   AV
White's Thrush

Accidental visitor: one shot at I. Ustica, 12 Oct 1974 (Massa *et al.* 1979).

271. TURDUS TORQUATUS   PM WV
Ring Ouzel

Scarce autumn passage migrant, early Oct to Nov, usually singly, occasionally up to 12 together; rare (and irregular?) winter visitor, Dec–Jan, and spring passage migrant, mid Mar to May. Occasional Sep. Both *T. t. torquatus* and *T. t. alpestris* occur, the latter apparently more numerous. Erroneously listed as breeder by Fusco Rao (1903–1907).

One recovery, of a bird ringed in Germany.

272. TURDUS MERULA   RB PM WV
Blackbird

Common resident breeder (*T. m. merula*), probably increasing. Colonised Aeolian Islands in early 1980s; one recent breeding record at I. Favignana (M. Sarà). Common autumn passage migrant (*T. m. merula*) and winter visitor, late Sep to mid Mar, mostly Nov-Jan. Occasional Apr at islets.

Breeding. T. m. merula. In every kind of well vegetated area, woods, groves, citrus plantations, valley bottoms, gardens, from sea level up to c. 2000 m (Aetna). High density in suburban areas of Palermo: 36 pairs per 10 ha (Lo Valvo *et al.* 1985). Nests in trees, occasionally on the ground. Eggs, C/2–5, usually C/3, late Mar to early Aug, recently fledged young mid Apr to early Sep, mostly late Apr to early Jul. Second broods usual, third probably occasional. Breeding success, 1–3 juveniles per pair.

5 recoveries, of birds ringed in Yugoslavia (2), Hungary (2) and Czechoslovakia (1).

273. TURDUS PILARIS   WV

Fieldfare

Scarce to locally fairly common winter visitor in highly variable numbers, Nov to Feb, mostly Dec–Jan. Once late Mar. Singly or up to 50 together, but local influxes of 100s sometimes reported.

274. TURDUS PHILOMELOS   PM WV

Song Thrush

Common autumn passage migrant and winter visitor (*T. p. philomelos*), first arrivals mid to late Sep, main passage mid Oct to early Dec, less numerous mid Dec to Feb. Spring passage Feb–Mar with a few till late Apr, usually fairly common. Occasional May and late Aug. No systematic count, but 100s in one day are common in many localities during main autumn passage, and in some also in spring (e.g. I. Ustica). Breeding stated by some authors (Doderlein 1869–74, Massa 1976b) was never confirmed, and seems unlikely.

4 recoveries, of birds ringed in Italy (2), Tunisia (1), Czechoslovakia (1). One ringed in Sicily recovered in Tunisia.

275. TURDUS ILIACUS   PM WV

Redwing

Scarce to uncommon autumn passage migrant and winter visitor (*T. i. iliacus*), Oct-Feb, peak numbers Nov-Dec. Singly or in parties up to 20. Slight evidence of spring passage at I. Ustica, Feb-Apr (Ajola 1959).

One recovery, of a bird ringed in Norway.

276. TURDUS VISCIVORUS   WV PM RB

Mistle Thrush

Winter visitor (*T. v. viscivorus*) in variable numbers, usually scarce, late Sep to late Mar; at islets some evidence of passage, late Sep to Nov and Mar; once late Aug and twice early Sep at I. Pantelleria.

Breeding. T. v. viscivorus. Scarce and local resident breeder at Madonie, Peloritani and Aetna Mts, probably also at Sicani Mts, from 400 up to c. 1700 m. Nests in deciduous woods. Few details: singing males recorded May, eggs, C/3, or unfledged young Jun-Jul.

SYLVIIDAE

277. CETTIA CETTI   RB

Cetti's Warbler

Common and widespread resident breeder (*C. c. cetti*), numbers probably increasing in recent years, as suggested by recent breeding at Aeolian Islands, where unrecorded by Moltoni & Frugis (1967). Malta has been colonised in last 25 years (Sultana & Gauci 1982).

Breeding. C. c. cetti. Occurs in wetlands, along rivers and canals, but also in well vegetated areas far from water: plantations, valley bottoms, maquis, brambles, also in suburban areas, from sea level up to c. 850 m. Highest densities in reedbeds: e.g. 6 pairs per 0·5 ha in a reedbed near Caltanissetta, where 3 young per nest were found early Jul (A. Dimarca).

The Sicilian race *Cettia cetti schiebeli* Rokitansky is a synonym of *C. c. cetti* (Vaurie 1959).

278. CISTICOLA JUNCIDIS   RB

Fan-tailed Warbler

C. j. cisticola at I. Pantelleria (Foschi 1968, Moltoni 1973), *C. j. juncidis* elsewhere. Common and widespread resident breeder and at some islets: Aeolian, Levanzo, Favignana, Pantelleria, and Ustica. In the latter it was unrecorded by Ajola (1959). No evidence of regular movements; one at I. Lampione, near I. Lampedusa, 26 Sep 1980.

Breeding. C. j. juncidis. Widespread in open areas from sea level up to c. 1000 m. Occurs in garigue, cultivated areas (mainly *Graminaceae*), meadows, wetlands. Few details; eggs, C/5, early May to mid Jul, double brooded.

279. LOCUSTELLA LUSCINIOIDES   AV

Savi's Warbler

Apparently an accidental visitor (*L. l. luscinioides*), recorded only by Stresemann (1943, 1954) at Biviere di Lentini, where breeding supposed, Apr 1943. Listed by Schembri (1843) as accidental near Catania and Siracusa. As it is almost annual at Malta (Sultana & Gauci 1982), this species is surely overlooked in Sicily.

280. ACROCEPHALUS MELANOPOGON   WV PM OB

Moustached Warbler

Uncommon autumn passage migrant and winter visitor, Nov to early Mar, mostly Dec-Feb. Up to 15 or 40 counted overwintering at large reedbeds, e.g. Siracusa salt-pan, Simeto and Biviere di Gela. Occasional on passage Apr and Oct.

Breeding. Priolo (1948, 1954) listed it as resident in wetlands near Catania, where he found one unfledged young, 12 Apr, but unrecorded there in breeding season since 1960s. Singles at L. Soprano, in suitable breeding habitat, 2 May 1982 and 15 Jul 1983 (A. Dimarca). Lynes (1912) listed it as abundant at Biviere di Lentini, where he found 14 nests, 6–8 Jun 1907, 6 of them empty, 6 with eggs, C/3–4.

281. ACROCEPHALUS PALUDICOLA   AV

Aquatic Warbler

Accidental visitor. 4 confirmed records: one at Castellamare, Aug 1924 and one near Palermo, 27 Apr 1936, specimens at MCT; one at Lake of Preola, Jun 1966, was probably a late migrant, not a breeder as supposed by Sorci *et al.* (1973); 1–3 recorded at Simeto, 5–9 Oct 1983 (A. Ciaccio). Doderlein (1869–74) listed it as common breeder in wetlands near Catania but gave no definite proof.

282. ACROCEPHALUS SCHOENOBAENUS   PM

Sedge Warbler

Uncommon to locally fairly common spring passage migrant, early Mar to mid May; up to 30 together regular at Siracusa salt-pan, early to mid Apr. Scarce on return passage, late Aug to late Oct. Easily overlooked. Erroneously listed in past as resident breeder and winter visitor (Stresemann 1943, Sorci *et al.* 1972, 1973).

283. ACROCEPHALUS PALUSTRIS   AV

Marsh Warbler

Accidental visitor. 2 confirmed records: one shot at Torto river, 18 Sep 1936, specimen now at MCT; one singing male at Misilmeri, 16 Apr 1953 (Steinbacher 1955b). Listed by Malherbe (1842–43) without details.

284. ACROCEPHALUS SCIRPACEUS   MB PM

Reed Warbler

Locally fairly common migrant breeder (*A. s. scirpaceus*), mainly along S and SE coasts; some evidence of passage, late Mar to May and late Aug to mid Oct. Once early Nov. Sorci *et al.* (1973) claimed that some birds overwintered, but this seems unlikely.

Breeding. A. s. scirpaceus. Nests in large or small reedbeds, wetlands, canals, rivers, from sea level up to 650 m. Breeding areas re-occupied late Mar to mid Apr, birds building nests recorded from early Apr, fledged young late May to Jul; one nest, C/4, in mid Jun was close to 2 others with recently fledged young (S. Baglieri). Most breeders probably leave by mid Aug. No complete census, but 20–30 pairs estimated at Biviere di Gela (A. Dimarca), 20–25 pairs at Siracusa salt-pan and nearby canals, May 1985 and c. 50 pairs at Pergusa, Jun 1981.

285. ACROCEPHALUS ARUNDINACEUS   PM MB

Great Reed Warbler

Uncommon passage migrant (*A. a. arundinaceus*) early Apr to mid May and mid Aug to mid Oct. Occasionally early Jun, once mid Nov.

Breeding. A. a. arundinaceus. Scarce and local migrant breeder at a few large reedbeds (Biviere di Gela, L. Soprano, Pergusa); breeding population less than 50 pairs. Much more common in past when breeding habitat was plentiful (Doderlein 1869–74). Few details: recorded in breeding sites mid-late Apr to mid Aug; nests, 55–145 cm above water level, eggs, C/4–5, Jun, recently fledged young late Jun to Jul.

286. HIPPOLAIS ICTERINA   PM

Icterine Warbler

Fairly common spring passage migrant, mainly at islets, mid Apr to early Jun, peaking mid May; usually fewer on return passage, mid Aug to late Oct. Doderlein (1869–74) claimed breeding at Favorita Park near Palermo, but gave no definite proof and confusion with *H. polyglotta* is likely.

2 recoveries, of birds ringed in Germany (1) and Sweden (1).

287. HIPPOLAIS POLYGLOTTA   PM OB

Melodious Warbler

Rare, irregular passage migrant, possibly overlooked, late Apr to May and late Aug to Sep, once Mar, Jun and Nov (Doderlein 1869–74, Steinbacher 1955b, Moltoni & Frugis 1967, Moltoni 1970, 1973a).

Breeding. One pair with recently fledged young Favorita Park, Jun 1973 (Massa 1976b). In the same area and in nearby Mt Pellegrino, Krampitz (1958) recorded singing males in May.

288. SYLVIA SARDA   RB PM WV
Marmora's Warbler

Scarce resident breeder (*S. s. sarda*) at I. Pantelleria (Doderlein 1869–74, Moltoni 1973a, Massa 1985). Rare and irregular passage migrant and winter visitor (*S. s. sarda*) along coasts and at islets, Nov-Mar; once Jun at I. Marettimo (Sorci *et al.* 1973) where doubtfully recorded in spring 1984 (F. Lo Valvo) and 1986 (U. F. Foschi). Decreased since last century: Doderlein (1869–74) recorded "many" at Mazara, Nov 1864, and some between Vittoria and Gela, autumn 1873.

Breeding. S. s. sarda. Confirmed only at Pantelleria, where Doderlein found it fairly common in spring. Nests in low and high maquis with *Quercus, Erica* and *Calycotome*. No details.

289. SYLVIA UNDATA   PM WV RB
Dartford Warbler

Uncommon autumn passage migrant and winter visitor (*S. u. undata*) along coasts, mainly E, and at wetlands, Nov to Mar. Also a scarce and local resident breeder at some islets, also locally at a few localities on the main island, but whether these are resident or migrant is unclear. Doderlein (1869–74) listed it as scarce along coasts (mainly near Gela and Mazara); Orlando (1937c) found one nest at Madonie Mts; Krampitz (1958) listed it as a possible breeder. Listed as resident at I. Pantelleria by Doderlein (1869–74) and Moltoni (1973), at Aeolian Islands by Moltoni & Frugis (1967); unrecorded at I. Marettimo by Krampitz (1957) and Steinbacher (1955b), but frequent there, Sep 1960 (Suchantke 1960) and breeding confirmed, spring 1969 (Krapp 1970). Breeding confirmed at Pantelleria, Marettimo, some Aeolian Islands, at 4 localities on Madonie and Peloritani Mts, and possibly bred on S coast, 1979–1983 (Massa 1985).

Breeding. S. u. undata. Nests, 20–80 cm above ground, in low maquis with *Erica* species, from sea level up to c. 1000 m. Eggs, C/3–5, late Apr to late May, probably single brooded. Recently fledged young early Jun to early Jul.

290. SYLVIA CONSPICILLATA   PM MB WV RB?
Spectacled Warbler

Fairly common to common spring passage migrant (*S. c. conspicillata*), first arrivals late Feb, mostly mid to late Mar, last on passage probably early to mid Apr. Some evidence of autumn passage along coasts, Sep to early Nov; scarce Nov to Feb, unrecorded nearly all years. Only a few are probably resident at I. Pantelleria (Moltoni 1973d), while in nearby Malta it is a fairly common resident (Sultana & Gauci 1982).

Breeding. S. c. conspicillata. Fairly common and widespread migrant breeder in low maquis, garigue, scrub, open areas, wet meadows, from sea level up to c. 2200 m (Aetna). No evidence of breeding at islets, except (probably) Pantelleria. Nests in tall shrubs, 15–35 cm above ground; birds building nests late Mar along coasts and mid Apr to mid May on higher grounds. Eggs, C/3–5, Apr-Jun, unfledged young till late Jun.

291. SYLVIA CANTILLANS   PM MB
Subalpine Warbler

Common spring passage migrant and common migrant breeder, occasional early Mar, first arrivals usually mid Mar, main passage late Mar to early Apr, last on passage early May; during main passage up to 50 together recorded in coastal areas. Apparently scarcer on return passage, mid Aug to early-mid Oct, while at Malta it is then much more common than in spring (Sultana & Gauci 1982). Both *S. c. cantillans* and *S. c. albistriata* occur, the latter identified only twice (Orlando 1958a), but there has been no proper ringing study of migrant *Sylvia* in Sicily.

Breeding. S. c. cantillans. Common migrant breeder in Sicily and Aeolian Islands in a variety of habitats: garigue, scrub, open areas with few bushes, woods, thickets, brambles, from sea level up to c. 1800 m. Nests in bushes, 40–120 cm above ground; birds building nests from early Apr. Eggs, C/3–4, mid Apr to mid Jun, mostly May.

292. SYLVIA MELANOCEPHALA   RB PM?
Sardinian Warbler

Abundant and widespread resident breeder all over Sicily and islets up to 1300 m, occasionally up to 1500 m. Probably an uncommon passage migrant, but no definite proof.

Breeding. S. m. melanocephala. Occurs in a variety of habitats: open areas with scattered shrubs, garigue, low and high maquis, copses and sometimes clearings of mature woods, cultivated areas, gardens and outskirts of urban areas, rarely in citrus plantations. Prefers low maquis, where a high density was found — 10–15 pairs per 10 ha. Sings throughout the year, especially Feb-Jun, within a shrub, 1–2 m above ground, sometimes up to 6–7 m, and frequently in flight. Nests in shrubs and little trees, 0·3–2 m above ground, usually 0·5–1 m. Double brooded. Nest building begins late Mar to early Apr. Eggs, C/2–5, usually C/3–4; clutch starts to be laid 1–25 days after nest building. Incubation, 13–14 days, begins after laying of penultimate egg. Young fledge after 12–13 days. Interval between fledging and second brood: 15–17 days; building of second nest usually mid May, laying late May, hatching early Jun, fledging mid to late Jun. Young depend on parents for at least 2 weeks. Above data refer mainly to N Sicily, from sea level up to c. 500 m, but along SE coasts an earlier breeding season seems to occur and first nests are usually found late Feb to early Mar.

According to Williamson (1976) some Sicilian specimens are close in plumage to the race *momus*.

293. SYLVIA RUEPPELLI   AV
Rüppell's Warbler

Accidental visitor. 6 records: one at Messina, 20 Mar 1882 (at FM, Arrigoni 1929); one at I. Ustica, 27 Mar 1959 (Giambona 1971); one at Cassibile, 31 Mar 1976, and one at Vendicari, 24 Mar 1977 (Massa *et al.* 1979); 2 at Capo Murro di Porco, 15 Mar 1979 (Iapichino & Baglieri 1982); all were adult males. One doubtful autumn record at I. Favignana, 16 Oct 1977 (Massa *et al.* 1979). A female carrying food recorded at I. Pantelleria, 25 Jun 1970, and breeding supposed (Moltoni 1973a).

294. SYLVIA HORTENSIS   AV
Orphean Warbler

Accidental visitor; 5 confirmed records: one at Ragusa, 19 Apr 1957 (Mebs 1957); 2 at I. Stromboli, 21–23 Aug 1959 (Moltoni & Frugis 1967); one at I. Favignana, late Mar 1971 and one at Mazara, Apr 1969 (Sorci *et al.* 1973); one at Siracusa, 1 May 1978. Brucher & Lehmann (1975) merely listed it for I. Pantelleria without comment. Benoit (1840) listed it as resident and common near Palermo, and Riera (1923) stated that it occurred occasionally in spring.

295. SYLVIA NISORIA   AV

Barred Warbler

Accidental visitor: one near Castelvetrano, 19 Oct 1905 (formerly in coll. Orlando, now lost) and one near Siracusa, 3 Nov 1974.

296. SYLVIA CURRUCA   PM

Lesser Whitethroat

Rare (and irregular?) passage migrant (*S. c. curruca*), late Mar to May and Sep-Oct. Once Jun. Unrecorded in many years, but easily overlooked. Doderlein (1869–74) stated that great numbers bred in Sicily, Orlando (1936a) and Mebs (1957) supposed breeding, but any breeding in Sicily seems unlikely.

297. SYLVIA COMMUNIS   PM MB

Whitethroat

Fairly common passage migrant (*S. c. communis*) at islets and along coasts, early Apr to early Jun, usually peaking late Apr to mid May, and mid Aug to mid Oct, peaking mid to late Sep. Occasional late Mar and late Jul.
Breeding. S. c. communis. Scarce and local migrant breeder in open areas with few shrubs, low maquis or garigue, from c. 500 up to c. 1800 m. Highest density recorded: 8 pairs per 10 ha in low maquis (Massa 1981b). Nests in shrubs, 25–45 cm above ground, eggs, C/2–5, late Apr to mid Jun, mainly May.
One recovery, of a bird ringed in Tunisia.

298. SYLVIA BORIN   PM

Garden Warbler

Fairly common passage migrant (*S. b. borin*), mid Apr to mid Jun and early Aug to late Oct, much more numerous on return passage. Doderlein (1869–74), Giglioli (1907) and Riera (1923) claimed breeding but gave no evidence. Ajola (1959) stated that numbers had greatly decreased at I. Ustica.
3 recoveries, of birds ringed in France (1), Czechoslovakia (1) and USSR (1). One ringed in Sicily (I. Linosa) recovered in S Italy (Apulia).

299. SYLVIA ATRICAPILLA   RB PM WV

Blackcap

Common resident breeder (see below), numbers augmented mid Sep to Mar, mainly from Nov, by large influxes of wintering birds. Some evidence of spring passage at islets, Mar-Apr, occasionally early May. *S. a. atricapilla* common in winter, but resident birds, according to wing formula and wing length, resemble *S. a. pauluccii* (Lo Valvo *et al.* 1986, 1988).
Breeding. S. a. pauluccii? Common and widespread resident, less numerous in E Sicily along coasts. Occurs in woods, gardens, plantations, urban areas, from sea level up to c. 1800 m. Nests in trees, 70–250 cm above ground. Eggs, C/2 to C/4 (usually C/3), early Apr to late Aug, mainly May, with fledged young till mid-late Sep; double brooded (Massa 1981). High density observed in surburban areas of Palermo: 45 pairs/10 ha (Lo Valvo *et al.* 1985).
One recovery, of a bird ringed in Germany.

300. PHYLLOSCOPUS INORNATUS   AV

Yellow-browed Warbler

Accidental visitor: one at I. Pantelleria, 9 Apr 1931 (Steinfatt 1934) and one at Capo Murro di Porco, 2 Dec 1980 (Iapichino & Baglieri 1982).

301. PHYLLOSCOPUS BONELLI   PM

Bonelli's Warbler

Scarce spring passage migrant (*P. b. bonelli* or *P. b. orientalis* could both occur), early Apr to mid May, mostly early May, usually singly. Some years unrecorded. Moltoni (1973a) reported winter sight records at I. Pantelleria: 2 on 14 Jan 1971 and one, 21 Feb 1973. Breeding claimed by Doderlein (1869–74) is unlikely.

302. PHYLLOSCOPUS SIBILATRIX   PM

Wood Warbler

Fairly common spring passage migrant, late Mar to late May, peaking mid to late Apr with 10s together at islets and at some coastal localities. Scarcer on return passage, late Aug to early Nov, mostly Sep. Once late Jul, early Aug and mid Nov. Breeding claimed by Doderlein (1869–74) is unlikely.

One recovery, of a bird ringed in Germany.

303 PHYLLOSCOPUS COLLYBITA   PM WV RB

Chiffchaff

Common autumn passage migrant and winter visitor (*P. c. collybita* and *P. c. abietinus* could occur), late Sep to early Apr, mostly early Nov to mid Mar, in every kind of habitat, also in towns. Evidence of small spring passage, mid Mar to late Apr, sometimes into May.

Breeding. P. c. collybita. Uncommon and local resident breeder, recorded only in wooded areas from 600 up to c. 1800 m (Madonie, Caronie and Peloritani Mts, Aetna), mainly in deciduous forests, less frequent in pine forest. Few details: recently fledged young, Jun-Jul.

4 recoveries, of birds ringed in England (1), Malta (1), Austria (1) and Yugoslavia (1).

304. PHYLLOSCOPUS TROCHILUS   PM

Willow Warbler

Common passage migrant (*P. t. trochilus*), late Mar to late May, peaking mid Apr, and mid Aug to late Oct, mostly late Sep to early Oct. Usually more numerous in spring, when 10s are regularly observed in one locality at islets and at some coastal areas. Occasional early Aug and Nov. Winter sight records at I. Pantelleria and I. Lampedusa, Dec-Feb 1968–1973 (Moltoni 1970, 1973a) need confirmation. Breeding claimed by Doderlein (1869–74) and Orlando (1936a) is unlikely.

There is one confirmed record of *P. t. acredula*, Palermo 1920 (Orlando 1939c, syn. *eversmanni*).

305. REGULUS REGULUS   WV PM
Goldcrest

Uncommon winter visitor (*R. r. regulus*) in woods, but also in town parks, singly or up to 10 in the same area, mid Oct to late Mar. Some evidence of slight autumn passage, mid Oct to Dec. Once late Sep (Kumerloeve 1968).

306. REGULUS IGNICAPILLUS   PM WV RB
Firecrest

Fairly common autumn passage migrant and winter visitor (*R. i. ignicapillus*), early Oct to Mar. Occasional Apr outside breeding areas. No information about possible winter movements of resident birds.

Breeding. R. i. ignicapillus. Uncommon and local resident breeder mainly in *Quercus* and *Fagus* woods, rarer in *Pinus* woods, from c. 400 up to c. 1800 m (Madonie, Caronie, Aetna and Peloritani Mts, Ficuzza wood). Few details: singing males mid Apr, birds building nests early May and recently fledged young from mid Jun.

MUSCICAPIDAE

307. MUSCICAPA STRIATA   PM MB
Spotted Flycatcher

Common passage migrant (*M. s. striata*), mid Apr to early Jun, peaking late Apr to mid May, when 10s or 100s in one day recorded at some coastal areas (e.g. Capo Murro di Porco) and on islets. Less numerous on return passage, mid Aug to early Nov. Occasional early Apr.

Breeding. M. s. striata. Uncommon and local migrant breeder, in wooded or cultivated areas (mixed citrus plantations) from sea level up to c. 900 m. Highest density (10 pairs per 10 ha) is found in plantations near Palermo (Lo Valvo *et al.* 1985). Also breeds at I. Marettimo and on some Aeolian Islands. Nests in trees, 65–420 cm above ground, eggs, C/2–3, late May to Jun, fledged young late Jun to early Jul. Breeding areas deserted Aug.

2 recoveries, of birds ringed in Sweden.

308. FICEDULA PARVA   PM
Red-breasted Flycatcher

Rare, but probably regular, autumn passage migrant (*F. p. parva*); only one spring record, one at I. Linosa, 28 Apr 1967 (Moltoni 1970). Up to 8 in a year recorded near Siracusa in 7 years between 1975–1983, mid Sep to late Oct (Massa *et al.* 1979, Iapichino & Baglieri 1982); 2 shot, Oct 1951 (Ajola 1959, Priolo 1956b); 6 recorded at Pelagian Islands, Oct 1967 (Moltoni 1970).

309. FICEDULA SEMITORQUATA   AV
Semi-collared Flycatcher

Accidental visitor: one male at I. Linosa, 2–4 May 1968 (Moltoni 1970).

310. FICEDULA ALBICOLLIS   PM OB
Collared Flycatcher

Uncommon spring passage migrant (*F. a. albicollis*), late Mar to mid May, mostly mid to late Apr, usually singly or up to 3–4. Occasional Jun.

Breeding. F. a. albicollis. Occasional breeder: one recently fledged young at Piano Zucchi (Madonie Mts), 28 Jul 1946 (MTC). Krampitz (1958) recorded one pair with male carrying food at Madonie, 1600 m, 14 Jun 1957.

311. FICEDULA HYPOLEUCA   PM

Pied Flycatcher

Fairly common spring passage migrant (*F. h. hypoleuca*), mid Mar to early Jun, peaking mid to late Apr, with up to 10–20 together in one locality, mainly along coasts and at islets. Scarce on return passage, mid Aug to mid Oct (occasionally late Oct), mostly Sep.
One recovery, of a bird ringed in Finland.

TIMALIIDAE

312. PANURUS BIARMICUS   FB AV

Bearded Tit (Reedling)

Former resident breeder (*P. b. biarmicus*) at Biviere di Lentini. Last known specimen from Lentini dated 1907, but probably became extinct between 1930s and 1940s (Orlando 1958i, Priolo 1954). Benoit (1840) listed it as fairly common at Lentini, Doderlein (1869–74) supposed it was more numerous in winter and partially migrant. Riera (1923) listed it as scarce at Biviere. Stresemann (1943) did not record it at the lake. Now an accidental visitor: one near Palermo, 23 Oct 1949 (at MCT); a flock of 10–15 at Siracusa salt pan, 6 Nov to late Dec 1980, 2–3 in the same period at Longarini marshes (Iapichino & Baglieri 1982).

AEGITHALIDAE

313. AEGITHALOS CAUDATUS   RB

Long-tailed Tit

Scarce and local resident (*A. c. siculus*), above c. 400 up to 1800 m in broadleaved woods of N Sicily (Ficuzza, Palazzo Adriano, Caronie, Peloritani, Aetna, especially Madonie Mts) and at Iblei Mts. Small local movements in winter in the same areas.
Breeding. A. c. siculus. Nests in trees, Feb-Mar to Jun-Jul, no details.
Sicilian form first described by Whitaker (1901). Detailed notes on plumage and taxonomy are given by Priolo (1979), who suggested that specific status could be applied to *siculus* and noted differences in plumage with *italiae* resident in Calabria, mainly in the head pattern; in *siculus* there is a band through the eye which is brown not black and is broader with fainter edges, so that the whole head appears dark with some whitish or fulvous on the crown. These plumage differences are much more evident than ones among other Palaearctic subspecies of the Long-tailed Tit.

PARIDAE

314. PARUS PALUSTRIS   RB

Marsh Tit

Rare or scarce local resident (*P. p. siculus*). Benoit (1840) listed it as common near Palermo, but this seems an error.

Breeding P. p. siculus. In beech woods between S. Fratello and Randazzo with rich undergrowth of *Ilex aquifolium, Prunus spinosa* and *Crataegus oxycantha*. Nests in holes in trees, occasionally in walls; eggs, C/6–9, May (A. Priolo).

De Burg described *P. p. siculus* from some Sicilian specimens of Arrigoni's collection; Vaurie (1959) states that *siculus* is not acceptable. Priolo (1954, 1969), however, confirmed that a small endemic population exists on the Caronie Mts above 1000–1200 m, and the Sicilian birds are distinguishable from the Italian ones (*italicus*), with wing length generally less than 60 mm.

315. PARUS ATER   RB PM?

Coal Tit

Locally fairly common resident breeder (*P. a. ater*) in copses and mature woods above 400 up to c. 1800 m, only in mountains areas (Madonie, Caronie, Peloritani and Aetna). Absent at Iblei Mts. Highest densities in pine forests, but is present also in broadleaved woods, especially beech. Regularly recorded in winter at low grounds, along coasts and in towns (e.g. Palermo). Altitudinal seasonal migration is even more likely than passage migration.

Breeding. P. a. ater. Nests in holes in trees or rocks, but also on the ground. Eggs, C/5–8, mid Apr to early Jun, recently fledged young mid May to early Jul. Double brooded.

316. PARUS CAERULEUS   RB

Blue Tit

Common resident breeder (*P. c. caeruleus*; at I. Pantelleria *P. c. ultramarinus* – Moltoni 1971, Brichetti & Violani 1986) from sea level, where usually scarcer, to c. 1850 m (Aetna and Madonie Mts).

Breeding. P. c. caeruleus. Occurs in pine, oak and beech woods, but also in cultivated areas (e.g. citrus plantations), gardens, parks, valley bottoms, urban areas. Nests in holes, in walls or trees, Mar-Apr (Jul), C/5–9, double brooded. At I. Pantelleria (*P. c. ultramarinus*) nests in high maquis with *Pinus pinaster, Quercus ilex*, etc.

317. PARUS MAJOR   RB

Great Tit

Common and widespread resident breeder (*P. m. major*), from sea level up to c. 1800 m.

Breeding. Resident in a large variety of habitats: deciduous or pine woods, plantations, groves, gardens, urban areas. Nests in holes, c. 1–4 m above ground; eggs, C/5–10, mostly C/7 late Mar to Jun, double brooded. Occasionally recorded at Egadi Islands (Sorci *et al.* 1973), once at I. Pantelleria (Steinfatt 1934) and some doubtful records at I. Ustica (Ajola 1959).

SITTIDAE

318. SITTA EUROPAEA   RB

Nuthatch

Uncommon and local resident breeder (*S. e. cisalpina*) in woody areas from 700 up to 1700 m, on Caronie, Madonie and Aetna Mts. Riera (1923) listed it as common at Iblei Mts, where now absent. Type of *S. e. siciliae*, described by

Kleinschmidt (= *cisalpina*), came from Enna, where this species has been recorded only once, in pine plantation near Aidone, 23 Apr 1957 (Mebs 1957).

Breeding. S. e. cisalpina. In coppice and mature woods, generally broadleaved (*Quercus* and *Fagus*); highest densities in old *Fagus* woods on Caronie (especially Mt Soro and surrounding woods). Less frequent at pine woods on Aetna where recorded in past (A. Priolo), but unrecorded 1979–1983 (Massa 1985), yet recorded again in 1984 and 1986 breeding seasons. Nests in holes in old trees from mid May. Eggs, C/4–7, recently fledged young mid-late Jun, sometimes early Jul. Post breeding family parties recorded till early Aug.

TICHODROMADIDAE

319. TICHODROMA MURARIA   AV

Wallcreeper

Accidental visitor. 5 records: one at Messina, spring 1842 (Graf 1842), one at Mazara, 26 Oct 1947 (Sorci *et al.* 1973), one at Novara di Sicilia, 19 Feb 1957 (Priolo 1972b), one at Piano Battaglia, Nov 1972 (C. Lauro), and one shot at Scillato, Nov 1985 (P. Failla). Doderlein (1869–74) listed it as rare but gave no records.

CERTHIIDAE

320. CERTHIA BRACHYDACTYLA   RB

Short-toed Treecreeper

Fairly common and widespread resident (*C. b. brachydactyla*).

Breeding. In any habitat with many trees: olive and almond tree plantations, pine or broadleaved woods, parks, from sea level up to c. 1800 m. Highest densities in natural woods: 5–8 pairs per 10 ha in an oak wood, 600 m above sea level (M. Sarà). Nests occupied mid Apr to late Jun, recently fledged young May-Jul.

Certhia brachydactyla siciliae Schiebel (from Sicily) is considered a synonym of *C. b. brachydactyla* (Vaurie 1959).

REMIZIDAE

321. REMIZ PENDULINUS   RB

Penduline Tit

Scarce and local resident breeder (*R. p. pendulinus*), more widespread in S and E Sicily, in freshwater wetlands and along rivers from sea level up to c. 600 m; up to 5–6 pairs recorded in the same locality. No regular movements, but family parties wander far from breeding areas Jul onwards.

Breeding. R. p. pendulinus. Population probably less than 100 pairs (Lo Verde & Massa 1985). Nests suspended from trees (usually *Salix* sp. or *Tamarix* sp.). Few details: birds building (or restoring) nests late Mar to early Aug, recently fledged young from mid May, mainly Jun (E. Giudice & R. Mascara).

ORIOLIDAE

322. ORIOLUS ORIOLUS   PM MB

Golden Oriole

Fairly common spring passage migrant (*O. o. oriolus*), singly or up to 15 together, early Apr to early Jun, peaking late Apr to early May. 158 counted at

Mt Ciccia (Messina Straits), 24 Apr to 2 May 1984. Occasional on passage mid Jun to early Jul. Scarcer on return passage, late Aug to Sep. Easily observed while feeding on fig (*Ficus* sp.) or Mulberry *Morus alba*.

Breeding. O. o. oriolus. Scarce and local migrant breeder, mainly at Madonie and Aetna Mts, in copses and mature woods or bottom of valleys with thick vegetation, up to c. 1500 m. Mating recorded from mid Apr, eggs, C/3–4, May (E. Giudice). One nest found in *Platanus orientalis* at Iblei Mts (S. Baglieri).

3 recoveries, of birds ringed in Hungary (2) and Poland (1).

LANIIDAE

323. LANIUS COLLURIO   PM MB
Red-backed Shrike

Scarce spring passage migrant (*L. c. collurio*), mid Apr to late May, some years unrecorded. Scarce but regular on return passage, late Aug to mid Oct, usually singly. Once early Jun and late Oct.

Breeding. L. c. collurio. Rare and local migrant breeder at Madonie, Caronie and Aetna Mts, up to 1400 m, in open areas with bushes and scattered trees. Nests in trees or bushes, eggs, C/5–6, May (A. Priolo), fledged young early Jul.

3 recoveries, of birds ringed in England (1), Tunisia (1) and Norway (1).

324. LANIUS MINOR   PM MB
Lesser Grey Shrike

Scarce passage migrant (*L. m. minor*), Apr-May and mid Aug to Sep, but usually very few records outside breeding areas.

Breeding. L. m. minor. Scarce and local migrant breeder, in Cen and NE Sicily, from 300 up to c. 900 m, in open areas with scattered trees (e.g. almond tree plantations). Nests in trees, c. 3–5 m above ground, eggs, C/4–5, Jun, recently fledged young mid to late Jul (Massa & Priolo 1981, Salvo 1982). Numbers have probably decreased this century; Doderlein (1869–74) and Giglioli (1907) listed it as common.

325. LANIUS EXCUBITOR   AV
Great Grey Shrike

Accidental visitor: 8 records since 1949: Nov (3), Jan, Mar, Dec (all *L. e. excubitor*); one shot near Ragusa, Sep 1969, referred to *L. e. pallidirostris* (Sorci *et al.* 1972); one shot near Siracusa, Nov 1976, referred to *L. e. meridionalis* (S. Baglieri).

326. LANIUS SENATOR   PM MB
Woodchat Shrike

Fairly common spring passage migrant, late Mar to early Jun, usually peaking mid to late Apr; less numerous on return passage, mid Aug to late Sep. Both *L. s. senator* and *L. s. badius* occur, *badius* being much less common and usually recorded at islets. *L. s. niloticus* collected once Messina, 21 Apr 1915 (Sturniolo 1923), now at MCT.

Breeding. L. s. senator. Widespread migrant breeder, mostly scarce, but locally uncommon. Marked decrease near Palermo in last 20 years. Bred at I. Favignana till 1970s, but now has disappeared. One pair belonging to *L. s. badius* bred there in 1987 (G. Lo Verde & F. Lo Valvo). Occurs in open areas with scattered trees from sea level up to c. 1800 m (Aetna). Nests in trees, c. 2–3 m above ground, eggs, C/5–6, May-Jun, fledged young Jun-Jul.

The Sicilian race *L. s. hensii* Clancey is considered a synonym of *L. s. senator* (Vaurie 1959).

9 recoveries, of birds ringed in Tunisia.

CORVIDAE

327. GARRULUS GLANDARIUS   RB
Jay

Common and widespread resident breeder, in natural and artificial woods and in areas with dense vegetation (e.g. citrus plantations), from sea level up to c. 1800 m. One record from islets: Favignana, winter 1967 (Sorci *et al.* 1973), but this lies only 13 km off Sicilian coast.

Breeding. Few details: eggs, C/3–6, Apr.

Vaurie (1959) listed *G. g. albipectus* for Sicily; later, Keve (1966) described a Sicilian race named *G. g. jordansi*, but further investigations are needed.

328. PICA PICA   RB
Magpie

Abundant and widespread resident breeder (*P. p. galliae*), mainly in open areas with scattered trees, but also in gardens and urban areas, from sea level up to c. 1900 m, more common along coasts. Numerous and increasing in E Sicily, where other Corvidae are scarcer.

Breeding. P. p. galliae. Mainly in open areas with scattered trees, but also in gardens and urban areas, from sea level up to c. 1900 m, more common along coasts. Breeds on I. Lunga very close to W coast; one pair bred at I. Favignana, 1986, where previously a single bird was recorded Sep 1970 (Sorci *et al.* 1973). In 1985 also colonised I. Lipari and I. Vulcano. Nests in bushes or trees, 1·5 to 10 m above ground, occasionally on electricity pylons. Nest building from mid Jan, eggs C/3–6, occasionally mid Mar, usually Apr, once mid Feb. From Jun onwards 10s up to 100 together recorded, mainly at rubbish tips.

329. PYRRHOCORAX PYRRHOCORAX   RB
Chough

Uncommon and local resident breeder (*P. p. erythrorhamphus*) in some calcareous mountains in N and Cen Sicily from 400 to 1600 m. Wanders in winter: post breeding and winter records at unusual localities, up to 20 km from breeding colonies.

Breeding. P. p. erythrorhamphus. On mountain grazings and high plateaux, generally inland, but 2 colonies only c. 1 km from the coast. Nests in holes and cavities on cliffs. Eggs, C/2–3 mid to late Apr, young fledge early to mid Jun. Very social; birds from different colonies may associate — up to 100–150 can occur together at Madonie Mts. Has decreased in last 20 years: c. 1000 individuals estimated (Sorci *et al.* 1971a), c. 350–400 pairs (Massa 1985), now probably c. 300 pairs in 13 colonies of 5–35 pairs. Some colonies are on verge of extinction, e.g. at Alcara Li Fusi and at Raffo Rosso; the latter discovered by Whitaker in the first years of this century, contained 20 pairs in 1967, 10 in 1970, 5 in 1973, 4 in 1979, 3 in 1980 and 2 in 1985.

330. CORVUS MONEDULA   RB
Jackdaw

Common to locally abundant resident (*C. m. spermologus*), absent from all islets, locally increasing. Post breeding flocks of 100s, sometimes 1000s, recorded Jun onwards. No evidence of passage.

Breeding. In a variety of habitats: mountains or hills with small cliffs, towns (e.g. Palermo), cultivated areas, from sea level up to c. 1500 m. Nests in colonies, exceptionally single pairs, in holes in cliffs or man made structures (buildings, viaducts). Birds building nests recorded from mid Mar; eggs, C/3–5, early May to mid Jun, newly hatched young early Jun to early Jul, recently fledged young mid Jun to late Jul, rarely Aug.

331. CORVUS FRUGILEUS   Former WV, AV
Rook

Former winter visitor (*C. f. frugilegus*), now accidental. Flocks of 30–40 regularly recorded last century, Nov to Mar (Benoit 1840, Whitaker 1904a,c) and till early 1950s (Orlando 1955a, Steinbacher 1955b); but one shot near Gela, Jan 1976 (G. Salvo), is the only record after 1955. Many specimens are in local collections and Museums. See also *C. corone.*

332. CORVUS CORONE   RB
Hooded Crow

Common and widespread resident breeder (*C. c. sardonius* – Vaurie (1965), but further studies needed), scarcer in SE Sicily along coasts. Breeds at I. Ustica, colonised c. 1975, and one pair bred at I. Favignana in 1986. Very social, winter flocks of 10s up to 100 common, mainly at rubbish tips. 6 old winter records of *C. c. corone* (Whitaker 1904a,c, Orlando 1955a, 1959b), labelled as such at WMB and at MCT, are in fact immature *C. frugilegus.*

Breeding. *C. c. sardonius* (see below). Nests in trees in a large variety of habitats, also in urban areas, from sea level up to c. 1800 m; eggs, C/2–5, early Apr to mid May (M. Siracusa).

Keve (1970) considers that Sicilian specimens have characteristics similar to *cornix* but influenced by *sardonius* and partially by *corone.*

333. CORVUS CORAX   RB
Raven

Fairly common resident breeder (*C. c. corax*) in all rocky areas, from sea level up to c. 1600 m. Also breeds at Aeolian and Egadi Islands; occasionally bred at I. Ustica (Ajola 1959). 10s up to 100, sometimes up to 200, together recorded in winter at roosts or feeding at rubbish tips: c. 200 at Piana Albanesi, Apr 1953 (Steinbacher 1955b), c. 70 at Campofiorito, 12 Feb 1978, 50 at I. Salina, 1 Oct 1977, 76 at Pantalica, 1 Dec 1986. Observed kleptoparasitizing *Milvus milvus* and *Neophron percnopterus* (Massa 1981a).

Breeding. *C. c. corax.* Nests in holes on cliffs; height of 15 nests, 3.5–50 m. Distance between 2 occupied nests sometimes only 200–300 m; Mebs (1957) counted 8 pairs in 5 km at Rocca Busambra, and 34 pairs were counted in 1100 km² in S Sicily (E. Giudice, R. Mascara). Eggs, C/3–5 from mid Mar, young usually fledge early Jun to early Jul.

STURNIDAE

334. STURNUS VULGARIS   PM WV RB
Starling

Abundant passage migrant and winter visitor (*S. v. vulgaris*) in open areas both inland and along coasts; occasionally recorded as early as mid Aug, first arrivals usually late Sep to mid Oct, peak numbers late Oct to Nov. Late autumn and winter roosts of 1000s, even 10,000s, commonly in towns, villages and reedbeds, but few accurate figures available: largest city roosts are at Catania, where more than 20,000 occupied a single roost, Jan 1984 (A. Ciaccio) and at Palermo, c. 30,000, 10 Feb 1978 and Dec 1987. Orlando (1965) recorded c. 100,000 at Biviere di Lentini reedbeds in early 1950s. Most leave early to mid Feb. Scarcer on return passage, Feb-Mar. Occasional Apr-May.

Breeding. S. v. vulgaris. A small, discrete breeding population was first recorded in the town of Siracusa in 1979, but probably had existed since 1974 at least (Iapichino & Baglieri 1979). Number of pairs increased from c.15 to c. 100, 1979–1987. Nests on buildings or palm trees in parks; fledged young mid May to late Jun.

22 recoveries, of birds ringed in Tunisia (6), Yugoslavia (4), Poland (3), Germany (2), Bulgaria (2), Czechoslovakia (2), USSR (1), Hungary (1) and N Italy (1).

335. STURNUS UNICOLOR   RB

Spotless Starling

Common resident breeder, with highest densities in Cen Sicily and Iblei Mts; absent in most of Messina province and in W Sicily, but 2 pairs colonised the town of Castellammare in 1986. Post breeding flocks of 10s or 100s, up to 500, recorded late Jun onwards, usually not far from breeding sites; a few winter and spring records from Trapani province (Steinbacher 1955b, Burgio 1977) and from Mt Aetna (A. Priolo), where it does not breed. Once at I. Pantelleria in Oct (Steinbacher 1956c).

Breeding. Widespread in open cultivated or rocky areas, cliffs, towns, villages, from sea level up to c. 1600 m. Colonies usually below 50 pairs. Calls throughout the year, especially Mar-Jun. Nests in holes on cliffs, buildings or other man made structures such as viaducts. Eggs, C/4–6, early Apr to mid Jun, hatching after 12–14 days; recently fledged young May to late Jul, mostly Jun. Some evidence of second broods.

336. STURNUS ROSEUS   AV

Rose-coloured Starling

Accidental visitor. 9 records of singles, only one this century: Messina, May 1834 (Benoit 1840); Catania, undated, Mt Pellegrino, autumn 1868, I. Ustica, 1871 and 1872 (Doderlein 1869–74); I. Ustica 1875 (shot by Doderlein, MM.); locality unknown, Oct 1881 (specimen at MM); Castelvetrano, 21 Jun 1899 (Venezia 1899b); I. Ustica, Apr 1958 (Ajola 1959). "Some" observed by Palazzotto (1801) near Gratteri seem doubtful.

PASSERIDAE

337. PASSER HISPANIOLENSIS   RB PM?

Spanish Sparrow

Abundant and widespread resident breeder throughout Sicily and islets. Some movements noted, Oct-Nov, along coasts probably refer to Sicilian vagrant birds. I. Ustica was colonised 3 times following elimination by farmers, but is now abundant (Doderlein 1869–74, Steinbacher 1955, Ajola 1959, Massa 1973). Post breeding and winter flocks recorded mainly Jun-Feb but may occur all month: roosts of 100s or 1000s common in towns or reedbeds.

Breeding. Occurs mainly in towns, villages and buildings, sometimes on cliffs, up to c. 1900 m (Aetna). Nests in holes and crevices in trees and electricity poles. Nest building from Mar, sometimes from Feb. Eggs, C/3–6 usually C/4–5, early Apr to Jul, double brooded, sometimes triple. Young fledge early May to early Aug.

A gynandromorph collected at I. Ustica, Feb 1980, had the pattern of one wing as male and the other one as female, but body pattern of a female.

Hartert (1903–23) named Sicilian and Maltese sparrows *P. h. maltae* but Vaurie (1959) considered *maltae* a hybrid *P. domesticus italiae* × *P. h. hispaniolensis*; Johnston (1969) considered the Sicilian sparrow to be *P. italiae*; others consider it as *P. hispaniolensis*, yet others as *P. h. italiae*. Lo Valvo & Lo Verde (1987) consider the Sicilian population to be differentiated from the Italian Sparrow *Passer italiae* and more like *hispaniolensis*, showing smaller black stripes on flanks and back than nominate *hispaniolensis*; so they include the Sicilian population in *P. hispaniolensis* and accept *P. h. maltae*. Aeolian Islands populations are still less striped black on flanks and are more similar to the Italian Sparrow.

338. PASSER MONTANUS   RB PM
Tree Sparrow

Fairly common resident breeder (*P. m. montanus*), more widespread in E Sicily, local in W and N Sicily, where probably increasing. Also breeds at Aeolian islands, I. Linosa and I. Ustica, the latter colonised in 1954 (Ajola 1959). Scarce passage migrant (*P. m. montanus*) at islets, Oct-Dec, and occasionally Mar (Moltoni 1973a, Ajola 1959). Post breeding parties of 5–10 are usual, but no larger winter flocks occur.

Breeding. P. m. montanus. In rocky and cultivated areas, towns and villages from sea level up to c. 1800 m (Aetna). Recorded building nests in Apr, sometimes late Mar. Nests in trees, buildings and cliffs; eggs, C/3–7, usually C/5, May to Jul; second broods usual, thirds exceptional. Young fledge 10–11 days after hatching.

339. PETRONIA PETRONIA   RB
Rock Sparrow

Uncommon to locally fairly common resident breeder (*P. p. petronia*), more widespread along NW coast, Cen Sicily and Iblei Mts, from sea level up to c. 1800 m. Breeds at I. Levanzo and I.Favignana; breeding at I. Lipari stated by Moltoni & Frugis (1967), but unrecorded there 1979–1983 (Massa 1985). No evidence of regular movements out of breeding season; occasional at I. Ustica (Ajola 1959) and at Aeolian Islands (Moltoni & Frugis 1967).

Breeding. P. p. petronia. In rocky habitats, occasionally in villages or ruins, usually in small colonies up to 20 pairs. Eggs, C/4–7, from late Apr, double brooded, recently fledged young till early Jul.

340. MONTIFRINGILLA NIVALIS   AV
Snow Finch

Accidental visitor, one record: 2 shot from a flock of 15 at I. Ustica, 16 Oct 1976 (Massa 1978a).

FRINGILLIDAE

341. FRINGILLA COELEBS   PM WV RB
Chaffinch

Common and widespread resident breeder, (*F. c. coelebs*), absent in parts of S Sicily and scarcer along the coast of E Sicily. Colonised some of Aeolian Islands in

1980s. Common autumn passage migrant and winter visitor (*P. c. coelebs*) mid Sep to early Apr, main autumn passage early Nov to early Dec; spring passage in variable numbers, mid Feb to early Apr.

Breeding. F. c. coelebs. In woods, cultivated areas with many trees (e.g. citrus plantations), gardens, also in urban areas, from sea level up to c. 1800 m. Highest density recorded in suburban area of Palermo: 30 pairs per 10 ha (Lo Valvo *et al.* 1985). Nests in trees, 165–250 cm above ground; eggs, C/2–5, from early Apr, recently fledged young till early Jul, double brooded.

One male *F. c. spodiogenys/africana* recorded at I. Pantelleria, 1 Jun 1987. A hybrid Chaffinch × Brambling, shot 2 May 1932, near Palermo (Orlando 1958a).

6 recoveries, of birds ringed in Hungary (5) and USSR (1).

342. FRINGILLA MONTIFRINGILLA   PM WV

Brambling

Scarce but probably regular autumn passage migrant and winter visitor, mid Nov to mid Mar, usually singly, occasionally up to 7 together. Once late Oct. (See *F. coelebs.*)

343. SERINUS SERINUS   RB MB? PM WV

Serin

Common and widespread breeder, but all breeders may not be strictly resident as some areas are deserted after breeding season. Reported as a scarce or doubtful breeder by most previous authors; the increase in recent decades being confirmed by first breeding records at Aeolian and Egadi Islands in early 1980s. Also common autumn passage migrant and winter visitor (*S. s. serinus*), first arrivals about mid Sep, main passage Nov; some evidence of spring passage, late Feb to late Mar, with a few into early May.

Breeding. S. s. serinus. In gardens, plantations, groves, pine woods, also in urban areas, much more common at low altitudes, but recorded up to c. 1800 m. High density in suburban area of Palermo: 50 pairs per 10 ha (Lo Valvo *et al.* 1985). Nest building first recorded mid Mar; nests in trees (mainly *Pinus* and *Cupressus*), 1–5 m above ground; eggs, C/2–4, Apr to Jul, occasionally late Aug; double brooded.

6 recoveries, of birds ringed in Czechoslovakia (4), Yugoslavia (1) and Cen Italy (1).

344. CARDUELIS CHLORIS   RB PM WV

Greenfinch

Fairly common resident breeder (*C. c. aurantiiventris*) from sea level up to 1850 m, absent from S coast and from some inland areas. Recently immigrated to some Aeolian Islands, but probably has now disappeared from I. Marettimo where it bred in 1970s. In mixed citrus plantations near Palermo densities vary between 3 and 10 pairs per 10 ha (La Mantia 1982, Lo Valvo *et al.* 1985). Fairly common autumn passage migrant and winter visitor, late Sep to mid Apr, main passage mid Oct to mid Nov, less numerous Dec-Feb; return passage Mar to mid Apr, occasionally into early May. No study has been carried out on the race/races migrating in Sicily.

Breeding. C. c. aurantiiventris. In groves, citrus plantations and pine woods. Calls from Feb. Nests in trees, 2–6 m above ground, eggs, C/4–5, early Mar to late Jun, double brooded, recently fledged young early Apr to mid Jul.

One recovery, of a bird ringed in Yugoslavia.

345. CARDUELIS CARDUELIS   RB PM WV

Goldfinch

Common and widespread resident breeder (*C. c. tschusii*) from sea level up to c. 1800 m, throughout, and on islets except Ustica and Linosa. Common passage migrant and winter visitor, mid Oct to early Apr, peak numbers usually late Oct to Nov. Some evidence of spring passage, mid Feb to Apr. No study has been carried out on race/races migrating in Sicily.

Breeding. C. c. tschusii according to Vaurie (1959). Foschi (1968) reported *tschusii* also from I. Pantelleria. Occurs in open areas, gardens, groves, plantations, woods and urban areas. 3–10 pairs per 10 ha counted in citrus planations near Palermo (La Mantia 1982, Lo Valvo *et al.* 1985). Nests in trees (usually *Citrus* sp., *Pinus* sp. or *Cupressus* sp.), eggs, usually C/4 mid Mar to early Sep (A. Dimarca), second broods common. Post breeding flocks of 10s or 100s recorded Jun onwards.

Carduelis c. bruniventris Schiebel (from Sicily) is considered a synonym of *C. c. tschusii* (Vaurie 1959).

3 recoveries, of birds ringed in Yugoslavia.

346. CARDUELIS SPINUS   PM WV OB or RB

Siskin

Scarce autumn passage migrant and winter visitor, late Sep to mid Apr, mostly mid Nov to Jan, singly or up to 20 together.

Breeding. Breeding recently proved at Aetna, c. 1850 m above sea level: 2 trapped females had brood patches, 18 May 1984; 2 family parties with recently fledged young, 12 Jun 1985.

One recovery, of a bird ringed in Hungary.

347. CARDUELIS CANNABINA   RB PM WV

Linnet

Abundant resident breeder in Sicily and at all islets, from sea level up to c. 2200 m (Aetna). Common autumn passage migrant and winter visitor (*C. c. cannabina*), in 10s or 100s, mid Oct to late Mar, main passage Nov; slight spring passage Feb to late Mar. In winter *C. cannabina, C. carduelis* and *Serinus serinus* usually flock together in 10s or 100s in open areas throughout.

Breeding. C. c. cannabina. In a large variety of habitats: scrub, garigue, low maquis, gardens, grove, plantations, salicornia beds and urban areas. Very high densities observed in citrus plantations near Palermo: 40–100 pairs per 10 ha (Lo Valvo *et al.* 1985). Nests in trees, mainly *Cupressus* sp. or *Pinus* sp., or in bushes, 40–470 cm above ground (mainly c. 200 cm); eggs, C/2–5, usually C/4, occasionally late Jan, mostly late Feb to early Jul, sometimes Aug, double brooded; incubation c. 11 days by female only, young fledge at 12–15 days (Lo Valvo & Lo Valvo 1987), recently fledged young till late Aug. Post breeding flocks are common after Jul.

7 recoveries, of birds ringed in Cen and N Italy (3), Yugoslavia (2), Austria (1) and Germany (1).

348. CARDUELIS FLAMMEA   AV

Redpoll

Accidental visitor (*C. f. cabaret*). 4 records: one near Palermo, Nov 1903; one at Acireale, Nov 1966 (Priolo 1972b); one near Alcamo, 5 Nov 1971 (Sorci *et al.* 1972); one at Madonie Mts, Dec 1974.

349. LOXIA CURVIROSTRA   RB PM WV

Crossbill

Local resident breeder at Aetna. Irregular summer-autumn migrant and winter visitor (*L. c. curvirostra*), Jun-Feb; influxes of 10s or 100s occasionally reported, e.g 1909–10, 1929–30, 1935–36, 1963–64, 1974–75. In an area near Messina, Sturniolo (1910) observed 10s from late Jun and 100s mid Jul to early Aug, with a decrease Sep to late Oct, 1908.

Breeding. First confirmed at Aetna in 1981 (Priolo & Sarà 1981). Occurs in *Pinus laricio* forest at 1300–1800 m. Song heard almost all the year (Jan–Apr, Jun, Aug, Oct, Nov). Breeds very early, Dec-Jan to Apr–May; recently fledged young Apr–May. No details on nests. Flocks of 10s recorded on Aetna, Jun–Oct (Krampitz 1956, B. Frochot, Priolo & Sarà 1981).

L. c. sub sp. A clinal form between *curvirostra* and *polyogina* can be biometrically separated: male, wing 95·8, bill length 19·8, bill depth 11·7 mm (Massa 1987b). Males are less red and females less green than nominate race. Although northern populations moult irregularly, Sicilian crossbills moult regularly, May–Sep.

350. BUCANETES GITHAGINEUS   PM

Trumpeter Finch

Rare and irregular migrant. 14 records, 1952–1979, mostly at I. Pantelleria and Pelagian Islands, where possibly regular, and along SE coasts: May (4), Jun (2), "spring" (4), once Feb, Jul, Oct and Nov. Usually singly or up to 4, but 10 at I. Linosa, 5 May 1967 (Moltoni 1970) and a flock of 20 near Siracusa, Jul 1977. A few specimens examined belonged to *B. g. githagineus* (Moltoni 1970, Massa *et al.* 1976). Priolo (1972b) reports 2 individuals flocking with *C. chloris*.

351. PYRRHULA PYRRHULA   AV

Bullfinch

Accidental visitor. 4 records of singles (race/races unknown): I. Ustica, Nov 1872 (Doderlein 1869–74), near Palermo, 1905 (coll. Bordonaro), Spartà, Dec 1933 (MCT), near Palermo, winter 1976 (G. Cangialosi).

352. COCCOTHRAUSTES COCCOTHRAUSTES   PM WV

Hawfinch

Scarce to occasionally uncommon autumn passage migrant and winter visitor (*C. c. coccothraustes*), late Sep to mid Mar, mostly late Nov to Jan, singly or up to 30 together. Once Apr.

One recovery, of a bird ringed in N Italy.

EMBERIZIDAE

353. PLECTROPHENAX NIVALIS   PM WV

Snow Bunting

Rare and irregular passage migrant and winter visitor (*P. n. nivalis*). 11 records of singles, late Oct to mid Jan (Ajola 1959, Moltoni 1973a, Massa *et al.* 1979, Iapichino *in* Toso 1981); but 2–5 at Simeto, from late Nov 1981 to 10 Jan 1982 (Ciaccio & Siracusa 1983) and 2 there, 30 Jan 1983.

354. EMBERIZA CITRINELLA   AV

Yellowhammer

Accidental visitor (*E. c. citrinella*). At least 6 records: one at Termini, Feb 1869, 6 at Mt S. Calogero, Jan 1870, "some" Oct 1881 (Doderlein 1869–74); one at Modica, 9 Dec 1892 (ITM); one at I. Levanzo, Mar 1971 (Sorci *et al.* 1973); one at Filaga, 3 Apr 1983. Giglioli (1890) listed it as very rare at Messina. Probably overlooked.

355. EMBERIZA CIRLUS   RB PM

Cirl Bunting

Common resident breeder (*E. c. cirlus*) from sea level up to c. 1800 m, in a variety of habitats: woods, plantations, cultivated or open areas with scattered trees, mainly on low hills. It also breeds at Aeolian Islands, and recently colonised I. Levanzo (M. Lo Valvo) and I. Favignana. Scarce and irregular passage migrant (*E. c. cirlus*) in W. Sicily, I. Ustica and I. Pantelleria, Nov-Dec and Feb-Apr (Steinbacher 1955b, Ajola 1959, Moltoni 1973a).
Breeding. E. c. cirlus. Nests in shrubs, occasionally in rock crevices, 20–200 cm above ground; eggs, C/4, mid Apr to early Jul, some evidence of second broods. Once recorded breeding Nov 1985 (La Mantia & Lo Valvo 1986).

356. EMBERIZA CIA   RB

Rock Bunting

Uncommon resident breeder (*Emberiza c. cia*), mainly in mountains in N. Sicily. No evidence of movements, but recorded 5 times at Malta (Sultana & Gauci 1982).
Breeding. Occurs in rocky open areas, garigue, on slopes with scattered trees, sometimes on outskirts of natural woods, from c. 400 up to 1800 m. Breeding season Apr to early Jul, no details.

357. EMBERIZA HORTULANA   PM

Ortolan Bunting

Scarce and decreasing spring passage migrant, late Mar to early May (Moltoni 1970), some years unrecorded; irregular on autumn passage, Sep-Oct (Kumerloeve 1968, Suchantke 1960), once early Nov. Usually singly, occasionally up to 15 together. Benoit (1840) listed it as a common migrant. Doderlein (1869–74) and Pistone (1888) considered it resident in Sicily, but this is unlikely.

358. EMBERIZA RUSTICA   AV

Rustic Bunting

Accidental visitor: one shot at Villa Forni near Palermo, 1926 (MCT).

359. EMBERIZA PUSILLA   AV

Little Bunting

Accidental visitor. 2 records: one at Catania, Sep 1958 (Priolo 1972b) and one at Vicari, Dec 1970 (Sorci *et al.* 1972).

360. EMBERIZA SCHOENICLUS   PM WV OB

Reed Bunting

Uncommon autumn passage migrant and winter visitor at wetlands with large reedbeds, late Sep to late Mar, mainly Nov to early Mar. Occasional Apr-Jul. Up to 20–30 together counted at Siracusa salt-pan and Biviere di Gela, Dec-Jan. Most birds belong to *E.s. schoeniclus*, but a few specimens were identified as *intermedia* (Massa 1976b).

Breeding. E. s. schoeniclus. Benoit (1840) and Doderlein (1869–74) listed it as breeding but gave no detail. Evidence of breeding at Capo Feto marsh confirmed twice recently: one nest with 3 newly hatched young, 25 May 1970; another C/3, 10 Jun 1979. Breeding suspected at Biviere di Gela, Jul 1983 (A. Dimarca).

361. EMBERIZA BRUNICEPS   AV

Red-heading Bunting

Accidental visitor: one shot at I. Ustica, 15 Sep 1974, reported to be in a flock of 11 (Massa *et al.* 1979).

362. EMBERIZA MELANOCEPHALA   PM

Black-headed Bunting

Rare and irregular spring passage migrant, but only 2 autumn records. 11 records: singles near Messina, 1847, 1857, 1863 (Doderlein 1869–74), 29 Dec 1882 and 10 May 1884 (Giglioli 1890); 2 specimens at MCT, Apr 1903 and 3 May 1923; 2 near Palermo, autumn 1952(Steinbacher 1955b); one at I. Levanzo, May 1970 (Sorci *et al.* 1973); one near Catania, Feb 1959 (coll. Priolo); 2 near Messina, May 1971 (G. Giambona). Breeding claimed by Massa (1881) considered an error by Doderlein (ms, c. 1890).

363. MILIARIA CALANDRA   RB PM

Corn Bunting

Common resident (*M. c. calandra*) from sea level up to c. 1600 m, in open cultivated areas or garigue. Recently has immigrated to I.Favignana and possibly I. Levanzo. Numbers of residents obscure passage, but probably a scarce to uncommon autumn passage migrant (*M. c. calandra*); slight evidence of spring passage at some islets, Mar-Apr.

Breeding. M. c. calandra. Nests usually on the ground; eggs, C/3–6, mid Apr to mid May, recently fledged young mid May to late Jun. Post breeding flocks of 10s recorded Jun onwards.

GAZETTEER

List of place names and geographical locations mentioned in the text, with some indication of their geographical position and other data. See also Figs 1, 4 and 6.

Acireale	North of Catania, c. 45,000 inhabitants (Fig. 4).
Aeolian Is.	Volcanic archipelago in the Tyrrhenian Sea, composed of 7 isles (Stromboli, Panarea, Vulcano, Lipari, Salina, Filicudi, Alicudi) (Figs 1, 4).
Aetna	Large volcano, 3350 m high, 1500 km², north of Catania (Fig. 1).
Agrigento	Chief town of province, c. 45,000 inhabitants (formerly called Girgenti) (Figs 1, 4).
Agrò	River whose mouth is close to Cape S. Alessio, north of Catania.
Aidone	Province of Enna, c. 7500 inhabitants (Fig. 4).
Alcamo	Province of Trapani, c. 41,000 inhabitants (Fig. 4).
Alcantara	Very small village, near the wonderful gorges of the R. Alcantara.
Alcara Li Fusi	Province of Messina, Caronie Mts, small village (c. 3000 inhabitants) at the foot of a high calcareous massif, where the last colony of Griffon Vultures bred (Figs 1, 4).
Alicudi	Isle of the Aeolian archipelago, 5·2 km² (Fig. 1).
Anapo	River flowing through the Iblei Mts, within deep calcareous valleys, called 'cave'. Its mouth is very close to the Ciane mouth, south of Siracusa, where the only Sicilian population of *Cyperus papyrus* lives (Fig. 1).
Augusta	Province of Siracusa, c. 35,000 inhabitants (Fig. 4).
Avola	Province of Siracusa, c. 30,000 inhabitants (Fig. 4).
Bagnara	In Calabria, a locality from which it is possible to observe raptor migration.
Baucina	Province of Palermo, c. 2000 inhabitants (Fig. 4).
Belice	River, which enters the sea on the south coast near the boundary between the provinces of Trapani and Agrigento (Fig. 1).
Bisacquino	Province of Palermo, c. 7000 inhabitants (Fig. 4).
Biviere di Cesarò	Freshwater lake on the Caronie Mts (1274 m) (Fig. 1).
Biviere di Gela	Freshwater lake near Gela (Figs 1, 6).
Biviere di Lentini	Lake near Lentini, drained dry finally in 1949; formerly a very important ornithological site.
Bivona	Province of Agrigento, c. 5000 inhabitants (Fig. 4).
Bronte	Province of Catania, between Adrano and Randazzo, Mt Aetna, c. 20,000 inhabitants.
Brucoli	Province of Siracusa, near Augusta, c. 700 inhabitants (Fig. 4).
Buonfornello	Coastal plain between Termini Imerese and Cefalù, close to the R. Imera mouth, formerly rich in marshes, now heavily industrialized.
Calascibetta	Province of Enna, c. 5500 inhabitants (Fig. 4).
Calatabiano	Province of Catania, near Taormina, c. 5000 inhabitants (Fig. 4).
Calatafimi	Province of Trapani, c. 8000 inhabitants (Fig. 4).
Caltagirone	Province of Catania, c. 35,000 inhabitants (Fig. 4).
Caltanissetta	Chief town of province, c. 55,000 inhabitants (Figs 1, 4).
Campofiorito	Province of Palermo, near Corleone, c. 1500 inhabitants (Fig. 4).
Camporeale	Province of Palermo, c. 5000 inhabitants (Fig. 4).
Cape S. Vito	see San Vito Lo Capo.
Capo Bianco	Province of Agrigento, south coast (Fig. 1).
Capodarso	Isolated inland rock (795 m) between Caltanissetta and Enna.
Capo dell'Armi	Calabrian locality important for raptor migration.
Capo d'Orlando	Province of Messina, north coast (Fig. 1).
Capo Feto	Marshy area near Mazara, province of Trapani (Figs 1, 6).
Capo Granitola	Cape on the coast east of Mazara (Fig. 1).
Capo Milazzo	Cape of the peninsula of Milazzo, province of Messina, north coast (Fig. 1).
Capo Murro di Porco	Cape near Siracusa; important site for visible migration (Fig. 1).
Capo Passero	Southeastern cape of Sicily, near Portopalo, province of Siracusa (Fig. 1).

Capo Peloro	Province of Messina, in front of Calabria (Fig. 1).
Capo S. Alessio	Cape near Taormina (Fig. 1).
Capo S. Marco	Coast south, between Agrigento and Mazara (Fig. 1).
Capo Zafferano	Promontory enclosing the eastern side of the Gulf of Palermo (Fig. 1).
Caronie Mts	Provinces of Messina, Catania and Enna, also called Nebrodi (term which formerly included the Madonie Mts); highest peak 1847 m (Mt Soro) (Fig. 1).
Cassibile	Province of Siracusa, c. 2500 inhabitants (Fig. 4).
Castanea	Small village in the Peloritani Mts (c. 2000 inhabitants) between Spartà and Mt Ciccia; important observation site for raptor migration.
Castelbuono	Province of Palermo, Madonie Mts, c. 10,500 inhabitants (Fig. 4).
Castellammare del Golfo	North coast, province of Trapani, c. 15,000 inhabitants (Fig. 4).
Castelvetrano	Province of Trapani, c. 30,000 inhabitants (Fig. 4).
Castrogiovanni	Former name of Enna.
Catania	Second town of Sicily, c. 500,000 inhabitants (Figs 1, 4).
Cefalù	Province of Palermo, north coast, c. 12,000 inhabitants (Figs 1, 4).
Cesarò	Province of Messina, Caronie Mts, c. 4500 inhabitants (Fig. 4).
Chiaramonte Gulfi	Province of Ragusa, c. 8000 inhabitants (Fig. 4).
Ciane	River in province of Siracusa which enters the sea close to R. Anapo mouth (Fig. 1).
Ciclopi	Lava reefs off the coast between Acireale and Catania.
Collesano	Madonie Mts, c. 5000 inhabitants (Fig. 4).
Conca d'Oro	Large inland plain of Palermo, formerly covered by citrus plantations, now much built up.
Corleone	Province of Palermo, c. 11,000 inhabitants (Fig. 4).
Cuba (= Pantano Cuba)	Seasonal salt marsh near Pachino, province of Siracusa.
Dinnammare	One of the peaks of the Peloritani Mts (1124 m), important for raptor migration (Fig. 4).
Dirillo (mouth)	South coast, between Gela and Scoglitti (Fig. 1).
Egadi Is.	Calcareous archipelago off the west coast of Trapani, consisting of 3 islets (Favignana, Levanzo and Marettimo) (Figs 1, 4).
Enna	Chief town of province, c. 28,000 inhabitants (formerly called Castrogiovanni) (Figs 1, 4).
Erei Mts	Central-eastern Sicily, provinces of Enna and Caltanissetta, highest peak 1000 m (Fig. 1).
Erice	Province of Trapani, c. 2000 inhabitants (Figs 1, 4).
Falconara	Coastal plain between Licata and Gela.
Faro Lake	Near Messina, between Ganzirri and Capo Peloro.
Faro Superiore	Near Messina, between Ganzirri and Spartà, c. 1500 inhabitants.
Favignana	The largest isle of the Egadi archipelago, 19 km^2 (Fig. 1).
Ficuzza	Province of Palermo, very small village in the similarly named oak wood; only 150 inhabitants (Fig. 1).
Filaga	Province of Palermo, small village between Prizzi and Lercara, of only 300 inhabitants.
Filicudi	Isle of the Aeolian archipelago, 9·5 km^2 (Fig. 1).
Filippazzo	Saddle which separates the Peloritani from the Caronie Mts.
Finale	Province of Palermo, north coast, near Pollina, c. 1000 inhabitants (Fig. 4).
Floresta	Province of Messina, Caronie Mts, c. 1000 inhabitants (Fig. 4).
Foce Birgj	Mouth of The Birgj river, south of Marsala, province of Trapani (Fig. 1).
Foce Simeto	Mouth of the Simeto river, South of Catania, important site for waterbirds (Nature Reserve) (Figs 1, 6).
Formica	Reef off Trapani.
Gangi	Village of the Madonie Mts, c. 10,000 inhabitants (Fig. 4). The saddle of Gangi and the Pollina river separate the Caronie from the Madonie Mts.
Ganzirri	Small village near Messina (Fig. 4).
Gela	Province of Caltanissetta, c. 70,000 inhabitants (formerly called Terranova); on the south coast (Figs 1, 4, 6).

Geraci Siculo	Province of Palermo, Madonie Mts, c. 3000 inhabitants (Fig. 4).
Giarre	Province of Catania, c. 20,000 inhabitants (Fig. 4).
Gibilmanna	Small village on the Madonie Mts, between Cefalù and Collesano; only c. 150 inhabitants.
Gibilrossa	Saddle between Palermo and Misilmeri.
Girgenti	Former name of Agrigento.
Gorgo Lake	see Montallegro Lake.
Gurrida Lake	Small freshwater lake near Randazzo, north of Mt Aetna.
I. Lunga	The largest isle of the Stagnone archipelago, province of Trapani; rich in salt-pans and marshes (now a Nature Reserve).
Iblei Mts	Southeastern part of Sicily, provinces of Ragusa and Siracusa; highest peak 986 m (Mt Lauro) (Fig. 1).
Imera	There are two Imera rivers originating from the Madonie Mts, one (Northern Imera) flowing to north coast, the other (Southern Imera) to the south and flowing into Salso river. The mouth of Northern Imera is near Termini Imerese (Fig. 1).
Isola delle Femmine	Islet off the small village west of Palermo of same name (Fig. 4).
Ispica	Province of Ragusa, c. 12,000 inhabitants (formerly called Spaccaforno) (Fig. 4).
Itala	Province of Messina, east coast, c. 1000 inhabitants (Fig. 4).
Lampedusa	Calcareous isle of the Pelagian archipelago, 20 km^2 (Fig. 1).
Lampione	Calcareous reef, 17 km off Lampedusa, 3 ha (Fig. 1).
Lascari	Province of Palermo, near Cefalù, c. 2500 inhabitants (Fig. 4).
Lentini	Province of Siracusa, c. 3200 inhabitants (Figs 1, 4).
Levanzo	Isle of the Egadi archipelago, 6 km^2 (Fig. 1).
Licata	Province of Agrigento, c. 41,000 inhabitants (Figs 1, 4).
Linosa	Volcanic isle of the Pelagian archipelago, 5 km^2 (Fig. 1).
Lipari	The largest isle of the Aeolian archipelago, 37·6 km^2 (Fig. 1).
Longarini	Seasonal salt marsh between Pachino and Pozzallo, province of Siracusa.
Lo Zucco Montelepre	Province of Palermo, between Terrasini and Partinico.
Macconi	Sand-dunal reefs on the southern coast between Gela and Scoglitti, near Vittoria.
Madonie Mts	High calcareous-dolomitic mountains in province of Palermo, highest peak 1979 m (Pizzo Carbonara) (Fig. 1).
Malabotte	East side of the Caronie Mts, on the boundary with the Peloritani Mts, covered by extensive beech woods.
Mandanici	Province of Messina, Peloritani Mts, c. 1000 inhabitants (Fig. 4).
Maraone	Reef off Trapani.
Marettimo	Isle of the Egadi archipelago, 12 km^2 (Fig. 1).
Marsala	Province of Trapani, c. 60,000 inhabitants (Figs 1, 4, 6).
Marzamemi	Province of Siracusa, near Portopalo, c. 350 inhabitants (Fig. 4).
Mazara (= Mazara del Vallo)	Province of Trapani, c. 40,000 inhabitants (Figs 1, 4).
Messina	Chief town of province, c. 250,000 inhabitants (Figs 1, 4).
Milazzo	Province of Messina, c. 25,000 inhabitants (Figs 1, 4).
Misilmeri	Province of Palermo, c. 15,000 inhabitants (Fig. 4).
Mistretta	Province of Messina, W Caronie Mts, c. 8000 inhabitants (Fig. 4).
Modica	Province of Ragusa, c. 40,000 inhabitants (Fig. 4).
Mondello	Formerly a large salt marsh, now the public beach of Palermo.
Monreale	Above Palermo, viewpoint of the 'Conca d'Oro', c. 20,000 inhabitants (Fig. 4).
Montallegro Lake (= Gorgo Lake)	Very small dam between Agrigento and Ribera (Fig. 6).
Montemaggiore (= M. Belsito)	Province of Palermo, c. 5000 inhabitants (Fig. 4).
Mozia	Islet of the Stagnone archipelago, province of Trapani, famous as an archaeological site, first excavated by J. Whitaker.
Mt Cammarata	Peak of the Sicani Mts (1584 m) (Fig. 1).
Mt Ciccia	One of the peaks of the Peloritani Mts (609 m), important observation site for raptor migration (Fig. 4).
Mt Cuccio	Inland of Palermo, 1050 m, circumscribes the 'Conca d'Oro'.
Mt Erice	Near Trapani, 751 m (formerly called Mt S. Giuliano) (Fig. 1).
Mt Ferro	One of the peaks of the Madonie Mts (1906 m), near Mt S. Salvatore.

Mt Gallo (or Cape Gallo)	Promontory, 561 m, enclosing the western side of the Gulf of Palermo.
Mt Grande	Peak of the Peloritani Mts (1374 m). There is another Mt Grande in the province of Trapani.
Mt Lauro	Peak of the Iblei Mts (986 m) (Fig. 1).
Mt Pellegrino	Promontory (606 m) north of Palermo, which Goethe described as "the most beautiful in the world" (Fig. 1).
Mt San Calogero	Isolated massif (1326 m) inland from Termini Imerese.
Mt S. Giuliano	Former name of Mt Erice.
Mt S. Salvatore	Second highest peak of the Madonie Mts, 1912 m.
Mt Soro	Peak of the Caronie Mts, 1847 m (Fig. 1).
Mussomeli	Province of Caltanissetta, c. 12,000 inhabitants (Fig. 4).
Naro	Province of Agrigento, c. 13,000 inhabitants. There are also a Naro river and a Naro reservoir in the same area (Figs 4, 6).
Nebrodi	See Caronie Mts.
Nicosia	Province of Enna, c. 15,000 inhabitants (Fig. 4).
Novara (di Sicilia)	Province of Messina, Caronie Mts, c. 2500 inhabitants (Fig. 4).
Ogliastro reservoir	At the boundary of the provinces of Enna and Catania, near Raddusa (Fig. 6).
Pachino	Province of Siracusa, c. 21,000 inhabitants (Figs 4, 6).
Palazzo Adriano	In the southern part of the province of Palermo, c. 3000 inhabitants (Fig. 4).
Palazzolo Acreide	Province of Siracusa, Iblei Mts, c. 9000 inhabitants (Fig. 4).
Palermo	Chief town of Sicily, c. 700,000 inhabitants (Figs. 1, 4).
Panarea	Isle of the Aeolian archipelago, 3·4 km² (Fig. 1).
Pantalica	Archaeological site (necropolis) along the Anapo river (now a Nature Reserve).
Pantelleria	Volcanic Isle (83 km²) in the Sicilian Channel, 100 km off Cape Granitola and 80 km off Cape Mustafà (Tunisia); its highest peak is 836 m (Fig. 1).
Parco della Favorita	Large gardens between Palermo and Mondello, inland of Mt Pellegrino.
Partanna	Province of Trapani, c. 11,000 inhabitants (Fig. 4). (There is another small village, close to Mondello, called Partanna.)
Partinico	Province of Palermo, c. 25,000 inhabitants (Fig. 4).
Paternò	Province of Catania, c. 40,000 inhabitants (Fig. 4).
Patti	Province of Messina, north coast, c. 12,000 inhabitants (Figs 1, 4).
Pelagian Is. (= Pelagic Is.)	Archipelago in the Sicilian Channel, composed of the isles of Linosa and Lampedusa and the reef of Lampione (Figs 1, 4).
Peloritani Mts	Province of Messina, highest peak 1374 m (Mt Grande) (Fig. 1).
Pergusa	Freshwater lake near Enna (called 'the navel of Sicily') (Figs 1, 4, 6).
Piana degli Albanesi	Province of Palermo, old Albanese village formerly called P. dei Greci, c. 6000 inhabitants. Near the village there is a reservoir of same name (Figs 1, 4, 6).
Piano Battaglia	Madonie Mts (1600 m), below Pizzo Carbonara (1979 m).
Piano Cervi	Madonie Mts, below Mt Cervi (1794 m). The place-name testifies the ancient presence of deer in Sicily.
Piano Zucchi	Madonie Mts, between Collesano and P. Battaglia.
Pietralonga	Rock within the plain of Tagliavia, province of Palermo.
Pizzo Carbonara	Highest peak of the Madonie Mts (1979 m).
Platani	River in province of Agrigento, reaching the sea between Agrigento and Sciacca (Fig. 1).
Pollina	Small village of the Madonie Mts, between Cefalù and Finale, c. 3000 inhabitants. The Pollina river and the saddle of Gangi separate the Caronie from the Madonie Mts.
Poma reservoir (= Iato)	Province of Palermo, near Partinico (Fig. 6).
Porto Empedocle	Harbour of the town of Agrigento, c. 15,000 inhabitants (Fig. 4).
Portopalo di Capo Passero	Province of Siracusa, c. 2500 inhabitants. Southeast point of Sicily (Fig. 1).
Pozzallo	Province of Ragusa, c. 12,000 inhabitants (Fig. 4).
Pozzillo reservoir	Province of Enna, near Regalbuto (c. 10,000 inhabitants) (Fig. 6).

Preola Lake	Freshwater lake near Mazara, Trapani province. There are three small ponds around the Preola lake, one called Murana and two called Gorghi Tondi.
Priolo	Province of Siracusa, c. 8000 inhabitants (Fig. 4).
Prizzi reservoir	Province of Palermo, near Prizzi (Figs 4, 6).
Punta Raisi	Plain near Terrasini, airport of Palermo.
Racalmuto	Province of Agrigento, c. 10,000 inhabitants (Fig. 4).
Raddusa	Province of Catania, c. 4000 inhabitants (Fig. 4).
Raffo Rosso	Rocky area peaking at 763 m, between Palermo and Isola delle Femmine.
Ragusa	Chief town of province, c. 60,000 inhabitants (Figs 1, 4).
Randazzo	Province of Catania, Mt Aetna, c. 11,000 inhabitants (Figs 1, 4).
Ribera	Province of Agrigento, c. 17,000 inhabitants (Fig. 4).
Rocca Busambra	Isolated calcareous massif, highest peak 1613 m, dominating the wood of Ficuzza, province of Palermo (Figs. 1, 4).
Rocca di Novara	Isolated calcareous massif of the Caronie Mts, 1340 m.
Roccalumera	Province of Messina, Peloritani Mts, a locality important for Raptor migration.
Roccapalumba	Province of Palermo, c. 3500 inhabitants (Fig. 4).
Rubino reservoir	Province of Trapani, near Salemi (Fig. 6).
S. Croce Camerina	Archaeological site near Scoglitti, province of Ragusa, south coast (Fig. 4).
S. Flavia	Province of Palermo, near Bagheria, c. 5000 inhabitants.
S. Fratello	Province of Messina, Caronie Mts, c. 6500 inhabitants (Fig. 4).
S. Giuseppe Iato	Province of Palermo, between Piana Albanesi and Partinico, c. 8000 inhabitants.
S. Mauro Castelverde	Eastern side of the Madonie Mts, between Castelbuono and Mistretta, c. 3000 inhabitants.
S. Nicola l'Arena	Between Bagheria and Termini Imerese.
S. Vito Lo Capo (= C. S. Vito)	Province of Trapani, at the tip of the similarly named peninsula, c. 3500 inhabitants (Fig. 1).
Salina	Isle of the Aeolian archipelago, 26·8 km² (Fig 1).
Salso	River, terminating on the south coast, close to Licata (Fig. 1).
Scanzano reservoir	Province of Palermo, between Marineo and Ficuzza (Fig. 6).
Sciacca	Province of Agrigento, c. 30,000 inhabitants (Fig. 4).
Scicli	Province of Ragusa, c. 20,000 inhabitants (Fig. 4).
Scillato	Province of Palermo, Madonie Mts, south of Collesano, c. 1000 inhabitants.
Scoglitti	Province of Ragusa, near Vittoria, c. 2000 inhabitants (Fig. 4).
Selinunte	Archaeological coastal site, south of Castelvetrano, province of Trapani.
Serradifalco	Province of Caltanissetta, c. 8000 inhabitants (Fig. 4).
Sicani Mts	Calcareous massifs between Belice and Platani rivers, highest peak 1584 m (Mt Cammarata) (Fig. 1).
Sicilian Channel	Sea between Sicily, Tunisia and Libya.
Simeto	The most important river of Sicily, province of Catania (Fig. 1).
Siracusa	Chief town of province, c. 100,000 inhabitants (Figs 1, 4).
Soprano Lake	Freshwater lake near Serradifalco, province of Caltanissetta.
Sosio	River flowing through the Sicani Mts, south of the province of Palermo (Fig. 1).
Spaccaforno	Former name of Ispica.
Spartà	Province of Messina, north coast, c. 500 inhabitants (Fig. 4).
Specchio di Venera	Small natural lake of I. Pantelleria, characterized by its warm sulphurous water.
Stagnone Is.	Islets off the coast of Marsala, south of Trapani (Fig. 1).
Stromboli	Isle of the Aeolian archipelago, 12·6 km² (Fig. 1).
Sutera	Province of Caltanissetta, c. 2500 inhabitants (Fig. 4).
Tagliavia	Hilly area between Corleone and Piana degli Albanesi.
Taormina	Province of Messina, c. 8000 inhabitants (Fig. 4).
Termini Imerese	Province of Palermo, c. 25,000 inhabitants (Figs 1, 4).
Terranova	Former name of Gela.
Terrasini	Province of Palermo, c. 8500 inhabitants (Figs 1, 4).
Tindari	North coast, province of Messina, near Patti, only 200 inhabitants (Fig. 4).

Trapani	Chief town of province, c. 70,000 inhabitants (Figs 1, 4).
Ustica	Volcanic isle, c. 70 km off Palermo coast, 8·1 km^2 (Fig. 4).
Valle del Bove	Large depression (5 × 7 km) on the east side of Mt Aetna.
Vendicari	Salt marsh between Noto and Pachino, in southeast Siracusa province; important site for waterfowl (Nature Reserve) (Figs 1, 6).
Vicari	Province of Palermo, c. 3500 inhabitants (Fig. 4).
Villabate	Suburb of Palermo (c. 10,000 inhabitants) (Fig. 4).
Vittoria	Province of Ragusa, c. 45,000 inhabitants (Fig. 4).
Vizzini	Province of Catania, c. 8500 inhabitants (Fig. 4).
Vulcano	Isle of the Aeolian archipelago, 21 km^2 (Fig. 1).
Zafferana Etnea	Province of Catania, Mt Aetna, c. 5000 inhabitants (Fig. 4).
Zingaro Nature Reserve	The first N.R. established in Sicily, now managed by the Azienda Foreste Demaniali, between S. Vito Lo Capo and Castellammare del Golfo, in extreme northwest (Fig. 4).

APPENDIX 1

SPECIES REJECTED FROM THE SICILIAN LIST

BLACK-FOOTED ALBATROSS *Diomedea nigripes.* One shot while settled on the beach near Messina, 10 Nov 1971 (Sorci *et al.* 1972); no other west Palaearctic records (Cramp & Simmons 1977, Harrison 1985), and release by sailors highly probable.

LITTLE SHEARWATER *Puffinus assimilis.* One sight record off Sicily (Fogolen 1962 *in* Toschi 1969); no details or description available and best regarded as doubtful.

EGYPTIAN GOOSE *Alopochen aegyptiacus.* Said to have been shot in Sicily, but no details (Temminck 1840).

VELVET SCOTER *Melanitta fusca.* Doderlein (1869–74) reported one shot near Catania by Zuccarello Patti, but no reference to this bird is found in Zuccarello's works.

BLACK VULTURE *Aegypius monachus.* Listed as rare breeder by Doderlein (1869–74) on Benoit's authority, but Benoit (1840) did not list it; reported as rare near Messina by Pistone (*in* Giglioli 1890). As Trischitta (1918a) pointed out, these authors seem to have misconstrued Benoit's statement on *Gyps fulvus* as referring to *Aegypius monachus.* The only claimed Sicilian specimen (Doderlein 1890 MS) in fact came from Sardinia (Trischitta 1918a).

BOBWHITE *Colinus virginianus.* Recently introduced to Mozia islet and Madonie Mts, but there is no evidence of breeding in the wild, though 2 males were recorded singing on Mozia, May 1986 (A. Carapezza).

CHUKAR *Alectoris chukar.* Sometimes introduced for shooting, always unsuccessfully (see also Rock Partridge *Alectoris graeca*).

BARBARY PARTRIDGE *Alectoris barbara.* Its claimed occurrence in Sicily (Temminck 1840, Malherbe 1843) seems unlikely.

PHEASANT *Phasianus colchicus.* Unsuccessfully introduced in the past century by Bourbons (Doderlein 1869–74) and, occasionally in this century, by C. Orlando (Krampitz 1958); also by hunters associations and forestry.

CROWNED CRANE *Balearica pavonina.* Swanson (1836 *in* Orlando 1958o) listed it for I. Lampedusa without details, but a specimen claimed to have been collected there in 1882 is preserved at MZUP. Arrigoni (1929) did not accept these records. 2 were recorded at Termini Imerese, autumn 1931 (Orlando 1935, 1958o), but there are no accepted Palaearctic records and the Sicilian birds were probably escapes.

SPUR-WINGED PLOVER (LAPWING) *Hoplopterus spinosus.* One shot at Ispica, 1955, (Di Carlo 1972) was in fact *Chettusia gregaria.* One undated specimen from Sicily is not accepted by Arrigoni (1929).

PURPLE SANDPIPER *Calidris maritima.* Doderlein (1869–74) stated that this species "sometimes" occurred in Sicily, but gave no record. One unlabelled specimen in coll. Trischitta was possibly imported.

GREAT BLACK-BACKED GULL *Larus marinus.* At least 2 were reported by Doderlein (1869–74) with inadequate details; and one was shot near Palermo, 17 Oct 1965, but its measurements as reported (Randazzo 1966) do not exclude confusion with *Larus fuscus* (skin lost).

ROSEATE TERN *Sterna dougallii.* One sight record off Palermo, 18 Jan 1971 (Sorci *et al.* 1972) is not confirmed by the description.

PIN-TAILED SANDGROUSE *Pterocles alchata.* Temminck (1840) said it was "common" in Sicily. Doderlein (1869–74, 1881) reported no record and listed it as a doubtful former visitor near Gela and Mazara.

RUFOUS TURTLE DOVE *Streptopelia orientalis.* One was shot near Noto, 11 Nov 1984 (S. Baglieri). This record was not accepted by National Homologation Committee (Brichetti *et al.* 1986).

RING-NECKED (ROSE-RINGED) PARAKEET *Psittacula krameri*. Sometimes recorded, but there is no evidence of its breeding in the wild, as has recently been shown in N and Cen Italy (Spanò & Truffi 1986).

MONK PARAKEET *Myiopsitta monachus*. 2 records near Siracusa: Sep 1984, 2 Aug 1985. Recently bred in wild in N Italy (Spanò & Truffi 1986).

PIED KINGFISHER *Ceryle rudis*. Malherbe (1843) obtained a specimen claimed to have been collected in Sicily, but gave no detail.

MIDDLE SPOTTED WOODPECKER *Dendrocopus medius*. Doderlein (1869–74) listed it as breeding on Madonie Mts on Minà Palumbo's authority (1861). Minà Palumbo, in his main work (1853–57), did not mention this species and published no ornithological paper in 1861. Giglioli (1890) considered it "rare" on Madonie, but gave no record. Orlando (1956c) stated this bird has never occurred in Sicily.

HOOPOE LARK *Alaemon alaudipes*. Temminck (1840) stated it had occurred in Sicily, but without detail.

DUPONT'S LARK *Chersophilus duponti*. Malherbe (1842–43) stated it had been shot in Sicily, but gave no detail.

PIED WHEATEAR *Oenanthe pleschanka*. One specimen from Ragusa at MM, 27 Apr 1971 (Di Carlo 1972) was in fact an *O. hispanica* (1975, E. Moltoni). One sight record at Rocca Busambra, 3 Apr 1972 (Cangialosi *in* Di Carlo 1972) has only inadequate details.

GRASSHOPPER WARBLER *Locustella naevia*. Listed by Malherbe (1843) as "rare" without details. Priolo (1954) stated its occurrence had never been confirmed in Sicily.

OLIVACEOUS WARBLER *Hippolais pallida*. There are 2 sight records, one at Capo Murro di Porco, 2 Sep 1979, and one at I. Linosa, 23 May 1982, but the descriptions do not exclude pale *H. icterina* beyond doubt. There are 7 records at Malta from 1960 (Sultana & Gauci 1982).

DESERT WARBLER *Sylvia nana*. One sight record at I. Pantelleria, 28 Aug 1974 (Brucher & Lehmann 1975). Brichetti & Massa (1984) include this record in the Italian Check-list, but the description of the individual observed in the field by Brucher & Lehmann (1975) is too brief to confirm identification.

NUTCRACKER *Nucifraga caryocatactes*. Doderlein (1881) wrote that "sometimes it arrives from the north". Listed by Mariani (1942) without details.

CITRIL FINCH *Serinus citrinella*. Malherbe (1843) listed it as rare in winter near Palermo, but his statements are often unreliable.

COMMON ROSEFINCH (SCARLET GROSBEAK) *Carpodacus erythrinus*. One reported by Doderlein (1881) with inadequate details. Arrigoni (1929) listed it as a rare migrant for Italy and isles, but gave no Sicilian record. Recorded 13 times at Malta (Sultana & Gauci 1982).

CRETZSCHMAR'S BUNTING *Emberiza caesia*. One undated specimen labelled "Sicily" in coll. Trischitta. Reported as a doubtful visitor by Doderlein (1869–74) and Zodda (1905).

APPENDIX 2

RINGING AND RECOVERIES

Data in this section are much less detailed than we had hoped to provide. The Istituto Nazionale di Biologia della Selvaggina (INBS) which runs the national ringing scheme is unfortunately still unable to supply copies of all recovery sheets. So information is based mainly on lists published by Orlando (1955g) and Moltoni (1966, 1973b, 1976a,b), who unfortunately omitted some important details (e.g. ringing co-ordinates, ring numbers) and, to a lesser extent, on works by Rydzewsky (1960), Arnould & Lachaux (1974), Caterini (1979), Osservatorio Ornitologico Siciliano (1979), Bendini (1983) and Lo Valvo (*in* Iapichino 1983, 1984).

We have complete details for only a small fraction of the total number of recoveries. For some recoveries we lack almost all details except ringing country: these are omitted from the appendix but are included in the summary of ringing under each species in the systematic list.

Many geographical names of ringing localities are extracted from the literature and not from recovery sheets, so some may be given erroneously, others may be too generic (e.g. "Black Sea"). The country of origin given refers to political boundaries at the time of ringing; recoveries from W and E Germany are combined. For each Sicilian locality we give the relevant administrative district with its initials in brackets: Palermo (PA), Catania (CT), Messina (ME), Siracusa (SR), Ragusa (RG), Caltanissetta (CL), Enna (EN), Agrigento (AG) and Trapani (TP). The number of recovered rings reported has dropped in recent years, following legal protection to the majority of birds most usually ringed; nearly all shooters now prefer to throw away the rings. Almost all the birds recovered were shot.

In the section on birds ringed in Sicily, recoveries within Sicily are included only if they occurred at earliest in the calendar year following ringing. Ringing in Sicily was only occasional in the past and was carried out only by Angelo Priolo. Since 1975, however, small numbers of birds are annually ringed; 5656 birds were ringed from 1982 to 1986, 3056 of them being *Calonectris diomedea*.

Foreign-ringed birds recovered in Sicily

Age symbols. 1 = pullus, 2 = adult, 3 = juvenile (first year bird), 4 = immature (post-first year)

SPECIES	Age	Date	RINGED Place	Date	RECOVERED Place
Podiceps nigricolis		8 Jun 65	Pardublice, Czechoslovakia	26 Oct 65	Raddusa (CT)
	3	5 Oct 79	Zbudov, **Czechoslovakia**	14 Oct 79	Near Palermo
Calonectris diomedea	2	30 May 74	I. Zembra, **Tunisia**	Sep 74	Off C. Murro di Porco (SR)
	2	18 Jun 77	Filfla, **Malta**	27 Mar 79	Siracusa
	3	20 Sep 78	I. Lavezzi, **Corsica, France**	15 Feb 84	Near Palermo
	3	4 Oct 78	Selvagem Grande, **Portugal**	16 May 87	I. Linosa (AG)
Puffinus puffinus	2	22 May 79	L-Ahrax, **Malta**	17 Jun 82	Avola (SR)
Hydrobates pelagicus		13 Jun 70	Filfla, **Malta**	29 Jul 76	Southern Ionian sea (SR)
	2	27 May 72	Filfla, **Malta**	20 Aug 72	Itala Marina (ME)
	2	27 May 72	Filfla, **Malta**	27 Apr 75	Off Siracusa
	2	28 Jun 73	Filfla, **Malta**	24 Jul 73	Pachino (SR)
	2	28 Jun 73	Filfla, **Malta**	15 Apr 75	Ionian sea (SR)
		6 Aug 73	**Malta**	15 Apr 75	25 km off Siracusa
	2	1 Jul 78	Filfla, **Malta**	7 Apr 79	Off Siracusa
Sula bassana	1	15 Jul 61	Bass Rock, **Great Britain**	19 Feb 64	Palermo
(continued)	1	4 Jul 64	Bass Rock, **Great Britain**	14 Nov 64	Porto Empedocle (AG)

SPECIES	Age	Date	RINGED Place	RECOVERED Date	Place
Sula bassana	1	1 Jul 66	Ailsa Craig, **Great Britain**	16 Dec 66	Catania
(cont.)	1	29 Jun 82	Wexford, **Ireland**	18 Jan 85	Punta Raisi (PA)
Phalacrocorax carbo		?	?, **Denmark**	6 Nov 78	Jato reservoir, Partinico (PA)
	1	30 Jun 28	Lekkerkerk, **Holland**	4 Oct 28	Termini Imerese (PA)
	1	29 May 31	Lekkerkerk, **Holland**	25 May 32	Mazara (TP)
	1	30 May 34	Pulitz, **Germany**	5 Nov 34	Siracusa
	1	3 May 36	Lekkerkerk, **Holland**	15 Jan 38	Biviere di Gela (CL)
		3 Jul 51	Koszalin, **Poland**	21 Mar 54	Milazzo (ME)
		31 May 57	Rostock, **Germany**	11 Nov 57	I. Linosa (AG)
		30 May 57	Niederhof, **Germany**	26 Nov 57	Selinunte (TP)
		1 Jun 57	Niederhof, **Germany**	20 Oct 59	Messina
	1	5 Jun 60	Svarto, **Sweden**	28 Sep 60	Messina
	1	29 Jun 62	Niederhof, **Germany**	1976	Mazara (TP)
		30 Jun 62	Niederhof, **Germany**	20 Oct 62	Marsala (TP)
	2	10 Jun 76	Varso Harsens Fjord-Jylland, **Denmark**	22 Jan 78	Castelvetrano (TP)
		30 May 78	Varso Harsens Fjord-Jylland, **Denmark**	25 Oct 78	Trinità reservoir (TP)
	1	13 May 79	Varso, Jylland, **Denmark**	10 Jun 84	Terrasini (PA)
Ixobrychus minutus	3	30 Jun 51	Osternienburg, **Germany**	24 Nov 51	Castel di Judica (CT)
	1	26 Jun 56	Zillebeke, **Belgium**	17 Sep 57	Milazzo (ME)
Nycticorax nycticorax			Kisbalaton, **Hungary**	27 Mar 31	Belice river (AG)
	1	16 Jun 13	Kisbalaton, **Hungary**	9 Sep 13	Acireale (CT)
	1	28 Jun 25	Kisbalaton, **Hungary**	4 Oct 25	Barcellona (ME)
	1	20 Jun 27	Kisbalaton, **Hungary**	14 Apr 29	Catania
		7 Jun 28	Kisbalaton, **Hungary**	18 Sep 29	Valguarnera (PA)
	1	2 Jun 31	Kisbalaton, **Hungary**	27 Mar 33	Castelvetrano (TP)
	1	5 Jun 31	Kisbalaton, **Hungary**	20 Sep 31	Catania
	1	20 Jun 31	Kisbalaton, **Hungary**	12 Sep 35	Corleone (PA)
	1	29 Jun 31	Sataraljaujlhely, **Hungary**	26 May 32	Paternò (CT)
	1	2 Jun 37	Camargue, **France**	5 Nov 37	Paternò (CT)
	1	22 Jul 39	Bologna, **Italy**	26 Oct 39	I. Pantelleria (TP)
	1	16 Jun 52	Enese, **Hungary**	22 May 66	Noto (SR)
	1	11 Jun 53	Kisbalaton, **Hungary**	6 Sep 53	Ficarazzi (PA)
	1	28 Jun 55	Vojvodina, **Yugoslavia**	14 Oct 55	Siracusa
	1	20 Jul 57	Kupinovo, **Yugoslavia**	5 Oct 57	Catania
	1	7 Jun 62	Coto Donana, **Spain**	1 May 63	Salemi (TP)
	1	10 Jun 65	Trebon, **Czechoslovakia**	20 Oct 65	Palazzo Adriano (PA)
	1	29 May 71	Lomnice nad Luznici, **Czechoslovakia**	15 Jun 74	Motta S. Anastasia (CT)
Ardeola ralloides	1	16 Jun 12	Obedska Bara, **Yugoslavia**	20 Apr 14	Selinunte (TP)
	3	21 Jun 50	Kisbalaton, **Hungary**	16 Apr 52	Gela (CL)
	1	27 Jun 57	Vojvodina, **Yugoslavia**	3 May 59	I. Lipari (ME)
	1	21 Jun 65	Vojvodina, **Yugoslavia**	21 Apr 67	Trapani
Egretta garzetta	1	5 Jun 34	Camargue, **France**	8 Apr 36	Catania
	1	14 Jun 34	Camargue, **France**	4 Aug 34	Messina
	1	26 Jun 55	Vojvodina, **Yugoslavia**	12 Sep 55	Pozzallo (RG)
	1	28 Jun 55	Carsko Blato, **Yugoslavia**	14 Oct 55	Siracusa
	1	19 Jun 56	Vojvodina, **Yugoslavia**	12 Oct 59	Siracusa
	1	11 Jun 60	Chikly, **Tunisia**	19 Mar 62	Sciacca (AG)
	1	15 Jul 62	I. Pillet, **France**	May 72	Portopalo (SR)
	1	27 May 66	Vojvodina, **Yugoslavia**	3 Oct 66	Milena (CL)
	1	1 Jul 69	Harvatska, **Yugoslavia**	11 Nov 69	Agrigento
	1	4 Jul 77	Vojvodina, **Yugoslavia**	13 Sep 77	Capo Zafferano (PA)
	3	4 Jul 77	Bezdan, **Yugoslavia**	13 Nov 77	Capo Zafferano (PA)
Egretta alba	1	18 Jun 56	Vojvodina, **Yugoslavia**	13 Apr 60	Gela (CL)
	1	5 Jul 57	Krasnodar, **USSR**	19 Oct 57	Mazara (TP)
Ardea cinerea		?	?, **USSR**	10 Dec 78	Roccapalumba (PA)
	1	27 May 27	Kisbalaton, **Hungary**	20 Oct 27	Pachino (SR)
	1	15 Jun 28	Kisbalaton, **Hungary**	1 Nov 28	Noto (SR)
	1	7 Jun 29	Schwarzort, **USSR**	9 Oct 30	Lentini (SP)
	3	7 Jun 31	L. Sakern, **Sweden**	3 Jan 31	Gela (CL)
	1	15 Jun 31	Kisbalaton, **Hungary**	14 Sep 31	Trapani
	1	16 May 34	Kruttinnen, **Poland**	29 Sep 34	Mazara (TP)
(continued)	1	25 Jun 49	L. Rybinskoe, **USSR**	29 Sep 49	Catania

SPECIES	Age	Date	RINGED Place	RECOVERED Date	Place
Ardea cinerea	1	25 Jun 49	L. Rybinskoe, **USSR**	6 Mar 50	S. Leone (AG)
(cont.)	1	19 Jun 55	Chevroux, **Switzerland**	5 May 57	Marsala (TP)
	1	3 Jul 57	Vyina-Estonya, **USSR**	22 Nov 57	Rosolini (SR)
	1	15 Jun 66	Valmiera, Latvia, **USSR**	Dec 66	Salt pans Siracusa
	1	16 Jun 70	Olsztyn, **Poland**	22 Jan 71	Agrigento
	1	12 May 73	L. Grand Lieu, **France**	26 Mar 77	Castelvetrano (TP)
	3	12 May 74	Kherson, Ukraine, **USSR**	Apr 81	Near Catania
		25 May 75	Beljaevka-Odessa, **USSR**	17 Dec 76	Mouth of Naro (AG)
Ardea purpurea	1	summer 10	Sarokerdo, **Hungary**	20 Apr 12	Mouth of Alcantara (CT)
	1	24 Jun 10	Sarokerdo, **Hungary**	Sep 10	Caccamo (PA)
	1	24 Jun 10	Sarokerdo, **Hungary**	1 Apr 14	Contessa Entellina (AG)
	1	Jul 10	Sarokerdo, **Hungary**	21 Oct 10	Scaletta (ME)
	1	20 Jun 12	Sarokerdo, **Hungary**	14 Oct 12	Messina
	1	11 Jul 12	Ujvidek-Novi Sad, **Yugoslavia**	15 Oct 12	Messina
	1	29 May 27	Kisbalaton, **Hungary**	28 Mar 32	Pozzillo (EN)
	1	16 Jun 29	Kisbalaton, **Hungary**	16 Oct 29	Alcamo (TP)
	1	18 Jun 31	Kisbalaton, **Hungary**	15 Oct 31	Ficarazzi (PA)
	1	19 Jun 31	Kisbalaton, **Hungary**	14 Sep 31	Trapani
	1	18 Jun 32	Kisbalaton, **Hungary**	7 Apr 35	Messina
	3	14 Jun 35	Valle Bonelli, **Italy**	13 Apr 40	Scicli (RG)
	3	16 Jun 39	Backo Gradiste, **Yugoslavia**	8 Apr 48	Pozzillo (EN)
	3	29 May 40	Valle Bonelli, **Italy**	15 Nov 40	Lentini (SR)
		15 Jun 53	Kisbalaton, **Hungary**	4 Apr 56	Messina
	1	19 Jun 55	Chevroux, **Switzerland**	5 May 57	Mazara (TP)
	1	2 Jun 56	Gabcikovo-Dunaj Streda, **Czechoslovakia**	22 Apr 59	Messina
	1	15 Jun 57	Noorden-Zuid, **Holland**	18 Oct 57	Marsala (TP)
		9 Jul 58	Kopacki, **Yugoslavia**	16 Aug 58	Salemi (TP)
		6 Jun 59	Noorden-Zuid, **Holland**	26 Apr 62	Marsala (TP)
	1	9 Jun 60	Kopacki-Bilje, **Yugoslavia**	13 Oct 60	Randazzo (CT)
		19 Jun 64	Kopacki, **Yugoslavia**	Sep 64	Sciara (PA)
	1	13 Jun 65	Szeged-Feherto, **Hungary**	1 Oct 68	Messina
		12 Jun 70	Noorden-Zuid, **Holland**	28 May 74	I. Ustica (PA)
		16 Jun 82	Zatin, Moravia, **Czechoslovakia**	15 Feb 84	Near Palermo
Ciconia ciconia	1	17 Jul 33	Luchow, **Germany**	19 Apr 37	Messina
	1	Jun 44	Bergum, **Holland**	27 Apr 47	Salemi (TP)
	1	May 46	Mirabeau, **Algeria**	11 May 46	Catania
	1	8 Jun 55	Altreu, **Switzerland**	17 May 58	Messina
	1	29 Jun 57	Gut Hodenberg, **Germany**	14 May 59	Marsala (TP)
Plegadis falcinellus	1	14 Jun 28	Kisbalaton, **Hungary**	15 May 33	Agrigento
	1	11 May 22	Kisbalaton, **Hungary**	19 Mar 25	Ispica (RG)
Platalea leucorodia	1	28 Jun 08	Obedska Bara, **Yugoslavia**	Oct 09	Marsala (TP)
		21 May 39	Dinnyés, **Hungary**	7 May 40	Agrigento
	1	14 Jun 40	Dinnyés, **Hungary**	18 Apr 46	Catania
	1	10 Jun 42	Kisbalaton, **Hungary**	24 Apr 46	Caltanissetta
	1	7 Jun 50	Oggau, **Austria**	15 Sep 50	Gela (CL)
	1	2 Jun 64	Hortbagy, **Hungary**	10 Sep 64	Salt pans Siracusa
Phoenicopterus ruber	1	1 Aug 54	Camargue, **France**	27 Aug 57	Capo Passero (SR)
		12 Jul 78	Camargue, **France**	25 Oct 78	L. Dirillo (CL)
	1	2 Aug 78	Camargue, **France**	8 Oct 78	Salt pans Siracusa
	1	2 Aug 78	Camargue, **France**	17 Sep 78	Vendicari (SR)
	1	Aug 78	Camargue, **France**	30 Oct 78	Jato reservoir, Partinico (PA)
Tadorna tadorna		?	?, **USSR**	25 Nov 58	Trapani
Anas penelope	3	13 Aug 49	Kedrovka, **USSR**	22 Nov 50	Gela (CL)
Anas crecca		?	?, **USSR**	2 Dec 54	Trapani
		17 Feb 53	Camargue, **France**	28 Apr 54	Trapani
		12 Dec 53	Abberton, **Great Britain**	6 Jun 54	Trapani
Anas acuta		28 Jul 32	Astrakhan, **USSR**	10 Nov 33	Trapani
		31 Jul 49	Astrakhan, **USSR**	29 Mar 50	Biviere di Gela (CL)

SPECIES	Age	RINGED Date	RINGED Place	RECOVERED Date	RECOVERED Place
Anas		26 Jul 49	Astrakhan, **USSR**	23 Mar 50	Torremuzza (CT)
querquedula		23 Jul 51	Astrakhan, **USSR**	16 Mar 52	Agnone (SR)
		4 Feb 78	Sevaré-Mopti, **Mali**	10 Mar 78	Termini Imerese (PA)
Pernis apivorus	1	27 Jul 48	Dalarna, **Sweden**	9 May 61	Sciacca (AG)
	1	3 Aug 62	Hulsingland, **Sweden**	1964 or 65	I. Pantelleria (TP)
	1	26 Jul 63	Rehakka, **Finland**	22 Dec 64	Rosolini (SR)
	1	4 Aug 64	Skane, **Sweden**	5 May 67	Castanea (ME)
	1	8 Aug 73	Angersjo, **Sweden**	Sep 73	Bagheria (PA)
	1	30 Jul 76	Sotkamo Oulun, Helsinki, **Finland**	9 Oct 76	Casteldaccia (PA)
Milvus migrans	1	19 Jun 37	Schwerin, **Poland**	14 Apr 39	Marineo (PA)
	1	17 Jul 54	Vaud, **Switzerland**	16 Apr 57	Messina
	1	12 Jun 59	Trebur, **Germany**	23 May 60	I. Ustica (PA)
Milvus milvus	3	2 Jul 31	Rumkogel b. Kratow, **Germany**	2 Nov 31	Sambuca (AG)
	3	17 Jun 38	Oberwesel a. Rhein, **Germany**	5 Mar 40	Trapani
Circus		?	?, **Poland**	Nov 73	Pachino (SR)
aeruginosus	1	29 Jun 52	Buchau, **Germany**	Oct 52	Trapani
Circus macrourus	2	8 Apr 55	C. Bon, **Tunisia**	12 Apr 55	Catania
	2	8 Apr 55	C. Bon, **Tunisia**	8 Nov 57	Bagheria (PA)
		7 Apr 63	C. Bon, **Tunisia**	31 Mar 67	Catania
Circus pygargus	3	4 Jul 53	Oland, **Sweden**	22 Apr 56	Marsala (TP)
	1	30 Jun 66	Grand Fontaine-Doubs, **France**	16 Apr 70	Punta Raisi (PA)
Accipiter nisus		6 Jul 52	Olberdorf, **Germany**	15 Oct 52	Palagonia (CT)
	1	29 Jun 74	Lilla Jolpan, **Sweden**	5 Dec 74	Palermo
Buteo buteo	3	26 Jun 30	Latvia, **USSR**	4 Nov 30	Noto (SR)
Buteo buteo		15 May 65	C. Bon, **Tunisia**	26 Nov 66	Mazara (TP)
vulpinus		11 May 67	C. Bon, **Tunisia**	28 May 67	I. Pantelleria (TP)
		24 May 67	C. Bon, **Tunisia**	20 May 68	Sferro (ME)
Pandion		?	**Finland**	23 Sep 79	Salt pans, Siracusa
haliaetus	3	9 Jul 28	Norra Ottajon, **Sweden**	21 Oct 28	I. Lipari (ME)
		16 Jul 33	Animskog, **Sweden**	2 Sep 33	Alcamo (TP)
	1	10 Jul 49	Lappora, **Finland**	15 Oct 49	I. Salina (ME)
		30 Jun 50	Djuron, **Sweden**	14 Apr 53	Misilmeri (PA)
		24 Jun 51	Svennevad, **Sweden**	30 Dec 52	Trapani
		26 Jul 54	Syvajarvi, **Finland**	9 Oct 54	Catania
		8 Jul 56	Mankaneva, **Finland**	5 May 58	Catania
	1	20 Jul 59	Solnuntaka, **Finland**	14 Nov 59	Messina
		22 Jul 62	Pentojarvi, **Finland**	6 Oct 63	Acireale (CT)
		15 Jul 64	Kaukkola, **Finland**	9 Oct 64	Lentini (SR)
	1	7 Jul 79	Karjalohja, Karislojo, **Finland**	15 Mar 82	Near Catania
	1	14 Jul 83	St Michel, Mikkelin, **Finland**	15 Oct 83	Jato reservoir, Partinico (PA)
Falco naumanni		18 Jun 55	Gran, **Austria**	19 Sep 55	Messina
	4	7 May 64	C. Bon, **Tunisia**	22 May 64	Mt Ciccia (ME)
Falco		?	**USSR**	13 Oct 57	Catania
tinnunculus	2	12 Apr 53	C. Bon, **Tunisia**	28 Apr 53	Mazara (TP)
		31 Mar 56	C. Bon, **Tunisia**	10 Oct 57	Aci Catena (CT)
		31 Mar 56	C. Bon, **Tunisia**	5 Apr 56	Paternò (CT)
		26 Jun 57	Pirkkala, **Finland**	14 Oct 57	Castelvetrano (TP)
	4	19 Apr 59	C. Bon, **Tunisia**	25 Apr 60	Mt Ciccia (ME)
	4	1 May 60	C. Bon, **Tunisia**	19 May 60	Near Messina
	1	17 Jul 60	Lappland, **Sweden**	Nov 60	Corleone (PA)
	2	22 Apr 62	C. Bon, **Tunisia**	27 Oct 64	Catania
	2	30 Apr 62	C. Bon, **Tunisia**	13 May 62	S. Filippo del Mela (ME)
	2	5 May 62	C. Bon, **Tunisia**	21 Nov 62	Castel di Lucio (ME)
	4	6 May 62	C. Bon, **Tunisia**	10 May 62	Marsala (TP)
	2	10 Apr 63	C. Bon, **Tunisia**	23 Mar 65	Messina
	4	24 Apr 63	C. Bon, **Tunisia**	19 May 63	Messina
	4	30 Apr 63	C. Bon, **Tunisia**	15 Jun 63	I. Stromboli (ME)
	4	4 May 63	C. Bon, **Tunisia**	25 Sep 66	Modica (RG)
(continued)		10 May 63	C. Bon, **Tunisia**	11 Jan 65	Bisacquino (PA)

SPECIES	Age	Date	Place	Date	Place
			RINGED		**RECOVERED**
Falco	4	9 May 64	C. Bon, **Tunisia**	10 Mar 68	Castanea (ME)
tinnunculus		28 Jun 64	Riedwihr, **France**	15 May 65	I. Ustica (PA)
(cont.)	4	21 Mar 65	C. Bon, **Tunisia**	19 Apr 65	Carini (PA)
	4	7 Apr 65	C. Bon, **Tunisia**	8 Jan 67	Carini (PA)
	4	9 Apr 65	C. Bon, **Tunisia**	12 May 65	Messina
		12 Apr 65	C. Bon, **Tunisia**	12 May 65	Messina
	2	12 Apr 65	C. Bon, **Tunisia**	28 Apr 65	Meri (ME)
	2	18 Apr 65	C. Bon, **Tunisia**	23 Apr 65	Partanna Mondello (PA)
		30 Apr 65	C. Bon, **Tunisia**	12 May 65	I. Ustica (PA)
	1	19 Jun 65	?, **Finland**	18 Apr 67	Bagheria (PA)
		4 May 66	C. Bon, **Tunisia**	20 Apr 67	Castanea (ME)
	2	7 May 66	C. Bon, **Tunisia**	16 May 66	Castanea (ME)
	2	15 May 66	C. Bon, **Tunisia**	22 May 66	S. Filippo del Mela (ME)
	2	8 Apr 67	C. Bon, **Tunisia**	24 Mar 68	Messina
	2	8 Apr 67	C. Bon, **Tunisia**	20 Apr 69	Messina
	2	13 Apr 67	C. Bon, **Tunisia**	4 Apr 69	Messina
	4	16 Apr 67	C. Bon, **Tunisia**	21 Apr 68	Messina
	4	13 May 67	C. Bon, **Tunisia**	3 Oct 71	Ganzirri (ME)
	4	15 May 67	C. Bon, **Tunisia**	29 May 67	S. Pier Niceto (ME)
	2	6 Apr 68	C. Bon, **Tunisia**	24 Apr 68	Castroreale Terme (ME)
	2	11 Apr 68	C. Bon, **Tunisia**	17 Apr 68	Messina
	4	11 Apr 68	C. Bon, **Tunisia**	17 Apr 68	Peloritani Mts (ME)
	4	18 Apr 68	C. Bon, **Tunisia**	28 Apr 68	Messina
	4	24 Apr 68	C. Bon, **Tunisia**	6 May 68	Marsala (TP)
Falco vespertinus		26 May 62	C. Bon, **Tunisia**	27 May 62	I. Levanzo (TP)
Coturnix	2	?	Paris, **France**	Spring 31	Messina
coturnix	2	8 May 30	Domsod, **Hungary**	26 Apr 31	Trapani
	2	12 May 30	Szigetszentmiklos, **Hungary**	1 Dec 31	Caltanissetta
		1 May 31	C. Bon, **Tunisia**	15 May 31	Messina
		6 May 34	C. Bon, **Tunisia**	18 May 34	Palermo
	2	16 Aug 36	Manerba (BS), **Italy**	28 Nov 37	Palermo
	2	17 May 38	Gaggiano (MI), **Italy**	27 Apr 39	S. Agata (ME)
	2	27 May 38	Lucca, **Italy**	14 May 39	Villafranca (ME)
	2	26 Apr 39	I. Scala, **Italy**	30 Apr 40	Palermo
	2	14 May 39	Modena, **Italy**	10 Sep 39	Lercara (PA)
	2	24 May 39	Stagliano, **Italy**	27 Apr 40	Palermo
	2	24 May 39	Modena, **Italy**	5 Oct 39	Partanna (TP)
	2	18 Jun 39	Loreto, **Italy**	26 Nov 39	Furnari (ME)
	2	25 Apr 40	Cerea (VR), **Italy**	12 Oct 40	Messina
	2	28 Apr 40	Modena, **Italy**	4 May 41	Faro (ME)
	2	30 Apr 40	Rovigo, **Italy**	6 Nov 40	Partinico (PA)
	2	2 May 40	Genova, **Italy**	11 May 41	Spartà (ME)
	2	20 May 40	Roma, **Italy**	14 Nov 40	Partinico (PA)
		2 Aug 40	Bologna, **Italy**	30 Apr 41	I. Pantelleria (TP)
	2	24 Apr 41	Mortara (PV), **Italy**	5 Aug 41	Catania
	2	14 May 41	Lucca, **Italy**	5 May 42	Messina
	2	2 Jun 42	Reggio Calabria, **Italy**	7 Sep 42	Pasquasia (EN)
	2	25 Apr 47	Mantova, **Italy**	8 May 48	Palermo
	2	14 May 47	Portogruaro, **Italy**	8 May 48	Palermo
	2	16 May 47	Brescia, **Italy**	25 Apr 48	Faro Superiore (ME)
	2	20 May 47	Monza (MI), **Italy**	21 Mar 48	Piano (CT)
	2	29 May 47	Verona, **Italy**	21 Mar 48	Passomartino (CT)
		5 May 48	Livorno, **Italy**	18 Sep 48	I. Pantelleria (TP)
		5 May 48	Padova, **Italy**	19 Aug 48	I. Ustica (PA)
	2	10 May 48	Firenze, **Italy**	14 Nov 48	Acireale (CT)
	2	12 May 48	Vigevano (PV), **Italy**	4 Nov 48	Trapani
	2	13 May 48	San Vincenzo, **Italy**	30 Apr 49	Alcamo (TP)
	2	15 May 48	Trecate (NO), **Italy**	19 Sep 49	Randazzo (CT)
	2	5 May 49	Vado Ligure (SV), **Italy**	18 Sep 49	Messina
	2	7 May 49	San Vincenzo, **Italy**	22 Sep 49	Riposto (CT)
		11 May 49	Livorno, **Italy**	24 Sep 50	I. Pantelleria (TP)
	2	31 May 49	Rieti, **Italy**	22 Apr 51	Pace (ME)
		10 May 50	Milano, **Italy**	4 Oct 50	I. Pantelleria (TP)
		10 May 50	Ravenna, **Italy**	25 Apr 51	I. Lipari (ME)
	2	10 May 50	Ferrara, **Italy**	2 May 51	Xitta (TP)
	2	15 May 50	Modena, **Italy**	14 Apr 51	Saponara (ME)
	2	15 May 50	Modena, **Italy**	15 Apr 51	Saponara (ME)
(continued)	2	15 May 50	Modena, **Italy**	4 May 51	Spartà (ME)

SPECIES	Age	RINGED		RECOVERED	
		Date	Place	Date	Place
Coturnix	2	18 May 50	Reggio Emilia, **Italy**	25 Apr 51	Ganzirri (ME)
coturnix	2	20 May 50	Portogruaro, **Italy**	7 May 51	San Lorenzo (ME)
(cont.)	2	Jun 50	Genova, **Italy**	8 May 51	Spartà (ME)
		2 Jun 50	Genova, **Italy**	4 Oct 50	I. Pantelleria (TP)
	2	2 Jun 50	Sampierdarena (GE), **Italy**	31 Oct 51	Ganzirri (ME)
		4 Jun 50	Genova, **Italy**	28 Apr 51	Mazara (TP)
	2	23 Jun 50	Bergamo, **Italy**	5 May 51	Camaro (ME)
	2	10 Jul 50	Roma, **Italy**	15 Sep 50	Sampieri (RG)
	2	24 Apr 51	Mortara (PV), **Italy**	4 Oct 51	Marsala (TP)
	2	2 May 51	Roccastrada, **Italy**	15 May 52	Piano Rame (ME)
	2	3 May 51	Pavia, **Italy**	24 Sep 51	I. Lipari (ME)
	2	5 May 51	Perugia, **Italy**	25 Sep 51	Pisano (CT)
		6 May 51	Casale Monferrato (AL), **Italy**	30 Dec 51	Paternò (CT)
		8 May 51	Cecina (LI), **Italy**	1 May 52	Santa Lucia (CT)
		12 May 51	Lugo (VR), **Italy**	21 Oct 51	Buccheri (SR)
		14 May 51	Bologna, **Italy**	1 Dec 51	Trapani
		28 May 51	Genova, **Italy**	10 Apr 52	Palmentazzo (ME)
		26 Apr 52	Savona, **Italy**	17 Apr 53	Salemi (TP)
		27 Apr 52	Cerea (VR), **Italy**	24 May 53	Custonaci (TP)
		28 Apr 52	Sesto Fiorentino (FI), **Italy**	14 Apr 53	Porticello (PA)
		30 Apr 52	Camisano (CR), **Italy**	26 Apr 53	Letoianni (ME)
		3 May 52	Como, **Italy**	29 Sep 52	S. Filippo del Mela (ME)
		4 May 52	Genova, **Italy**	16 Sep 52	Rilievo (TP)
		4 May 52	San Remo (IM), **Italy**	20 Mar 53	I. Pantelleria (TP)
		7 May 52	Genova, **Italy**	29 Sep 53	I. Ustica (PA)
		23 May 52	Genova, **Italy**	15 May 53	Mandanici (ME)
		1 May 53	Roma, **Italy**	12 May 53	Granateri (ME)
		1 May 53	Roma, **Italy**	8 May 53	Faro Superiore (ME)
		10 May 53	C. Bon, **Tunisia**	11 May 53	Messina
		11 May 53	Mantova, **Italy**	16 Dec 53	Castelvetrano (TP)
		14 May 53	Casale Monferrato (AL), **Italy**	20 Sep 53	Santo (ME)
		22 May 53	Piacenza, **Italy**	12 Nov 53	Manciamele (SR)
		23 May 53	Torino, **Italy**	21 Sep 53	Giampilieri (ME)
		29 Apr 54	C. Bon, **Tunisia**	19 Mar 54	Messina
		9 May 54	C. Bon, **Tunisia**	22 Aug 54	Cammarata (AG)
		29 May 54	Cremona, **Italy**	4 Oct 54	I. Pantelleria TP)
		2 Apr 55	C. Bon, **Tunisia**	13 Oct 55	Siracusa
		3 Apr 55	C. Bon, **Tunisia**	4 May 55	Messina
		3 Apr 55	C. Bon, **Tunisia**	6 May 55	Messina
		1 May 55	C. Bon, **Tunisia**	3 May 55	Taormina (CT)
		7 May 55	Genova, **Italy**	22 Sep 55	I. Pantelleria (TP)
		7 May 55	C. Bon, **Tunisia**	11 May 55	Messina
		1 May 56	C. Bon, **Tunisia**	22 Aug 56	Messina
		9 May 56	C. Bon, **Tunisia**	16 May 56	Messina
		11 May 56	C. Bon, **Tunisia**	13 May 56	Messina
		11 May 56	C. Bon, **Tunisia**	16 May 56	Messina
		13 May 56	C. Bon, **Tunisia**	3 May 57	Casteldaccia (PA)
		29 Apr 57	Padova, **Italy**	1957	I. Pantelleria (TP)
		4 May 57	C. Bon, **Tunisia**	19 Aug 57	Catania
		4 May 57	C. Bon, **Tunisia**	26 May 57	Messina
	2	4 May 57	C. Bon, **Tunisia**	28 Apr 58	Alì (ME)
		1 Aug 57	Lyss, **Switzerland**	17 Dec 57	Siracusa
	2	23 Apr 59	C. Bon, **Tunisia**	4 May 59	Near Messina
	2	25 Apr 59	C. Bon, **Tunisia**	3 May 59	Zaffaria (ME)
	4	30 Apr 59	C. Bon, **Tunisia**	12 May 59	Near Messina
	2	30 Apr 59	C. Bon, **Tunisia**	16 May 59	Giardini (ME)
	2	30 Apr 59	C. Bon, **Tunisia**	16 May 59	Villafranca Tirrena (ME)
	4	2 May 59	C. Bon, **Tunisia**	13 May 59	I. Levanzo (TP)
	2	2 May 59	C. Bon, **Tunisia**	16 May 59	Riviera Contemplazione (ME)
	2	2 May 59	C. Bon, **Tunisia**	17 May 59	Near Messina
	2	29 Mar 60	C. Bon, **Tunisia**	13 Apr 60	Bagheria (PA)
	2	26 Apr 60	C. Bon, **Tunisia**	25 Apr 61	Near Messina
	2	27 Apr 60	C. Bon, **Tunisia**	28 Apr 60	Castellana Sicula (PA)
		15 May 61	Savona, **Italy**	15 Apr 62	I. Levanzo (TP)
(continued)	2	14 Apr 62	C. Bon, **Tunisia**	5 May 63	Sperone (ME)

SPECIES	Age	Date	Place (RINGED)	Date	Place (RECOVERED)
Coturnix	2	28 Apr 62	C. Bon, **Tunisia**	9 May 62	Faro superiore (ME)
coturnix	2	28 Apr 62	C. Bon, **Tunisia**	4 May 62	Ganzirri (ME)
(cont.)	2	29 Apr 62	C. Bon, **Tunisia**	4 Oct 63	Gesso (ME)
	2	19 Apr 63	C. Bon, **Tunisia**	5 May 63	Saba (ME)
	2	24 Apr 63	C. Bon, **Tunisia**	24 Apr 65	Ganzirri (ME)
	2	2 May 63	Draa ben Jourder, **Tunisia**	20 May 64	Messina
	2	5 May 63	C. Bon, **Tunisia**	19 May 63	S. Lucia (ME)
	4	14 Apr 65	C. Bon, **Tunisia**	4 May 65	Gianquinto (TP)
	2	21 Apr 65	C. Bon, **Tunisia**	7 May 65	Targia (SR)
	2	21 Apr 65	C. Bon, **Tunisia**	9 May 67	S. Giorgio (ME)
	2	21 Apr 65	C. Bon, **Tunisia**	30 Apr 65	Casazza (ME)
Gallinula	2	24 May 56	Poznam, **Poland**	30 Dec 56	Marsala (TP)
chloropus	3	11 Sep 80	Ismaning, Speichersee, **Germany**	20 Nov 81	Near Palermo
Fulica atra		?	?, **USSR**	21 Jan 57	Biviere di Gela (CL)
	3	13 Aug 53	Kisbalaton, **Hungary**	4 Dec 53	Biviere di Gela (CL)
Charadrius	1	1 Jul 65	Freiberg, **Germany**	27 Mar 70	Siracusa
dubius	2	3 Jul 76	Horovce, Moravia, **Czechoslovakia**	30 Jun 83	Near Catania
Charadrius alexandrinus		29 Apr 31	Apaj, **Hungary**	1 Dec 31	Gela (CL)
Vanellus vanellus		16 Nov 38	Ferrara, **Italy**	31 Dec 38	I. Ustica (PA)
	1	26 May 57	Tjurholnem, **Sweden**	1964 (?)	I. Pantelleria (TP)
	1	31 May 61	Vlijnen, **Holland**	17 Mar 62	Villafranca (ME)
		16 Oct 67	Kirchain, **Germany**	24 Jan 68	Milena (CL)
Calidris alba		30 Aug 37	Revtangen, **Norway**	26 May 38	Catania
Calidris minuta	2	9 Apr 66	Ghadira, **Malta**	19 Apr 66	Messina
		4 Sep 69	Radés, **Tunisia**	5 Sep 69	Near Catania
		8 Sep 78	Torhamn-Blekinge, **Sweden**	8 Oct 78	Mouth of Salso (CL)
Calidris ferruginea		9 Sep 46	Ottenby, **Sweden**	9 May 48	Agrigento
		20 Nov 73	Banc D'Arguin, **Mauritania**	May 74	Salt pans Siracusa
Calidris alpina		4 Oct 58	Munchen, **Germany**	11 Nov 58	Trapani
		9 Sep 73	Senné, **Czechoslovakia**	30 Aug 74	Pachino (SR)
Philomachus	2	6 Jul 51	Ottenby, **Sweden**	10 Mar 52	Trapani
pugnax		23 Aug 57	Rummelo, **Finland**	15 Sep 57	Agrigento
	3	27 Sep 58	Pori, **Finland**	21 Oct 58	Marsala (TP)
		18 Aug 59	Pori, **Finland**	25 Sep 59	Vallelunga (CL)
		3 Aug 78	Nesseby-Finmark, **Norway**	3 Sep 78	Catania
		22 Oct 80	Radés, **Tunisia**	30 Sep 81	Termini Imerese (PA)
Lymnocryptes minimus		2 Oct 76	Hannover Niedersachsen, **Germany**	1 Dec 76	Siracusa
Limosa limosa		1 Jun 80	Heves, **Hungary**	21 Apr 82	Trapani
Tringa		?	**Czechoslovakia**	Dec 81	Catania
erythropus		11 Jul 63	Kettila, **Finland**	7 Sep 63	Fiumetorto (PA)
Tringa totanus		18 Jun 17	Riems, Pomerania, **Germany**	24 Dec 17	Trapani
	1	28 May 50	Oksnoes, **Denmark**	13 Apr 51	Augusta (SR)
Tringa glareola	3	1 Sep 38	Ottenby, **Sweden**	17 Apr 40	Siracusa
		9 Aug 58	Pori, **Finland**	1 May 59	Agrigento
		25 Aug 60	Ledskar, **Sweden**	25 Sep 60	Caltanissetta
Actitis	1	17 Jul 50	Backsele, **Sweden**	10 Sep 50	Catania
hypoleucos		18 Jul 59	Leipzig, **Germany**	28 Apr 61	Misilmeri (PA)
Stercorarius skua (continued)		15 Jul 76	Foula, Shetland, **Great Britain**	10 Jan 85	Pozzillo (CT)

SPECIES	Age	Date	RINGED Place	RECOVERED Date	Place
Stercorarius skua (cont.)	1	15 Jul 79	Foula, Shetland, **Great Britain**	5 Sep 79	Off Siracusa
Larus melanocephalus		?	Orlov, **USSR**	16 Oct 51	Plaia (CT)
		6 Jul 30	Orlov, **USSR**	21 Nov 30	Mouth of Simeto (CT)
		6 Jul 30	Orlov, **USSR**	23 Feb 31	Mouth of Dirillo (CL)
		9 Apr 47	Orlov, **USSR**	25 May 50	Siracusa
		30 Jun 48	Orlov, **USSR**	13 Jan 49	Near Agrigento
		30 Jun 48	Orlov, **USSR**	14 Jan 49	Gela (CL)
		30 Jun 48	Orlov, **USSR**	24 Jan 49	Near Messina
		30 Jun 48	Orlov, **USSR**	24 May 49	Near Catania
		30 Jun 48	Orlov, **USSR**	7 Feb 49	Licata (AG)
		30 Jun 48	Orlov, **USSR**	9 Feb 49	Licata (AG)
		30 Jun 48	Orlov, **USSR**	27 Feb 49	Near Agrigento
		30 Jun 48	Orlov, **USSR**	9 Nov 49	Buonfornello (PA)
		2 Jul 48	Orlov, **USSR**	19 Dec 49	I. Pantelleria (TP)
		2 Jul 48	Orlov, **USSR**	20 Jan 49	Castellammare (TP)
		3 Jul 48	Orlov, **USSR**	Feb 49	Salso river (AG)
		2 Jul 49	Orlov, **USSR**	? 49	Near Palermo
		2 Jul 49	Orlov, **USSR**	6 Jun 50	Messina
		2 Jul 49	Orlov, **USSR**	15 Sep 50	Near Palermo
		2 Jul 49	Orlov, **USSR**	22 Jan 50	Solunto (PA)
		2 Jul 49	Orlov, **USSR**	22 Jan 50	Near Palermo
		2 Jul 49	Orlov, **USSR**	23 Oct 49	Near Palermo
		2 Jul 49	Orlov, **USSR**	25 May 50	Near Siracusa
		2 Jul 49	Orlov, **USSR**	28 Jan 51	Near Palermo
		2 Jul 49	Orlov, **USSR**	29 Dec 52	Near Palermo
		2 Jul 49	Orlov, **USSR**	Nov 49	Near Trapani
		2 Jul 49	Orlov, **USSR**	9 Nov 49	Near Palermo
		2 Jul 49	Orlov, **USSR**	19 Nov 49	Mazara (TP)
		2 Jul 49	Orlov, **USSR**	1 Mar 50	Near Palermo
		2 Jul 49	Orlov, **USSR**	8 Mar 50	Near Palermo
		2 Jul 49	Orlov, **USSR**	19 Mar 50	Near Palermo
		2 Jul 49	Orlov, **USSR**	3 Apr 50	Cannizzaro (CT)
		2 Jul 49	Orlov, **USSR**	10 Apr 50	Near Palermo
		2 Jul 49	Orlov, **USSR**	16 Mar 51	Near Palermo
		2 Jul 49	Orlov, **USSR**	24 Mar 51	Near Palermo
		2 Jul 49	Orlov, **USSR**	7 Nov 52	Near Palermo
		3 Jul 49	Orlov, **USSR**	Nov 49	Mazara (TP)
		26 Jun 50	Orlov, **USSR**	16 Mar 51	Near Palermo
		29 Jun 50	Orlov, **USSR**	13 Dec 50	Near Palermo
		29 Jun 50	Orlov, **USSR**	19 Dec 50	Near Palermo
		29 Jun 50	Orlov, **USSR**	28 Jan 51	Near Palermo
		29 Jun 50	Orlov, **USSR**	29 Dec 52	Near Palermo
		29 Jun 50	Orlov, **USSR**	9 Mar 51	Near Palermo
		29 Jun 50	Orlov, **USSR**	11 Mar 51	Near Palermo
		29 Jun 50	Orlov, **USSR**	24 Mar 51	Near Palermo
		29 Jun 50	Orlov, **USSR**	28 Mar 51	Near Palermo
		30 Jun 50	Orlov, **USSR**	13 Dec 50	Near Palermo
		30 Jun 50	Orlov, **USSR**	26 Mar 52	Near Palermo
		30 Jun 51	Orlov, **USSR**	1 Jan 52	Mouth of Simeto (CT)
		30 Jun 51	Orlov, **USSR**	10 Dec 52	Sciacca (AG)
		30 Jun 51	Orlov, **USSR**	22 Dec 51	Augusta (SR)
		30 Jun 51	Orlov, **USSR**	26 Jan 52	Near Messina
		30 Jun 51	Orlov, **USSR**	26 Mar 52	Near Messina
		30 Jun 51	Orlov, **USSR**	8 Nov 51	Near Catania
		30 Jun 51	Orlov, **USSR**	28 Nov 51	Ragusa
		30 Jun 51	Orlov, **USSR**	14 Feb 52	Ragusa
		30 Jun 51	Orlov, **USSR**	10 Feb 53	Mouth of Gela (CL)
		30 Jun 51	Orlov, **USSR**	19 Mar 53	Near Messina
		30 Jun 51	Orlov, **USSR**	23 Mar 53	Near Messina
		24 Jun 52	Orlov, **USSR**	2 Jan 53	Near Trapani
		24 Jun 52	Orlov, **USSR**	8 Dec 52	Near Palermo
		24 Jun 52	Orlov, **USSR**	10 Dec 52	Sciacca (AG)
		24 Jun 52	Orlov, **USSR**	17 Feb 53	Near Siracusa
		5 Jul 52	Orlov, **USSR**	30 Nov 52	Near Siracusa
		28 Jun 56	Orlov, **USSR**	30 Dec 57	Campofelice (PA)
	1	28 Jun 56	Orlov, **USSR**	Dec 56	I. Lampedusa (AG)
		15 Jun 70	Orlov, **USSR**	15 Oct 70	Anapo (SR)
	3	16 Jun 75	Kerson, **USSR**	28 Nov 76	Portopalo (SR)
(continued)		19 Jun 75	Kerson, **USSR**	Dec 75	Portopalo (SR)

SPECIES	Age	RINGED Date	RINGED Place	RECOVERED Date	RECOVERED Place
Larus	3	23 Jun 76	Kerson, **USSR**	28 Nov 76	Portopalo (SR)
melanocephalus	3	17 Jun 81	Kerson, **USSR**	14 Mar 82	Termini Imerese (PA)
(cont.)					
Larus minutus	3	1 Jul 34	Babit, Latvia, **USSR**	7 Mar 35	Palermo
Larus ridibundus	1	19 Jun 08	L. Velencze, **Hungary**	16 Mar 09	Near Palermo
	1	4 Jun 09	L. Velencze, **Hungary**	1 Dec 09	Galati (ME)
	3	summer 13	Lantersee, **Poland**	17 Dec 13	Near Palermo
	1	3 Jun 13	L. Velencze, **Hungary**	10 Jan 15	Siracusa
	1	Jun 14	L. Velencze, **Hungary**	14 Jan 15	Palermo
		17 Jun 28	?, **Finland**	3 Feb 29	Messina
	1	17 Jun 28	Vik, **Finland**	3 Feb 29	Near Messina
	3	16 Jun 29	L. Babit, **USSR**	26 Dec 29	Near Palermo
	1	10 Jun 32	Borga, **Finland**	12 Dec 32	Near Catania
	3	12 Jun 32	L. Babit, **USSR**	16 Jan 33	Near Messina
	1	30 May 33	Vik, **Finland**	28 Feb 34	Mouth of Gela (CL)
	1	6 Jun 34	Matsalu, Estonia, **USSR**	30 Nov 36	Near Catania
	3	15 Jun 34	Vaarso, **Denmark**	1937/38	Near Catania
	3	15 Jun 35	Petes, **Sweden**	1 Jan 36	Near Catania
	1	8 Jul 35	Karlo, **Finland**	4 Aug 37	Near Palermo
		12 May 36	Eisgrub, **Czechoslovakia**	Oct 36	I. Ustica (PA)
	1	6 Jun 36	Chropyne, **Czechoslovakia**	2 Feb 37	Near Palermo
	1	7 Jun 36	Vysoke Myto, **Czechoslovakia**	2 Dec 36	Near Palermo
	1	7 Jun 36	Karlo, **Finland**	29 Jan 37	Near Messina
	1	18 Jun 36	Bohdanec, **Czechoslovakia**	18 Mar 37	Near Siracusa
	1	21 Jun 38	Stare Jezero u Treb, **Czechoslovakia**	12 Jan 39	Sciacca (AG)
	1	11 Jun 40	Rétszilas, **Hungary**	26 Nov 40	Near Siracusa
	1	16 Jun 45	Bukovina, **Czechoslovakia**	4 Dec 47	Near Trapani
	1	20 May 50	Cernicovice, **Czechoslovakia**	Mar 52	Licata (AG)
	1	3 Jun 50	Lednice, **Czechoslovakia**	14 Jan 53	Granatello (SR)
		17 Jun 51	Chrudim, **Czechoslovakia**	29 Jan 52	Mouth of Salso (CL)
		27 Jun 52	L. Babit, **USSR**	2 Apr 53	Siracusa
	1	7 Jun 54	Rétszilas, **Hungary**	1 Mar 55	Near Messina
	1	9 Jun 54	Rétszilas, **Hungary**	14 Dec 54	Siracusa
	1	9 Jun 54	Rétszilas, **Hungary**	22 Nov 54	Catania
	1	18 Jul 54	Szeged, **Hungary**	28 Dec 58	Altavilla (PA)
		12 Jun 55	L. Babit, **USSR**	2 Jan 56	Agrigento
	1	12 Jun 55	Rétszilas, **Hungary**	28 Dec 55	Messina
		13 Jun 55	Apetlon, Burgenland, **Austria**	10 Feb 56	Near Messina
	1	2 Jul 55	Helsinki, **Finland**	19 Jan 58	Messina
	1	16 Jun 56	Rétszilas, **Hungary**	2 Jan 57	Scicli (RG)
	1	17 Jun 56	Rétszilas, **Hungary**	Winter 56/7	Messina
	1	17 Jun 56	Szeged-Feherto, **Hungary**	23 Nov 56	Messina
	1	28 Jun 56	Virolahti, **Finland**	22 Dec 56	Messina
	1	2 Jun 57	Szeged, **Hungary**	14 Feb 59	Augusta (SR)
	1	18 May 58	Szeged, **Hungary**	11 Jan 59	Pachino (SR)
	1	23 May 58	Szeged, **Hungary**	31 Dec 58	Catania
	1	15 Jun 58	Szeged, **Hungary**	28 Dec 58	Barcellona (ME)
	1	15 Jun 58	Szeged, **Hungary**	28 Feb 59	Near Messina
	1	28 May 60	Kloostri, Matsalu, **USSR**	4 Jan 62	Palermo
	1	5 Jun 60	Szeged-Feherto, **Hungary**	19 Feb 62	Messina
	1	28 May 61	Szeged-Feherto, **Hungary**	1 Oct 62	Milazzo (ME)
	1	28 May 61	Szeged-Feherto, **Hungary**	5 May 62	Messina
	1	27 May 62	Szeged-Feherto, **Hungary**	24 Dec 62	Tremestieri (CT)
	1	14 Jun 62	Porvoo, **Finland**	13 Mar 63	Near Palermo
	3	30 Jun 62	Riistavesi, **Finland**	15 Mar 63	I. Stromboli (ME)
	3	8 Jul 63	Harvatska, **Yugoslavia**	29 Nov 67	Gela (CL)
	1	7 Jun 64	Szeged-Feherto, **Hungary**	13 Jan 65	Faro (ME)
	1	7 Jun 64	Szeged-Feherto, **Hungary**	12 Feb 65	Messina
		13 Jun 64	Gizycko, **Poland**	Jan 65	Salt pans Siracusa
	1	11 Jun 66	Miletin, **Czechoslovakia**	3 Dec 67	Messina
		29 May 69	Bardaca, **Yugoslavia**	2 Dec 69	Marsala (TP)
(continued)	1	2 Jun 70	Bardaca, **Yugoslavia**	27 Feb 71	Mouth of Simeto (CT)

SPECIES	Age	Date	RINGED Place	RECOVERED Date	Place
Larus ridibundus	2	16 Aug 78	L. Bytynskie, **Poland**	27 Nov 78	Near Messina
(cont.)	1	20 Jun 79	Haademeeste, Estonia, **USSR**	27 Dec 79	Palermo
Larus genei	3	30 Jun 48	Orlov, **USSR**	7 Nov 48	Near Palermo
	3	30 Jun 48	Orlov, **USSR**	8 Apr 49	Near Catania
		30 Jun 48	Orlov, **USSR**	7 Nov 48	Near Siracusa
	3	3 Jul 49	Orlov, **USSR**	Sep 49	Near Palermo
		26 Jun 50	Orlov, **USSR**	9 Oct 51	Near Siracusa
		26 Jun 50	Orlov, **USSR**	20 Jan 51	Mouth of Irminio (RG)
		26 Jun 50	Orlov, **USSR**	Jan 51	Salt pans S. Teodoro (TP)
	3	26 Jun 50	Orlov, **USSR**	30 Dec 50	Near Siracusa
		26 Jun 50	Orlov, **USSR**	28 Jan 51	Near Palermo
	3	30 Jun 50	Orlov, **USSR**	26 Oct 50	Near Siracusa
		16/18 Jun 52	Orlov, **USSR**	18 Oct 53	Near Trapani
		16/18 Jun 52	Orlov, **USSR**	20 Oct 52	S. Leone (AG)
		16/18 Jun 52	Orlov, **USSR**	21 Dec 52	Near Siracusa
		16/18 Jun 52	Orlov, **USSR**	22 Aug 52	Between Licata and Agrigento
		16/18 Jun 52	Orlov, **USSR**	22 Oct 52	Near Trapani
		16/18 Jun 52	Orlov, **USSR**	24 Oct 52	Marausa (TP)
		16/18 Jun 52	Orlov, **USSR**	27 Dec 52	Licata (AG)
		16/18 Jun 52	Orlov, **USSR**	13 Nov 52	Near Siracusa
		16/18 Jun 52	Orlov, **USSR**	4 Feb 55	Near Agrigento
	3	16/18 Jun 52	Orlov, **USSR**	27 Nov 52	Near Catania
		18 Jun 53	Orlov, **USSR**	23 Mar 54	Near Siracusa
		18 Jun 53	Orlov, **USSR**	20 Nov 54	Near Catania
		18 Jun 53	Orlov, **USSR**	30 Dec 54	Near Siracusa
		24 Jun 53	Orlov, **USSR**	4 Jan 54	Near Catania
		24 Jun 53	Orlov, **USSR**	9 Oct 53	Near Messina
		24 Jun 53	Orlov, **USSR**	12 May 54	Near Trapani
		24 Jun 53	Orlov, **USSR**	7 Nov 53	Near Siracusa
		24 Jun 53	Orlov, **USSR**	15 Nov 53	Near Trapani
	3	22 Jun 54	Orlov, **USSR**	2 Dec 54	Near Trapani
	3	22 Jun 54	Orlov, **USSR**	3 Jun 55	Near Trapani
	3	22 Jun 54	Orlov, **USSR**	9 Dec 54	Near Siracusa
	3	22 Jun 54	Orlov, **USSR**	13 Jan 55	Near Trapani
	3	22 Jun 54	Orlov, **USSR**	16 Dec 54	Near Siracusa
	3	22 Jun 54	Orlov, **USSR**	9 Nov 54	Near Catania
	3	22 Jun 54	Orlov, **USSR**	10 Nov 54	Near Catania
	3	22 Jun 54	Orlov, **USSR**	21 Nov 54	Near Catania
	3	22 Jun 54	Orlov, **USSR**	30 Nov 54	Near Trapani
	3	22 Jun 54	Orlov, **USSR**	23 Feb 55	Near Messina
	3	23 Jun 54	Orlov, **USSR**	19 Nov 54	Near Messina
	3	23 Jun 54	Orlov, **USSR**	28 Nov 54	Near Trapani
	1	13 Jun 72	Chott el Djon, **Tunisia**	Jan 73	I. Pantelleria (TP)
		1 Jul 77	Cagliari, **Italy**	? 80	Pachino (SR)
Larus fuscus	3	12 Jul 35	Yttre Flackholmen, **Sweden**	14 Dec 35	Termini Imerese (PA)
	3	27 Jun 36	Graesholm, **Denmark**	2 Dec 37	Mouth of Simeto (CT)
	3	12 Jul 36	St Rossen, **Sweden**	Dec 36	Catania
	3	22 Jul 36	Tvarminne, **Finland**	24 Sep 36	S. Flavia (PA)
	3	29 Jun 41	Graesholm, **Denmark**	Nov 41	Palermo
	3	26 Aug 56	Farne Is, **Great Britain**	16 Nov 56	Siracusa
	1	13 Jul 73	Anholt, **Denmark**	18 Feb 76	Siracusa
	1	12 Jul 75	Anholt, **Denmark**	16 Feb 76	Siracusa
	3	31 Jul 82	Vaasan Laani, **Finland**	13 Aug 86	Siracusa
Rissa tridactyla		?	?, **USSR**	22 Oct 52	Near Trapani
		7 Jul 56	Farne Is, **Great Britain**	9 Mar 57	Palermo
Sterna caspia		?	Matsalu, Estonia, **USSR**	7 Nov 79	Siracusa
		?	**USSR**	3 Oct 81	Catania
		9 Jun 37	?, **Finland**	17 Dec 37	Scicli (RG)
		19 Jun 56	Kyrkslatt, **Finland**	8 Nov 64	Gela (CL)
		22 Jul 56	Kyrkslatt, **Finland**	5 Sep 65	Catania
		12 Jul 57	Tasenlelto, **Finland**	16 Sep 64	Mascali (CT)
		10 Jun 59	Kyrkslatt, **Finland**	26 Oct 59	Messina
		19 Jun 60	Pernaja, **Finland**	11 Nov 60	Siracusa
(continued)		13 Jun 61	Eckero, **Finland**	17 Sep 65	Catania

SPECIES	Age	Date	Place	Date	Place
			RINGED		**RECOVERED**
Sterna caspia (cont.)	1	8 Jun 63	Razdolnoe, Crimea, **USSR**	24 Sep 68	Salt pans Siracusa
	1	20 Jul 64	Raldolnoie, Crimea, **USSR**	Nov 64	Salt pans Siracusa
	1	26 Jun 65	Sodermanland, **Sweden**	4 Sep 71	Salt pans Priolo (SR)
		29 Jun 65	Snoppertuna, **Finland**	17 Sep 65	Catania
		4 Jul 70	Klyndrorna, **Sweden**	15 Oct 70	Siracusa
	1	6 Jul 71	Bjorkoby Vaasan Luani, **Finland**	6 Nov 76	Fiumetorto (PA)
	1	10 Jun 72	Klyndrorna, **Sweden**	10 Oct 72	Vendicari (SR)
		17 Jun 72	Svartlogafjarden, **Sweden**	29 Sep 74	Salt pans Priolo (SR)
	1	28 Jun 72	Kirkkonumm, **Finland**	28 Oct 76	Pachino (SR)
	1	7 Jul 72	Perna Laani, **Finland**	12 Oct 74	Sicily
	1	10 Jun 73	Algsbadarna, **Sweden**	12 Nov 75	Pantano Longarini (SR)
	1	13 Jun 73	Estonia, **USSR**	Sep 76	Pachino (SR)
	1	15 Jun 74	Bromaru Laani, **Finland**	10 Nov 76	Salt pans Priolo (SR)
	1	24 Jun 74	Vuidenmann, **Finland**	11 Nov 74	Sicily
	1	9 Jul 74	Matsalu, Estonia, **USSR**	4 Sep 74	Salt pans Priolo (SR)
	1	12 Jun 76	Kallskaren, Stockholm, **Sweden**	Oct 76	Pantano Cuba, Pachino (SR)
		20 Jun 76	Bjorkoby Vaasan Laani, **Finland**	19 Sep 76	Imera river (PA)
	1	21 Jun 76	Klyndrorna, **Sweden**	Oct 76	Pachino (SR)
	1	1 Jul 76	Kirkkonummi Laani, **Finland**	12 Sep 76	Salt pans Priolo (SR)
	3	7 Oct 76	Oulun Laani, **Finland**	15 Nov 76	Salt pans Priolo (SR)
	1	15 Jun 76	Ostergotland, **Sweden**	12 Sep 76	Salt pans Priolo (SR)
	1	19 Jun 76	Orskar, **Sweden**	Sep 82	Siracusa
	1	26 Jun 80	Matsalu, Estonia, **USSR**	Sep 82	Siracusa
	1	26 Jun 83	Sipelgarahu, Estonia, **USSR**	2 Oct 83	Palermo
Sterna sandvicensis		?	?, **USSR**	7 Nov 52	I. Lachea (CT)
	3	5 Jul 49	Black Sea, **USSR**	13 Nov 49	I. Levanzo (TP)
	3	3 Jun 58	Black Sea, **USSR**	28 Dec 58	Marsala (TP)
		Jul 58	Black Sea, **USSR**	20 Dec 58	Messina
		7 Jul 58	Black Sea, **USSR**	26 Dec 58	Torre Faro (ME)
		16 Jun 59	Black Sea, **USSR**	5 Jan 60	Marina di Ragusa (RG)
		15 Jul 55	Black Sea, **USSR**	19 Apr 57	Aci Castello (CT)
		15 Jun 70	Orlov, **USSR**	30 Oct 70	Siracusa
Chlidonias niger		9 May 40	Pisa, **Italy**	8 May 47	Catania
		7 Jun 55	**Holland**	21 Apr 59	Marsala (TP)
Columba palumbus		2 Nov 54	Lecunberry, **France**	31 Oct 55	Ragusa
Streptopelia turtur			?, **Czechoslovakia**	Sep 69	I. Pantelleria (TP)
	3	13 Jun 12	Sibyllernort, **Poland**	30 Jul 14	Marsala (TP)
	3	3 Aug 40	Zleby, **Czechoslovakia**	28 May 41	Agnone (SR)
		4 Jul 54	Ronov, **Czechoslovakia**	21 Apr 56	Mazara (TP)
	2	30 Apr 63	C. Bon, **Tunisia**	14 May 63	Campofelice (PA)
	2	1 May 64	C. Bon, **Tunisia**	30 Apr 67	Scicli (RG)
		24 Apr 69	Forlì, **Italy**	late Apr 69	I. Pantelleria (TP)
Otus scops	2	7 Apr 60	C. Bon, **Tunisia**	9 May 60	Villaggio Contemplazione (ME)
Caprimulgus europaeus	1	30 Jun 35	Ferrara, **Italy**	20 Oct 35	Sortino (SR)
Alcedo atthis	3	5 Jun 48	Zadverice, **Czechoslovakia**	6 Sep 48	Mazara (TP)
		21 Aug 59	Munchen, **Germany**	3 Oct 59	Palermo
		27 Jul 76	Domsod-Donau, Budapest, **Hungary**	17 Oct 76	Eleuterio river (PA)
Upupa epops	1	4 Jul 35	Weisenheim, **Germany**	24 Sep 35	Cipponeri (TP)
	3	13 Jun 52	?, **Poland**	30 Mar 54	Messina
Jynx torquilla	1	18 Jun 29	Budapest, **Hungary**	13 Sep 32	Caltagirone (CT)
	1	15 Jun 32	Diosjeno, **Hungary**	15 Aug 32	I. Pantelleria (TP)
	3	29 Jun 53	Luopioinen, **Finland**	18 Apr 54	Messina
		29 Jun 59	Holm, **Finland**	11 Sep 60	Messina

SPECIES	Age	Date (Ringed)	Place (Ringed)	Date (Recovered)	Place (Recovered)
Riparia riparia	2	5 Jun 68	Ousvala, **Sweden**	10 Oct 69	Catania
Hirundo rustica	1	30 Jul 26	Samso, **Denmark**	9 May 27	Palermo
	2	26 Aug 31	Karise, **Denmark**	29 Jun 34	Castelvetrano (TP)
	1	24 Jul 34	Pyritz, **Poland**	18 Apr 35	Misilmeri (PA)
	3	8 Jul 53	Aneboda, **Sweden**	1 Oct 53	Trapani
		6 May 57	Camargue, **France**	25 Jun 57	Sciacca (AG)
	2	30 Apr 67	C. Bon, **Tunisia**	12 Sep 69	Scordia (CT)
		31 Aug 67	Theux, **Belgium**	13 Oct 67	Palermo
	2	7 Apr 68	C. Bon, **Tunisia**	19 Apr 68	Caltanissetta
Delichon urbica		1 Sep 76	Leigh Marsh, Essex, **Great Britain**	10 Nov 76	Mazara (TP)
Anthus cervinus		5 Oct 58	Ottenby, **Sweden**	9 Nov 58	Messina
Motacilla flava		17 Dec 63	Kano, **Nigeria**	25 Mar 65	Messina
		28 Apr 78	Piani-Lavagna (GE), **Italy**	Mar 79	Pachino (SR)
Motacilla cinerea	3	6 Nov 71	Lunzjata, **Malta**	8 Jan 73	Castelvetrano (TP)
Motacilla alba		4 May 54	Tahi, **Hungary**	15 Jan 57	Catania
Erithacus rubecula	2	12 Sep 30	Lampertheim, **Germany**	30 Jan 32	Mendola (TP)
	2	27 Sep 31	Brieg, **Poland**	22 Oct 31	Villagrazia (PA)
	3	2 Sep 47	Polna, **Czechoslovakia**	1 Dec 47	Barcellona (ME)
		3 Oct 56	Ottenby, **Sweden**	16 Nov 56	Catania
		14 Oct 58	Rybacki, **USSR**	2 Jan 60	Caltagirone (CT)
		9 Oct 59	Rybacki, **USSR**	26 Nov 60	Palermo
		25 Oct 59	K. Marx Stadt, **Germany**	18 Jan 60	Mazara (TP)
		11 Apr 63	Hel, **Poland**	12 Dec 63	Alcamo (TP)
	3	5 Jul 64	Trencin, **Czechoslovakia**	21 Jan 65	Marsala (TP)
		14 Apr 66	Marchegj, **Austria**	2 Feb 67	Bagheria (PA)
	2	19 Nov 68	Lunzjata, **Malta**	1 Nov 69	Giardini (ME)
		16 Sep 69	Porvoo, **Finland**	Jan 70	Palermo
		20 May 82	Csobanka, **Hungary**	31 Oct 82	Valdina (ME)
Phoenicurus ochruros	3	9 Jun 30	Nassau, **Germany**	4 Nov 31	I. Pantelleria (TP)
Oenanthe oenanthe	3	23 Jun 25	Budapest, **Hungary**	30 Sep 25	I. Pantelleria (TP)
	2	31 Mar 65	C. Bon, **Tunisia**	5 Sep 66	Randazzo (CT)
	2	4 Apr 65	C. Bon, **Tunisia**	8 Apr 66	Palermo
Turdus torquatus	1	25 Mar 37	Rostock, **Germany**	30 Dec 37	Palermo
Turdus merula	2	15 Oct 60	Budakeszi, **Hungary**	18 Nov 61	Catania
	1	30 May 63	Banja Luka, **Yugoslavia**	22 Dec 63	Messina
	1	2 May 64	Dolovo, **Yugoslavia**	22 Feb 65	Mascalucia (CT)
	3	5 Jul 64	Starà Turà, **Czechoslovakia**	21 Jan 65	Marsala (TP)
	2	21 Apr 74	Budakeszi, **Hungary**	15 Jan 76	Mandanici (ME)
Turdus philomelos	3	14 May 36	Letomysl, **Czechoslovakia**	13 Nov 36	Vallelunga (CL)
	2	20 Oct 37	Castel Fusano (Roma), **Italy**	10 Feb 38	Paternò (CT)
	2	19 Oct 62	Draa ben Jourder, **Tunisia**	20 Jan 67	Corleone (PA)
		12 Oct 77	La Roncade-Vazzola (TV), **Italy**	5 Mar 78	Campobello di Mazara (TP)
Turdus iliacus	1	14 Jun 58	Trysil, **Norway**	4 Nov 59	Adrano (CT)
Hippolais icterina	1	1 Jul 55	Zettau, **Germany**	8 Sep 55	Aci S. Antonio (CT)
		22 Aug 56	Falsterbo, **Sweden**	29 Sep 56	Messina
Sylvia communis	2	28 Apr 60	C. Bon, **Tunisia**	10 May 60	I. Ustica (PA)
Sylvia borin		22 May 54	Lednice, **Czechoslovakia**	5 Sep 54	Messina
		17 Sep 58	Camargue, **France**	7 Oct 58	Mazara (TP)
	2	12 Jul 67	Strutele, Latvia, **USSR**	Sep 67	Partanna (TP)
Sylvia atricapilla		8 Sep 65	Munchen, **Germany**	19 Mar 66	Patti (ME)
Phylloscopus sibilatrix	1	7 Jun 53	Fim-Fechenheim, **Germany**	4 Sep 55	Catania

SPECIES	Age	Date	RINGED Place	RECOVERED Date	Place
Phylloscopus		25 Aug 57	Karnten, **Austria**	19 Feb 58	Messina
collybita	3	9 Oct 65	I. May, **Great Britain**	22 Mar 66	Trapani
	2	14 Jan 67	Lunzjata, **Malta**	11 Dec 67	Pedara (CT)
		27 Sep 75	Zalog, **Yugoslavia**	27 Jan 78	Catania
Muscicapa striata	1	5 Jul 54	Narke, **Sweden**	30 Apr 60	I. Ustica (PA)
	2	8 Jun 55	Ottenby, **Sweden**	Sep 56	Messina
Ficedula	1	2 Jul 80	?, **Finland**	25 Apr 81	Termini Imerese (PA)
hypoleuca					
Oriolus oriolus		?	**Poland**	4 Sep 81	Palermo
	1	22 Jun 23	Szeged, **Hungary**	6 May 28	Alcamo (TP)
	1	5 Jun 52	Szeged, **Hungary**	30 Jun 56	Marsala (TP)
Lanius collurio		?	**Norway**	1980	Partinico (PA)
	3	28 Aug 54	Seahouses, **Great Britain**	24 Sep 54	Marsala (TP)
	2	23 Apr 55	C. Bon, **Tunisia**	3 May 55	Messina
Lanius senator		1 May 55	C. Bon, **Tunisia**	22 Aug 55	Augusta (SR)
		16 Apr 56	Gabès, **Tunisia**	21 Jun 57	Acireale (CT)
		22 Apr 56	C. Bon, **Tunisia**	13 Sep 56	Pachino (SR)
	2	26 Apr 59	Gabès, **Tunisia**	21 Aug 59	Solarino (SR)
	4	28 Apr 59	Gabès, **Tunisia**	12 Oct 60	Sortino (CT)
	2	4 May 59	Gabès, **Tunisia**	20 Apr 60	Mascalucia (CT)
	2	22 Apr 62	C. Bon, **Tunisia**	2 Sep 62	Paternò (CT)
		19 Apr 64	C. Bon, **Tunisia**	8 May 65	Rometta (ME)
		14 Apr 65	C. Bon, **Tunisia**	25 May 67	Bagheria (PA)
Sturnus vulgaris	2	29 Jul 30	Kustendil, **Bulgaria**	25 Dec 30	Aci S. Antonio (CT)
	3	22 May 36	Premsendorf, **Germany**	22 Jan 38	Catania
	1	20 Jun 36	Skalbania, **Poland**	23 Oct 36	Marsala (TP)
	1	20 Jun 36	Kolonia Lisowska, **Poland**	4 Jan 38	Catania
	2	26 Jan 37	Manerba, **Italy**	28 Nov 37	Palermo
	1	14 May 37	Zehuby, **Czechoslovakia**	3 Nov 37	S. Caterina (CL)
	1	1 Jun 38	Zeitz, **Germany**	29 Oct 38	Palermo
	1	1 Jun 40	Kesarovo, **Bulgaria**	1941	Castelvetrano (TP)
	1	10 May 54	Krapina, **Yugoslavia**	18 Oct 54	Palermo
		26 Feb 57	Enfidaville, **Tunisia**	7 Dec 57	Catania
		27 Feb 57	Enfidaville, **Tunisia**	1 Sep 57	Alimena (PA)
		27 Feb 57	Enfidaville, **Tunisia**	15 Oct 57	Palermo
		27 Feb 57	Enfidaville, **Tunisia**	31 Oct 57	Enna
		27 Feb 57	Enfidaville, **Tunisia**	31 Oct 59	Alcamo (TP)
		27 Feb 57	Enfidaville, **Tunisia**	6 Mar 57	Messina
	1	30 May 58	Stari Sacz, **Poland**	15 Oct 58	Ribera (AG)
	1	31 May 58	Szeged, **Hungary**	11 Oct 58	Menfi (AG)
	1	7 May 59	Gunaros Srbja, **Yugoslavia**	17 Oct 59	Marsala (TP)
	1	21 Jun 63	Michelovce, **Czechoslovakia**	11 Jan 64	Regalbuto (EN)
	1	19 May 68	Smederevo, **Yugoslavia**	2 Oct 68	Messina
	3	21 May 75	Ryazań Region, **USSR**	30 Nov 75	Campofiorito (PA)
		22 Apr 82	Mokrice, Hrvatska, **Yugoslavia**	14 Feb 84	Giarre (CT)
Fringilla coelebs	1	7 Aug 55	Budakeszi, **Hungary**	21 Nov 57	Catania
		17 Apr 56	Budapest, **Hungary**	7 Feb 57	Caltanissetta
		29 Sep 56	Paty, **Hungary**	4 Nov 58	Messina
	2	19 Mar 57	Pestlorinc, **Hungary**	12 Feb 61	Messina
		2 Jun 57	Matrahasca, **Hungary**	25 Dec 57	S. Pantaleo (ME)
		29 Sep 58	Rybacki, **USSR**	Oct 59	Zimardo (RG)
Serinus serinus		12 Jul 31	Ljubljana, **Yugoslavia**	21 Mar 37	Messina
	2	29 Apr 37	Bullendorf, **Czechoslovakia**	24 Dec 37	Catania
		14 Jul 50	Pisa, **Italy**	14 Dec 51	Messina
	1	17 May 51	Zbraslav, **Czechoslovakia**	19 Jan 52	Nesina (CT)
	1	9 Jun 62	Beroum, **Czechoslovakia**	22 Feb 65	Milazzo (ME)
	3	7 Aug 65	Praha-Deivice, **Czechoslovakia**	8 Dec 65	Messina
Carduelis chloris		21 Oct 56	Rijeke, **Yugoslavia**	28 Mar 57	Messina

SPECIES	Age	Date	Place	Date	Place
			RINGED		RECOVERED
Carduelis carduelis	2	13 Jan 48	Split, **Yugoslavia**	25 Dec 48	Piana degli Albanesi (PA)
		26 Oct 59	Hrvatska, **Yugoslavia**	10 Feb 60	Catania
	3	31 Jul 60	Hrvatska, **Yugoslavia**	21 Feb 61	Riposto (CT)
Carduelis spinus		22 May 57	Nagykovacsi, **Hungary**	23 Feb 58	Agrigento
Carduelis cannabina		18 Oct 51	Munchen, **Germany**	17 Feb 52	Ragusa
	3	22 Jul 54	Manojilovac, **Yugoslavia**	5 Apr 55	Messina
		1955 ?	Split, **Yugoslavia**	6 Nov 55	Catania
		13 Sep 64	Wien, **Austria**	25 Oct 64	Vittoria (RG)
		20 Oct 71	Pesaro, **Italy**	Oct 72	I. Pantelleria (TP)
		1972	?, **Italy**	6 Feb 73	I. Pantelleria (TP)
		14 Oct 80	L. Patria (NA), **Italy**	15 Feb 81	Roccapalumba(PA)
Coccothraustes coccothraustes		11 Oct 77	La Roncade-Vazzola (TV), **Italy**	1978	Campobello di Mazara (TP)

Birds ringed in Sicily and recovered in Sicily and localities outside Sicily

SPECIES	Age	Date	Place	Date	Place
			RINGED		RECOVERED
Calonectris diomedea	2	6 Sep 81	I. Linosa (AG)	26 Aug 82	I. Linosa (AG)
	2	6 Sep 81	I. Linosa (AG)	26 Apr 82	I. Linosa (AG)
	2	7 Sep 81	I. Linosa (AG)	13 Sep 83	I. Linosa (AG)
	2	7 Sep 81	I. Linosa (AG)	29 Aug 82	I. Linosa (AG)
	2	25 Apr 82	I. Linosa (AG)	21 Apr 84	I. Linosa (AG)
	2	25 Apr 82	I. Linosa (AG)	13 Sep 83	I. Linosa (AG)
	2	26 Apr 82	I. Linosa (AG)	22 Apr 84	I. Linosa (AG)
	2	27 Apr 82	I. Linosa (AG)	5 Jun 84	I. Linosa (AG)
	2	27 Apr 82	I. Linosa (AG)	5 Jun 84	I. Linosa (AG)
	2	27 Apr 82	I. Linosa (AG)	21 Apr 84	I. Linosa (AG)
	2	27 Apr 82	I. Linosa (AG)	22 Apr 84	I. Linosa (AG)
	2	27 Apr 82	I. Linosa (AG)	22 Apr 84	I. Linosa (AG)
	2	28 Apr 82	I. Linosa (AG)	21 Apr 84	I. Linosa (AG)
	2	28 Apr 82	I. Linosa (AG)	5 Jun 84	I. Linosa (AG)
	2	29 Apr 82	I. Linosa (AG)	24 Apr 84	I. Linosa (AG)
	2	29 Apr 82	I. Linosa (AG)	5 Jun 84	I. Linosa (AG)
	2	29 Apr 82	I. Linosa (AG)	28 Aug 84	I. Linosa (AG)
	2	29 Apr 82	I. Linosa (AG)	21 Apr 84	I. Linosa (AG)
	2	21 May 82	I. Linosa (AG)	10 Mar 83	Jijel, **Algeria**
	2	21 May 82	I. Linosa (AG)	21 Apr 84	I. Linosa (AG)
	2	21 May 82	I. Linosa (AG)	21 Apr 84	I. Linosa (AG)
	2	22 May 82	I. Linosa (AG)	5 Jun 84	I. Linosa (AG)
	2	22 May 82	I. Linosa (AG)	21 Mar 84	Thyna, **Tunisia**
	2	23 May 82	I. Linosa (AG)	5 Jun 84	I. Linosa (AG)
	2	23 May 82	I. Linosa (AG)	22 Apr 84	I. Linosa (AG)
	2	23 May 82	I. Linosa (AG)	22 Apr 84	I. Linosa (AG)
	2	23 May 82	I. Linosa (AG)	5 Jun 84	I. Linosa (AG)
	2	23 May 82	I. Linosa (AG)	5 Jun 84	I. Linosa (AG)
	2	23 May 82	I. Linosa (AG)	5 Jun 84	I. Linosa (AG)
	2	23 May 82	I. Linosa (AG)	5 Jun 84	I. Linosa (AG)
	2	23 May 82	I. Linosa (AG)	28 Aug 84	I. Linosa (AG)
	2	23 May 82	I. Linosa (AG)	21 Apr 84	I. Linosa (AG)
	2	23 May 82	I. Linosa (AG)	21 Apr 84	I. Catania (AG)
	2	23 May 82	I. Linosa (AG)	21 Apr 84	I. Linosa (AG)
	2	23 May 82	I. Linosa (AG)	21 Apr 84	I. Linosa (AG)
	2	23 May 82	I. Nagykovacsi (AG)	22 Apr 84	I. Linosa (AG)
	2	23 May 82	I. Linosa (AG)	22 Apr 84	I. Ragusa (AG)
	2	23 May 82	I. Linosa (AG)	22 Apr 84	I. Messina (AG)
	2	23 May 82	I. Linosa (AG)	22 Apr 84	I. Linosa (AG)
	2	23 May 82	I. Linosa (AG)	22 Apr 84	I. Vittoria (AG)
	2	24 May 82	I. Linosa (AG)	5 Jun 84	I. Linosa (AG)
	2	24 May 82	I. Linosa (AG)	28 Aug 84	I. Linosa (AG)
	2	24 May 82	I. Linosa (AG)	21 Apr 84	I. Linosa (AG)
	2	24 May 82	I. Linosa (AG)	21 Apr 84	I. Linosa (AG)
	2	24 May 82	I. Linosa (ΛG)	21 Apr 84	I. Linosa (ΛG)
	2	24 May 82	I. Linosa (ΛG)	22 Apr 84	I. Linosa (AG)
(continued)	2	25 May 82	I. Linosa (AG)	20 Mar 83	Jijel, **Algeria**

SPECIES	Age	RINGED Date	Place	RECOVERED Date	Place
Calonectris	2	25 May 82	I. Linosa (AG)	20 Mar 83	I. Linosa (AG)
diomedea	2	25 May 82	I. Linosa (AG)	22 Apr 84	I. Linosa (AG)
(cont.)	2	26 May 82	I. Linosa (AG)	22 Apr 84	I. Linosa (AG)
	2	26 May 82	I. Linosa (AG)	5 Jun 84	I. Linosa (AG)
	2	26 May 82	I. Linosa (AG)	5 Jun 84	I. Linosa (AG)
	2	26 May 82	I. Linosa (AG)	22 Apr 84	I. Linosa (AG)
	2	28 May 82	I. Linosa (AG)	5 Jun 84	I. Linosa (AG)
	2	28 May 82	I. Linosa (AG)	21 Apr 84	I. Linosa (AG)
	2	30 May 82	I. Linosa (AG)	21 Apr 84	I. Linosa (AG)
	2	30 May 82	I. Linosa (AG)	22 Apr 84	I. Linosa (AG)
	2	21 Aug 82	I. Linosa (AG)	21 Apr 84	I. Linosa (AG)
	2	21 Aug 82	I. Linosa (AG)	29 Aug 84	I. Linosa (AG)
	2	22 Aug 82	I. Linosa (AG)	11 Sep 83	I. Linosa (AG)
	2	23 Aug 82	I. Linosa (AG)	21 Apr 84	I. Linosa (AG)
	2	23 Aug 82	I. Linosa (AG)	22 Apr 84	I. Linosa (AG)
	2	26 Aug 82	I. Linosa (AG)	21 Apr 84	I. Linosa (AG)
	2	26 Aug 82	I. Linosa (AG)	22 Apr 84	I. Linosa (AG)
	2	27 Aug 82	I. Linosa (AG)	21 Apr 84	I. Linosa (AG)
	2	27 Aug 82	I. Linosa (AG)	21 Apr 84	I. Linosa (AG)
	2	27 Aug 82	I. Linosa (AG)	21 Apr 84	I. Linosa (AG)
	2	28 Aug 82	I. Linosa (AG)	21 Apr 84	I. Linosa (AG)
	2	28 Aug 82	I. Linosa (AG)	21 Apr 84	I. Linosa (AG)
	2	28 Aug 82	I. Linosa (AG)	21 Apr 84	I. Linosa (AG)
	2	28 Aug 82	I. Linosa (AG)	22 Apr 84	I. Linosa (AG)
	2	28 Aug 82	I. Linosa (AG)	22 Apr 84	I. Linosa (AG)
	2	10 Apr 83	I. Linosa (AG)	22 Apr 84	I. Linosa (AG)
	2	10 Apr 83	I. Linosa (AG)	21 Apr 84	I. Linosa (AG)
	2	11 Apr 83	I. Linosa (AG)	5 Jun 84	I. Linosa (AG)
	2	11 Apr 83	I. Linosa (AG)	21 Apr 84	I. Linosa (AG)
	2	11 Apr 83	I. Linosa (AG)	22 Apr 84	I. Linosa (AG)
	2	12 Apr 83	I. Linosa (AG)	22 Apr 84	I. Linosa (AG)
	2	12 Apr 83	I. Linosa (AG)	5 Jun 84	I. Linosa (AG)
	2	12 Apr 83	I. Linosa (AG)	28 Aug 84	I. Linosa (AG)
	2	12 Apr 83	I. Linosa (AG)	5 Jun 84	I. Linosa (AG)
	2	12 Apr 83	I. Linosa (AG)	21 Apr 84	I. Linosa (AG)
	2	12 Apr 83	I. Linosa (AG)	21 Apr 84	I. Linosa (AG)
	2	13 Apr 83	I. Linosa (AG)	21 Apr 84	I. Linosa (AG)
	2	13 Apr 83	I. Linosa (AG)	24 Apr 84	I. Linosa (AG)
	2	24 May 83	I. Linosa (AG)	24 Apr 84	I. Linosa (AG)
	2	24 May 83	I. Linosa (AG)	21 Apr 84	I. Linosa (AG)
	2	27 May 83	I. Linosa (AG)	21 Apr 84	I. Linosa (AG)
	2	28 May 83	I. Linosa (AG)	21 Apr 84	I. Linosa (AG)
	2	21 Apr 84	I. Linosa (AG)	28 Aug 84	I. Linosa (AG)
	2	21 Apr 84	I. Linosa (AG)	26 Apr 86	I. Linosa (AG)
	2	21 Apr 84	I. Linosa (AG)	27 Apr 86	I. Linosa (AG)
	2	21 Apr 84	I. Linosa (AG)	27 Apr 86	I. Linosa (AG)
	2	21 Apr 84	I. Linosa (AG)	27 Apr 86	I. Linosa (AG)
	2	21 Apr 84	I. Linosa (AG)	27 Apr 86	I. Linosa (AG)
	2	21 Apr 84	I. Linosa (AG)	27 Apr 86	I. Linosa (AG)
	2	21 Apr 84	I. Linosa (AG)	29 Apr 86	I. Linosa (AG)
	2	21 Apr 84	I. Linosa (AG)	25 Apr 86	I. Linosa (AG)
	2	22 Apr 84	I. Linosa (AG)	26 Apr 86	I. Linosa (AG)
	2	22 Apr 84	I. Linosa (AG)	27 Apr 86	I. Linosa (AG)
	2	22 Apr 84	I. Linosa (AG)	27 Apr 86	I. Linosa (PAG)
	2	22 Apr 84	I. Linosa (AG)	28 Apr 86	I. Linosa (AG)
	2	23 Apr 84	I. Linosa (AG)	25 Apr 86	I. Linosa (AG)
	2	23 Apr 84	I. Linosa (AG)	27 Apr 86	I. Linosa (AG)
	2	23 Apr 84	I. Linosa (AG)	27 Apr 86	I. Linosa (AG)
	2	23 Apr 84	I. Linosa (AG)	28 Apr 86	I. Linosa (AG)
	2	23 Apr 84	I. Linosa (AG)	29 Apr 86	I. Linosa (AG)
	2	24 Apr 84	I. Linosa (AG)	28 Apr 86	I. Linosa (AG)
	2	5 Jun 84	I. Linosa (AG)	23 Apr 87	I. Linosa (AG)
	2	5 Jun 84	I. Linosa (AG)	29 Apr 86	I. Linosa (AG)
	2	5 Jun 84	I. Linosa (AG)	23 Apr 87	I. Linosa (AG)
	2	28 May 85	I. Linosa (AG)	25 Apr 86	I. Linosa (AG)
	2	28 May 85	I. Linosa (AG)	25 Apr 86	I. Linosa (AG)
	2	21 Apr 86	I. Linosa (AG)	23 Apr 87	I. Linosa (AG)
	2	21 Apr 86	I. Linosa (AG)	13 May 87	I. Linosa (AG)
(continued)	2	25 Apr 86	I. Linosa (AG)	13 May 87	I. Linosa (AG)

SPECIES	Age	RINGED Date	Place	RECOVERED Date	Place
Calonectris	2	25 Apr 86	I. Linosa (AG)	13 May 87	I. Linosa (AG)
diomedea	2	26 Apr 86	I. Linosa (AG)	23 Apr 87	I. Linosa (AG)
(cont.)	2	26 Apr 86	I. Linosa (AG)	23 Apr 87	I. Linosa (AG)
	2	26 Apr 86	I. Linosa (AG)	23 Apr 87	I. Linosa (AG)
	2	26 Apr 86	I. Linosa (AG)	13 May 87	I. Linosa (AG)
	2	26 Apr 86	I. Linosa (AG)	16 May 87	I. Linosa (AG)
	2	26 Apr 86	I. Linosa (AG)	16 May 87	I. Linosa (AG)
	2	26 Apr 86	I. Linosa (AG)	26 Aug 87	I. Linosa (AG)
	2	26 Apr 86	I. Linosa (AG)	23 Apr 87	I. Linosa (AG)
	2	27 Apr 86	I. Linosa (AG)	23 Apr 87	I. Linosa (AG)
	2	27 Apr 86	I. Linosa (AG)	23 Apr 87	I. Linosa (AG)
	2	27 Apr 86	I. Linosa (AG)	23 Apr 87	I. Linosa (AG)
	2	27 Apr 86	I. Linosa (AG)	23 Apr 87	I. Linosa (AG)
	2	27 Apr 86	I. Linosa (AG)	13 May 87	I. Linosa (AG)
	2	27 Apr 86	I. Linosa (AG)	13 May 87	I. Linosa (AG)
	2	27 Apr 86	I. Linosa (AG)	14 May 87	I. Linosa (AG)
	2	27 Apr 86	I. Linosa (AG)	16 May 87	I. Linosa (AG)
	2	27 Apr 86	I. Linosa (AG)	26 Aug 87	I. Linosa (AG)
	2	27 Apr 86	I. Linosa (AG)	26 Aug 87	I. Linosa (AG)
	2	27 Apr 86	I. Linosa (AG)	23 Apr 87	I. Linosa (AG)
	2	27 Apr 86	I. Linosa (AG)	8 Mar 87	Cherchell, **Algeria**
	2	28 Apr 86	I. Linosa (AG)	23 Apr 87	I. Linosa (AG)
	2	28 Apr 86	I. Linosa (AG)	23 Apr 87	I. Linosa (AG)
	2	28 Apr 86	I. Linosa (AG)	23 Apr 87	I. Linosa (AG)
	2	28 Apr 86	I. Linosa (AG)	14 May 87	I. Linosa (AG)
	2	28 Apr 86	I. Linosa (AG)	14 May 87	I. Linosa (AG)
	2	28 Apr 86	I. Linosa (AG)	14 May 87	I. Linosa (AG)
	2	28 Apr 86	I. Linosa (AG)	14 May 87	I. Linosa (AG)
	2	28 Apr 86	I. Linosa (AG)	14 May 87	I. Linosa (AG)
	2	28 Apr 86	I. Linosa (AG)	16 May 87	I. Linosa (AG)
	2	28 Apr 86	I. Linosa (AG)	16 May 87	I. Linosa (AG)
	2	28 Apr 86	I. Linosa (AG)	16 May 87	I. Linosa (AG)
	2	28 Apr 86	I. Linosa (AG)	26 Aug 87	I. Linosa (AG)
	2	28 Apr 86	I. Linosa (AG)	26 Aug 87	I. Linosa (AG)
	2	29 Apr 86	I. Linosa (AG)	23 Apr 87	I. Linosa (AG)
	2	29 Apr 86	I. Linosa (AG)	23 Apr 87	I. Linosa (AG)
	2	29 Apr 86	I. Linosa (AG)	23 Apr 87	I. Linosa (AG)
	2	29 Apr 86	I. Linosa (AG)	13 May 87	I. Linosa (AG)
	2	29 Apr 86	I. Linosa (AG)	14 May 87	I. Linosa (AG)
	2	29 Apr 86	I. Linosa (AG)	14 May 87	I. Linosa (AG)
	2	29 Apr 86	I. Linosa (AG)	16 May 87	I. Linosa (AG)
Hydrobates	2	2 Jun 86	I. Marettimo (TP)	16 Jul 87	I. Marettimo (TP)
pelagicus	2	2 Jun 86	I. Marettimo (TP)	16 Jul 87	I. Marettimo (TP)
	2	2 Jun 86	I. Marettimo (TP)	16 Jul 87	I. Marettimo (TP)
	2	2 Jun 86	I. Marettimo (TP)	16 Jul 87	I. Marettimo (TP)
	2	2 Jun 86	I. Marettimo (TP)	16 Jul 87	I. Marettimo (TP)
	2	2 Jun 86	I. Marettimo (TP)	16 Jul 87	I. Marettimo (TP)
	2	2 Jun 86	I. Marettimo (TP)	16 Jul 87	I. Marettimo (TP)
	2	2 Jun 86	I. Marettimo (TP)	16 Jul 87	I. Marettimo (TP)
	2	2 Jun 86	I. Marettimo (TP)	16 Jul 87	I. Marettimo (TP)
	2	2 Jun 86	I. Marettimo (TP)	16 Jul 87	I. Marettimo (TP)
	2	2 Jun 86	I. Marettimo (TP)	16 Jul 87	I. Marettimo (TP)
	2	2 Jun 86	I. Marettimo (TP)	16 Jul 87	I. Marettimo (TP)
	2	2 Jun 86	I. Marettimo (TP)	16 Jul 87	I. Marettimo (TP)
	2	2 Jun 86	I. Marettimo (TP)	16 Jul 87	I. Marettimo (TP)
	2	2 Jun 86	I. Marettimo (TP)	16 Jul 87	I. Marettimo (TP)
	2	2 Jun 86	I. Marettimo (TP)	16 Jul 87	I. Marettimo (TP)
	2	2 Jun 86	I. Marettimo (TP)	16 Jul 87	I. Marettimo (TP)
	2	2 Jun 86	I. Marettimo (TP)	16 Jul 87	I. Marettimo (TP)
	2	2 Jun 86	I. Marettimo (TP)	16 Jul 87	I. Marettimo (TP)
	2	2 Jun 86	I. Marettimo (TP)	16 Jul 87	I. Marettimo (TP)
	2	2 Jun 86	I. Marettimo (TP)	16 Jul 87	I. Marettimo (TP)
	2	2 Jun 86	I. Marettimo (TP)	16 Jul 87	I. Marettimo (TP)
	2	2 Jun 86	I. Marettimo (TP)	16 Jul 87	I. Marettimo (TP)

SPECIES	Age	Date	RINGED Place	Date	RECOVERED Place
Coturnix	2	30 Apr 51	Catania	Nov 51	**Malta**
coturnix	2	23 May 60	Catania	1964	**Malta**
Himantopus himantopus	1	26 Jun 80	Vendicari (SR)	Aug 80	Ferrara, **Italy**
Scolopax rusticola		13 Dec 77	Madonie Mts (loc. Volpignano) (PA)	30 Dec 79	Madonie Mts (loc. Volpignano) (PA)
		4 Jan 80	Madonie Mts. (loc. Volpignano) (PA)	19 Nov 81	Madonie Mts (loc. Piano Zucchi) (PA)
		23 Dec 80	Ficuzza (PA)	15 Feb 81	Godrano (PA)
Larus cachinnans	1	25 May 84	I. Levanzo (TP)	6 Sep 85	Capo S. Marco (AG)
Erithacus	2	23 Oct 83	Palermo (loc. Favorita)	2 Dec 84	Palermo (loc. Favorita)
rubecula	2	22 Oct 82	Palermo (loc. Micciulla)	3 Oct 85	Palermo (loc. Micciulla)
	2	20 Oct 81	Palermo (loc. Borgo Molara)	8 Dec 82	Palermo (loc. Borgo Molara)
	2	6 Nov 81	Misilmeri (PA)	20 Mar 84	Misilmeri (PA)
	2	13 Nov 81	Misilmeri (PA)	9 Jan 83	Misilmeri (PA)
	2	7 Dec 81	Termini Imerese (PA)	21 Mar 82	Termini Imerese (PA)
	2	24 Oct 82	Misilmeri (PA)	15 Feb 83	Misilmeri (PA)
	2	26 Nov 82	Torretta (PA)	15 Oct 83	Torretta (PA)
	2	27 Nov 83	Palermo (loc. Favorita)	14 Mar 84	Palermo (loc. Favorita)
	2	2 Dec 84	Palermo (loc. Favorita)	27 Jan 85	Palermo (loc. Favorita)
	2	18 Nov 84	Palermo (loc. Favorita)	27 Jan 85	Palermo (loc. Favorita)
Luscinia megarhynchos		3 May 60	Gurrida, Randazzo (CT)	5 Apr 61	Tripoli, **Libya**
Turdus merula	1	22 May 81	Palermo (loc. Micciulla)	2 Oct 83	Palermo (loc. Micciulla)
	1	14 Jun 81	Palermo (loc. Favorita)	7 Apr 82	Palermo (loc. Favorita)
	1	14 Jun 81	Palermo (loc. Favorita)	14 Mar 84	Palermo (loc. Favorita)
	2	21 Mar 82	Palermo (loc. Favorita)	20 Mar 83	Palermo (loc. Favorita)
	2	21 Mar 82	Palermo (loc. Favorita)	16 Oct 83	Palermo (loc. Favorita)
	2	21 Mar 82	Palermo (loc. Favorita)	4 Nov 84	Palermo (loc. Favorita)
	2	2 Apr 83	Palermo (loc. Favorita)	14 Mar 84	Palermo (loc. Favorita)
	2	2 Apr 83	Palermo (loc. Favorita)	3 Feb 85	Palermo (loc. Favorita)
	2	2 Apr 83	Palermo (loc. Favorita)	10 Feb 85	Palermo (loc. Favorita)
	2	29 May 83	Palermo (loc. Favorita)	10 Feb 85	Palermo (loc. Favorita)
	2	16 Oct 83	Palermo (loc. Favorita)	14 Mar 84	Palermo (loc. Favorita)
	2	19 Jun 83	Palermo (loc. Favorita)	3 Feb 85	Palermo (loc. Favorita)
Turdus		14 Nov 60	Randazzo (CT)	29 Jan 61	Adrano (CT)
philomelos	2	15 Nov 61	Gurrida, Randazzo (CT)	4 Mar 63	Domaine de Montarneau, **Tunisia**
Sylvia borin		27 Apr 82	I. Linosa (AG)	4 Sep 83	Ugento, Lecce, **Italy**
Sylvia atricapilla	2	4 Apr 82	Palermo (loc. Favorita)	29 May 83	Palermo (loc. Favorita)
	3	16 Oct 83	Palermo (loc. Favorita)	14 Mar 84	Palermo (loc. Favorita)
	2	18 Dec 83	Palermo (loc. Favorita)	27 Jan 85	Palermo (loc. Favorita)
	2	18 Dec 83	Palermo (loc. Favorita)	2 Dec 84	Palermo (loc. Favorita)
Phylloscopus collybita		14 Mar 84	Palermo (loc. Favorita)	2 Dec 84	Palermo (loc. Favorita)
Parus major	2	10 Oct 82	Palermo (loc. Favorita)	25 May 84	Palermo (loc. Favorita)
	2	23 Oct 83	Palermo (loc. Favorita)	5 May 85	Palermo (loc. Favorita)
	2	4 Nov 84	Palermo (loc. Favorita)	5 May 85	Palermo (loc. Favorita)
	2	18 Nov 84	Palermo (loc. Favorita)	5 May 85	Palermo (loc. Favorita)
	2	2 Dec 84	Palermo (loc. Favorita)	27 Jan 85	Palermo (loc. Favorita)
		2 Nov 85	Piana degli Albanesi (PA)	11 May 86	Piana degli Albanesi (PA)
Sturnus vulgaris		30 Nov 60	Randazzo (CT)	15 Jan 61	Bronte (CT)
Fringilla coelebs	2	4 Apr 82	Palermo (loc. Favorita)	20 Mar 83	Palermo (loc. Favorita)
	2	29 May 83	Palermo (loc. Favorita)	5 May 85	Palermo (loc. Favorita)
	3	16 Oct 83	Palermo (loc. Favorita)	5 May 85	Palermo (loc. Favorita)
	3	16 Oct 83	Palermo (loc. Micciulla)	10 Feb 85	Palermo (loc. Micciulla)
	3	16 Oct 83	Palermo (loc. Favorita)	17 Feb 85	Palermo (loc. Favorita)
	1	26 May 83	Palermo (loc. Favorita)	20 Aug 84	Palermo (loc. Favorita)
Emberiza cirlus		2 Sep 60	Randazzo (CT)	12 Mar 61	Randazzo (CT)

BIBLIOGRAPHY

Includes all Sicilian ornithological references up to 1987

AJOLA, G. 1939. Catture interessanti per la provincia di Palermo. *Riv. Ital. Orn.* 9: 211–214.

————— 1948a. Catture di uccelli interessanti. *Plinia* 1: 1–4.

————— 1948b. La quinta cattura dell'Aquila imperiale in Italia (*Aquila heliaca* Sav.). *Riv. Ital. Orn.* 8: 135–137.

————— 1950. Osservazioni sui Gabbiani e deduzioni sulle loro abitudini. *Riv. Ital. Orn.* 20: 125–139.

————— 1951a. Comparsa di *Sula bassana* (L.) nel litorale di Palermo–Gabbiani inanellati presi in Sicilia. *Riv. Ital. Orn.* 21: 112–115.

————— 1951b. Insolita abbondanza di Rapaci notturni in Sicilia. *Riv. Ital. Orn.* 21: 87–88.

————— 1955. La *Sula bassana* (L.) presente ogni anno nel mare palermitano. *Riv. Ital. Orn.* 25: 137–139.

————— 1959. Gli uccelli dell'isola di Ustica. *Riv. Ital. Orn.* 29: 89–128.

ALLAVENA, S. 1965. Elenco degli uccelli riscontrati a Panarea (Isole Eolie) del 12 al 22 agosto 1964. *Riv. Ital. Orn.* 35: 156–159.

AMARI, G. 1937. Avifauna siciliana scomparsa. *Diana* 22: 1083.

ANGELINI, G. 1892. Nota sulla Quaglia tridattila (*Turnix sylvatica*). *Boll. Soc. Romana Staz. Zool.* 1: 95–99.

————— 1893. Sulla permanenza invernale di alcune specie di Uccelli in Sicilia. *Boll. Soc. Romana Staz. Zool.* 2: 15–18.

————— 1896. Contributo allo studio delle migrazioni ornitiche con osservazioni fatte specialmente attorno allo stretto di Messina. *Boll. Soc. Romana Staz. Zool.* 5: 21–29.

ARNONE, M., DAMICO, M., DIMARCA, A., GARITO, P., GIUDICE, E., LONGO, A., ROMANO, M. & MEDORO, R. 1985. *Il Biviere di Gela.* Lega Italiana Protezione Uccelli, Caltanissetta.

ARNOULD, M. & LACHAUX, M. 1974. Baguage, reprises et controles en Tunisie 1967—1971. *Institut de Rech. Sc. et Techn. de Tunis.*

ARRIGONI DEGLI ODDI, E. 1902. *Atlante Ornitologico.* Hoepli, Milano.

————— 1913. *Merula torquata alpestris. Riv. Ital. Orn.* 2: 254.

————— 1922. Notizie sopra due specie estinte dell'avifauna italiana. *Corriere del Cacciatore* 4 (December): 6–8.

————— 1929. *Ornitologia italiana.* Hoepli, Milano

BACCETTI, N. & MONGINI, E. 1981. Uccelli marini nel Mediterraneo e Canale di Sicilia. *Avocetta* 5: 25–38.

BAGLIERI, S. 1972a. Osservazioni di nidificazione del Fratino (*Charadrius a. alexandrinus*, Linneo) nelle saline di Siracusa. *Riv. Ital. Orn.* 42: 176–180.

————— 1972b. Cattura di Ubara asiatica nella Sicilia orientale. *Riv. Ital. Orn.* 42: 445.

————— 1973a. Contributo alla conoscenza dell'avifauna siciliana. Frequenza degli uccelli di ripa nelle saline di Siracusa. *Riv. Ital. Orn.* 43: 439–453.

————— 1973b. Monachella del deserto a Siracusa. *Riv. Ital. Orn.* 43: 482–484.

————— 1973c. Stercoraridi al largo di Siracusa. *Riv. Ital. Orn.* 43: 507–508.

————— 1974a. Prime segnalazioni per l'Italia di Culbianco isabellino (*Oenanthe isabellina* Temminck). *Riv. Ital. Orn.* 44: 206–209.

————— 1974b. Due catture di Gambecchio frullino nella Sicilia orientale. *Riv. Ital. Orn.* 44: 158–160.

————— 1977. La Rondine rossiccia (*Hirundo daurica rufula* Temminck) nella Sicilia orientale. *Gli Uccelli d'Italia* 2: 13–16.

BAGLIERI, S. & FAGOTTO, F. 1977. La Rondine di mare maggiore, *Hydroprogne tschegrava* (Lepechin), nella Sicilia orientale. *Riv. Ital. Orn.* 47: 229–234.

—————, ————— 1978. Accertata la sopravvivenza del Gufo reale (*Bubo bubo* (L.)) in Sicilia. *Naturalista Sicil.* 2: 85–86.

—————, ————— 1980. Il Nibbio reale negli Iblei siracusani (Sicilia orientale). *Gli Uccelli d'Italia* 5: 219–222.

BAGLIERI, S. & IAPICHINO, C. 1974. Il Fraticello (*Sterna a. albifrons* Pallas) nidifica in Sicilia. *Riv. Ital. Orn.* 44: 293–295.

BAGLIERI, S. & IAPICHINO, C. 1979. Prima comparsa di Calandra asiatica (*Melanocorypha bimaculata* Ménètr.) in Sicilia. *Naturalista Sicil.* 3: 17–21.

BAGLIERI, S., IAPICHINO, C., MIRABELLA, F. & SCELSI, F. 1980. Un nido di Gabbiano comune (*Larus ridibundus*) in Sicilia. *Riv. Ital. Orn.* 50: 228–229.

BALDUCCI, E. 1901. La nuova cattura in Italia di un *Pelecanus crispus* Bruch. *Riv. Ital. Orn.* 1: 68–71.

BANNERMAN, D. A. & BANNERMAN, W. M. 1983. *The Birds of the Balearics.* Croom Helm Ltd, London.

BENDINI, L. 1983. Ricatture in: *Bollettino dell'attività di inanellamento.* 2. Istituto Nazionale di Biologia della Selvaggina, Bologna.

BENOIT, L. 1840. *Ornitologia Siciliana.* Stamperia G. Fiumara, Messina.

BIRBECK, R. 1854. Notes on the birds of Italy and Sicily made in 1853. *The Zoologist* 12: 4249–4251.

BLONDEL, J. 1982. Caractérisation et mise en place des avifaunes dans le bassin méditerranéen. *Ecologia Mediterranea* 8: 253–272.

——————— 1986. *Biogéographie évolutive.* Masson, Paris.

BOCCHI, G. D., MAINARDI, D. & ORLANDO, C. 1960. Gruppi sanguigni e ibridazione interspecifica in Pesci e in Uccelli. *Rend. Ist. Lombardo Accad. Sci. Lett.* 94: 63–74.

BORG, S. 1973. A brief visit to Lipari Island. *Il Merill* 12: 13.

BRICHETTI, P., FASOLA, M. & TOSO, S. 1986. Comitato di omologazione delle specie accidentali. 4. *Riv. Ital. Orn.* 56: 245–246.

BRICHETTI, P. & MASSA, B. 1984. Check-list degli Uccelli Italiani. *Riv. Ital. Orn.* 54: 3–37.

BRICHETTI, P. & VIOLANI, C. 1986. Une population nicheuse de *Parus caeruleus ultramarinus* Bp. sur l'ile de Pantelleria (Canal de Sicile). *Oiseau et R.F.O.* 56: 77–81.

BROWN, I. R. F., BANNISTER, W. H. & DE LUCCA, C. 1970. A comparison of Maltese and Sicilian Sparrow haemoglobins. *Comp. Biochem. Physiol.* 34: 557–562.

BRUCHER, VON H. & LEHMANN, VON E. 1975. Vogelbeobacthungen auf der Insel Pantelleria (Pelag. Inseln) im Sommer 1974. *Gesellschaft Naturforsch. Fr. Berlin* 15: 70–78.

BURGIO, A. 1977a. Notizie sulla permanenza del Pollo sultano nella palude di Murana (Mazara del Vallo). *Gli Uccelli d'Italia* 2: 122.

——————— 1977b. Comunicazioni *in*: Caterini, R. Brevi note sulla Sicilia. *Gli Uccelli d'Italia* 2: 229.

CAIRONE, A. 1982. Successo riproduttivo di Gheppio, Grillaio e Poiana nel territorio di Roccapalumba (Sicilia). *Avocetta* 6: 35–40.

CALCARA, P. 1842. Catalogo Uccelli *in*: Descrizione dell'Isola di Ustica. *Giorn. Letterario*, 229.

——————— 1846. *Rapporto del viaggio scientifico eseguito nelle Isole di Lampedusa, Linosa e Pantelleria e di altri punti della Sicilia.* Palermo.

——————— 1847. *Descrizione dell'Isola di Lampedusa.* Tip. R. A. Pagano, Palermo.

——————— 1851a. Elenco di alcuni Uccelli *in*: *Ricerche sulla Storia Naturale dei dintorni di Nicosia.* Stamperia M. A. Console, Palermo.

——————— 1851b. Elenco di alcuni Uccelli *in*: *Descrizione dell'Isola di Linosa.* Tip. R. A. Pagano, Palermo.

CAMBI, D. 1977. Nuova segnalazione di *Burhinus oedicnemus saharae* (Occhione del Sahara). *Riv. Ital. Orn.* 47: 278–281.

——————— 1978. Note su alcune specie di rilevante interesse ornitologico. *Gli Uccelli d'Italia* 3: 75–76.

CAMBI, L. & CAMBI, D. 1977. Osservazioni ornitologiche compiute a Pantelleria dal 29 aprile al 6 maggio 1976. *Gli Uccelli d'Italia* 2: 197–200.

CANGIALOSI, G. 1969a. Nuova cattura di Uccello delle tempeste codaforcuta. *Riv. Ital. Orn.* 39: 224–226.

——————— 1969b. Catture interessanti. *Riv. Ital. Orn.* 39: 226–227.

CASEMENT, M. B. 1966. Migration across the Mediterranean observed by radar. *Ibis* 108: 461–491.

CASTRONOVO, G. 1873. *Erice oggi Monte San Giuliano.* Notizie fisiche e naturali. Tip. Lao, Trapani.

CATALISANO, A., LO VALVO, F., LO VERDE, G. & MASSA, B. in press. Dati biometrici sull'Uccello delle tempeste (*Hydrobates pelagicus*). *Atti IV Conv. Ital. Orn., Naturalista Sicil.* 12 (suppl.).

CATALISANO, A. & MASSA, B. 1987a. Considerations on the structure of the diet of the Barn Owl (*Tyto alba*) in Sicily (Italy). *Boll. Zool.* 54: 69–73.

————, ———— 1987b. Confronto tra le comunità di uccelli del Teide (Tenerife, Canarie) e dell'Etna (Sicilia). *Riv. Ital. Orn.* 57: 173–186.

CATERINI, F. 1938. Catture rare e interessanti. *Riv. Ital. Orn.* 8: 138–139.

CATERINI, R. 1978. La Sicilia: osservazioni e censimenti. *Gli Uccelli d'Italia* 3: 29–35.

CAVENDISH TAYLOR, E. 1886. Letter on *Porphyrio coeruleus*. *Ibis* Ser 5(4): 378.

CIACCIO, A. 1986. Il Martin pescatore, *Alcedo atthis*, nidifica in Sicilia. *Riv. Ital. Orn.* 56: 108–109.

———— in press. Svernamento di un'Oca colombaccio, *Branta bernicla*, in Sicilia. *Riv. Ital. Orn.* 58.

CIACCIO, A., DIMARCA, A., LO VALVO, F. & SIRACUSA, M. in press. Primi dati sulla biologia e lo status del Lanario (*Falco biarmicus*) in Sicilia. *Ric. Biol. Selvaggina* 12 (Suppl.).

CIACCIO, A., MASCARA, R. & SIRACUSA, M. 1983. Il Grillaio, *Falco naumanni*, sverna in Sicilia. *Riv. Ital. Orn.* 53: 195.

CIACCIO, A. & SIRACUSA, M.1983a. Interessanti osservazioni ornitologiche alla foce del Simeto (Catania, Sicilia). *Riv. Ital. Orn.* 53: 37–40.

————, ———— 1983b. Il Gruccione, *Merops apiaster*, nidifica in Sicilia. *Riv. Ital. Orn.* 53: 95–96.

————, ———— 1984. Prima prova di nidificazione della Moretta tabaccata, *Aythya nyroca*, in Sicilia. *Riv. Ital. Orn.* 54: 91–92.

————, ———— 1985a. Un caso di svernamento di Fraticello, *Sterna albifrons*, in Sicilia. *Riv. Ital. Orn.* 55: 75.

————, ———— 1985b. Prime prove di nidificazione per il Gufo comune, *Asio otus*, in Sicilia. *Riv. Ital. Orn.* 55: 76.

————, ———— 1985c. Accertata nidificazione di Svasso maggiore, *Podiceps cristatus*, in Sicilia. *Riv. Ital. Orn.* 55: 201–202.

————, ———— 1987. Nuovi dati sulla nidificazione dello Svasso maggiore, *Podiceps cristatus*, in Sicilia. *Riv. Ital. Orn.* 57: 114.

CONTOLI, L., RAGONESE, B. & TIZI, L. 1978. Sul sistema trofico "Micromammiferi-*Tyto alba*" nei Pantani di Vendicari. (Noto, Sicilia S–E.) *Animalia* 5: 79–105 (also published in *Atti II Conv. Sicil. Ecol.* 275–295).

COSTANTINO, G. 1918. Un Gipaeto a Messina. *Riv. Ital. Orn.* 4: 36.

CRAMP, S. 1985. *The Birds of the Western Palearctic. Vol. IV.* Terns to Woodpeckers. Oxford Univ. Press.

CRAMP, S. & SIMMONS, K. E. L. 1977. *The Birds of the Western Palearctic. Vol. I.* Ostrich to Ducks. 1980. *Vol. II.* Hawks to Bustards. *Vol. III.* Waders to Gulls. Oxford University Press.

CUPANI, F. 1713. *Pamphiton Siculum.* 3 Vols. Ex Typogr. Regia A. Epiro, Palermo.

DE GREGORIO, A. 1910. Cattura di un grosso Avvoltoio, *Vultur (Gyps) fulvus. Naturalista Sicil.* 21: 271.

———— 1915. Sulla cattura di un Airone (*Ardea purpurea*) e di un Gabbiano (*Larus ridibundus*) provvisti di un anello in Sicilia e sul passaggio delle Rondini. *Naturalista Sicil.* 22: 202–204.

———— 1923. Appunti ornitologici. *Naturalista Sicil.* 24: 19–22.

———— 1926. Sull'*Ardea purpurea. Naturalista Sicil.* 24: 129.

DEJONGHE, J. F. 1980. Analyse de la migration prénuptiale des rapaces et des cigognes au Cap Bon (Tunisie). *Oiseau et R.F.O.* 50: 125–147.

DE MURS, O. 1844. Analyse de la 'Faune Ornithologique de la Sicile' de M. A. Malherbe. *Rev. Zool.*, 21–24.

DE STEFANI PEREZ, T. 1883. Gli Uccelli utili all'agricoltura in Sicilia. *La Sicilia Agricola* 1: 1–129.

———— 1887a. Proteggiamo gli uccelletti (Ricordi agli agricoltori e alla gioventù). *La Sicilia Agricola* 5: 1–4.

———— 1887b. Gli animali dannosi della Sicilia. *La Sicilia Agricola* 5: 1002, 1017–1022.

———— 1896. Note diverse. Ornitologia. *Naturalista Sicil.* 1 (N.S.): 45–59.

———— 1897. *Stercorarius crepidatus* Gml. nuova specie per il Golfo di Palermo. *Avicula* 1: 7 and *Naturalista Sicil.* 2 (N.S.): 131.

DE STEFANI PEREZ, T. 1898. Cattura di alcuni rari uccelli in Sicilia. *Avicula* 2: 101–103.

———— 1905a. Importante cattura ornitologica fatta in Sicilia. *Naturalista Sicil.* 18: 51–52. (Also published and rectified in *Avicula*, 1905, 9: 157–158.)

———— 1905b. Note ornitologiche. *Naturalista Sicil.* 18: 116–118.

———— 1918. Il Regio Istituto di Zoologia di Palermo. *La Scienza per tutti* 10: 1–14.

———— 1923. Cattura di uccelli rari in Sicilia. *Boll. R. Ist. Zool. Palermo* 1: 23–24.

DI CARLO, E. A. 1973. Aspetti della migrazione degli Uccelli attraverso il ponte delle isole circum-siciliane. *Lav. Soc. It. Biogeogr.* 3: 815–852.

DIMARCA, A. & FALCI, A. 1983. Accertata nidificazione di Moriglione (*Aythya ferina* L.) in Sicilia. *Naturalista Sicil.* 7: 82.

DIMARCA, A., GIUDICE, E. & LONGO, A. 1986. Nuove osservazioni di Piro piro fulvo, *Tryngites subruficollis*, in Sicilia. *Riv. Ital. Orn.* 56: 250

————, ———— 1987. Nuove nidificazioni di uccelli al Biviere di Gela. *Naturalista Sicil.* 10 (1986): 15–19.

DIMARCA, A. & IAPICHINO, C. 1984. La migrazione, dei Falconiformi sullo Stretto di Messina. Primi dati e problemi di conservazione. *Lega Italiana Protezione Uccelli*, Parma.

DIMARCA, A., IAPICHINO, C. & LONGO, A. in press. Distribuzione e fluttuazioni degli uccelli acquatici in Sicilia. *Atti IV Conv. Ital. Orn., Naturalista Sicil.* 12 (Suppl.).

DIMARCA, A. & LO VALVO, M. 1987. Dati sulla biologia riproduttiva della Rondine, *Hirundo rustica*, in Sicilia. *Riv. Ital. Orn.* 57: 85–96.

DI PALMA, M. G. 1979. Il Museo di Zoologia dell'Università di Palermo. *Naturalista Sicil.* 3: 3–16.

DI PALMA, M. G. & MASSA, B. 1981. Contributo metodologico per lo studio dell'alimentazione dei Rapaci. *Atti I Conv. Ital. Orn.* 69–76.

DODERLEIN, P. 1869–74. Avifauna del Modenese e della Sicilia. *Giorn. Sci. Nat. Econom.* 5: 137–195; 6: 187–236; 7: 9–72; 8: 40–124; 9: 28–93; 10: 35–71 and 133–148.

———— 1872. Alcune generalità sulla fauna sicula dei Vertebrati. *Ann. Soc. Natur. in Modena* 6: 1–60.

———— 1881. Rivista della fauna sicula dei Vertebrati. *Nuove Effemeridi Siciliane* 11: 1–92.

———— 1883a. Sulla accidentale comparsa di una *Sula bassana* nelle vicinanze di Palermo. *Naturalista Sicil.* 2: 138–140.

———— 1883b. Sulla immigrazione in Sicilia del *Turdus torquatus* L. *Naturalista Sicil.* 2: 217–220.

———— 1893. Avifauna Sicula. Rapaces. *Atti R. Accad. Sc. Lett. Arti Palermo* 2: 1–33.

———— c.1890. Handwritten notes on Doderlein's 1869–74 original copy.

EERDEN, VAN M. R. & MUNSTERMAN, M. J. 1986. Importance of the Mediterranean for wintering Cormorants *Phalacrocorax carbo sinensis*. In: *Mediterranean Marine Avifauna*: 123–141. Medmaravis & Monbaillìu.

ELLIOTT, H. F. I. & MONK, J. F. 1952. Land-bird migration over the Suez route to East Africa. *Ibis* 94: 528–530.

ERHARDT, A. 1931. Bermerkungen zur Avifauna Siziliens und der Umgebung Neaples. *Verh. Orn. Ges. Bay.* 19: 366–379.

FAGOTTO, F. 1976. Il Pollo sultano nelle Saline di Siracusa. *Gli Uccelli d'Italia* 1: 115–117.

———— 1982a. Aspetti eco-faunistici della zona costiera di Vendicari (Sicilia). *Quad. Struttura Zoocenosi Terrestri CNR*: 185–198.

———— 1982b. Avifauna della foce del fiume Simeto (Sicilia). *Quad. Struttura Zoocenosi Terrestri CNR*: 199–210.

FAGOTTO, F. & BAGLIERI, S. 1976. Ornitofauna e vegetazione delle Saline di Siracusa. *Animalia* 3: 81–103.

————, ———— 1978a. Uccelli nidificanti e ambiente dell'alta valle dell'Anapo (Siracusa, Sicilia). *Animalia* 5: 107–121.

————, ———— 1978b. L'ambiente palustre di Priolo: appunti su un biotopo ormai fortemente degradato. *Atti II Conv. Sicil. Ecol.* 115–118.

FALCONE, S. 1987. Un caso di necrofagia di Lanario *Falco biarmicus*. *Naturalista Sicil.* 10 (1986): 105.

———— in press. Rapaci abbattuti illegalmente in Sicilia. *Ric. Biol. Selvaggina* 12 (Suppl.).

FALCONE, S. & SEMINARA, S. 1981. Premières données sur le statut et la biologie du Faucon Pelerin *Falco peregrinus* en Sicile. *Rapaces Méditerranéens. Ann. du CROP* 1: 116–118.

FANTIN, G. 1975. L'Usignolo d'Africa (*Agrobates galactotes*). *Riv. Ital. Orn.* 45: 55–60.

———— 1982. Terza presenza in Italia del Corriere asiatico *Charadrius asiaticus*. *Gli Uccelli d'Italia* 7: 155–162.

FASCE, P. & FASCE L. 1984. L'Aquila reale in Italia. Ecologia e conservazione. *Lega Italiana Protezione Uccelli*, Parma.

FAVERO, L. 1959. I pellicani sono comparsi ancora in Italia. *Riv. Ital. Orn.* 29: 52–53.

FAZIO, G. 1976. Avvistamento di un Grifone (*Gyps fulvus*) in Sicilia. *Riv. Ital. Orn.* 46: 170.

FLINT, P. R. & STEWART, P. F. 1983. *The Birds of Cyprus*. British Ornithologists' Union.

FOCARDI, G. & SPINA, F. 1986. Rapporto sui censimenti invernali degli Anatidi e della Folaga in Italia (1982–1985). *Istituto Nazionale di Biologia della Selvaggina*, Bologna.

FOSCHI, F. 1968. Monografia sugli uccelli dell'isola di Pantelleria. *Riv. Ital. Orn.* 38: 1–44.

FRUGIS, S. & SCHENK, H. 1981. Red List of Italian Birds. *Avocetta* 5: 133–141.

FUSCO RAO, A. 1903–1907. Note ornitologiche da servire per la compilazione di un'Avifauna catanese. *Avicula* 7: 49–50, 74–79 and 150–151; 8: 102–105 and 155–159; 9: 95–96 and 154–155; 10: 19–24; 11: 37–38.

GALEA, C. & MASSA, B. 1985. Notes on the Raptor migration across the Central Mediterranean. *ICBP Techn. Publ.* 5: 257–261.

GALVAGNI, G. 1839–43. Fauna Etnea. *Atti Accad. Gioenia* 14 (1839): 171–300; 19 (1842): 245–259; 20 (1843): 167–185.

GATTO, A. 1975. Vittime dell'industrializzazione. *Riv. Ital. Orn.* 45: 374–376.

———— 1977. Osservazioni nell'area del Porto di Termini Imerese. *Gli Uccelli d'Italia* 2: 285–289.

———— 1980. Osservazioni nell'area del Porto di Termini Imerese. *Gli Uccelli d'Italia* 5: 38–47.

———— 1982a. Osservazioni ornitologiche durante l'anno 1980 alla foce del torrente Barratina (Palermo). *Gli Uccelli d'Italia* 7: 163–172.

———— 1982b. Riprese di uccelli inanellati. *Riv. Ital. Orn.* 52: 214–215.

———— 1985. Dormitorio di Ballerina bianca *Motacilla alba*. *Gli Uccelli d'Italia* 10: 38–41.

GIAMBONA, G. 1971. Nuove aggiunte all'avifauna di Ustica (Palermo, Sicilia). *Riv. Ital. Orn.* 41: 117–121.

GIGLIOLI, H. E. 1886. *Avifauna Italica*. Le Monnier, Firenze.

———— 1889–1890. Primo resoconto dei risultati dell'Inchiesta Ornitologica. Parte I. *Avifauna Italica (1889)*. Parte II. *Avifaune locali (1890)*. Le Monnier, Firenze.

———— 1907. Secondo resoconto dei risultati dell'Inchiesta Ornitologica in Italia. *Avifauna Italica*. Tip. S. Giuseppe, Firenze.

GIORDANO, D. 1907. Specie ornitologiche stazionarie o di passo nelle due Raguse. *Atti Congr. Natur. Ital.* 737–743.

GLUTZ VON BLOTZHEIM, U. N. & BAUER, W. 1982. *Handbuch der Vogel mitteleuropas*. Vol. 8/1. Akad Verlagsgesellschaft, Wiesbaden.

GOZENBACH, VON T. 1863. Beobachtungen uber die Vogel in der Gegend von Messina. *Bericht u.thatigkeit St. Gallischen Natur. Gesellsch. wahrend ver:* 104–136.

GRAF, G. 1842. Lettera diretta al Sig. Scuderi (*Tichodroma muraria*). Lettera e descrizione di un Avvoltoio grifone. Published by the Author, Messina.

GUERCIO, V., CARACAPPA, S., CORRAO, A., GALOFARO, V. & GALLO, L. 1984. Anatidi selvatici come rilevatori biologici dell'inquinamento del lago di Pergusa. *Atti Soc. Ital. Sc. Veterinarie* 38: 650–652.

HARRISON, P. 1985. *Seabirds, and Identification Guide*. Croom Helm Ltd, London.

HARTERT, E. 1903–1923. *Die Vogel der Palaarktischen Fauna*. Friedlander.

HEMERY, G. & D'ELBEE, E. 1985. Discrimination morphologique des populations atlantique et méditerranéenne de Petrel tempete *Hydrobates pelagicus*. In: *Oiseaux marins nicheurs du Midi et de la Corse. Ann. du CROP* 2: 63–67.

IANNIZZOTTO, M. 1910a. Pernice bianca. *Avicula* 14: 60.

———— 1910b. *Nisaetus fasciatus. Avicula* 14: 162.

IAPICHINO, C. 1978. Prime osservazioni ornitologiche nell'Oasi faunistica di Vendicari. *Laboratorio* 2: 3–12.

IAPICHINO, C. 1983. Rapporto Ornitologico Sicilia 1982. *Lega Italiana Protezione Uccelli*, Palermo.

───────── 1984a. *Sula bassana*, Stercoraridae e *Larus melanocephalus* nella Sicilia orientale. *Riv. Ital. Orn.* 54: 38–44.

───────── 1984b. Rondine di mare del Ruppell, *Sterna bengalensis*, in Sicilia, *Riv. Ital. Orn.* 54: 96–97.

───────── 1984c. Rapporto Ornitologico Sicilia 1983. *Picus* 10: 115–143.

───────── 1985a. La Riserva Naturale di Vendicari. L'avifauna. *Natura e Montagna* 32: 39–48.

───────── 1985b. Rapporto Ornitologico Sicilia 1984. *Picus* 11: 131–159.

───────── 1985c. Migration of the Sandwich Tern in East Sicily. *Il Merill* 23: 7–8.

IAPICHINO, C. & BAGLIERI, S. 1978. Nidificazioni di Corriere piccolo, *Charadrius dubius curonicus* Gmelin, e di Cavaliere d'Italia, *Himantopus h.himantopus* (L.) in zone umide costiere del Siracusano. *Riv. Ital. Orn.* 48: 327–332.

─────────, ───────── 1979. Prime nidificazioni di Storno (*Sturnus vulgaris* L.) in Sicilia. *Riv. Ital. Orn.* 49: 236–238.

─────────, ───────── 1981. Sulla nidificazione della Schiribilla (*Porzana parva*) in Sicilia. *Riv. Ital. Orn.* 51: 257.

─────────, ───────── 1982a. Il Lui forestiero, *Phylloscopus inornatus*, è regolare nel Mediterraneo? *Riv. Ital. Orn.* 52: 208–209.

─────────, ───────── 1982b. Alcuni dati sulle migrazioni in Sicilia. *Riv. Ital. Orn.* 52: 210–212.

IAPICHINO, C., LO VALVO, F. & MASSA, B. 1983. Biometria della Berta maggiore (*Calonectris diomedea*) dell'Isola di Linosa (Pelagie). *Riv. Ital. Orn.* 53: 145–152.

JANY, E. 1959. Vogelkundliche Beobachtungen in Italien und Sizilien. *Vogelwelt* 80: 47–52.

JOHNSTON, R. F. 1969a. Taxonomy of House Sparrows and their allies in the Mediterranean basin. *Condor* 71: 129–139.

───────── 1969b. Character variation and adaptation in European Sparrows. *Syst. Zool.* 18:206–231.

───────── 1972. Color variation and natural selection in Italian Sparrows. *Boll. Zool.* 39: 351–362.

KEVE, A. 1966. Studi sulle variazioni della Ghiandaia (*Garrulus glandarius* L.) d'Italia. *Riv. Ital. Orn.* 36: 315–323.

───────── 1970. Le Cornacchie grigie d'Italia. *Riv. Ital. Orn.* 40: 37–42.

KRAMPITZ, H. E. 1956a. Biologische Streifzuge durch sizilianische Hohenwalder. *Natur u. Volk* 86: 41–48.

───────── 1956b. Die Brutvogel Siziliens. *J. Orn.* 97: 310–334.

───────── 1957. Beobachtungen auf der Mittelmeerinsel Marettimo im Mai 1955. *Vogelring* 26: 35–37.

───────── 1958. Weiteres uber die Brutvogel Siziliens. *J. Orn.* 99: 39–58.

KRAPP, F. 1970. Vogelbeobachtungen wahrend des Fruhjahrszuges 1969 auf den Agadischen Inseln. *Orn. Beobachter* 67: 280–294.

KUMERLOEVE, H. 1968. Osservazioni sul passo autunnale (1967) nella zona di Catania. *Riv. Ital. Orn.* 38: 59–66.

LA MANTIA, T. 1982. Dati quantitativi sull'avifauna nidificante in una zona suburbana di Palermo. *Avocetta* 6: 41–46.

LA MANTIA, T. & LO VALVO, M. 1986. Nidificazione in novembre di Zigolo nero, *Emberiza cirlus*, in Sicilia. *Riv. Ital. Orn.* 56: 120.

LEBRETON, P. & LEDANT, J. P. 1981. Remarques d'ordre biogéographique et écologique sur l'avifaune méditerranéenne. *Vie et Milieu* 30: 195–208.

LEONARDI, C. 1893. *Gli Uccelli del territorio di Girgenti*. Tip. Formica & Gaglio, Agrigento.

───────── 1897. Cattura di una *Fratercula arctica* (L. ex Clus.) in Girgenti. Sue accidentali apparizioni. *Avicula* 1: 8.

LILFORD, LORD. 1862. On the extinction in Europe of the Common Francolin (*Francolinus vulgaris* Steph.). *Ibis* Ser. 1(4): 352–356.

LO VALVO, F. & LO VERDE, G. 1987. Studio della variabilità fenotipica delle popolazioni italiane di Passere e loro posizione tassonomica. *Riv. Ital. Orn.* 57: 97–110.

LO VALVO, F., LO VERDE, G. & LO VALVO, M. 1986. Dati biometrici per uno studio tassonomico preliminare della Capinera siciliana *Sylvia atricapilla. Atti III Conv. Ital. Orn.* 279–281.

——————, ——————, —————— 1988. Relationships among wing length, wing shape and migration in Blackcap *Sylvia atricapilla* populations. *Ring. & Migr.* 9: 51–54.

LO VALVO, M. 1983. Accertata nidificazione di Codirossone (*Monticola saxatilis*) in Sicilia. *Naturalista Sicil.* 7: 81.

—————— 1986. La Fauna del Parco della Favorita e di Monte Pellegrino (Palermo). *Naturalista Sicil.* 10 (suppl.): 91–163.

LO VALVO, M., LA MANTIA, T. & MASSA, B. 1985. Bird population of Palermo's urban and suburban areas. *Boll. Zool.* 52: 347–354.

LO VALVO, M. & LO VALVO, F. 1987. Riproduzione del Fanello (*Carduelis cannabina*) in un agrumeto della Sicilia. *Avocetta* 11: 145–149.

LO VALVO, M. & MASSA, B. in press a. Analisi multivariata di alcune variabili che influenzano la ricchezza specifica in isole mediterranee e macaronesiche. *Atti IV Conv. Ital. Orn., Naturalista Sicil.* 12 (suppl.).

——————, —————— in press b. Les communautés d'oiseaux nicheurs dans des successions à *Quercus ilex* en Sicile et en Corse. *Alauda* 57.

LO VALVO, M. & SARÁ, M. 1982. Nidificazione del Cavaliere d'Italia (*Himantopus himantopus*) nella Scilia occidentale. *Naturalista Sicil.* 5: 97–98.

LO VERDE, G. 1987. Osservazione di Codirosso algerino *Phoenicurus moussieri* nell'isola di Lampedusa (Pelagie, Agrigento). *Riv. Ital. Orn.* 57: 260.

LO VERDE, G. & MASSA, B. 1985. Lista rossa delle specie nidificanti in Sicilia. *In*: Atlas Faunae Siciliae–Aves. *Naturalista Sicil.* 9 (spec.): 1–242.

——————, —————— in press. Abitudini alimentari della Civetta (*Athene noctua*) in Sicilia. *Atti IV Conv. Ital. Orn. Naturalista Sicil.,* 12 (suppl.).

LYNES, H. 1912. Field-notes on a collection of birds from the Mediterranean (with systematic notes by H. F. Witherby). *Ibis* Ser. 9(6): 121–187.

MACK SMITH, D. 1968. *A History of Sicily*. Medieval Sicily: 800–1713. Modern Sicily: after 1713. Chatto & Windus. London.

MAGGIO, I. 1898. Cigni selvatici. *Avicula* 2: 6.

MALHERBE, A. 1842–1843. *Faune Ornithologique de la Sicile.* Mem. Acad. Royale Metz.; and 1843, Typ. S. Lamort, Metz.

MARIANI, M. 1942. *Gli Uccelli di Sicilia.* Tip. Boccone del Povero, Palermo.

MARTORELLI, G. 1906. *Gli Uccelli d'Italia* (1931 and 1960: 2nd and 3rd eds. revised and improved by Moltoni, E. & Vandoni, C.). Rizzoli, Milano.

MASCARA, R. 1984a. Nuovi dati sulla nidifcazione del Gruccione, *Merops apiaster*, in Sicilia. *Riv. Ital. Orn.* 55: 90–91.

—————— 1984b. Il Biancone, *Circaetus gallicus*, sverna in Sicilia. *Riv. Ital. Orn.* 55: 91–92.

—————— 1984c. Censimento e note sulla biologia riproduttiva di alcuni Falconiformi nella Sicilia centro-meridionale. *Naturalista Sicil.* 8: 3–12.

—————— 1985. Elenco sistematico, consistenza e status degli uccelli presenti nel Biviere di Gela. *Gli Uccelli d'Italia* 10: 107–118.

—————— 1986. Consistenza e note sulla biologia riproduttiva del Lanario, *Falco biarmicus*, nella Sicilia meridionale. *Riv. Ital. Orn.* 56: 203–212.

—————— 1987a. Accertata nidificazione di Pernice di mare, *Glareola pratincola*, in un'area cerealicola della Sicilia. *Riv. Ital. Orn.* 57: 137

—————— 1987b. La Ghiandaia marina (*Coracias garrulus*) in un'area della Sicilia meridionale. *Naturalista Sicil.* 11: 47–49.

MASSA, B. 1968. In memoria di Gino Ajola. *Riv. Ital. Orn.* 38: 448–450.

—————— 1969. Catture interessanti per la provincia di Palermo. *Riv. Ital. Orn.* 39: 233–235.

—————— 1973a. Considerazioni su alcuni Rapaci diurni e notturni in Sicilia. *Rapaci Oggi* 57–62.

—————— 1973b. L'Avifauna estiva degli arcipelaghi delle Egadi e dello Stagnone (Trapani, Sicilia). *Atti Accad. Gioenia Sc. Nat. Catania* 5: 63–95.

—————— 1974a. Appunti sulla biogeografia delle Isole Egadi. *L'Universo* 54: 789–804.

MASSA, B. 1974b. La Procellaria del Capo (*Daption capensis* (L.)) è giunta anche nel Mediterraneo. *Riv. Ital. Orn.* 44:210–212.

———— 1975a. Falchi sullo Stretto. *Pro Avibus* 13 (4–5): 4-7.

———— 1975b. Il declino dell'avifauna in Sicilia. Proposte di conservazione. *Atti IV Simp. Naz. Conserv. Nat.* 2: 259–268.

———— 1975c. The situation of the Falconiformes in Sicily. *World Conf. on Birds of Prey*, 131–132.

———— 1976a. I Falconiformi della fauna siciliana. *Atti I Conv. Sicil. Ecol.* 117–134.

———— 1976b. Considerazioni sulla situazione dell'avifauna siciliana. Problemi di conservazione. *Ric. Biol. Selvaggina* 7 (suppl.): 427–474.

———— 1976c. Una specie in via di estinzione: l'Aquila del Bonelli. In: *S.O.S. Fauna*, WWF, Camerino.

———— 1976d. Nozioni utili per lo studio e la salvaguardia della Coturnice di Sicilia (*Alectoris graeca whitakeri* Schiebel, 1934). *Atti V Simp. Naz. Conserv. Nat.* 1: 309–316.

———— 1977a. Carlo Orlando (1898–1976). *Riv. Ital. Orn.* 47: 86–92.

———— 1977b. Studio della popolazione di Fratini (*Charadrius a.alexandrinus*) delle Saline di Trapani. *Naturalista Sicil.* 1: 3–15.

———— 1978a. Nuovi dati sulla migrazione del Fringuello alpino (*Montifringilla nivalis* (L.)) in Italia. *Riv. Ital. Orn.* 48: 172–175.

———— 1978b. Observations on Eleonora's Falcon *Falco eleonorae* in Sicily and surrounding islets. *Ibis* 120: 531–534.

———— 1978c. Studio dei Laro-limicoli di Sicilia (*Aves, Charadriiformes*). *Atti II Conv. Sicil. Ecol.* 71–114.

———— 1978d. Nuovi dati sulla biologia invernale di *Upupa epops* in Italia. *Avocetta* 1: 19–24.

———— 1978e. Rapaci sullo Stretto. *Pro Avibus* 13 (4–5): 4–6.

———— 1980. Ricerche sui Rapaci in un'area-campione della Sicilia. *Naturalista Sicil.* 4(3–4): 59–72.

———— 1981a. Le régime alimentaire de quatorze espèces de Rapaces en Sicile. *Rapaces méditerranéens, Ann. du CROP* 1: 119–129.

———— 1981b. Primi studi sulla nicchia ecologica di cinque Silvidi (genere *Sylvia*) in Sicilia. *Riv. Ital. Orn.* 51: 167–178.

———— 1982a. Il gradiente faunistico nella penisola italiana e nelle Isole. *Atti Soc. It. Sci. Nat. Museo Civ. Stor. Nat. Milano* 123: 353–374.

———— 1982b. Sauver les Rapaces en Sicile. *L'Homme et l'Oiseau* 20: 221–223.

———— 1983. Predazione su *Ocneridia nigropunctata* (Orthoptera Pamphagidae) polimorfiche da parte di *Falco naumanni*. *Riv. Ital. Orn.* 53: 174–176.

———— (ed.) 1985. *Atlas Faunae Siciliae–Aves. Naturalista Sicil.* 9 (spec.): 1–242.

———— 1987a. Comparaison entre les populations de Beccroisés Méditerranéens. *Acta Biol. Mont.* 7: 193–196.

———— 1987b. Variations in Mediterranean Crossbills *Loxia curvirostra*. *Bull. Brit. Orn. Cl.* 107: 118–130.

———— 1987c. Considerazioni sui popolamenti di uccelli terrestri delle Isole Mediterranee. *Biogeographia, Lav. Soc. It. Biogeogr.* 10: 163–186.

———— 1987d. Joseph Whitaker, ornitologo. *Atti Conv. 'I Naturalisti e la Cultura Scientifica siciliana nell'800'* (Palermo, 5–7 Dec 1984): 533–540.

———— in press. Bird communities along an ecological succession in Mediterranean and Canary Islands. *Atti Conv. Accad. Naz. Lincei.*

MASSA, B., BAGLIERI, S. & CANGIALOSI, G. 1976. Contributo allo studio delle migrazioni in Sicilia: appunti sulle specie orientali e nord-africane. *Riv. Ital. Orn.* 46: 1–14.

————, ————, ———— 1979. Nouvelles données pour l'etude des migrations à travers la Méditerranée centrale. *Alauda* 47: 17–27.

MASSA, B. & CANGIALOSI, G. 1969a. Beccapesci maggiore in Sicilia. *Riv. Ital. Orn.* 39: 408–410.

————, ———— 1969b. Nuova cattura di Piro piro codalunga (*Bartramia longicauda*). *Riv. Ital. Orn.* 39: 410–411.

————, ———— 1970a. Uccelli riscontrati in una gita a Favignana (Isole Egadi). *Riv. Ital. Orn.* 40: 25–36.

MASSA, B. & CANGIALOSI, G. 1970b. Insolita abbondanza di rapaci notturni in Sicilia. *Riv. Ital. Orn.* 40:61–64.

MASSA, B. & CATALISANO, A. 1986a. Observations on the Mediterranean Storm Petrel *Hydrobates pelagicus* at Marettimo Isle. *Avocetta* 10: 125–127.

————, ———— 1986b. Status and conservation of the Storm Petrel *Hydrobates pelagicus* in Sicily. In: *Mediterranean Marine Avifauna:* 143–151, Medmaravis & Monbailliu.

MASSA, B. & DI PALMA, M. G. in press. Uccelli, Rettili e Anfibi delle Isole circum-siciliane. *Actes Coll. Int. sur les Vert. Terr. et Dulcaq. Iles Médit.*

MASSA, B. & LO VALVO, M. 1986. Biometrical and biological considerations on the Cory's Shearwater *Calonectris diomedea.* In: *Mediterranean Marine Avifauna:* 293–313, Medmaravis & Monbailliu.

MASSA, B., LO VALVO, M. & CATALISANO, A. in press. Bird communities of Etna (Sicily). *Bull. Zool.* 56.

MASSA, B., MARCHESE, L. & SEMINARA, S. 1975. Proposta di un Parco Naturale Regionale sulle Madonie (Sicilia). *Atti IV Simp. Naz. Conserv. Nat.* 2: 451–475.

MASSA, B. & PRIOLO, A. 1981. A proposito della nidificazione dell'Averla cenerina, *Lanius minor*, in Sicilia. *Riv. Ital. Orn.* 51: 250–251.

MASSA, B. & SARÁ, M. 1982. Dieta comparata del Barbagianni (*Tyto alba* (Scopoli)) in ambienti boschivi, rurali e suburbani della Sicilia. *Naturalista Sicil.* 6(1–2): 3–15.

MASSA, B. & SCHENK, H. 1983. Similarità tra le avifaune della Sicilia, Sardegna e Corsica. *Lav. Soc. It. Biogeogr.* 8: 757–799.

MASSA, C. 1890. Passaggio dei Cigni (*Cygnus musicus*) nel Pantano di Lentini (Siracusa). *Agricolt. Calabro-sicula* (Dec.).

———— 1891. Gli Uccelli della Sicilia. *Naturalista Sicil.* 10: 172–205.

MAYAUD, N. 1956. Etude sur la migration et les zones d'hivernage des Sternes caspiennes *Hydroprogne caspia* (Pallas) d'Europe. *Alauda* 24: 206–218.

MEBS, T. 1957. Ornithologische Beobachtungen in Sizilien. *Vogelwelt* 78: 169–176.

———— 1959. Beitrag zur Biologie des Feldeggsfalken (*Falco biarmicus feldeggi*). *Vogelwelt* 80: 142–149.

MINÁ-PALUMBO, F. 1853. Catalogo degli Uccelli delle Madonie. I. *Atti Accad. Sc. Lett. Arti Palermo*, 2: 1–32. 1857. II. Continuazione e fine. *Atti Accad. Sc. Lett. Arti Palermo*, 3: 1–45.

———— 1859. *Osservazioni sull'Albinismo degli Uccelli.* Published by the Author.

———— 1883. *Turdus torquatus* Linn. *Naturalista Sicil.* 2: 175–177.

MINA-PALUMBO, F. & MORICI-MINÁ, M. 1898–99. Avifauna sicula. Metacromatismo. *Avicula*, 2: 140–143; 3: 16–20.

MOLTONI, E. 1933. Il Cuculo americano in Italia. *Riv. Ital. Orn.* 3: 157–161.

———— 1957. Gli uccelli rinvenuti durante una escursione ornitologica all'Isola di Pantelleria, Prov. di Trapani, nel giugno-luglio 1954 (29 giugno-21 luglio) con notizie su quelli noti per l'Isola. *Riv. Ital. Orn.*, 27: 1–41.

———— 1960. Uccelli rinvenuti durante una gita ornitologica a Stromboli (Isole Eolie) dal 21 al 29 agosto 1959. *Riv. Ital. Orn.* 30: 78–87.

———— 1966. Altre notizie su uccelli inanellati all'estero e ripresi in Italia ed in Libia. *Riv. Ital. Orn.* 36: 109–314.

———— 1970. Gli uccelli ad oggi riscontrati nelle Isole Linosa, Lampedusa e Lampione (Isole Pelagie, Canale di Sicilia, Mediterraneo). *Riv. Ital. Orn.* 40: 77–283.

———— 1971. La Cinciarella algerina *Parus caeruleus ultramarinus*, Bonaparte, é uccello sedentario nell'isola di Pantelleria (Trapani). *Riv. Ital. Orn.* 41: 25–27.

———— 1973a. Gli uccelli fino ad oggi rinvenuti o notati all'isola di Pantelleria (Provincia di Trapani, Sicilia). *Riv. Ital. Orn.* 43: 173–437.

———— 1973b. Elenco di parecchie centinaia di uccelli inanellati all'estero e ripresi in Italia ed in Libia. *Riv. Ital. Orn.* 43 (suppl.): 1–182.

———— 1976a. Nuovi dati su uccelli inanellati all'estero e ripresi in Italia ed in Libia. *Riv. Ital. Orn.* 46 (suppl.): 3–71.

———— 1976b. Uccelli inanellati presi alle Isole Pelagie, Pantelleria, Egadi ed in Libia. *Ric. Biol. Selvaggina* 7 (suppl.): 491–511.

MOLTONI, E. & FRUGIS, S. 1967. Gli Uccelli delle Isole Eolie (Messina, Sicilia). *Riv. Ital. Orn.* 37: 93–234.

MOLTONI, E. & PIROVANO, S. 1980. Osservazioni ornitologiche autunnali a Panarea ed Uccelli ad oggi noti per l'isola (Eolie). *Riv. Ital. Orn.* 50: 3–18.

MONGITORE, R. 1742. *Della Sicilia ricercata nelle cose memorabili.* Stamp. F. Valenza, Palermo.

MOREAU, R. E. 1953. Migration in the Mediterranean area. *Ibis* 95: 329–364.

——————— 1961. Problems of Mediterranean-Saharan migration. *Ibis.* 103a: 373–427 and 580–623.

——————— 1972. *The Palaeartic-African Bird Migration Systems.* Academic Press, London.

MORICI-MINÁ, M. 1886–87. Osservazioni di Ornitologia Nebrodense. *Boll. Natur.* 6: 18–19 and 67–68; 7: 9–10 and 75–76.

MORICI-MINÁ, M. 1886–88. Osservazioni sull'albinismo. *Boll. Natur.* 6: 4; 7: 89–90; 8: 26.

MUTH, G. P. 1870. Die Vogel auf Sizilien. *Zoologischer Garten*: 143

NAGY, J. 1912. Ornithologische Beobachtungen auf den Vulkanen Italiens im Juni 1911. *Aquila* 19: 459–462.

NAVEH, Z. & LIEBERMAN, A. S. 1984. *Landscape Ecology. Theory and Application.* Springer-Verlag, New York.

NOCITO, G. 1844. *Catalogo degli Uccelli del Territorio di Girgenti.* Published by the Author.

NORANTE, N. 1982. Piro piro terek *Xenus cinereus* in Sicilia. *Gli Uccelli d'Italia* 7: 137.

NOVELLETTO, A. & PETRETTI, F. 1980. Sull'Uccello delle tempeste codaforcuta, *Oceanodroma leucorhoa* (Vieillot), in Italia. *Riv. Ital. Orn.* 50: 155–157.

ORLANDO, C. 1935a. Brevi note sull'Avifauna Siciliana. *Riv. Ital. Orn.* 5: 114–116.

——————— 1935b. Seguito alle "Brevi note sull'Avifauna Siciliana". Note su catture siciliane di Sula bassana. La Gru pavonina in Italia. *Riv. Ital. Orn.* 5: 216–223.

——————— 1935c. Nota sul passo primaverile in provincia di Palermo. Nota su alcune osservazioni eseguite nei boschi di Isnello e Collesano durante l'inverno 1934–1935 (Palermo). *Riv. Ital. Orn.* 5: 295–296.

——————— 1936a. Specie nidificanti nella zona litoranea tra i Golfi di Palermo e di Castellammare. *Riv. Ital. Orn.* 6: 61–72 and 201–205.

——————— 1936b. Note sull'Avifauna Siciliana. *Riv. Ital. Orn.* 6: 83–92.

——————— 1936c. Sulla presunta abbondanza di Cesene (*Turdus pilaris* L.) nel passo autunnale del 1935 nell'isola di Marettimo-Egadi. Cattura di Aquile in Sicilia. Esemplari siciliani di Avvoltoio degli agnelli (*Gypaetus barbatus grandis* Storr.) esistenti nelle raccolte locali. Alcune note tratte dal mio giornale. *Riv. Ital. Orn.* 6: 291–294.

——————— 1937a. Catture di Aquile in Sicilia. *Riv. Ital. Orn.* 7: 141.

——————— 1937b. Francesco Venezia. *Riv. Ital. Orn.* 7: 151–154.

——————— 1937c. Alcune note tratte dal mio giornale. *Riv. Ital. Orn.* 7: 222–224.

——————— 1937d. Joseph I. S. Whitaker. *Riv. Ital. Orn.* 7: 240–244.

——————— 1937e. In merito alle varietà di Becaccia. *Diana* 32 (7): 312.

——————— 1937f. Una invasione di Gabbiani tridattili in Sicilia. *Diana* 32 (10): 480–481.

——————— 1938. Esemplari siciliani di *Sula bassana.* Cattura di Storno inanellato. Alcune note tratte dal mio giornale. Catture di Aquile in Sicilia. Rettifiche a precedenti comunicazioni. *Riv. Ital. Orn.* 8: 94–97.

——————— 1939a. *Sylvia cantillans*, Pallas (1764). *Riv. Ital. Orn.* 9: 148–177.

——————— 1939b. *Sula bassana* L. *Riv. Ital. Orn.* 9: 205–208.

——————— 1939c. Luì siberiano, Luì boreale e Luì grosso nordico orientale. *Riv. Ital. Orn.* 9: 241–244.

——————— 1939d. Note tratte dal mio giornale. *Riv. Ital. Orn.* 9: 245–248.

——————— 1940a. Il Corvo imperiale (*Corvus corax* L.). *Riv. Ital. Orn.* 10: 22–40.

——————— 1940b. Osservazioni su un caso di nidificazione della Ballerina gialla (*Motacilla cinerea cinerea* Tunst.). *Riv. Ital. Orn.* 10: 51–55.

——————— 1943a. *Alauda arvensis* (a proposito di Lodole nane). *Riv. Ital. Orn.* 13: 51–54.

——————— 1943b. Note tratte dal mio giornale. *Riv. Ital. Orn.* 13: 123–125.

——————— 1954. Una nuova cattura per l'Italia di Poiana dalla coda bianca (*Buteo rufinus rufinus* (Cretzschmar)). *Riv. Ital. Orn.* 24: 208–212.

——————— 1955a. La Cornacchia nera (*Corvus corone*, L.) in Sicilia. *Riv. Ital. Orn.* 25: 74–76.

——————— 1955b. "... *Poianas quos Itali vocent*" (Aldrovandi) (Contributo allo studio della *Buteo buteo* (L.)). *Riv. Ital. Orn.* 25: 105–131.

——————— 1955c. Avifauna Sicula. *Riv. Ital. Orn.* 25: 140–141.

ORLANDO, C. 1955d. Cuculo dal ciuffo, *Clamator glandarius* (L.). *Riv. Ital. Orn.* 25: 163–170.

——————— 1955e. Catture di Aquile in Sicilia. *Riv. Ital. Orn.* 25: 195–197.

——————— 1955f. Sulla legittimità del genere *Buteaetos* del Moschler (*typus B. ferox*). *Riv. Ital. Orn.* 25: 207–208.

——————— 1955g. *Promemoria per l'Assessorato Agricoltura e Foreste della Regione sulla opportunità di creare Osservatori Ornitologici e stazioni di inanellamento in Sicilia.* Tip. Priulla, Palermo.

——————— 1956a. La Coturnice di Sicilia (*Alectoris graeca whitakeri*, Schiebel, 1934). *Riv. Ital. Orn.* 26: 1–12.

——————— 1956b. Il Pellicano riccio in Sicilia e le differenze tra le due specie *onocrotalus* e *crispus* a proposito dei contestati individui catturati nel mar di Pozzallo nel gennaio 1877. *Riv. Ital. Orn.* 26: 38–42.

——————— 1956c. I Picini (sottofamiglia *Picinae*) in Sicilia. *Riv. Ital. Orn.* 26: 78–81.

——————— 1956d. Dati e date sulla Beccaccia. *Riv. Ital. Orn.* 26: 144–145.

——————— 1956e. Nuove notizie sulla frequenza del Cuculo dal ciuffo (*Clamator glandarius*, L.) in Italia. *Riv. Ital. Orn.* 26: 174–177.

——————— 1956f. *Sulla Beccaccia*. Printed by the Author.

——————— 1957a. Contributo allo studio delle forme europee del *Bubo bubo* (L.). *Riv. Ital. Orn.* 27: 42–57.

——————— 1957b. Il Rusignolo d'Africa (*Agrobates g. galactotes* (Temm.)) in Sicilia. *Riv. Ital. Orn.* 27: 115–116.

——————— 1957c. Contributo allo studio del genere *Cisticola juncidis*, Bonaparte con particolare riferimento alle due forme *juncidis* (Rafinesque) 1810, *carmelae* Orlando 1937. *Riv. Ital. Orn.* 27: 125–131.

——————— 1957d. Contributo allo studio del Lanario (*Falco biarmicus*) in Italia. *Riv. Ital. Orn.* 27: 147–153.

——————— 1957e. L'Occhiocotto (*Sylvia melanocephala* Gmelin) in Italia. *Riv. Ital. Orn.* 27: 168–170.

——————— 1958a. Una doppia cattura per l'Italia di Sterpazzolina orientale (*Sylvia cantillans albistriata*, (Brehm)). *Riv. Ital. Orn.* 28: 80–82

——————— 1958b. Cattura di un Albatro urlatore (*Diomedea e. exulans*, L.) in Sicilia. *Riv. Ital. Orn.* 28: 101–113.

——————— 1958c. Ibrido fra Fringuello e Peppola (*Fringilla coelebs × Fringilla montifringilla*). *Riv. Ital. Orn.* 28: 133–135

——————— 1958d. Nuove catture per la Sicilia di Pellicani (*Pelecanus onocrotalus*, Linnaeus). *Riv. Ital. Orn.* 28: 135–137.

——————— 1958e. La Gallina prataiola *Otis tetrax* (L.). *Venatoria Sicula* 12: 234.

——————— 1958f. Il Pollo sultano *Porphyrio porphyrio* (L.). *Venatoria Sicula* 12: 252.

——————— 1958g. Il Grifone *Gyps fulvus* (Habliz). *Venatoria Sicula* 12: 268.

——————— 1958h. L'Avvoltoio degli Agnelli (*Gypaetus barbatus* (L.)). *Venatoria Sicula* 12: 284.

——————— 1958i. Il Basettino *Panurus biarmicus* (L.). *Venatoria Sicula* 12: 298.

——————— 1958l. Il Francolino *Francolinus francolinus* (L.). *Venatoria Sicula* 12: 328.

——————— 1958m. La Quaglia tridattila *Turnix sylvatica* (Desf.). *Venatoria Sicula* 12: 342–344.

——————— 1958n. L'Occhione *Burhinus oedicnemus* (L.). *Venatoria Sicula* 12: 364.

——————— 1958o. *La Gru pavonina* Balearica pavonina (L.) *in Italia*. Printed by the Author.

——————— 1959a. Contributo per una migliore conoscenza del genere *Jynx torquilla*, L. *Riv. Ital. Orn.* 29: 22–29.

——————— 1959b. *Corvus corone* L. e *Corvus cornix* L. *Riv. Ital. Orn.* 29: 47–50.

——————— 1962. Aquile in Sicilia. *Riv. Ital. Orn.* 32: 317.

——————— 1965. La presenza degli Storni a Palermo. *Boll. Rotary Club Palermo* (2045): 1–7.

——————— 1967a. Il Sordone *Prunella collaris* (Scopoli) in Sicilia. *Riv. Ital. Orn.* 37: 61–63.

——————— 1967b. Catture di Sule in Sicilia. *Riv. Ital. Orn.* 37: 72–73.

——————— 1967c. La Cesena (*Turdus pilaris*) in Sicilia. *Riv. Ital. Orn.* 37: 73.

——————— 1967d. Una sconosciuta monografia sull'Avifauna di Erice (Monte S. Giuliano). *Riv. Ital. Orn.* 37: 254–256.

ORLANDO, C. 1967e. Contributo per una migliore conoscenza della *Alectoris g. graeca* (Meisner), 1804 e forme affini europee con particolare riguardo alla *saxatilis* del Meyer, 1805. *Riv. Ital. Orn.* 37: 307–313.

ORLANDO, V. E. 1978. La raccolta Iannizzotto a Chiaramonte Gulfi (Ragusa). *Riv. Ital. Orn.* 48: 337–339.

———————— 1979. Gli Uccelli nidificanti nell'entroterra del Golfo di Castellammare. *Riv. Ital. Orn.* 49: 187–196.

OSSERVATORIO ORNITOLOGICO SICILIANO. 1979. Riprese in Sicilia di uccelli inanellati 1972/1979. *Naturalista Sicil.* 3: 79–80.

PALAZZOTTO, B. c.1810. *Trattato di Ornitologia Siciliana*. MS.

———————— 1826. Lettera intorno ad un Uccello di singolare forma nella conformazione del becco (*Corvus graculus*). *Giorn. Sc. Lett. Arti. Sicilia* 22: 137–152.

PERCO, F., LAMBERTINI, M., LO VALVO, M. & MILONE, M. 1987. Gabbiano reale *Larus cachinnans* Pallas 1811. In: Fasola, M. (ed.), *Distribuzione e popolazioni dei Laridi e Sternidi nidificanti in Italia*. Ric. Biol. Selvaggina 11 (suppl.): 53–72.

PETERKEN, G. 1981. *Woodland Conservation and Management*. Chapman and Hall, London and New York.

PETERSON, R. T., MOUNTFORT, G. & HOLLOM, P. A. D. 1954. *A Field Guide to the Birds of Britain and Europe*. Collins, London.

PICCHI, C. 1902. *L'Acredula sicula* Whit. *Avicula* 6: 3–5.

PISTONE, A. 1888. *Ornitologia Siciliana*. Tip. Davì, Messina.

———————— 1890a. Metacromatismo, ossia clorocroismo, geraiocroismo, melanismo e eritrismo in alcuni uccelli. *Naturalista Sicil.* 10: 9–16.

———————— 1890b. Disseminazione zoofila per uccelli fitofagi. *Naturalista Sicil.* 9: 221–225 and 229–234.

PRATESI, F. 1976. Tre storie di uccelli: il Francolino, la Quaglia tridattila e la Gallina prataiola. In: *SOS Fauna*. WWF, Camerino.

PRESTON, F. W. 1962. The canonical distribution of commonness and rarity. Part I and Part II. *Ecology* 43: 185–215 and 410–432.

PRIOLO, A. 1946. Cattura di Succiacapre dal collo rosso in Sicilia. *Riv. Ital. Orn.* 16: 173–174.

———————— 1948. Catture interessanti in Sicilia. *Riv. Ital. Orn.* 18: 52–54.

———————— 1949. La Casarca in Sicilia. *Riv. Ital. Orn.* 19: 124–125.

———————— 1954. Quadro sinottico delle osservazioni ornitologiche svolte in Sicilia dal 1940 al 1953. *Avocetta* 1: 1–13.

———————— 1956a. Catture di Aquile in Sicilia. *Riv. Ital. Orn.* 26: 36.

———————— 1956b. Catture interessanti. *Riv. Ital. Orn.* 26: 37.

———————— 1965a. La Sula. *Venatoria sicula* 19 (2): 29–30.

———————— 1965b. Il Sordone in Sicilia. *Venatoria sicula* 19 (4): 62.

———————— 1967. Distrutti i Grifoni delle Caronie? *Riv. Ital. Orn.* 37: 7–11.

———————— 1968a. Precisazioni in merito al Succiacapre dal collo rosso ucciso in Sicilia nel 1946. *Riv. Ital. Orn.* 38: 74.

———————— 1968b. Contributo allo studio dei caratteri e delle affinità del Gabbiano roseo (*Larus genei*, Brème). *Riv. Ital. Orn.* 38: 45–46.

———————— 1969a. La Cincia bigia, *Parus palustris*, in Sicilia. *Riv. Ital. Orn.* 39: 198–205.

———————— 1969b. Gli Uccelli, un patrimonio da salvare. *Sud 70* 1 (2): 85–88.

———————— 1970. Affinità della Coturnice, *Alectoris graeca*, e conseguenze dei ripopolamenti effettuati nei distretti da essa abitati ricorrendo alla Coturnice orientale, *Alectoris chukar*. *Riv. Ital. Orn.* 40: 441–445.

———————— 1972a. Rapporti di parentela ed evoluzione del Gabbiano corallino (*Larus melanocephalus*, Temminck). *Riv. Ital. Orn.* 42: 227–231.

———————— 1972b. Brevi note ornitologiche dalla Sicilia orientale. *Riv. Ital. Orn.* 42: 430–434.

———————— 1973. Nidificazione dell'Aquila reale (*Aquila chrysaetos*) sull'Appennino siculo. *Uccelli del Mondo e Animali da Compagnia* 1: 5–7.

———————— 1974a. Osservazioni alla foce del Simeto presso Catania (1972–73). *Riv. Ital. Orn.* 44: 43–52.

PRIOLO, A. 1974b. Accertata la sopravvivenza del Grifone in Sicilia. *Riv. Ital. Orn.* 44: 213–214.

———— 1975. Osservazioni e ricerche sul Gabbiano corso, *Larus audouinii* Payraudeau, in Sicilia. *Riv. Ital. Orn.* 45: 359–365.

———— 1976. Airone schistaceo, *Egretta gularis schistacea* (Hemprich & Ehrenberg), osservato in Sicilia alla foce del Simeto. *Riv. Ital. Orn.* 46: 253–256.

———— 1977. Note sul comportamento del Gabbiano roseo (*Larus genei*). *Riv. Ital. Orn.* 47: 110–113.

———— 1979. Note sul Codibugnolo siciliano *Aegithalos caudatus siculus*, Whitaker. *Gli Uccelli d'Italia* 4: 5–13.

———— 1984. Variabilità in *Alectoris graeca* e descrizione di *A. g. orlandoi* subsp. nova degli Appennini. *Riv. Ital. Orn.* 54: 45–76.

———— in press. Le forme geografiche degli uccelli siciliani. *Atti IV Conv. Ital. Orn., Naturalista Sicil.* 12 (suppl.).

PRIOLO, A. & SARÁ, M. 1981. Nidificazione del Crociere, *Loxia curvirostra*, in Sicilia. *Riv. Ital. Orn.,* 51: 249.

————, ———— 1986. Problemi di conservazione della Coturnice di Sicilia *Alectoris graeca whitakeri. Atti III Conv. Ital. Orn.* 39–41.

RAFINESQUE SCHMALTZ, C. S. 1810. *Caratteri di alcuni nuovi generi e nuove specie di animali e di piante della Sicilia, con varie osservazioni sopra i medesimi.* Tip. S. Filippo, Palermo.

RANDAZZO, G. R. 1964. Nuova cattura della *Sula bassana* (L.) in Sicilia. *Atti Soc. Peloritana. Sc.* 10: 471–476.

———— 1966. Su di una cattura di *Larus marinus* Linn. in Sicilia. *Riv. Ital. Orn.* 36: 366–367.

———— 1972a. Duplice cattura di *Ciconia nigra* L. nell'Isola di Ustica (PA). *Venatoria Sicula* 7: 101.

———— 1972b. Su di una cattura di *Aquila imperialis* Mogilnik nella provincia di Palermo. *Venatoria Sicula* 8: 3–7.

———— 1972c. Cattura in Sicilia di un esemplare di *Sterna caspia* (Pall.) (Beccapesci maggiore). *Venatoria Sicula* 9: 137–138.

———— 1977a. Alcune interessanti notizie sul mimetismo, sul dimorfismo e sull'ibridismo negli Uccelli. *Venatoria Sicula* 31: 107.

———— 1977b. La *Nycticorax nycticorax* in Sicilia. *Venatoria Sicula* 31: 138.

RANDI, E., SPINA, F. & MASSA, B. in press. Variabilità genetica nella Berta maggiore (*Calonectris diomedea*). Analisi elettroforetica di campioni provenienti da colonie del Mar Mediterraneo e dell'Atlantico. *Atti IV Conv. Ital. Orn., Naturalista Sicil.* 12 (suppl.).

RENZONI, A., FOCARDI, S., FOSSI, C., LEONZIO, C. & MAYOL, J. 1986. Comparison between concentrations of Mercury and other contaminants in eggs and tissues of Cory's Shearwater *Calonectris diomedea* collected on Atlantic and Mediterranean Islands. *Environm. Poll.* 40: 17–35.

RIERA, E. 1923. Note sugli uccelli osservati nella provincia di Siracusa. *Riv. Ital. Orn.* 7: 8–17.

RIGGIO, G. 1892. Corrispondenze scientifiche moderne degli animali figurati, Artropodi e Vertebrati, nel Pamphiton Siculum del Cupani. *Naturalista Sicil.* 12: 31–36, 69–73 and 115–122 (birds).

———— 1894. Metacromatismo. *Naturalista Sicil.* 14: 133–137.

RIGGIO, G. & DE STEFANI PEREZ, T. 1894. Appunti e note di Ornitologia Siciliana. *Nauralista Sicil.* 14: 1–3, 29–39, 75–83 and 128–132.

RIGGIO, S. 1976. Degradazione dell'ambiente ed estinzione della fauna vertebrata in Sicilia. *Atti I Conv. Sicil. Econ.* 69–93.

RIGGIO, S. & MASSA, B. 1975. Problemi di conservazione, della natura in Sicilia. 1° Contributo. Dati preliminari per un'analisi della degradazione ambientale ed elenco delle aree dell'isola di maggiore interesse naturalistico. *Atti IV Simp. Naz. Cons. Nat.* 2: 299–425.

ROSSO, E. T. 1844. *Per l'inaugurazione del Gabinetto di Storia Naturale ed Archeologia del la R. Accademia di Caltagirone.* Tip. G. Musumeci Papale, Caltagirone.

RUSSO, F. 1698. *Breve descrizione di tutte le sorte di Uccelli conosciuti in Sicilia.* MS.

RYDZEWSKI, W. 1960. Recoveries of ringed birds. Mediterranean Islands. *Riv. Ital. Orn.* 30: 1–77.

SABATINI, G. 1913. Note ornitologiche delle Isole Eolie. *Riv. Ital. Orn.* 2: 255–258.

———— 1915. Elenco degli Uccelli catturati o osservati nelle Isole Eolie. *Atti Soc. Toscana Sc. Nat. Mem.* 30: 3–21.

SALEM, V. 1908. Uccelli rari e metacromatici catturati in Sicilia. *Naturalista Sicil.* 20: 211–216.

SALVADORI, T. 1872. *Fauna d'Italia. Uccelli.* Vallardi, Milano.

SALVO, G. 1982. Ulteriori dati sulla nidificazione dell'Averla cenerina, *Lanius minor*, in Sicilia. *Riv. Ital. Orn.* 52: 220.

———— 1984a. Prime nidificazioni di Codirossone, *Monticola saxatilis*, in provincia di Agrigento. *Riv. Ital. Orn.* 54: 101.

———— 1984b. Primi dati sulla biologia del Lanario, *Falco biarmicus*, nella Sicilia centro-meridionale. *Riv. Ital. Orn.* 54: 244–248.

———— in press. Dati sulla dieta alimentare dell'Aquila del Bonelli (*Hieraaetus fasciatus*) in Sicilia. *Atti IV Conv. Ital. Orn., Naturalista Sicil.* 12 (suppl.).

SARÁ, M. 1983. Comportamento e abitudini alimentari della Berta maggiore (*Calonectris diomedea*) nel Canale di Sicilia. *Riv. Ital. Orn.* 53: 183–193.

———— in press. Dati preliminari sulla densità dell'Allocco (*Strix aluco*) in Sicilia. *Ric. Biol. Selvaggina* 12 (Suppl.).

SARÁ, M. & MASSA, B. 1985. Considerazioni sulla nicchia trofica dell'Allocco (*Strix aluco*) e del Barbagianni (*Tyto alba*). *Riv. Ital. Orn.* 55: 61–73.

SARÁ, M., SIRACUSA, M. & CIACCIO, A. 1987. Estinzione del Gufo reale, *Bubo bubo*, in Sicilia. *Riv. Ital. Orn.* 57: 50–56.

SARÁ, M. & ZANCA, L. in press. Nicchia trofica di *Tyto alba* in ambienti insulari del Mediterraneo. *Atti IV Conv. Ital. Orn., Naturalista Sicil.* 12 (suppl.).

SAUNDERS, H. 1869. Notes on the Ornithology of Italy and Spain. *Ibis* Ser. 2(5): 391–403.

SCHEMBRI, A. 1843. *Quadro comparativo. Le Ornitologie di Malta, Sicilia, Roma, Toscana, Liguria, Nizza, e la provincia di Gard.* Tip. Anglo-Maltese, Malta.

SCHENK, H., CHIAVETTA, M., FALCONE, S., FASCE, P., MASSA, B., MINGOZZI, T. & SARACINO, U. 1985. *The Ecology of the Peregrine Falcon in Italy: first results from five sample areas.* ICBP Techn. Publ. 5: 367–380.

SCOTT, D. A. 1980. *A preliminary Inventory of Wetlands of International Importance for Waterfowl in West Europe and Northwest Africa.* IWRB special Publ. 2.

SIRACUSA, M. & CIACCIO, A. 1985. Dieta del Barbagianni, *Tyto alba*, e sue variazioni stagionali in un'area della Sicilia sud-occidentale. *Riv. Ital. Orn.* 55: 151–160.

SIRACUSA, M., LO VALVO, F., MASSA, B., CIACCIO, A. & DIMARCA, A. in press. Nicchia trofica di Lanario (*Falco biarmicus*) e Pellegrino (*F. peregrinus*) in una regione di simpatria. *Atti IV Conv. Ital Orn., Naturalista Sicil.* 12 (suppl.).

SORCI, G., MASSA, B. & CANGIALOSI, G. 1971a. Ricerche, osservazioni, consistenza attuale del Gracchio corallino (*Pyrrhocorax p. erythrorhamphus*) in Sicilia. *Riv. Ital. Orn.*, 41: 1–10.

————, ————, ———— 1971b. Passo autunnale e primaverile 1969–70 di acquatici e trampolieri in Sicilia. *Riv. Ital. Orn.*, 41: 61–85.

————, ————, ———— 1971c. Il genere *Stercorarius* Brisson è regolare nel Mediterraneo. *Riv. Ital. Orn.* 41: 161–198.

————, ————, ———— 1972. Osservazioni e catture interessanti in Sicilia. *Riv. Ital. Orn.* 42: 232–247.

————, ————, ———— 1973. Avifauna delle Isole Egadi con notizie riguardanti quella della provincia di Trapani (Sicilia). *Riv. Ital. Orn.* 43: 1–119.

SPALLANZANI, L. 1792. *Viaggi alle due Sicilie e in alcune parti dell'Appennino*: Chapter 24: 107–110 and 123. Tip. Comini.

SPANÓ, S., TRAVERSO, G. & SARÁ, M. 1986. Distribuzione attuale di *Alectoris graeca* e *A. barbara* in Italia. *Atti III Conv. Ital. Orn.* 58–61.

SPANÓ, S. & TRUFFI, G. 1986. Il Parrocchetto dal collare *Psittacula krameri*, allo stato libero in Europa, con particolare riferimento alle presenze in Italia, e primi dati sul Pappagallo monaco, *Myopsitta monachus*. *Riv. Ital. Orn.* 56: 231–239.

SPINA, F., SCHENK, H. & MASSA, B. 1985. *Status and Conservation of Eleonora's Falcon in Italy.* ICBP Techn. Publ. 5: 143–146.

STEINBACHER, J. 1954a. Uber den Fruhlings-Vogelzug auf Sizilien. *Vogelwelt* 75: 129–139.

———— 1954b. Uber die Sperlings-Formen von Sardinien und Sizilien. *Senck. Biol.* 34: 307–310.

STEINBACHER, J. 1955a. Vogelleben und vogelzug in Sizilien. *Natur. u. Volk.* 85: 1–11.

———— 1955b. Sull'ecologia e distribuzione degli uccelli in Sicilia. *Riv. Ital. Orn.* 25: 42–68.

———— 1956a. Herbst-Vogelleben in Sardinien und Sizilien. *Vogelwelt* 77: 1–12.

———— 1956b. Zur variation des Gefieders und Verhaltens ben den Sperlingen Sardiniens und Siziliens. *Senck. Biol.* 37: 213–219.

———— 1956c. Uber den Herbst-Vogelzug auf Pantelleria. *Vogelring* 25: 2–6.

———— 1956d. Herbst-Vogelleben in Sizilien. *Gefied. Welt.* 80: 76–77, 92–93, 115–116, 135–136 and 157–158.

———— 1956e. Uber den Herbstzug des Schwalben (*Hirundo rustica* and *Delichon urbica*) in Sardinien und Sizilien. *Die Vogelwarte* 18: 211–212.

———— 1959. Pantelleria, Insel zwischen Europa und Afrika. *Natur. u. Volk* 89: 1–11.

STEINFATT, O. 1931. Beobachtungen uber den Vogelzug in Italien, Sizilien und NordAfrika. *Kocsag* 4: 95–100.

———— 1934. Vogelwelt und Vogelzug auf der Insel Pantelleria. *J. Orn.* 82: 409–419.

STRESEMANN, E. 1922. Rafinesque's Benennungen sizilianischer Vogel. *J. Orn.* 70: 128–129.

———— 1943. Die Brutvogel des Sees von Lentini, Sizilien. *Orn. Monabster* 51: 116–122.

———— 1955. Bemerkungen zu den Verbreitung-skarten in: Peterson-Mountfort-Hollom, Die Vogel Europas. *J. Orn.* 96: 107–114.

STURNIOLO, G. 1905–1907. Continuazione del contributo allo studio degli Uccelli Siciliani del dott. Zodda. *Avicula* 9: 145–151; 10: 40–43; 11: 9–12 and 97–101.

———— 1910. Il passo dei Crocieri in Messina nell'estate del 1909. *Avicula* 14: 50–52.

———— 1913a. La *Terekia cinerea* (Gould) in Sicilia. *Riv. Ital. Orn.* 2: 200–202.

———— 1913b. Un caso di melanismo completo nella *Coturnix communis* (Bonat.). *Riv. Ital. Orn.* 2: 202–203.

———— 1923. Il *Lanius senator niloticus* Bp. in Sicilia. *Riv. Ital. Orn.* 6: 39–41.

SUCHANTKE, A. 1960. September-Beobachtungen auf der Agadischen Insel Marettimo. *Orn. Beob.* 57: 223–240.

SUFFERN, C. 1919. Notes on the migration of birds over the Mediterranean Sea. *Br. Birds* 13: 173–181.

SULTANA, J. & GAUCI, C. 1982. *A New Guide to the Birds of Malta.* Malta Orn. Soc.

SULTANA, J., GAUCI, C. & BEAMAN, M. 1975. *A Guide to the Birds of Malta.* Malta Orn. Soc.

SURDO, S. 1987. Prima nidificazione dell'Avocetta, *Recurvirostra avosetta*, in Sicilia. *Riv. Ital. Orn.* 57: 150.

TEMMINCK, C. J. 1840. *Manuel d'Ornithologie.*

THIBAULT, J. C. 1983. *Les Oiseaux de la Corse.* Parc Nat. Reg. Corse, Ajaccio.

THIOLLAY, J. M. 1975. Migration de printemps au Cap Bon. *Nos Oiseaux* 33: 109–121.

———— 1977. Importance des populations de rapaces migrateurs au Méditerranée occidentale. *Alauda* 45: 115–121.

TOSCHI, A. 1969. *Avifauna Italiana.* Ed. Olimpia, Firenze.

TOSO, S. 1981. Nuovi avvistamenti. *Avocetta* 5: 41–44.

———— 1985. Nuovi avvistamenti. *Avocetta* 9: 89–92.

TRISCHITTA, A. 1918a. Sulla pretesa esistenza del *Vultur monachus* L. in Sicilia. *Boll. Ist. Zool. R. Univ. Palermo* 1: 43–46.

———— 1918b. La *Fratercula arctica* L. nel Messinese. *Riv. Ital. Orn.* 4: 12–15.

———— 1919a. Il *Phalacrocorax (Microcarbo) pygmaeus* (Pallas) in Sicilia. *Riv. Ital. Orn.* 5: 1–3.

———— 1919b. Il gen. *Stercorarius* Brisson in Sicilia. *Riv. Ital. Orn.* 5: 4–6.

———— 1919c. Sull'esistenza del Picchio nero (*Dryocopus martius* (L.)) in Sicilia. *Boll. Ist. Zool. R. Univ. Palermo* 1: 77–80.

———— 1922. Note ornitologiche. *Atti Soc. It. Sc. Nat.* 61: 121–131.

———— 1923a. L'*Anser albifrons* Scop. in Sicilia. *Riv. Ital. Orn.* 6: 20–21.

———— 1923b. Catture di Uccelli rari a Messina. *Riv. Ital. Orn.* 6: 44–45.

———— 1939a. Il Falco biarmicus erlangeri *Kleinschm. in Sicilia.* Tip. Arti Grafiche Solunto, Bagheria.

———— 1939b. *Alcune nuove forme di Uccelli italiani.* Tip. Arti Grafiche Solunto, Bagheria.

TRISCHITTA, A. 1939c. *Altre nuove forme di Uccelli italiani* (*lettera diretta al Sig. Dott. Renzo Ragioneri*). Tip. Arti Grafiche Solunto, Bagheria.

——— 1958–60. Le Falco-Aquile facenti parte dell'avifauna italica: l'Aquila minore e l'Aquila del Bonelli. *Il Cacciatore Sicil.* 3: 87–88, 99–100 and 110–111; 5: 64–65, 70–74 and 98–99.

——— 1963. Un'altra cattura in Sicilia del Falco della Regina. *Il Cacciatore Sicil.* 8: 63–64.

VAUGHAN, R. 1980. Notes on Cory's Shearwater (*Calonectris diomedea*) and some other birds on Linosa, Pelagic Isles. *Riv. Ital. Orn.* 50: 143–154.

VAURIE, C. 1959. *The Birds of the Palearctic Fauna.* I. *Passeriformes.* 1965. II. *Non Passeriformes.* Witherby, London.

VENEZIA, F. 1897a. *Phoenicopterus roseus. Monticola saxatilis. Avicula* 1: 67.

——— 1897b. *Haematopus ostralegus* L. (Beccaccia di mare). *Avicula* 1: 126.

——— 1897c. *Platalea leucorodia* (Spatola). *Avicula* 1: 163.

——— 1897d. *Phoenicopterus roseus* Pall. e *Cygnus ferus* Ray. *Avicula* 1: 163.

——— 1898a. Cigno. *Avicula* 2: 6.

——— 1898b. *Falcinellus autunnalis. Avicula* 2: 13.

——— 1898c. Cattura di una *Fratercula arctica. Avicula* 2: 34–35.

——— 1898d. *Himantopus candidus, Petrocinella cyanea. Avicula* 2: 35.

——— 1898e. Da Castelvetrano. *Avicula* 2: 73.

——— 1898f. *Aquila chrysaetos* L. (Aquila reale), *Coracias garrula* L. (Ghiandaia marina). *Avicula* 2: 106.

——— 1898g. *Ciconia nigra. Avicula* 2: 148–149.

——— 1899a. Da Castelvetrano. *Avicula* 3: 85.

——— 1899b. *Pastor roseus* (Storno roseo). *Avicula* 3: 139.

——— 1900a. Cattura di una *Fratercula arctica* e di un Gabbiano roseo. *Avicula* 4: 27.

——— 1900b. Lodola cappellaccia (*Galerida cristata*). *Avicula* 4: 133.

——— 1901. *Sula bassana, Glareola pratincola. Avicula* 5: 117–118.

——— 1904. Da Castelvetrano. *Avicula* 7: 85.

——— 1912. Cattura di *Merops persicus. Riv. Ital. Orn.* 1: 283.

——— 1934. Cattura di Fenicotteri. *Avicula* 4: 86.

VOOUS, K. H. 1973, 1977. List of recent Holarctic Bird species. *British Ornithologists' Union*, London. Reprinted from *Ibis* 115: 612–638; 119: 223–250, 376–406.

WARNKE, G. 1941. Vom Schwalben-Fruhjahrsug an der sizilianischen kuste. *Vogelzug* 12: 20–23.

WHITAKER, J. 1882. Sulla migrazione degli uccelli, specialmente in Sicilia. *Naturalista Sicil.* 1: 121–127.

——— 1896. *Turnix sylvatica* in Sicily. *Ibis* Ser. 7(2): 290–291.

——— 1899a. Sulla riproduzione in cattività del Pollo sultano (*Porphyrio coeruleus* Vandelli) volg. sic. gaddo fagiano o gaddu fascianu. *Naturalista Sicil.* 3: 17–20.

——— 1899b. Letter on a *Caprimulgus aegyptius* caught near Palermo. *Ibis* Ser. 7(5): 475–476.

——— 1899c. On the breeding of the Purple Gallinule in captivity. *Ibis* Ser. 7(5): 502–505.

——— 1899d. The passage of the *Cuculus canorus* L. in Sicily. *Aquila* 6: 99–100.

——— 1901. On a new species of *Acredula* from Sicily. *Bull. Brit. Orn. Cl.* 11: 51–52.

——— 1902. Further information on two recently described species of Passerine Birds. *Ibis* Ser. 8(2): 54–59.

——— 1903. On the occurrence of *Porphyrio alleni* in Italy and Tunis. *Ibis* Ser. 8(3): 431–432.

——— 1904a. Il *Corvus corone*, la *Linota rufescens* e la *Glareola melanoptera* in Sicilia. *Avicula* 8: 56.

——— 1904b. La *Glareola melanoptera* in Sicilia. *Avicula* 8: 84–85.

——— 1904c. *Corvus corone, Linota rufescens* and *Glareola melanoptera* in Sicily. *Ibis* Ser. 8(4): 477–478.

——— 1905. *The Birds of Tunisia.* Published by the Author.

——— 1910a. On the great invasion of Crossbills in 1909. *Ibis* Ser. 9(4): 331–351.

WHITAKER, J. 1910b. Letter on *Pterocles senegallus* in Sicily. *Ibis* Ser. 9(4): 567–568.

———————— 1910c. Cattura di *Pterocles senegallus* in Sicilia. *Avicula* 14: 102.

———————— c.1920. *The Birds of Sicily*. MS.

WILLIAMSON, K. 1976. *Identification for Ringers. The Genus* Sylvia (*Revised*). British Trust for Ornithology, Tring.

WILLIAMSON, M. 1981. *Island Populations*. Oxford Univ. Press, Oxford.

WOLDHEK, S. 1980. Bird killing in the Mediterranean. *European Committee for the Prevention of Mass destruction of Migratory birds*, Zeist/Netherlands.

ZAVATTARI, E. (ed.). 1960. Biogeografia delle Isole Pelagie. *Rendic. Accad. Naz. XL* 11: 1–471.

ZODDA, G. 1901–1905. Contributo allo studio degli Uccelli Siciliani. *Avicula* 5: 155–158; 6: 14–23, 36–40, 100–102 and 134–137; 7: 45–48, 65–70, 108–114 and 142–145; 8: 72–75; 9: 9–14.

ZUCCARELLO PATTI, M. 1844a. Osservazioni e ricerche su di un vago uccellino siciliano appartenente al gen. *Sylvia* di Latham (*Sylvia atricapilla*). *Atti Accad. Gioenia Sc. Nat. Catania* 1: 139–142.

———————— 1844b. Osservazioni ornitologiche sopra molti uccelli siciliani. *Atti Accad. Gioenia Sc. Nat. Catania* 1: 143–148.

———————— 1845. Osservazioni e descrizioni ornitologiche. *Atti Accad. Gioenia Sc. Nat. Catania* 2: 321–335.

———————— 1846. Sulla grande Ottarda, sull'Anitra casarca e sul Pellicano bruno. *Atti Accad. Gioenia Sc. Nat. Catania* 3: 431–437.

INDEX OF SCIENTIFIC NAMES

Accipiter gentilis, 51
  nisus, 52
Acrocephalus arundinaceus, 24, 99
  melanopogon, 23, 98
  paludicola, 98
  palustris, 99
  schoenobaenus, 98
  scirpaceus, 22, 99
Actitis hypoleucos, 71
acuta, Anas, 18, 20, 44
Aegithalos caudatus, 11, 22, 30, 105
Aegypius monachus, 124
aegyptiacus, Alopochen, 124
aegyptius, Caprimulgus, 82
aeruginosus, Circus, 10, 23, 50
Alaemon alaudipes, 125
Alauda arvensis, 19, 22, 87
alaudipes, Alaemon, 125
alba, Calidris, 67
alba, Egretta, 40
alba, Motacilla, 19, 91
alba, Tyto, 80
albellus, Mergus, 46
albicilla, Haliaeetus, 49
albicollis, Ficedula, 104
albifrons, Anser, 42
albifrons, Sterna, 23, 77
Alca torda, 77
Alcedo atthis, 24, 83
alchata, Pterocles, 124
Alectoris barbara, 124
  chukar, 58, 124
  graeca, 11, 24, 25, 30, 58, 124
alexandrinus, Charadrius, 22, 65
alleni, Porphyrula, 60
Alopochen aegyptiacus, 124
alpestris, Eremophila, 88
alpina, Calidris, 68
aluco, Strix, 30, 81
americanus, Coccyzus, 80
Ammomanes cincturus, 86
Anas acuta, 18, 20, 44
  clypeata, 45
  crecca, 19, 44
  penelope, 18, 19, 43
  platyrhynchos, 23, 44
  querquedula, 19, 20, 23, 44
  strepera, 43
angustirostris, Marmaronetta, 45
Anser albifrons, 42
  anser, 43
  erythropus, 43
  fabalis, 42
Anthropoides virgo, 62
Anthus campestris, 89
  cervinus, 90
  novaeseelandiae, 89
  pratensis, 19, 90
  spinoletta, 90
  trivialis, 90

apiaster, Merops, 24, 84
apivorus, Pernis, 18, 20, 25, 47
apricaria, Pluvialis, 66
Apus apus, 22, 82
  melba, 83
  pallidus, 83
aquaticus, Rallus, 22, 59
Aquila chrysaetos, 24, 53
  clanga, 53
  heliaca, 53
  pomarina, 53
arborea, Lullula, 87
arctica, Fratercula, 78
arctica, Gavia, 34
Ardea cinerea, 18, 21, 40
  purpurea, 10, 23, 39, 40
Ardeola ralloides, 39
Arenaria interpres, 18, 72
aristotelis, Phalacrocorax, 23, 37
arquata, Numenius, 70
arundinaceus, Acrocephalus, 24, 99
arvensis, Alauda, 19, 22, 87
asiaticus, Charadrius, 66
Asio flammeus, 82
  otus, 24, 82
assimilis, Puffinus, 124
ater, Parus, 22, 106
Athene noctua, 81
atra, Fulica, 18, 19, 22, 25, 61
atricapilla, Sylvia, 19, 22, 30, 33, 102
atthis, Alcedo, 24, 83
audouinii, Larus, 21, 23, 74
auritus, Podiceps, 34
avosetta, Recurvirostra, 63
Aythya ferina, 18, 19, 24, 45
  fuligula, 46
  marila, 46
  nyroca, 20, 23, 46

Balearica pavonina, 124
barbara, Alectoris, 124
barbatus, Gypaetus, 11, 23, 49
Bartramia longicauda, 70
bassana, Sula, 19, 37
bengalensis, Sterna, 76
bernicla, Branta, 43
biarmicus, Falco, 23, 24, 27, 56
biarmicus, Panurus, 11, 23, 105
bimaculata, Melanocorypha, 86
Bombycilla garrulus, 91
bonelli, Phylloscopus, 103
borin, Sylvia, 18, 102
Botaurus stellaris, 38
brachydactyla, Calandrella, 22, 86
brachydactyla, Certhia, 107
Branta bernicla, 43
bruniceps, Emberiza, 117
Bubo bubo, 23, 30, 81
Bubulcus ibis, 39
Bucanetes githagineus, 17, 115

Bucephala clangula, 46
Burhinus oedicnemus, 24, 64
Buteo buteo, 22, 30, 52
    lagopus, 53
    rufinus, 52

cachinnans, Larus, 23, 33, 75
caeruleus, Parus, 106
caesia, Emberiza, 125
calandra, Miliaria, 24, 117
calandra, Melanocorypha, 24, 86
Calandrella brachydactyla, 22, 86
    rufescens, 17, 87
Calidris, alba, 67
    alpina, 68
    canutus, 67
    ferruginea, 21, 68
    maritima, 124
    melanotos, 68
    minuta, 21, 67
    temminckii, 67
Calonectris diomedea, 23, 27, 35, 36
campestris, Anthus, 89
cannabina, Carduelis, 19, 22, 30, 114
canorus, Cuculus, 79
cantillans, Sylvia, 22, 30, 100
canus, Larus, 74
canutus, Calidris, 67
capense, Daption, 35
Caprimulgus aegyptius, 82
        europaeus, 22, 82
        ruficollis, 82
carbo, Phalacrocorax, 18, 23, 37
Carduelis cannabina, 19, 22, 30, 114
        carduelis, 19, 22, 25, 114
        chloris, 113
        flammea, 114
        spinus, 22, 24, 30, 114
Carpodacus erythrinus, 125
caryocatactes, Nucifraga, 125
caspia, Sterna, 18, 76
caudatus, Aegithalos, 11, 23, 30, 105
Cercotrichas galactotes, 17, 92
Certhia brachydactyla, 107
cervinus, Anthus, 90
Ceryle rudis, 125
Cettia cetti, 24, 97
Charadrius alexandrinus, 22, 65
        asiaticus, 66
        dubius, 22, 65
        hiaticula, 65
        morinellus, 66
cherrug, Falco, 57
Chersophilus duponti, 125
Chettusia gregaria, 66, 124
        leucura, 66
Chlamydotis undulata, 62
Chlidonias hybridus, 21, 77
        leucopterus, 21, 77
        niger, 18, 77
chloris, Carduelis, 113
chloropus, Gallinula, 22, 60
chrysaetos, Aquila, 24, 53
chukar, Alectoris, 58, 124
cia, Emberiza, 30, 116

Ciconia, ciconia, 41
    nigra, 26, 41
Cinclus cinclus, 24, 91
cincturus, Ammomanes, 86
cinerea, Ardea, 18, 21, 40
cinerea, Motacilla, 91
cinereus, Xenus, 71
Circaetus gallicus, 26, 50
Circus spp., 51
Circus aeruginosus, 10, 23, 50
        cyaneus, 51
        macrourus, 51
        pygargus, 51
cirlus, Emberiza, 22, 24, 116
Cisticola juncidis, 22, 98
citreola, Motacilla, 91
citrinella, Emberiza, 116
citrinella, Serinus, 125
Clamator glandarius, 17, 79
clanga, Aquila, 53
clangula, Bucephala, 46
clypeata, Anas, 45
Coccothraustes coccothraustes, 115
Coccyzus americanus, 80
coelebs, Fringilla, 19, 22, 30, 112
colchicus, Phasianus, 124
Colinus virginianus, 124
collaris, Prunella, 19, 92
collurio, Lanius, 108
collybita, Phylloscopus, 19, 22, 30, 103
Columba livia, 54, 78
        oenas, 30, 78
        palumbus, 79
columbarius, Falco, 56
columbianus, Cygnus, 42
communis, Sylvia, 18, 22, 102
conspicillata, Sylvia, 22, 30, 100
Coracias garrulus, 24, 84
corax, Corvus, 110
corone, Corvus, 22
Corvus corax, 110
        corone, 22, 24, 110
        frugilegus, 110
        monedula, 24, 54, 109
Coturnix coturnix, 21, 24, 58
crecca, Anas, 19, 44
Crex crex, 60
crispus, Pelecanus, 38
cristata, Fulica, 61
cristata, Galerida, 22, 24, 87
cristatus, Podiceps, 23, 34
Cuculus canorus, 79
curruca, Sylvia, 102
Cursorius cursor, 64
curvirostra, Loxia, 22, 24, 30, 115
cyaneus, Circus, 51
Cygnus columbianus, 42
        cygnus, 42
        olor, 42

Daption capense, 35
dauma, Zoothera, 96
daurica, Hirundo, 89
decaocto, Streptopelia, 79
Delichon urbica, 20, 21, 22, 89

Dendrocopus major, 85
    medius, 125
    minor, 24, 86
deserti, Oenanthe, 95
diomedea, Calonectris, 23, 27, 35, 36
Diomedea exulans, 35
Diomedea nigripes, 124
dominica, Pluvialis, 66
dougallii, Sterna, 124
Dryocopus martius, 85
dubius, Charadrius, 22, 65
duponti, Chersophilus, 125

Egretta alba, 40
    garzetta, 21, 39, 40
    gularis, 39
eleonorae, Falco, 23, 56
Emberiza bruniceps, 117
    caesia, 125
    cia, 30, 116
    cirlus, 22, 24, 116
    citrinella, 116
    hortulana, 116
    melanocephala, 10, 117
    pusilla, 116
    rustica, 116
    schoeniclus, 117
epops, Upupa, 19, 22, 84
Eremophila alpestris, 88
Erithacus rubecula, 19, 25, 93
erythrinus, Carpodacus, 125
erythropus, Anser, 43
erythropus, Tringa, 70
europaea, Sitta, 22, 30, 106
europaeus, Caprimulgus, 22, 82
excubitor, Lanius, 108
exulans, Diomedea, 35

fabalis, Anser, 42
falcinellus, Limicola, 68
falcinellus, Plegadis, 41
Falco biarmicus, 23, 24, 27, 56
    cherrug, 57
    columbarius, 56
    eleonorae, 23, 56
    naumanni, 20, 24, 54
    pelegrinoides, 57
    peregrinus, 23, 24, 27, 57
    subbuteo, 24, 56
    tinnunculus, 20, 22, 25, 55
    vespertinus, 20, 25, 55
fasciatus, Hieraaetus, 24, 54, 57
ferina, Aythya, 18, 19, 24, 45
ferruginea, Calidris, 21, 68
ferruginea, Tadorna, 43
Ficedula albicollis, 104
    hypoleuca, 105
    parva, 104
    semitorquata, 104
flammea, Carduelis, 114
flammeus, Asio, 82
flava, Motacilla, 21, 90
Francolinus francolinus, 23, 58

Fratercula arctica, 78
Fringilla coelebs, 19, 22, 30, 112
    montifringilla, 113
frugilegus, Corvus, 110
Fulica atra, 18, 19, 22, 25, 61
    cristata, 61
fulicarius, Phalaropus, 72
fuligula, Aythya, 46
fulvus, Gyps, 23, 50, 124
fusca, Melanitta, 124
fuscus, Larus, 19, 75

galactotes, Cercotrichas, 17, 92
Galerida cristata, 22, 24, 87
gallicus, Circaetus, 26, 50
Gallinago gallinago, 19, 69
    media, 69
Gallinula chloropus, 22, 60
garrulus, Bombycilla, 91
garrulus, Coracias, 24, 84
Garrulus glandarius, 109
garzetta, Egretta, 21, 39, 40
Gavia arctica, 34
    stellata, 33
Gelochelidon nilotica, 21, 75
genei, Larus, 17, 18, 74
gentilis, Accipiter, 51
githagineus, Bucanetes, 17, 115
glandarius, Clamator, 17, 79
glandarius, Garrulus, 109
Glareola nordmanni, 65
    pratincola, 64
glareola, Tringa, 71
graeca, Alectoris, 11, 24, 25, 30, 58, 124
gregaria, Chettusia, 66, 124
grisegena, Podiceps, 34
griseus, Puffinus, 36
Grus grus, 18, 21, 61
gularis, Egretta, 39
Gypaetus barbatus, 11, 23, 49
Gyps fulvus, 23, 50, 124

Haematopus ostralegus, 18, 63
Haliaeetus albicilla, 49
haliaetus, Pandion, 23, 54
heliaca, Aquila, 53
hiaticula, Charadrius, 65
Hieraaetus fasciatus, 24, 54, 57
    pennatus, 54
Himantopus himantopus, 23, 63
Hippolais pallida, 125
    icterina, 99, 125
    polyglotta, 99
Hirundo daurica, 89
    rustica, 18, 21, 22, 88
hirundo, Sterna, 76
hispanica, Oenanthe, 95
hispaniolensis, Passer, 22, 111
Hoplopterus spinosus, 124
hortensis, Sylvia, 101
hortulana, Emberiza, 116
hybridus, Chlidonias, 21, 77
Hydrobates pelagicus, 23, 33, 36
hypoleuca, Ficedula, 105
hypoleucos, Actitis, 71

ibis, Bubulcus, 39
icterina, Hippolais, 99, 125
ignicapillus, Regulus, 104
iliacus, Turdus, 97
inornatus, Philloscopus, 103
interpres, Arenaria 18, 72
isabellina, Oenanthe, 17, 94
Ixobrychus minutus, 24, 38

juncidis, Cisticola, 22, 98
Jynx torquilla, 85

krameri, Psittacula, 125

lagopus, Buteo, 53
Lanius collurio, 108
    excubitor, 108
    minor, 30, 108
    senator, 22, 24, 108
lapponica, Limosa, 69
Larus audouinii, 21, 23, 74
    cachinnans, 23, 33, 75
    canus, 74
    fuscus, 19, 75
    genei, 17, 18, 74
    marinus, 124
    melanocephalus, 17, 18, 19, 21, 73
    minutus, 21, 73
    ridibundus, 18, 19, 21, 74
leucocephala, Oxyura, 10, 23, 47
leucopterus, Chlidonias, 21, 77
leucorhoa, Oceanodroma, 37
leucorodia, Platalea, 41
leucura, Chettusia, 66
leucura, Oenanthe, 95
Limicola falcinellus, 68
Limosa lapponica, 69
    limosa, 20, 69
livia, Columba, 54, 78
lobatus, Phalaropus, 72
Locustella luscinioides, 11, 98
    naevia, 125
longicauda, Bartramia, 70
longicaudus, Stercorarius, 73
Loxia curvirostra, 22, 24, 30, 115
Lullula arborea, 87
Luscinia megarhynchos, 22, 93
    svecica, 93
luscinioides, Locustella, 11, 98
Lymnocryptes minimus, 69

macrourus, Circus, 51
major, Dendrocopus, 85
major, Parus, 22, 106
marila, Aythya, 46
marinus, Larus, 124
maritima, Calidris, 124
Marmaronetta angustirostris, 45
martius, Dryocopus, 85
media, Gallinago, 69
medius, Dendrocopus, 125
megarhynchos, Luscinia, 22, 93
Melanitta fusca, 124
    nigra, 46

melanocephala, Emberiza, 10, 117
melanocephala, Sylvia, 22, 101
melanocephalus, Larus, 17, 18, 19, 21, 73
Melanocorypha bimaculata, 86
    calandra, 24, 86
melanopogon, Acrocephalus, 23, 98
melanotos, Calidris, 68
melba, Apus, 83
merganser, Mergus, 47
Mergus albellus, 46
    merganser, 47
    serrator, 47
Merops apiaster, 24, 84
    superciliosus, 84
merula, Turdus, 22, 24, 30, 96
migrans, Milvus, 18, 20, 24, 25, 30, 48
Miliaria calandra, 24, 117
Milvus migrans, 18, 20, 24, 25, 30, 48
    milvus, 24, 30, 48
minimus, Lymnocryptes, 69
minor, Dendrocopus, 24, 86
minor, Lanius, 30, 108
minuta, Calidris, 21, 67
minutus, Ixobrychus, 24, 38
minutus, Larus, 21, 73
modularis, Prunella, 92
monachus, Aegypius, 124
monachus, Myiopsitta, 125
monedula, Corvus, 24, 54, 109
montanus, Passer, 112
Monticola saxatilis, 22, 24, 96
    solitarius, 96
montifringilla, Fringilla, 113
Montifringilla nivalis, 112
morinellus, Charadrius, 66
Motacilla alba, 19, 91
    cinerea, 91
    citreola, 91
    flava, 21, 90
moussieri, Phoenicurus, 94
muraria, Tichodroma, 107
Muscicapa striata, 18, 21, 104
Myiopsitta monachus, 125

naevia, Locustella, 125
nana, Sylvia, 125
naumanni, Falco, 20, 24, 54
nebularia, Tringa, 71
Neophron percnopterus, 24, 26, 49
Netta rufina, 23, 45
niger, Chlidonias, 18, 77
nigra, Ciconia, 26, 41
nigra, Melanitta, 46
nigricollis, Podiceps, 18, 23, 35
nigripes, Diomedea, 124
nilotica, Gelochelidon, 21, 75
nisoria, Sylvia, 102
nisus, Accipiter, 52
nivalis, Montifringilla, 112
nivalis, Plectrophenax, 115
noctua, Athene, 81
nordmanni, Glareola, 65
novaeseelandiae, Anthus, 89
Nucifraga caryocatactes, 125

Numenius arquata, 70
  phaeopus, 70
  tenuirostris, 70
Nycticorax nycticorax, 17, 24, 39, 40
nyroca, Aythya, 20, 23, 46

Oceanodroma leucorhoa, 37
ochropus, Tringa, 71
ochrurus, Phoenicurus, 93
oedicnemus, Burhinus, 24, 64
Oenanthe deserti, 95
  hispanica, 95
  isabellina, 17, 94
  leucura, 95
  oenanthe, 18, 21, 95
  pleschanka, 125
oenas, Columba, 30, 78
olor, Cygnus, 42
onocrotalus, Pelecanus, 38
orientalis, Streptopelia, 124
Oriolus oriolus, 107
ostralegus, Haematopus, 63
Otis tarda, 63
otus, Asio, 24, 82
Otus scops, 80
Oxyura leucocephala, 10, 23, 47

pallida, Hippolais, 125
pallidus, Apus, 83
paludicola, Acrocephalus, 98
palumbus, Columba, 79
palustris, Acrocephalus, 99
palustris, Parus, 11, 22, 30, 33, 105
Pandion haliaetus, 23, 54
Panurus biarmicus, 11, 23, 105
paradisaea, Sterna, 76
parasiticus, Stercorarius, 72, 73
Parus ater, 22, 106
  caeruleus, 106
  major, 22, 106
  palustris, 11, 22, 30, 33, 105
parva, Ficedula, 104
parva, Porzana, 59
Passer hispaniolensis, 22, 111
  montanus, 112
pavonina, Balearica, 124
pelagicus, Hydrobates, 23, 33, 36
Pelecanus crispus, 38
  onocrotalus, 38
pelegrinoides, Falco, 57
pendulinus, Remix, 107
penelope, Anas, 18, 19, 43
pennatus, Hieraaetus, 54
percnopterus, Neophron, 24, 26, 49
peregrinus, Falco, 23, 24, 27, 57
Pernis apivorus, 18, 20, 25, 47
Petronia petronia, 112
phaeopus, Numenius, 70
Phalacrocorax aristotelis, 23, 37
  carbo, 18, 23, 37
  pygmaeus, 38
Phalaropus fulicarius, 72
  lobatus, 72
Phasianus colchicus, 124
Philomachus pugnax, 20, 25, 68

philomelos, Turdus, 19, 21, 97
Phoenicopterus ruber, 27, 41
Phoenicurus moussieri, 94
  ochruros, 93
  phoenicurus, 18, 21, 22, 30, 94
Phylloscopus bonelli, 103
  collybita, 19, 22, 30, 103
  inornatus, 103
  sibilatrix, 103
  trochilus, 18, 103
Pica pica, 22, 24, 109
Picus viridis, 24, 85
pilaris, Turdus, 19, 97
Platalea leucorodia, 21, 27, 41
platyrhynchos, Anas, 23, 44
Plectrophenax nivalis, 115
Plegadis falcinellus, 41
pleschanka, Oenanthe, 125
Pluvialis apricaria, 66
  dominica, 66
  squatarola, 66
Podiceps auritus, 34
  cristatus, 23, 34
  grisegena, 34
  nigricollis, 18, 23, 35
polyglotta, Hippolais, 99
pomarina, Aquila, 53
pomarinus, Stercorarius, 72, 73
Porphyrio porphyrio, 10, 23, 60
Porphyrula alleni, 60
Porzana parva, 59
  porzana, 59
  pusilla, 59
pratensis, Anthus, 19, 90
pratincola, Glareola, 64
Prunella collaris, 19, 92
  modularis, 92
Psittacula krameri, 125
Pterocles alchata, 124
  senegallus, 78
Ptyonoprogne rupestris, 88
Puffinus assimilis, 124
  griseus, 36
  puffinus, 23, 36
pugnax, Philomachus, 20, 25, 68
purpurea, Ardea, 10, 23, 39, 40
pusilla, Emberiza, 116   ·
pusilla, Porzana, 59
pygargus, Circus, 51
pygmaeus, Phalacrocorax, 38
Pyrrhocorax pyrrhocorax, 24, 109
Pyrrhula pyrrhula, 115

querquedula, Anas, 10, 20, 23, 44

ralloides, Ardeola, 39
Rallus aquaticus, 22, 59
Recurvirostra avosetta, 63
Regulus ignicapillus, 104
  regulus, 104
Remiz pendulinus, 107
ridibundus, Larus, 18, 19, 21, 74
Riparia riparia, 18, 88
Rissa tridactyla, 75
roseus, Sturnus, 111

rubecula, Erithacus, 19, 25, 93
ruber, Phoenicopterus, 27, 41
rubetra, Saxicola, 94
rudis, Ceryle, 125
rueppelli, Sylvia, 101
rufescens, Calandrella, 17, 87
ruficollis, Caprimulgus, 82
ruficollis, Tachybaptus, 22, 34
rufina, Netta, 23, 45
rufinus, Buteo, 52
rupestris, Ptyonoprogne, 88
rustica, Emberiza, 116
rustica, Hirundo, 18, 21, 22, 88
rusticola, Scolopax, 19, 25, 69

sandvicensis, Sterna, 17, 18, 76
sarda, Sylvia, 100
saxatilis, Monticola, 22, 24, 96
Saxicola rubetra, 94
        torquata, 22, 94
schoeniclus, Emberiza, 117
schoenobaenus, Acrocephalus, 98
scirpaceus, Acrocephalus, 22, 99
Scolopax rusticola, 19, 25, 69
scops, Otus, 80
semitorquata, Ficedula, 104
senator, Lanius, 22, 24, 108
senegalensis, Streptopelia, 79
senegallus, Pterocles, 78
Serinus citrinella, 125
        serinus, 22, 24, 113
serrator, Mergus, 47
sibilatrix, Phylloscopus, 103
Sitta europaea, 22, 30, 106
skua, Stercorarius, 73
solitarius, Monticola, 96
spinoletta, Anthus, 90
spinosus, Hoplopterus, 124
spinus, Carduelis, 22, 24, 30, 114
squatarola, Pluvialis, 66
stagnatilis, Tringa, 71
stellaris, Botaurus, 38
stellata, Gavia, 33
Stercorarius, spp., 72, 73
        longicaudus, 73
        parasiticus, 72, 73
        pomarinus, 72, 73
        skua, 73
Sterna albifrons, 23, 77
        bengalensis, 76
        caspia, 18, 76
        dougallii, 124
        hirundo, 76
        paradisaea, 76
        sandvicensis, 17, 18, 76
strepera, Anas, 43
Streptopelia decaocto, 79
        orientalis, 124
        senegalensis, 79
        turtur, 21, 22, 25, 79
striata, Muscicapa, 18, 21, 104
Strix aluco, 30, 81
Sturnus roseus, 111
        unicolor, 111
        vulgaris, 19, 21, 24, 30, 110

subbuteo, Falco, 24, 56
subruficollis, Tryngites, 68
Sula bassana, 19, 37
superciliosus, Merops, 84
svecica, Luscinia, 93
sylvatica, Turnix, 23, 61
Sylvia atricapilla, 19, 22, 30, 33, 102
        borin, 18, 102
        cantillans, 22, 30, 100
        communis, 18, 22, 102
        conspicillata, 22, 30, 100
        curruca, 102
        hortensis, 101
        melanocephala, 22, 101
        nana, 125
        nisoria, 102
        rueppelli, 101
        sarda, 100
        undata, 100

Tachybaptus ruficollis, 22, 34
Tadorna ferruginea, 43
        tadorna, 43
tarda, Otis, 63
temminckii, Calidris, 67
tenuirostris, Numenius, 70
Tetrax tetrax, 23, 62
Tichodroma muraria, 107
tinnunculus, Falco, 20, 22, 25, 55
torda, Alca, 77
torquata, Saxicola, 22, 94
torquatus, Turdus, 96
torquilla, Jynx, 85
totanus, Tringa, 70
tridactyla, Rissa, 75
Tringa erythropus, 70
        glareola, 71
        nebularia, 71
        ochropus, 71
        stagnatilis, 71
        totanus, 70
trivialis, Anthus, 90
trochilus, Phylloscopus, 18, 103
Troglodytes troglodytes, 22, 30, 92
Tryngites subruficollis, 68
Turdus iliacus, 97
        merula, 22, 24, 30, 96
        philomelos, 19, 21, 97
        pilaris, 19, 97
        torquatus, 96
        viscivorus, 97
Turnix sylvatica, 23, 61
turtur, Streptopelia, 21, 22, 25, 79
Tyto alba, 80

undata, Sylvia, 100
undulata, Chlamydotis, 62
unicolor, Sturnus, 111
Upupa epops, 19, 22, 84
urbica, Delichon, 20, 21, 22, 89

Vanellus vanellus, 19, 67
vespertinus, Falco, 20, 25, 55
virginianus, Colinus, 124
virgo, Anthropoides, 62

viridis, Picus, 24, 85
viscivorus, Turdus, 97
vulgaris, Sturnus, 19, 21, 24, 30, 110

Xenus cinereus, 71

Zoothera dauma, 96

INDEX OF ENGLISH NAMES

Accentor, Alpine, 19, 92
Albatross, Black-footed, 124
    Wandering, 35
Avocet, 63

Bee-eater, 24, 84
    Blue-cheeked, 84
Bittern, 38
    Little, 24, 38
Blackbird, 22, 24, 30, 96
Blackcap, 19, 22, 30, 33, 102
Bluethroat, 93
Bobwhite, 124
Brambling, 113
Bullfinch, 115
Bunting, Black-headed, 10, 117
    Cirl, 22, 24, 116
    Corn, 24, 117
    Cretzschmar's, 125
    Little, 116
    Ortolan, 116
    Red-headed, 117
    Reed, 117
    Rock, 30, 116
    Rustic, 116
    Snow, 115
Bush Chat, Rufous, 17, 92
Bustard, Great, 63
    Houbara, 62
    Little, 23, 62
Buzzard, 22, 30, 52
    Honey, 18, 20, 25, 47
    Long-legged, 52
    Rough-legged, 53

Chaffinch, 19, 22, 30, 112
Chiffchaff, 19, 22, 30, 103
Chough, 24, 109
Chukar, 58, 124
Coot, 18, 19, 22, 25, 61
    Crested, 61
Cormorant, 18, 23, 37
    Pygmy, 38
Corncrake, 60
Courser, Cream-Coloured, 64
Crake, Baillon's, 59
    Little, 59
    Spotted, 59
Crane, Common, 18, 21, 61
    Crowned, 124
    Demoiselle, 62
Crossbill, 22, 24, 30, 115
Crow, Hooded, 22, 24, 110
Cuckoo, 79
    Great Spotted, 17, 79
    Yellow-billed, 80
Curlew, 70
    Slender-billed, 70
    Stone, 24, 64

Dipper, 24, 91
Diver, Black-throated, 33
    Red-throated, 34
Dotterel, 66
Dove, Collared, 79
    Palm, 79
    Rock, 54, 78
    Rufous Turtle, 124
    Stock, 30, 78
    Turtle, 21, 22, 25, 79
Duck, Ferruginous, 20, 23, 46
    Tufted, 46
    White-headed, 10, 23, 47
Dunlin, 68
Dunnock, 92

Eagle, Bonelli's, 24, 54, 57
    Booted, 54
    Golden, 24, 53
    Imperial, 53
    Lesser Spotted, 53
    Short-toed, 26, 50
    Spotted, 53
    White-tailed, 49
Egret, Cattle, 39
    Great White, 40
    Little, 21, 39, 40

Falcon, Barbary, 57
    Eleonora's, 23, 56
    Lanner, 23, 24, 27, 56
    Red-footed, 20, 25, 55
Fieldfare, 19, 97
Finch, Citril, 125
    Snow, 112
    Trumpeter, 17, 115
Firecrest, 104
Flamingo, Greater, 27, 41
Flycatcher, Collared, 104
    Pied, 105
    Red-breasted, 104
    Semi-collared, 104
    Spotted, 18, 21, 104
Francolin, Black, 23, 58

Gadwall, 43
Gallinule, Allen's, 60
    Purple, 10, 23, 60
Gannet, 19, 37
Garaganey, 19, 20, 23, 44
Godwit, Bar-tailed, 69
    Black-tailed, 20, 69
Goldcrest, 104
Goldeneye, 46
Goldfinch, 19, 22, 25, 114
Goosander, 47
Goose, Bean, 42
    Brent, 43
    Egyptian, 124

Goose, Greylag, 43
   Lesser White-fronted, 43
   White-fronted, 42
Goshawk, 51
Grebe, Black-necked, 18, 23, 35
   Great Crested, 23, 34
   Little, 22, 34
   Red-necked, 34
   Slavonian, 34
Greenfinch, 113
Greenshank, 71
Gull, Audouin's, 21, 23, 74
   Black-headed, 18, 19, 21, 74
   Common, 74
   Great Black-backed, 124
   Lesser Black-backed, 19, 75
   Little, 21, 73
   Mediterranean, 17, 18, 19, 21, 73
   Slender-billed, 17, 18, 74
   Yellow-legged Herring, 23, 33, 75

Harrier, Hen, 51
   Marsh, 10, 23, 50
   Montagu's 51
   Pallid, 51
Hawfinch, 115
Hemipode, Andalusian, 23, 61
Heron, Grey, 18, 21, 40
   Night, 17, 24, 39, 40
   Purple, 10, 23, 39, 40
   Squacco, 39
   Western Reef, 39
Hobby, 24, 56
Hoopoe, 19, 22, 84

Ibis, Glossy, 41

Jackdaw, 24, 54, 109
Jay, 109

Kestrel, 20, 22, 25, 55
   Lesser, 20, 24, 54
Kingfisher, 24, 83
   Pied, 125
Kite, Black, 18, 20, 24, 25, 30, 48
   Red, 24, 30, 48
Kittiwake, 75
Knot, 67

Lammergeier, 11, 23, 49
Lapwing, 19, 67
Lark, Bar-tailed Desert, 86
   Bimaculated, 86
   Calandra, 24, 86
   Crested, 22, 24, 87
   Dupont's, 125
   Hoopoe, 125
   Lesser Short-toed, 17, 87
   Shore, 88
   Short-toed, 22, 86
Linnet, 19, 22, 30, 114

Magpie, 22, 24, 109
Mallard, 23, 44
Martin, Crag, 88

Martin, House, 20, 21, 22, 89
   Sand, 18, 88
Merganser, Red-breasted, 47
Merlin, 56
Moorhen, 22, 60

Nightingale, 22, 93
Nightjar, 22, 82
   Egyptian, 82
   Red-necked, 82
Nutcracker, 125
Nuthatch, 22, 30, 106

Oriole, Golden, 107
Osprey, 23, 54
Ouzel, Ring, 96
Owl, Barn, 80
   Eagle, 23, 30, 81
   Little, 81
   Long-eared, 24, 82
   Scops, 80
   Short-eared, 82
   Tawny, 30, 81
Oystercatcher, 18, 63

Parakeet, Monk, 125
   Ring-necked, 125
Partridge, Barbary, 124
   Rock, 11, 24, 25, 30, 58, 124
Pelican, Dalmatian, 38
   White, 38
Peregrine, 23, 24, 27, 57
Petrel, Leach's, 37
   Storm, 23, 33, 36
Phalarope, Grey, 72
   Red-necked, 72
Pheasant, 124
Pigeon, Cape, 35
Pintail, 18, 20, 44
Pipit, Meadow, 19, 90
   Red-throated, 90
   Richard's, 89
   Tawny, 89
   Tree, 90
   Water, 90
Plover, Caspian, 66
   Golden, 66
   Grey, 66
   Kentish, 22, 65
   Lesser Golden, 66
   Little Ringed, 22, 65
   Ringed, 65
   Sociable, 66
   Spur-winged, 124
   White-tailed, 66
Pochard, 18, 19, 24, 45
   Red-crested, 23, 45
   White-eyed, 46
Pratincole, 64
   Black-winged, 65
Puffin, 78

Quail, 21, 24, 25, 58

Rail, Water, 22, 59
Raven, 110

Razorbill, 77
Redpoll, 114
Redshank, 70
    Spotted, 70
Redstart, 18, 21, 22, 30, 94
    Black, 93
    Moussier's, 94
Redwing, 97
Robin, 19, 25, 93
Roller, 24, 84
Rook, 110
Rosefinch, Common, 125
Ruff, 20, 25, 68

Saker, 57
Sanderling, 67
Sandgrouse, Pin-tailed, 124
    Spotted, 78
Sandpiper, Broad-billed, 68
    Buff-breasted, 68
    Common, 71
    Curlew, 21, 68
    Green, 71
    Marsh, 71
    Pectoral, 68
    Purple, 124
    Terek, 71
    Upland, 70
    Wood, 71
Scaup, 46
Scoter, Common, 46
    Velvet, 124
Serin, 22, 24, 113
Shag, 23, 37
Shearwater, Cory's, 23, 27, 35, 36
    Little, 124
    Manx, 23, 36
    Sooty, 36
Shelduck, 43
    Ruddy, 43
Shoveler, 45
Shrike, Great Grey, 108
    Lesser Grey, 30, 108
    Red-backed, 108
    Woodchat, 22, 24, 108
Siskin, 22, 24, 30, 114
Skua, Arctic, 72, 73
    Great, 73
    Long-tailed, 73
    Pomarine, 72, 73
Skylark, 19, 22, 87
Smew, 46
Snipe, 19, 69
    Great, 69
    Jack, 69
Sparrow, Rock, 112
    Spanish, 22, 111
    Tree, 112
Sparrowhawk, 52
Spoonbill, 21, 27, 41
Starling, 19, 21, 24, 30, 110
    Rose-coloured, 111
    Spotless, 111
Stilt, Black-winged, 23, 63

Stint, Little, 21, 67
    Temminck's, 67
Stonechat, 22, 94
Stork, Black, 26, 41
    White, 41
Swallow, 18, 21, 22, 88
    Red-rumped, 89
Swan, Bewick's, 42
    Mute, 42
    Whooper, 42
Swift, 22, 82
    Alpine, 83
    Pallid, 83

Teal, 19, 44
    Marbled, 45
Tern, Arctic, 76
    Black, 18, 77
    Caspian, 18, 76
    Common, 76
    Gull-billed, 21, 75
    Lesser Crested, 76
    Little, 23, 77
    Roseate, 124
    Sandwich, 17, 18, 76
    Whiskered, 21, 77
    White-winged Black, 21, 77
Thrush, Blue Rock, 96
    Mistle, 97
    Rock, 22, 24, 96
    Song, 19, 21, 97
    White's 96
Tit, Bearded, 11, 23, 105
    Blue, 106
    Coal, 22, 106
    Great, 22, 106
    Long-tailed, 11, 22, 30, 105
    Marsh, 11, 22, 30, 33, 105
    Penduline, 107
Treecreeper, Short-toed, 107
Turnstone, 18, 72

Vulture, Black, 124
    Egyptian, 24, 26, 49
    Griffon, 23, 50, 124

Wagtail, Citrine, 91
    Grey, 91
    White, 19, 91
    Yellow, 21, 90
Wallcreeper, 107
Warbler, Aquatic, 98
    Barred, 102
    Bonelli's, 103
    Cetti's 24, 97
    Dartford, 100
    Desert, 125
    Fan-tailed, 22, 98
    Garden, 18, 102
    Grasshopper, 125
    Great Reed, 24, 99
    Icterine, 99, 125
    Marmora's 100
    Marsh, 99
    Melodious, 99

Warbler, Moustached, 23, 98
   Olivaceous, 125
   Orphean, 101
   Reed, 22, 99
   Rüppell's, 101
   Sardinian, 22, 101
   Savi's, 11, 98
   Sedge, 98
   Spectacled, 22, 30, 100
   Subalpine, 22, 30, 100
   Willow, 18, 103
   Wood, 103
   Yellow-browed, 103
Waxwing, 91
Wheatear, Black, 95
   Black-eared, 95
   Common, 18, 21, 95
   Desert, 95
   Isabelline, 17, 94
   Pied, 125

Whimbrel, 70
Whinchat, 94
Whitethroat, 18, 22, 102
   Lesser, 102
Wigeon, 18, 19, 43
Woodcock, 19, 69
Woodlark, 87
Woodpecker, Black, 85
   Great Spotted, 85
   Green, 24, 85
   Lesser Spotted, 24, 86
   Middle Spotted, 125
Woodpigeon, 79
Wren, 22, 30, 92
Wryneck, 85

Yellowhammer, 116